Meet up!

ANGLAIS 2de B1

DIRECTION D'OUVRAGE ET AUTEUR :

Erwan GOURAUD
FORMATEUR
ENSEIGNANT AU LYCÉE JEAN-JACQUES ROUSSEAU, SARCELLES (95)

AUTEUR·E·S :

Bryce ANGOT
ENSEIGNANT DANS L'ACADÉMIE D'AMIENS (80)

Hugues AZAÏS
ENSEIGNANT AU LYCÉE DÉODAT DE SÉVERAC, TOULOUSE (31)

Joël CASCADE
ENSEIGNANT AU LYCÉE BELLEPIERRE, SAINT-DENIS-DE-LA-RÉUNION (974)

Élodie DAVO-VERDAVOIR
ENSEIGNANTE AU LYCÉE SAINTE-MARIE GRAND LEBRUN, BORDEAUX (33)

Véronique DORGET
ENSEIGNANTE AU LYCÉE LOUIS LAPICQUE, ÉPINAL (88)

Sylvie DOUGLADE-VAL
FORMATRICE
ENSEIGNANTE AU LYCÉE CLAUDE GELLÉE, ÉPINAL (88)

Françoise DU
FORMATRICE
ENSEIGNANTE AU LYCÉE BREQUIGNY, RENNES (35)

Pierre GUENDOUZ
FORMATEUR
ENSEIGNANT AU LYCÉE JACQUES DUHAMEL, DOLE (39)

Axel JACOBIN
FORMATEUR
ENSEIGNANT AU LYCÉE MONTALEMBERT, COURBEVOIE (92)

Amal NAVAILH
ENSEIGNANTE AU LYCÉE JACQUES PRÉVERT, BOULOGNE-BILLANCOURT (92)

Isabelle VALENTIN
FORMATRICE
ENSEIGNANTE AU LYCÉE DES MÉTIERS PIERRE DORIOLE, LA ROCHELLE (17)

Fatima ZAÂZOUI
ENSEIGNANTE AU LYCÉE LÉO LAGRANGE, BONDY (93)

Avec la participation de Cathy LIRIA
ENSEIGNANTE AU LYCÉE JEAN STURM, STRASBOURG (67)

Hatier

Merci à tou·te·s les enseignant·e·s qui nous ont aidé·e·s à élaborer cette nouvelle collection lors des rencontres à Paris et avec nos délégué·e·s pédagogiques, en particulier Véronique JAUBERT et Tony CARTWRIGHT pour leurs relectures et leurs conseils avisés.

Conception graphique : Primo&Primo, Gudrun Challe
Mise en page : Gudrun Challe
Édition : Annika Sanchez, Anne-Laure Culière, Olivier Martin, Catherine de Bernis, Pauline Gaberel
Illustrations : Philippe Gady, Nicolas Haverland, Louise Plantin, Isa Python
Infographies : Henri-Olivier, Robin Laperche
Iconographie : Véronique Foz, Hatier illustration
Cartographie : L'atelier cartographik
Droits : Andréa Freire

Merci à Kay Steggles, Brendan McCann, à toute l'équipe et aux élèves de la British School of Paris pour les vidéos de l'unité « Join The Club » !

Les auteur·e·s tiennent également à remercier tou·te·s les élèves qui ont testé les unités du manuel en classe.

ISBN : 978-240-1-05319-9

Discover the English-speaking world and improve your skills!

Bienvenue dans votre manuel !

Nous avons créé ce manuel autour de vous, autour de votre expérience d'élève de seconde. Vous arrivez dans un nouvel établissement avec un nouveau cadre, de nouveaux·elles professeur·e·s, de nouveaux·elles camarades et de nouveaux programmes ! Vous verrez que, dès le début du manuel, une unité vous permettra de faire le pont avec le collège et d'entrer dans votre peau de lycéen·ne grâce aux clubs, un phénomène bien anglo-saxon !

Ce manuel est conçu pour s'adapter à votre niveau de compétence dans chaque activité langagière. Vous travaillerez toutes ces activités langagières à travers l'étude des documents de chaque unité ! Nous incluons également des propositions de médiation, à l'articulation de ces activités langagières.

Dès la page d'ouverture, vous pourrez comprendre quel est l'angle d'attaque de l'unité, c'est-à-dire sa problématique : un terme que vous entendrez bien souvent au lycée ! Des mots clés sous forme de **hashtags** vous indiqueront l'orientation que prendra votre unité.

Les rubriques **Improve your writing skills**, qui reviennent sur des points clés d'écriture, et les activités proposées en grammaire (**Practise your grammar**) et en phonologie (**Improve your pronunciation**) ainsi que pour travailler le lexique (**Build up your vocabulary**) vous permettront de consolider vos compétences à l'écrit et à l'oral.

Votre manuel est imaginé pour vous permettre de progresser tout au long de l'année. Ainsi, les logos *Pédagogie différenciée* vous indiquent que vous, ou votre professeur·e, pouvez choisir votre parcours, celui qui est le plus adapté à vos compétences à un moment précis de l'année. Cela vous permettra de gagner en confiance et en compétences, et cela facilitera, *in fine*, votre progression au cours de l'année.

Vous verrez que le manuel vous propose de multiples aides pour la langue, la culture et la méthodologie. Il ne reste plus qu'à vous servir !

Enfin, ce manuel, c'est aussi et surtout une invitation au voyage, à la découverte. Grâce à des documents, tous authentiques, nous explorons les axes du programme qui constituent le socle de la culture anglo-saxonne aujourd'hui.

Il nous reste donc à vous souhaiter de progresser, de faire de belles découvertes et surtout de passer une très bonne année avec **Let's Meet Up!**

Les auteur·e·s

Quelques pistes pour bien utiliser

Pour vous repérer

Réception

Compréhension écrite

Compréhension orale

Production

Expression écrite

Expression orale

Interaction écrite

Interaction orale

Médiation

Expliquer un discours lu ou entendu

Pédagogie différenciée

Pédagogie différenciée

› Deux **approches différentes** d'un même document pour arriver à la même conclusion.
› Plusieurs documents de niveaux différents pour **travailler en groupes**.

Mémorisation active

Memory Challenge

Une manière ludique de retenir les contenus essentiels de chaque double-page.

Pour vous entraîner

Dans votre manuel :

grammaire, phonologie, écriture et vocabulaire pour chaque séquence.

Practise your grammar
› L'essentiel de la règle
› Un ou deux exercices

Improve your pronunciation
› L'essentiel de la règle
› Des exemples fournis en MP3
› Un ou deux exercices

Work on your writing skills
› Une démarche simple accompagnée d'exemples en contexte
› Un ou deux exercices

Build up your vocabulary
› Une carte mentale
› Deux exercices en contexte
› Quizlet

Sur la plateforme :

lexique, grammaire, prononciation, compréhension et expression orales ou écrites.

www.reussirenlangues.com/letsmeetup2de

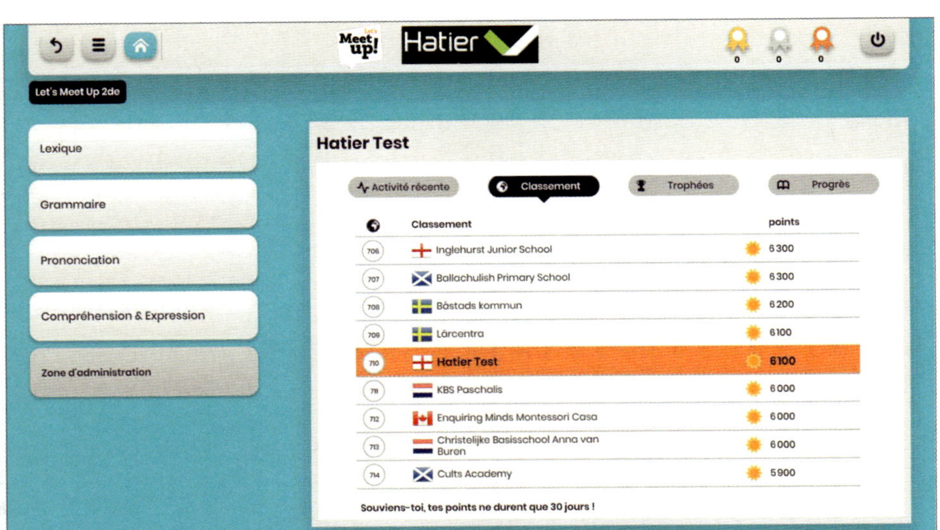

› Une **interface** très fonctionnelle et facile à utiliser
› Des **activités** ludiques en lien avec les contenus de chaque séquence
› Un **enregistreur** pour la production orale
› La possibilité d'**envoyer vos productions** directement à votre professeur·e
› Un **suivi de vos résultats**

LET'S MEET UP!

Pour lire, écouter de l'anglais en dehors du cours

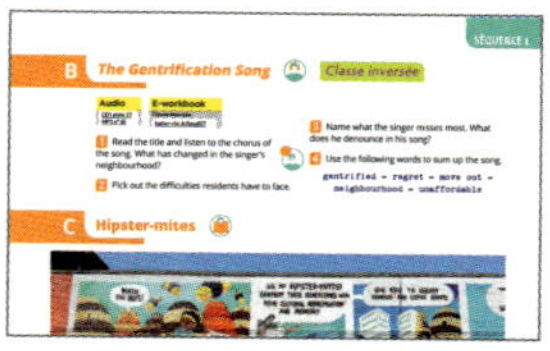

La classe inversée Classe inversée

› Un **document** accompagné d'une **fiche du E-workbook** (à télécharger) pour préparer la mise en commun en classe et/ou travailler à votre rythme.

› Ces éléments sont disponibles en ligne en tapant la mini-URL indiquée dans la boîte !

E-workbook
Classe inversée
hatier-clic.fr/lmu040

Go4it

› **Des conseils pour prolonger la séquence** : lectures, séries, films, romans graphiques, chansons… Il y en a pour tous les goûts – la priorité est votre immersion dans la langue anglaise !

Le site de téléchargement :

Retrouvez tous les MP3 et les fiches du *E-workbook* en un seul clic !

https://langues-eleves.editions-hatier.fr

Sommaire des MP3

Sommaire des annexes

TRANSITION collège/lycée

Join the club?

Les clubs scolaires au Royaume-Uni et aux États-Unis.

Project #1: You are the president of two clubs in an American or British high school. Present them in a video.

Project #2: You are a student in an American or British high school. Write an email to the school's headmaster or mistress to create a new club.

Pictures
Drama club at the British School of Paris; Steam Club; Key Club; UNICEF Club; Drama Club; Math Club

AXE 1 Intergenerational relationships — Vivre

SÉQUENCE 1 How is the Irish heritage passed on?

Les liens intergénérationnels en Irlande : entre héritage et sentiment d'appartenance.

Project #1: Conduct an interview for a talk show. The topic is "what is great about being Irish".

Project #2: Create an infographic related to Irish culture and identity.

Pictures
The Irish heritage; I am Irish, RTÉ 2

Text
Claddaghs

Audio
Claddaghs; Questioning cultural identity

SÉQUENCE 2 How can the born-free generation build its

Comment la génération post-apartheid forge une nouvelle Afrique du Sud.

Project #1: Make a portrait of a member of the born-free generation for a documentary.

Project #2: Write an article showcasing the new face of post-apartheid South Africa.

Picture
The born-free generation

Videos
South Africa's Post Apartheid Generation, Journeyman Pictures; *Trailer for* Bayeza, 10and5

AXE 2 Professional fields, the world of work

SÉQUENCE 1 Do gap years really prepare for work life?

L'année de césure prépare-t-elle les jeunes anglo-saxons à leur futur professionnel ?

Project #1: Take part in the competition: "Win a free gap year abroad!" Prepare a video to show you are the best candidate.

Project #2: Write an email to apply for an internship during your gap year abroad.

Videos
Studying abroad, University of Adelaide; *Graduate career advice,* Newcastle University

Audio
A year off before College, The Wall Street Journal

SÉQUENCE 2 Is Canada a dream job country?

Le Canada : nouvel Eldorado pour les jeunes diplômés ?

Project #1: Act out a phone conversation between a potential immigrant and a Canadian immigration advisor.

Project #2: Create a poster to encourage young people to move to Canada for a contest set up by the Canadian government.

Infographics
Young Canadians' dream jobs; American or Canadian dream?

Videos
Empowering Canadian Youth for the Jobs of Tomorrow, RBC; *International Experience Canada*

AXE 3 Village, neighbourhood, city Le village,

SÉQUENCE 1 How does gentrification impact US cities?

Phénomène urbain ou signe des temps ? L'appropriation de certains quartiers par des personnes plus aisées change radicalement le profil de la ville américaine.

Project #1: Participate in a town meeting about the construction of a new block of flats in your neighbourhood.

Project #2: Create a poster for your residents' association to raise awareness on the dangers of gentrification.

Texts

Diagnosing gentrification, HuffPost; *Them,* Atria Books

Audio

The Gentrification Song, The Gift of Gab; *Interview,* Guadalis Del Carmen

SÉQUENCE 2 What are the challenges facing Indian cities?

L'Inde face aux défis de l'urbanisation.

Project #1: Give an inauguration speech as the mayor of a new suburban city near Mumbai.

Project #2: Write a post on your travel blog. Explain the specificities of Indian cities to your international readers.

Videos

India: Crowded Cities, UN Stories; *Mumbai: Maximum City under Pressure,* Urban-Think Tank; *Journey Through India,* CNBC International; *India's smart city plan,* ORF

AXE 4 Self-representation and relationship to

SÉQUENCE 1 How do stereotypes impact women's empower-

Évolution des codes vestimentaires, du regard sur les femmes, quelle est l'image de la femme américaine aujourd'hui ?

Project #1: Convince the producers of your TV show to invite a celebrity who is trying to end stereotypes on women.

Project #2: For International Women's Day, create a leaflet to denounce stereotypes and encourage women's empowerment.

Pictures

Seventeen magazine; Instagram post, Essena O'Neill; *Instagram post,* Beyoncé

Videos

Gender stereotypes in advertising; RBG, Julie Cohen and Betsy West

SÉQUENCE 2 How are Native Americans represented in the

Les indiens d'Amérique, loin des clichés...

Project #1: Choose a misconception about Native Americans and explain why it is wrong in a 90-second speech.

Project #2: Write a blog post describing how Native American culture has been represented in the USA.

Pictures

Photographs, Edward Curtis; *Indian memes; Pocahontas,* Lithograph; Elle Magazine*'s cover*

Texts

Custer Died for Your Sins: An Indian Manifesto, Vine Deloria Jr.; *Pocahontas,* Historian Camilla Townsend

le quartier, la ville

others Représentation de soi et rapport à autrui

AXE 5 Sports and society Sports et société

SÉQUENCE 1 Does American football bring people together?

Le Super Bowl : plus qu'une commémoration, le symbole de l'unité d'un pays.

Project #1: Record the video that a football player who took a knee, posted for his fans on his Facebook page.

Project #2: Take part in a discussion on an NFL online forum about whether the Super Bowl brings Americans together.

Pictures

The Atlanta Falcons entering the field at Super Bowl 51; Idina Menzel sings the national anthem prior to Super Bowl XLIX; Colin Kaepernick, Time Magazine

Texts

What is the Super Bowl?, CBSSports; Mediapost; Wonderpolis; Forbes; *The national anthem in sports,* HuffPost

SÉQUENCE 2 Is football a medium of social inclusion in the

Le football made in UK : ciment d'une nation et vecteur de progrès sociaux ?

Project #1: Act out the interview of a British football player. Discuss the values and role of football in the UK.

Project #2: Create a brochure for a British football club presenting its history and values.

Pictures

World Cup 1966; England women's national football team

Audios

The secret story of football, University of Leicester

Texts

Football and social classes, Dr Andy Clark; *The women's struggle is not over,* The Telegraph; *Manchester United Club Charter*

AXE 6 Creation and relation to arts La création

SÉQUENCE 1 Does rap rhyme with poetry?

Et si le rap, invention d'une nouvelle langue, expression d'une émotion à travers les mots, était une forme moderne de poésie ?

Project #1: Record a speech to convince your teacher to include a rap artist in a poetry project.

Project #2: Create a poster for the rappers' Hall of Fame. Show the link between rap and poetry.

Pictures

Mural on Clink Street, Jimmy C; *Shakespearean swag*

Videos

What does rap mean?; Shakespeare in rap

SÉQUENCE 2 How do musicals reflect the English-speaking

Les comédies musicales comme interprétation des faits de sociétés qui ont marqué le Royaume-Uni et les États-Unis.

Project #1: Become a YouTube influencer. Record a video to push tourists to see a live musical.

Project #2: Write a blog entry to recommend a musical reflecting the American or British society.

Blog

Meaningful entertainement

Text

Hair, *the 60s*

et le rapport aux arts

AXE 7 Saving the planet, imagining possible

SÉQUENCE 1 How do British citizens deal with sustainability?

Enjeu qui n'est pas nouveau au Royaume-Uni, la protection de l'environnement prend de nouvelles formes qu'il convient d'explorer.

Project #1: On your YouTube channel, announce five new habits you will adopt for a more sustainable lifestyle.

Project #2: You are a member of a youth council in London. Write to the mayor to share your ideas for a more sustainable city.

Audio

Zero-waste tips, Sustainably Vegan; *A day a week without meat,* Meat Free Monday

Infographics

Green fashion, Fashion Revolution

SÉQUENCE 2 Can cli-fi save the world?

L'imagination au pouvoir : et si la science-fiction « climatique » était le meilleur lanceur d'alerte ?

Project #1: Let's debate! Can cli-fi change people's behaviour on climate?

Project #2: Create the back cover of a cli-fi story taking place in an English-speaking country.

Texts

Three cli-fi novels; Carbon Diaries; Saci Lloyd; *Can 'cli-fi' actually make a difference?*

AXE 8 The past in the present Le passé dans le

SÉQUENCE 1 Do American symbols still represent the USA?

Un poids de l'histoire qui n'est pas toujours facile à assumer...

Project #1: Discuss American symbols in a debate.

Project #2: Create a poster for the hall of fame of American symbols.

Texts

The Great Seal; The Stars and Stripes; Independence Day; The Star-Spangled Banner; Traditions stronger than change, The New York Times

Video

Harriet Tubman to replace Andrew Jackson on the $20 bill, ABC

SÉQUENCE 2 How were Asian immigrants welcomed into

Longtemps oubliée, l'histoire de l'immigration asiatique aux États-Unis (notamment via Angel Island) fait aujourd'hui l'objet d'un travail de mémoire important.

Project #1: Make a speech to pay tribute to the Asian immigrants who came to the USA through Angel Island.

Project #2: Write an article to present Angel Island and Asian immigration to the USA.

Pictures

An interrogation at the Angel Island Immigration Station; Monument near the United States Immigration Station; the Angel Island Immigration Station today

Videos

US immigration history preserved on Angel Island, AP Archive; *Preserving Angel Island's role in US immigration history,* Assembly CA

futures Sauver la planète, penser les futurs possibles

	P. 148		Options pédagogiques
Texts *Upcycling clothes*, University of Chester; *Ban on plastic*, CNBC **Videos** *BedZED - The need for sustainable communities*, Bioregional; *T-charge*, ITN	**Grammaire** les adjectifs composés, le futur **Phonologie** la prononciation de la voyelle *a* **Écriture** les nombres **Vocabulaire** le développement durable	Let's RECAP P. 164 AUTO évaluation P. 154 GO4IT P. 165	Pédagogie différenciée P. 151 Classe inversée P. 149 Médiation P. 150

	P. 156		Options pédagogiques
Pictures *Geostorm; Truth to Power*, Al Gore **Video** *Definition of a genre; Al Gore talks about* Truth to Power, IMDb	**Grammaire** *can* et *could*, l'hypothèse avec *if* / la projection **Phonologie** le suffixe *-ion* **Écriture** la rédaction d'une 4e de couverture **Vocabulaire** la fiction climatique	Let's RECAP P. 164 AUTO évaluation P. 162 GO4IT P. 165	Pédagogie différenciée P. 159 Classe inversée P. 158

présent

	P. 168		Options pédagogiques
Audio *Taking down Confederate symbols* **Picture** *The Confederate States of America*	**Grammaire** le passif, la détermination (Ø et *the*) **Phonologie** l'accent américain **Écriture** l'orthographe américaine **Vocabulaire** les symboles, les valeurs	Let's RECAP P. 184 AUTO évaluation P. 174 GO4IT P. 185	Pédagogie différenciée P. 169 Classe inversée P. 171 Médiation P. 170

the USA?	P. 176		Options pédagogiques
Texts *Historical testimonies in poems; David, 8 years old: "paper son"; Don Lee: my arrival and my interrogation* **Audio** *Paper sons*	**Grammaire** le prétérit en *be* + V-*ing*, le *present perfect* **Phonologie** les sons /ɪ/ et /iː/ **Écriture** la rédaction d'un article **Vocabulaire** l'immigration, Angel Island	Let's RECAP P. 184 AUTO évaluation P. 182 GO4IT P. 185	Pédagogie différenciée P. 178 Classe inversée P. 177

TRANSITION
COLLÈGE/LYCÉE

in partnership with

THE BRITISH SCHOOL
OF PARIS

Join the club?

Projects

Project #1: You are the president of two clubs in an American or British high school. Present them in a video.

Project #2: You are a student in an American or British high school. Write an email to the school's headmaster or mistress to create a new club.

Tools

Grammaire poser des questions, le présent simple, décrire un document, les adverbes d'intensité

Phonologie les questions

Vocabulaire l'école et moi

#meandmyschool #highschoolclubs

#mytastes #extracurricularactivities

Drama club at the British School of Paris

A Speed class meeting

E-workbook
Fiche à imprimer
hatier-clic.fr/lmu001

1 ***GROUP WORK*** Find five questions you would ask someone you meet for the first time. Then select your group's best three questions.

2 As a class, select the best ten questions.

3 Write down the questions chosen with the class and answer them for yourself.

4 Ask four classmates ten questions and write down their answers.

5 ***PAIR WORK*** Write a short paragraph where you describe one of your classmates and introduce a lie. Then, read your description to a classmate and make him or her guess what the lie is.

REMEMBER HOW TO

Pronounce questions

What's your favourite school subject? ↘

Do you like maths? ↗

Audio
CD1 piste 02
MP3 n° 02

REMEMBER HOW TO

Ask questions

Pour poser une question en anglais, il faut respecter l'ordre des mots suivant :

(mot interrogatif) + auxiliaire + sujet + verbe + (complément)?

Where	*do*	*you*	*live?*
mot interrogatif	aux.	sujet	verbe

Do	*you*	*like*	*watching series?*
aux.	sujet	verbe	complément

⚠

Who	*is*	*your favourite singer?*
sujet	verbe	complément

REMEMBER HOW TO

Talk about yourself

Age: I am 15 years old. ⚠ Be

Place of living: I live in + city.

Family: I have … (half-)brothers or (half-)sisters. I don't have any brothers or sisters.

Hobbies: I like / love + *V*-ing. I like / love to + *V*. I like / love + noun.

I like / love watching series. I like / love to watch series.
I like / love series.

Dislikes: I don't like / hate + *V*-ing. I don't like / hate to + *V*.
I don't like / hate + noun.

I don't like / hate watching *Modern Family*.
I don't like / hate to watch *Modern Family*.
I don't like / hate *Modern Family*.

B Clubs of the British School of Paris

costumes
interests theatre natural
plays Drama
acting stage

THE BRITISH SCHOOL
OF PARIS

calculus
train understand numbers
algebra Math
opportunity
competitions

show
music songs
perform Choir public
sing
instruments

library discussion spoiling
read Book review
quizzes
covers

Vidéo DVD

E-workbook Fiche à imprimer hatier-clic.fr/lmu002

1 Watch the video.
Write down all the words you can hear for each club.
Bonus: some words are in the word clouds!

2 Watch the video again and complete your notes.

3 ***GROUP WORK*** Write a short description of one club. Report to the class.

4 You are the president of the film club at the British School of Paris, present your club.

REMEMBER HOW TO

Use the simple present

Au présent, les verbes se conjuguent avec un **s** à la 3e personne du singulier.

She loves rugby, he prefers tennis.

REMEMBER HOW TO

Talk about school

lunch break

subject: topic you study at school (maths, history, PE = Physical Education...)

break (*UK*), recess (*US*): morning or afternoon pause between lessons

form (*UK*): a class of pupils

gather: be together

revise

join: become a member of

act

debate

C Clubs in American high schools

1 Match each image with the correct club name.

Key club - Video games club - Anime club - Democrats / Republicans / Independents club - Chess club

a

b

c

d

e

2 Vocabulary competition! In the texts, find the words corresponding to the equivalents or definitions below. May the best team win!

Team 1

outing - help the people you live with - gathering things that people wear - picking up litter / rubbish - talk / chat about

Team 2

a game with a king and a queen - an assembly - taking the food people bring for charity - organise

3 Match each description with a club.

1. *Discuss new political events, volunteer for a campaign, host a public viewing of a political debate, plan a political rally, gather signatures of support for a bill.*

2. *Host a chess competition between members, bring in chess masters to discuss chess strategy, watch famous chess movies and documentaries.*

3. *Perform acts of service in your community such as cleaning up parks, collecting clothing and organizing food drives. Join the oldest and largest service program for high school students founded in 1925.*

4. *Host a video game competition, discuss the evolution of technology in this industry, bring in a person who works at a video game company to discuss possible careers in the gaming world.*

5. *Learn to speak some Japanese, read anime and discuss it as a group, watch anime TV shows and movies, plan a club trip to an anime convention or draw your own anime character!*

4 ***PAIR WORK*** Choose the club you would like to join. Knowing there are only two spots left, convince the president of the club to choose you.

Student A You want to join the club. Explain the reasons why.

Student B You are the president, select the best students to join your club.

REMEMBER HOW TO

Organise your thoughts

Structurer	*first or firstly, second or secondly, third or thirdly, then…*
Expliciter	*because, that's why…*
Donner des exemples	*for example, for instance…*
Conclure	*to conclude, all in all…*

REMEMBER HOW TO

Talk about your personality

outgoing: extrovert
sociable: friendly
shy: introvert, reserved
amusing: funny
down-to-earth: pragmatic
creative
clever: smart, intelligent, bright

REMEMBER HOW TO

Be more precise

On peut utiliser des adverbes pour varier les degrés d'intensité.
a bit • a little • quite • rather • very • really
I am ***very*** *funny!*

D Let's practise and get better!

Pédagogie différenciée GROUP WORK

1 Write down the following information about your club: name, time, place, goal, trips and events. Then, describe your group's poster.

2 Prepare questions to ask the other groups (name of the club, time, place, goal, trips and events).

3 Talk to your classmates to find information about the other clubs.

4 Choose the club you would like to join and explain why.

REMEMBER HOW TO
Describe a document

Pour décrire, je peux utiliser les formules suivantes :

I can see / there is + singulier
There are + pluriel
It is written...
The different characters depicted are...
It shows / indicates / suggests that...
It makes us feel that...
What I find the most striking / incredible / interesting / impressive is that...

I ***can see*** *a computer on the poster,* ***there is*** *a boy standing.* ***It is written*** *that the club starts at 4 pm.*

GROUP A **STEAM CLUB**

GROUP B **KEY CLUB**

GROUP C **UNICEF CLUB**

Help the world's children with UNICEF!

Participate in various UNICEF campaigns like Trick-or-Treat for UNICEF or Live Below the Line!
Prepare fun fundraising events!
Help raise awareness about children's issues around the world.

Let's meet up every Monday at 4:30 PM in Mr Perrez's room 106 (next to the IT room).

GROUP D **DRAMA CLUB**

KEEP CALM AND JOIN THE DRAMA CLUB!

Let's prepare a great end-of-year show!
First meeting September 4 then every Tuesday from 3 to 4 pm in the drama studio.
Email: brendanmc@highschoolmeetup.com to join the club!

GROUP E **MATH CLUB**

Math is all around us!

Who: Everyone!
When: Thursdays after school
Where: Mrs Ruby's room
Why: Do homework, prepare for tests, help other students, resolve fun math problems, take part in math competitions!

We are counting on you!

REMEMBER HOW TO

Write an email or a letter

Commencez par *Hi* ou *Hello* + le prénom ou *Dear* + *Mr / Mrs* + nom, pour quelqu'un que vous ne connaissez pas.

Pour demander des informations, vous pouvez utiliser : *I would like to know if... / Could I have more information about... / Can you please tell me if...*

Si vous écrivez à vos ami·e·s, vous pouvez utiliser les contractions (*you're, I'm, don't, there's...*).

Pour conclure, écrivez : *I hope to hear from you soon* ou *I'm looking forward to hearing from you soon* + *Take care / See you soon* ou *Kind regards* pour être plus formel·le.

Pour finir, n'oubliez pas de signer en écrivant votre prénom ou votre nom et prénom pour quelqu'un que vous ne connaissez pas.

5 Write an email to the president of the British School of Paris's video game club.

You should – introduce yourself (hobbies, dislikes...);
– ask for more information about the club (day and time, members, events, trips...);
– ask how to join.

Tools in the Spotlight

Entraînez-vous sur la plateforme *Let's Meet Up!*
reussirenlangues.fr

Practise your grammar

Précis grammatical, p. 192

Poser des questions

1 Mettez les mots dans l'ordre afin de poser des questions.

a. you / how / are / ?
b. join / did / club / video games / you / the / ?
c. like / you / do / serving / community / your / ?
d. good / you / arithmetic / at / are / ?

2 Posez les questions ayant pour réponse les éléments soulignés.

a. She is joining the math club.
b. Spanish club is held on Thursdays and Fridays at 3.30 pm.
c. Katie is the president of the Democrats club.
d. Film club takes place in Mrs. Turner's classroom.

Le présent simple

3 Réécrivez les phrases suivantes avec *he* ou *she* pour sujet.

a. I don't like swimming.
b. They understand math better when they go to math club.
c. Do you watch cool movies during film club?
d. Mrs Brown and Nittolo love romance anime and they host a festival each year.

4 Complétez le paragraphe avec les verbes suivants.

focus • believe • encourage • say • not sound • think

My sports teacher ... us to join the chess club because he ... that it will help us ... when we are in class. But my friend ... it ... cool enough. She ... this club is too nerdy.

5 Écrivez un court paragraphe pour décrire le *Key club*.

generous • help the community • take responsabilities • clean parks • collective work

It is important to...
Key club helps people to...

Décrire un document

6 Décrivez cette affiche (voir p. 20).

Les adverbes d'intensité

7 Utilisez certains des intensifs suivants dans les phrases. Attention au sens ! (Plusieurs réponses sont possibles.)

very • quite • rather • really • a bit • a little

a. Film club is ... interesting if you love to go to the cinema.
b. It is ... cool to be part of the debate team.
c. If you love anime, then you are ... interested in Japanese culture.
d. I am not part of the drama club as I'm ... shy.
e. What we do at the science club is ... surprising.

Improve your pronunciation

Précis de phonologie, p. 242

Les questions

8 **Écoutez les questions suivantes. Ont-elles une intonation descendante ↘ ou ascendante ↗ ?**

Audio
CD1 piste 03
MP3 n° 03

a. What are your hobbies?
b. Do you like playing video games?
c. Where does the book club take place?
d. Did you write to the president of Key club?
e. Are you a member of the maths club?

9 **Complétez les phrases avec les mots « descendante » ou « ascendante ».**

On retrouve l'intonation ..., dans les questions ouvertes (introduites par un interrogatif souvent en *wh*-).
What's your favourite club?
On retrouve l'intonation ... dans les questions fermées (réponse par oui ou non).
Do you have a favourite club?

Build up your vocabulary

Audio
CD1 piste 04

Le lycée en Angleterre et aux États-Unis

	UK (England only)	US
14 to 15 years	Year 10	9th Grade (Freshman)
15 to 16 years	Year 11	10th Grade (Sophomore)
16 to 17 years	Year 12	11th Grade (Junior Year)
17 to 18 years	Year 13	12th Grade (Senior Year)

Quizlet
hatier-clic.fr/lmu003

Me, myself and school

My environment — MP3 n°04

I am + age.
I live in + city.
I am from + country / city.
I was born in + country / city.
I have ... (half-)brothers or (half-)sisters.
I don't have any brothers or sisters.

My personality — MP3 n°05

outgoing: extrovert
sociable: friendly
shy: introvert, reserved
amusing: funny
down-to-earth: pragmatic
creative
clever: smart, intelligent, bright
pessimistic ≠ optimistic
absent-minded
hardworking
be a social butterfly

My tastes — MP3 n°08

like, love ≠ dislike, hate
be keen on
be fond of
be crazy about
enjoy
In my free time / After school, I...
My favourite (school subject, actor, pop group, sport) is... because...

School — MP3 n°07

subject: topic you study at school (maths, history, PE = Physical Education...)
recess (*US*): break (*UK*): morning or afternoon pause between lessons
lunch break
form (*UK*): class of pupils
gather: come together
revise

High school clubs — MP3 n°06

after-school clubs
extracurricular activities
join outings / field trips / excursions / trips abroad
enhance (= improve) the academic experience
develop relationships
volunteer
meet people with similar interests
gain leadership experience
help the community
act
debate

Project #1

You are the president of two clubs in an American or British high school. Present them in a video.

1 Choose two clubs that you can find in an American or British high school.

- ✓ Choose clubs of the unit or go on the internet to find other ones.
- ✓ They must be clubs which can be found in an American or British high school.

2 Explain what students will be able to do in the clubs.

- ✓ Present your clubs.
- ✓ List all the activities, outings and events that are organised.
- ✓ Use linking words: **first**, **second**, **third**, **in addition**, **for example**.

3 Write notes and practise.

- ✓ Make a list of five keywords for each club.
- ✓ Use an (online) dictionary to check the pronunciation of difficult words.

4 Action!

- ✓ Don't read your notes.
- ✓ Speak at least 1 minute and 30 seconds.
- ✓ Look at the camera and act as a president!

➤ Fiche de méthodologie N°12 p. 266 N°20 p. 280

Project #2

You are a student in an American or British high school. Write an email to the school's headmaster or mistress to create a new club.

1 Choose a club that you can find in an American or British high school.

- ✓ Choose a club of the unit or go on the internet to find another one.
- ✓ It must be a club which can be found in an American or British high school.

2 Explain why this club should be created.

- ✓ Present the club and all the activities, outings and events that will be organised.
- ✓ Try to find original and irrefutable arguments.
- ✓ Use linking words: **in addition**, **for example**, **because**, **that's why**...

3 Use the correct vocabulary.

- ✓ Don't forget you are writing to your school's headmaster or mistress and not to your friends.
- ✓ Use **Dear Mr / Mrs XX** (at the beginning) and **Kind regards** (before you sign).

4 Add images to illustrate your proposal.

- ✓ Find photos or drawings to illustrate your request. Use **Please find attached**...
- ✓ You email must be convincing!

Fiche de méthodologie N°22 p. 284

AXE 1

Intergenerational relationships

Vivre entre générations

SÉQUENCE 1 How is the Irish heritage passed on?

Projects

Project #1: Conduct an interview for a talk show. The topic is "what is great about being Irish".

Project #2: Create an infographic related to Irish culture and identity.

Tools

Grammaire	le génitif, la place des adjectifs qualificatifs
Phonologie	la prononciation du -*s* à la fin des mots
Écriture	la virgule et le point-virgule
Vocabulaire	l'Irlande, l'immigration

SÉQUENCE 2 How can the born-free generation build its future?

Projects

Project #1: Make a portrait of a member of the born-free generation for a documentary.

Project #2: Write an article showcasing the new face of post-apartheid South Africa.

Tools

Grammaire	le présent simple, la proposition relative
Phonologie	les sons /ʊ/ et /uː/
Écriture	les majuscules
Vocabulaire	la culture, la politique

#generations #heritage #traditions #Irishness #culturaldiversity

#IamIrish, a project for a more diverse representation of Irish identity

#thinkdifferently #bornfreegeneration #intergenerational #mandelaslegacy

Smarteez girl, Chris Saunders

SÉQUENCE 1

How is the Irish heritage passed on?

A Irish symbols

GROUP WORK

GROUP A

GROUP B

GROUP C

1 Describe your group's pictures and identify as many Irish symbols as you can.

2 Explain what aspect of the Irish culture your pictures represent.

3 Prepare a short presentation about your group's pictures to the class.
Be ready to answer your classmates' questions.

Word Spot

Irish folklore
Gaelic /geɪlɪk/: a Celtic /keltɪk/ language spoken in Ireland
custom: tradition
cultural roots: cultural heritage
sense of unity
sense of belonging
respect traditions
share cultural references
be bilingual /baɪlɪŋgwəl/
have a strong significance: mean sthg important
pass along: transmit
be culturally rich
embrace /ɪmbreɪs/ your culture: welcome your culture
celebrate: honour, praise
preserve

Grammar Spot

Genitive Tools → p. 32
"My dad's wedding ring is a Claddagh."

B The Irish heritage

✦ The Claddagh ring

Growing up in a very Irish family, Claddaghs were everywhere. My dad's wedding ring is a Claddagh. Almost every anniversary gift that my dad got for my mom was from the Irish shop, and consisted of some form of a Claddagh. My grandma had the Claddagh in various forms. It was a symbol that was part of my family, and from a young age I fell in love with the story and symbolism behind it. I would like to share that story with you.

In Claddagh, Ireland, a fishing village, there was a young man and woman who were just a week away from being married. Pirates came into their village and took the men to sell them into slavery. Mr. Richard Joyce, the young man who was to be married, was sold to a Turkish goldsmith[1]. While he was working for this goldsmith, he never forgot about his true love back home. He crafted[2] a ring that he hoped to eventually[3] return home and give to the love of his life. This ring is now called the Claddagh. He was eventually freed from slavery, and was able to return home. When he got home he found his love and gave her the ring. After receiving the ring, they got married and their love lasted[4] forever. [...] The Claddagh has been such an important part of my heritage, and I am excited to share it with my children in the future. It is one of the most beautiful symbols of love. I hope that you will go out and share this story with other people!

Shannan McQuade

✦ www.theodysseyonline.com, Oct 11, 2016

1. jewellery maker and seller 2. created 3. finally 4. continued

1 Describe the ring. Guess what each element of the ring represents.

2 ***PAIR WORK*** Find out what the Claddagh ring symbolises and its origins using the two different documents (the text and the recording). Then share your findings with your partner.

Audio CD1 piste 05

Student A — **E-workbook** Fiche à imprimer hatier-clic.fr/lmu004

Student B — **E-workbook** Fiche à imprimer hatier-clic.fr/lmu005

3 Explain in a short paragraph why offering a Claddagh ring on Valentine's Day is symbolic.

C Irishness

1 Read the caption and describe the background and the people. Find elements which make you think about Ireland.

2 Guess the topics addressed by the people in the documentary.

`culture - emigration - heritage - music - identity`

✦ Gareth Alcorn and Trish Archer in the documentary *I am Irish* by journalist Una Mullally for RTÉ 2, April 2016

Prepare your project

PAIR WORK Act out an interview!

Student A You are an American journalist writing about Irish traditions and heritage.

Student B You are an Irish citizen. Talk about your Irish culture and heritage and how it is passed on by your family.

Grammar Tip Précis → p. 214

Pay attention to the word order in your **questions**.

Memory Challenge

Explain it to me! Choose a word related to Irish heritage and ask your classmate to explain it.

D Sharing a legendary heritage

Vidéo DVD

Pédagogie différenciée

TRAIL A

1. Watch the video and pick out keywords that define "Irish".
2. Focus on images, verbs, and words that refer to the Irish. Show that Charlotte's heritage is her guiding force.
3. Pick out the words showing she is proud of her culture.
4. List the forms Irish music takes in the video and say how important music is for her and the Irish.

TRAIL B

1. Watch the video and rephrase Charlotte's definition of being Irish.
2. Find elements she associates with her heritage.
3. Identify her views and her illustrations of Irish culture (events, people).
4. Explain Charlotte's opinion about Irish music.

Meet up! Define the concept of Irishness according to Charlotte in a one-minute presentation.

E Questioning cultural identity

Audio CD1 piste 06

#IamIrish — celebrating diversity —

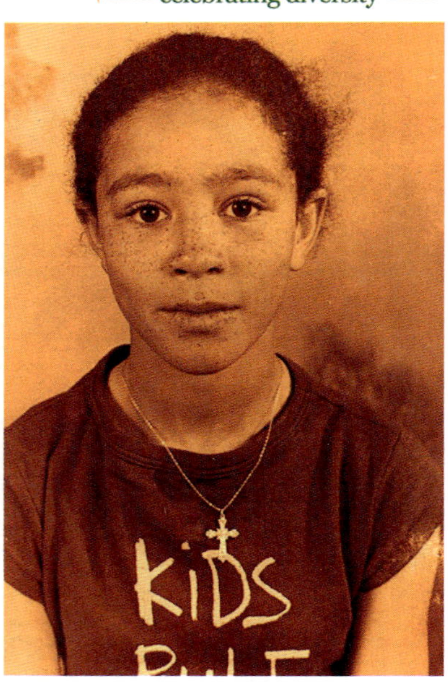

✦ Lorraine Maher age nine.

1. Listen to the recording and choose the subjects that Lorraine Maher addresses:

   `heritage - places of origin and living - childhood - future - history - Irish identity - politics.`

2. Focus on Lorraine's story of emigration and write down the verbs of movement, places and feelings. Narrate her journey in your own words.
3. Find elements Lorraine connects to her Irish heritage.
4. Describe Lorraine's experience of Irishness as a mixed-race person. Would you say it was positive? Justify your answer.

Culture Tip

Lorraine Maher is the creative director of the #IamIrish exhibition. The exhibition explored the Irish identity and features the diversity of the Irish by showing photographs of Irish people of mixed heritage.

Grammar Spot

Adjectives TOOLS → p. 32

"I grew up in a very **strong proud** Irish household."

Word Spot

community
diversity
diaspora /daɪæspərə/: a group of people from one country who spread to other countries
investigate: examine
identify /aɪdentɪfaɪ/ as
explore your roots
go abroad: go to another country
settle: start living somewhere
be of Irish descent

F Generations flying the same flag?

Classe inversée

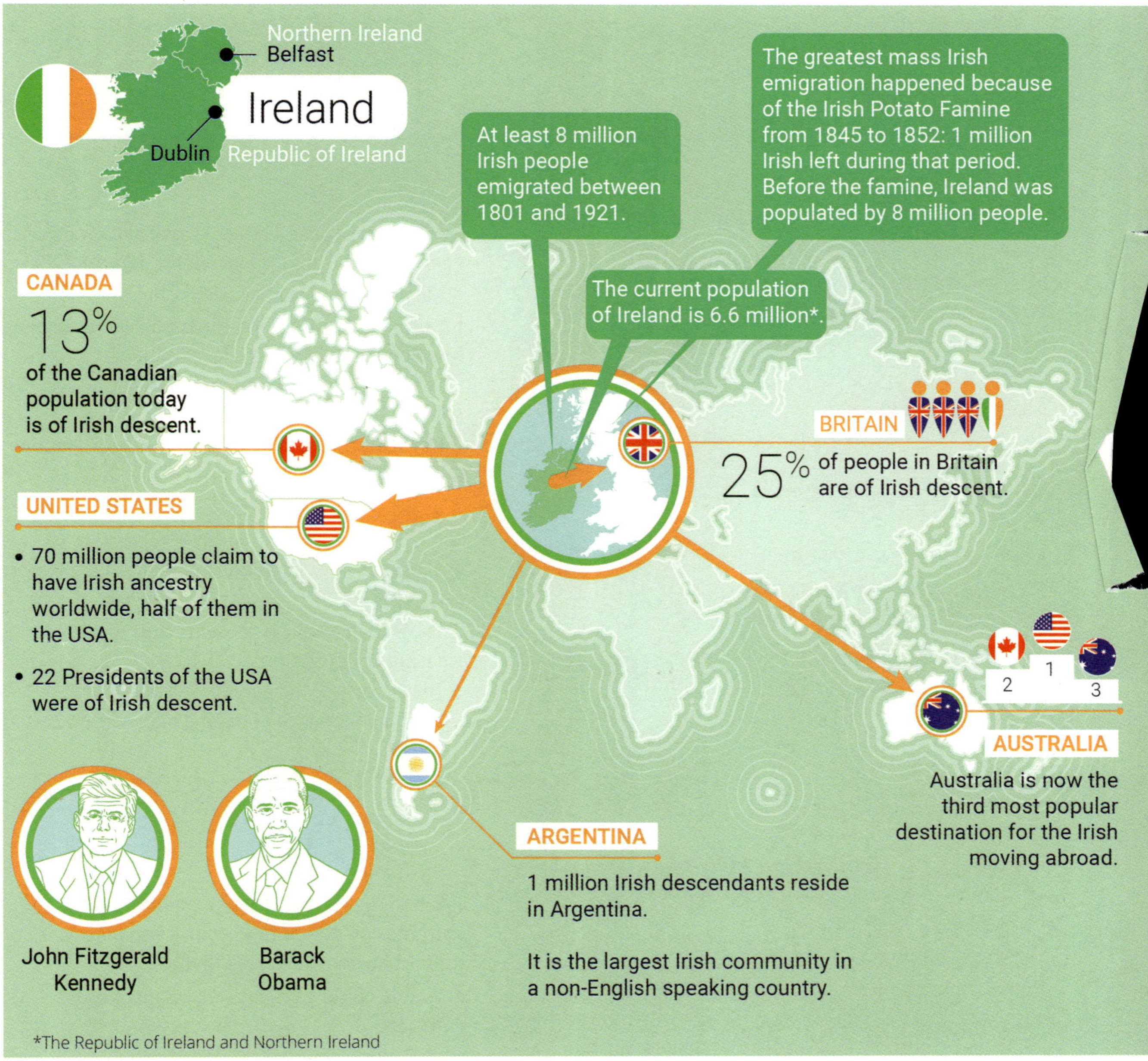

E-workbook
Classe inversée
hatier-clic.fr/lmu006

1 Look at the content and the flags used in the infographic and guess the topic.

2 Look at the numbers and the countries on the map. Explain what they reveal about the population of Ireland.

3 Look at the dates. Specify the cause of the Irish mass migration.

4 Barack Obama visited Ireland in 2011. Use elements from the infographic to write the speech he delivered when he arrived. Deliver your speech to the class explaining why Ireland is so important in the English-speaking world.

Prepare your project

You are an Irish-American writing an entry on your blog about your Irish roots. Tell your story and say why you are proud to be Irish.

Grammar Tip Précis → p. 228

Use the **passive voice** to show how the Irish culture was passed on to you.

Memory Challenge

Say all the words that come to your mind when you think about people of Irish origin.

Tools in the Spotlight

Practise your grammar

Précis grammatical, p. 192

Le génitif

Pour exprimer la **possession**, on peut utiliser le génitif. Il est généralement utilisé avec des mots désignant un être humain. Il peut aussi être utilisé avec des noms d'animaux, de lieux, d'institutions, d'objets liés à une activité humaine et avec des repères temporels.

Il se forme ainsi :

- nom singulier + **'s** + nom ;

This is my dad's wedding ring.
➔ C'est l'alliance de mon père.

- nom pluriel en s + **'** + nom.

These are my parents' wedding rings.
➔ Ce sont les alliances de mes parents.

⚠ Pas d'article devant un nom propre.
James Joyce's novels are great.

1 Remplacez l'adjectif possessif souligné par un génitif en utilisant les mots entre parenthèses.

a. Most of its sheep have a black head. (Ireland)
b. During the conference, his action was praised. (the President).
c. This *Book of Kells* was their copy. (Frank and Margaret)
d. Her sculpture was inaugurated in 1992. (Jeanne Rynhart)

2 Transformez le groupe nominal souligné avec un génitif.

a. The Dublin museum presents the most beautiful treasures of the Celts.
b. The success of the parade was fantastic.
c. The independence of Ireland began in 1922.

La place des adjectifs qualificatifs

- Les adjectifs se trouvent :
  - devant un **nom** (adjectifs épithètes) ;

*I just love our **rich** history.* (history : nom)

  - après un verbe d'**état** (l'adjectif est alors attribut du sujet) : *be*, *become*, *appear*, *feel*, *look*, *remain*, *seem*, *sound*...

*Tradition is really **strong** and I feel really **proud** of my culture.* (is, feel : verbe d'état)

- Lorsque plusieurs adjectifs sont utilisés devant un nom, ils doivent respecter l'ordre OTACOM :

Opinion **T**aille **Â**ge **C**ouleur **O**rigine **M**atière

A lovely big old green Irish steel shamrock.
(O) (T) (A) (C) (O) (M)

3 Indiquez si les adjectifs qualificatifs sont épithètes ou attributs. Pensez à leur place par rapport au nom qu'ils qualifient !

a. Ireland has always enjoyed a dynamic and rich culture.
b. Irish music sounds so unique to me.
c. The Irish culture is internationally famous.
d. To me, it's an instinctive identification with the history of the country.

4 Mettez dans l'ordre les adjectifs entre parenthèses.

a. For many, Ireland is a (small / beautiful) island.
b. The country also has (large / green) fields.
c. I'm definitely a (Irish / young / happy) person.
d. I think it's a (brilliant / short) documentary about Irishness.
e. It contributes to fighting against (racial / harmful) stereotypes.
f. Contrary to popular opinion only a few Irish men have (red / short / curly) hair.

Improve your pronunciation

Précis de phonologie, p. 242

La prononciation du -s à la fin des mots

Audio
CD1 piste 07
MP3 n° 09

Il existe trois façons différentes de prononcer un -*s* à la fin d'un mot : /s/, /z/ ou /ɪz/.

- Le -*s* à la fin d'un mot se prononce /s/ après les sons consonnes **t**, **k**, **p** et **th** : *pets*, *takes*, *cups*, *baths*.

- Le -*s* à la fin d'un mot se prononce /ɪz/ après les sons consonnes **s**, **sh**, **x**, **ch** et **z**. Ces mots forment leur pluriel par l'ajout de -*es*. Cette marque de **pluriel** se prononce /ɪz/ et constitue donc une syllabe supplémentaire : *brush* → *brushes*, *box* → *boxes*, *branch* → *branches*.

La marque de la **3e personne du présent simple** se prononce également /ɪz/ lorsque le verbe se termine par le son /ʃ/ ou /tʃ/ : *he or she washes*, *he or she catches*.

- Le -*s* se prononce /z/ dans tous les autres cas : *bags*, *cars*, *tables*, *drives*.

5 Prononcez ces mots et dites si le -*s* final se prononce /s/, /z/ ou /ɪz/. Puis vérifiez avec l'enregistrement.

Audio
CD1 piste 08
MP3 n° 10

a. fears b. tears c. faces d. pirates e. hopes f. woes g. Paul's h. bridges i. crops j. promises

6 Prononcez les mots et écrivez la bonne prononciation : /s /, /z/ ou /ɪz/. Écoutez l'enregistrement pour vérifier vos réponses.

Audio
CD1 piste 09
MP3 n° 11

a. boxes b. dreams c. dances d. plants e. Celtics f. causes g. emigrants h. moves i. cliffs j. passages

Work on your writing skills

La virgule et le point-virgule

- **La virgule** (*comma* en anglais) sépare les éléments d'une même phrase ou indique une pause.
En revanche, **le point-virgule** (*semicolon*) sépare des propositions indépendantes reliées logiquement entre elles.

- **La virgule** clarifie le sens d'une phrase ou souligne un élément, un point ou une signification. Elle sert par exemple à énumérer, séparer des adjectifs qui décrivent un nom. Elle sert aussi à interpeler ou attirer l'attention.

In Claddagh, Ireland, a fishing village, there was a young man and woman who were just a week away from being married.

- **Le point-virgule** sépare des propositions de même nature et sert à mettre en parallèle deux propositions pour éviter l'utilisation d'une conjonction (*and*, *but*).

I am sorry for not having written to you earlier; we really need to catch up on each other's news.

⚠ Contrairement au français, on ne met pas d'espace avant le point-virgule en anglais.

7 Insérez une virgule ou un point-virgule si nécessaire.

a. Irish history is full of stories of ... battles ... adventures and invasions.
b. The Celts' rich imagination has inspired fabulous ... fantastic ... stories.
c. He moved to Ireland ... she preferred to stay in America with her family.
d. He was crazy about meeting ... his favourite singer who played his favourite tunes.
e. When I watched the video you sent me from Ireland ... I felt I needed to go there.
f. The Galway team won the rugby match ... we lost the game by six points.
g. Film directors love filming sunsets ... they get the best light in Ireland.
h. Angus asked ... "What do you want for lunch?"
i. I visited the Cobh Heritage Centre ... it was a breathtaking experience about Irish history.

Build up your vocabulary

Audio
CD1 piste 10

Irishness

Culture
MP3 n°12

- speech: language
- Irish folklore
- Gaelic /geɪlɪk/: a Celtic /keltɪk/ language spoken in Ireland
- custom: tradition
- cultural roots: cultural heritage
- landscape: scenery
- national music
- share cultural references
- be bilingual /baɪlɪŋgwəl/
- have a strong significance: mean sthg important
- pass along: transmit
- be culturally rich
- embrace /ɪmbreɪs/ your culture: welcome your culture
- preserve

Heritage
MP3 n°15

- homeland: country of origin
- history
- ancestors ≠ descendants
- heritage: patrimony
- legacy
- sense of unity
- sense of belonging
- origin
- family tradition
- respectful
- celebrate: commemorate
- honour
- respect traditions
- symbolise

Identity
MP3 n°13

- diversity ≠ similarity
- citizenship
- otherness
- community
- diverse /daɪvɜːs/
- proud: showing pride
- unmistakable
- maintain: keep in existence
- explore your roots
- be of Irish descent
- identify /aɪdentɪfaɪ/ as

Migration
MP3 n°14

- diaspora /daɪæspᵊrə/: a group of people from one country who spread to other countries
- native /neɪtɪv/
- toward: in the direction of
- emigrate
- settle: start living somewhere
- go abroad: go to another country
- move: move house
- spread: disperse
- look backward ≠ look forward

Apprenez et révisez le vocabulaire !

Utilisez Quizlet pour vous entraîner en vous amusant.

Quizlet
hatier-clic.fr/lmu007

Utilisez le vocabulaire en contexte.

1 Complétez les phrases suivantes avec des mots de la carte mentale.

a. The island of Ireland is often named the Emerald Isle after the colour of the sea and the green ... .
b. In Ireland people learn two languages at school: English and ... . They are ... .
c. Many Irish people wear a Claddagh. The Claddagh ring ... love.
d. In the mid 1800s Irish people ... because of the potato famine.
e. The Irish have an original culture and they are proud to ... it to their children.
f. Many American people are of ... .

2 Écrivez un paragraphe sur les spécificités de la culture irlandaise en utilisant la traduction en anglais de ces mots, que vous trouverez dans la carte mentale.

héritage | langue | transmettre | préserver | fierté

AUTO évaluation

Faites le quiz interactif en ligne et suivez les conseils pour vous préparer à l'évaluation.

Quiz
hatier-clic.fr/lmu008

Project #1

Conduct an interview for a talk show on Raidió Teilifís Éireann. The topic is "what is great about being Irish".

1 Student A: the host

- Prepare the interview with a few questions. Use proper word order in your questions: **(WH-) + auxiliary + subject + verb (+ object)**.
- Present your talk show: introduce the topic and your guest.
- Thank the guest for coming.

2 Student B: the guest

- Choose who you are (name, age, hobbies) and where you come from in Ireland.
- Select a few symbols or celebrations that you enjoy as an Irish person.
- Explain what image you have of Irish people.

3 Student A and Student B: act out the talk show.

- Listen carefully to each other.
- Be polite and friendly.

4 Student A and Student B: conclude the talk show.

- Explain how the concept of Irishness can be different from one person to another.
- Remind the audience that Ireland is a multicultural society.

➤ Fiche de méthodologie N°19 p. 278

Project #2

To celebrate Irishness, create an infographic related to Irish culture and identity.

1 Choose a topic and do some research.

- Pick up a topic that you like about Irish culture or identity.
- Select some information but do not copy everything from a website.
- Make sure the information comes from a source you can trust like an encyclopedia.

2 Organise your findings.

- Find fun facts to make your infographic appealing.
- Use eye-catching keywords or titles and **superlatives**.

3 Create your infographic.

- Go online to find a template.
- Pay attention to the colours and the way you present the information.
- Use typically Irish pictures.

4 Sound Irish!

- Go online and find an Irish saying in Gaelic. Don't forget to write the translation in English.

➤ Fiche de méthodologie N°9 p. 261 N°10 p. 262

SÉQUENCE 2

How can the born-free generation build its future?

A The born-free generation

1 Describe the scene, the people and the atmosphere.

2 Identify the elements that refer to unity.

3 Say how this photograph portrays South Africa's youth and imagine what the event could be.

4 Create a caption for this photograph using the following words.

Soweto - march - anniversary

B Mandela's legacy

Vidéo DVD

✦ *South Africa's Post Apartheid Generation*, Journeyman Pictures, 2014

Culture Tip

Apartheid was a system that legally separated people on the basis of their skin colour. It started in 1948 and ended in 1991. The elections of 1994, which saw Nelson Mandela become the first president, changed the history of the country. Since then, South Africa has been called the **Rainbow Nation** promoting a free, multiracial and democratic society.

1 Define the topic of this video in one sentence.

2 Describe the young people featured in the video (physical appearance, mood, activities).

3 Using the photos in black and white and the Culture Tip, say all you can about life under apartheid.

4 Explain the role of culture for the born-free generation.

Grammar Spot

Present simple Tools → p. 40

"I **feel** like it's continuing what the youth of 1976 started."

Word Spot

- opportunity
- equality
- freedom
- a multicultural society
- diversity
- youth: youngsters
- a means of expression
- pop culture /kʌltʃəʳ/
- revolutionary
- express your creativity
- thrive /θraɪv/: succeed
- identify as

C The Smarteez

[The Smarteez are] part of a young generation of South Africans who were born after the struggles against apartheid. [They] admit to being different from the preceding generation; they are less committed[1] to political issues[2] and instead struggle[3] against blandness[4] and conformity by fighting for self-expression and challenging stereotypes. In their refusal to be defined by roots or race, the Smarteez take control of their identity, repositioning themselves as bold[5], original and creative in their approach to fashion and style, the makers of a whole new fashion scene in South Africa.

✦ makingafrica.net, April, 2015 (adapted)

1. dedicated 2. problems 3. fight
4. monotony 5. audacious

✦ Young designers in Soweto, Per-Anders Pettersson

1 Describe the picture as precisely as possible.

2 Read the text and say how the young generation differs from the previous generation of South Africans.

3 Describe how the Smarteez express their identity.

4 Explain who the Smarteez are to your history teacher (in French or in English).

D Portraying the South African youth

Vidéo
DVD

✦ Trailer for *Bayeza*, 10and5, 2017

1 Watch the video without the sound. Identify the places, the actions and the people. Guess what the video is about.

2 Choose the adjectives that describe the South African youth in the video. Justify your answers.

joyful – strange – pessimistic – cool – conscious – diverse – rebellious

3 Watch the video with the sound. List the adjectives the young South Africans use to describe themselves.

4 Record a one-minute video about the born-free generation which would follow these portraits.

Prepare your project

Create the cover of a magazine about the born-free generation. Find a title and the topics discussed in the magazine. Use a powerful photograph.

Grammar Tip Précis → p. 193

Pay attention to **articles** and capital letters.

Memory Challenge

In pairs, select five words that best symbolise the South African born-free generation.

E Being part of a new generation

Ballet dancer Thabang Mabaso grew up in Orange Farm, a poor township[1] outside Johannesburg, before going to art school. There he started to train as a dancer and is now a professional dancer in the Johannesburg ballet company.
He gives ballet lessons in the townships and knows his life would have been very different under apartheid.
"If we hadn't gained democracy in 1994," he says, "I'd have been perhaps a gardener but definitely not a ballet dancer."
He readily[2] acknowledges[3] that few blacks attend[4] his performances and adds that there has been opposition to his chosen profession closer to home.
"My mum never saw my ballet as a proper[5] job or career, she would always say: 'Oh you're going to go play ballet now?'"
However, Thabang believes that South Africa has the diversity and the potential to develop like the United States.
"I think we have similar histories and I believe that South Africa definitely could become like America."

✦ www.bbc.com, April 25, 2014

1. segregated area for non-white people during apartheid
2. easily 3. admits 4. go to 5. real

1 Identify the words related to dance. Complete the sentences to sum up Thabang's experience.
Thabang Mabaso studied in ... . After having started as ... , he became ... and now teaches ... .

2 In the following list, select the challenges that Thabang faced. Make a sentence explaining how Thabang's life became a success story.

people's opinion – previous political context – career – economic background – current political context

3 Pick out verbs describing speech and opinion. Focus on what comes after them and show that Thabang is optimistic.

4 Write a short paragraph to conclude the article.
In the next few years Thabang hopes...

F Opportunities or challenges?

Classe inversée

Audio
CD1 piste 11
MP3 n° 16

E-workbook
Classe inversée
hatier-clic.fr/lmu009

1 Note down information on Sharlote Mona and introduce her.

2 List the words related to politics in South Africa. Explain why the majority of the population is hopeful.

3 Pick out numbers about unemployment in the country. Comment on the situation of black South Africans today.

4 Use all the information in the recording and list the opportunities and challenges of the born-free generation in South Africa.

Grammar Spot

Relative clauses Tools → p. 40
"Sharlote escaped life under apartheid **which** kept blacks poor and uneducated."

Word Spot

- hope
- dream
- democratic elections
- apartheid /əpɑ:teɪt/
- youth: youngsters
- Rainbow Nation
- post-apartheid
- democracy
- discrimination
- (un)employment
- disillusion: disappointment
- optimistic ≠ pessimistic
- hopeful
- happy ≠ dissatisfied
- fulfil one's hopes
- have potential

G Expressing the born-free's freedom

In her photo essay, Alexia Webster looks at the lives of some young South Africans born in the very first years of democracy and asks them about what it means to be free.

Asandiswa Makapela, 20 years old - Langa, Cape Town
"I feel like a lot of change has been brought about since apartheid [...]. Black kids can go to white schools and we can even communicate with white people but it was hard back then[1]. But [...] people don't have opportunities, they are still poor and don't even have a good education".

Brode Gleeson, 17 years old - Camps Bay, Cape Town
"In certain ways the term freedom has changed. My parents were able to walk around freely at night, whereas[2] nowadays we don't have the same freedom. But our parents had to follow what their parents said or go into the army and I don't have that [...]. I wish I could be more safe, like in other countries."

✦ www.alexiawebster.com, 2012

1. in those days 2. while on the contrary

Pédagogie différenciée

TRAIL A

1 Read both texts and introduce the two characters in one sentence.

2 Explain the positive consequences the end of apartheid has had on the two youngsters.

3 List the three issues that still have to be solved in South Africa.

TRAIL B

1 Describe both pictures and imagine the characters' living conditions.

2 Oppose these two characters' lives with their parents'. Say what has changed for them.

3 List the difficulties South Africa still has to overcome.

Meet up! Imagine a meeting between Asandiswa Makapela and Brode Gleeson. They talk about their lifestyle and how it is different from their parents' generation. They also talk about their hopes for the future. Act out their conversation.

Prepare your project

Prepare a podcast for your school's radio station where you explain what the born-free generation is and what their hopes are.

Grammar Tip Précis → p. 217

Use **modal verbs** to express what people couldn't do and what they can do today.

Memory Challenge

Spell it out! Memorise as many words referring to South Africa as possible, then spell them out for your partner.

Tools in the Spotlight

Entraînez-vous sur la plateforme *Let's Meet Up!* **reussirenlangues.fr**

Practise your grammar

Précis grammatical, p. 192

Le présent simple

- On utilise le présent simple pour **caractériser** quelqu'un ou quelque chose : parler de son état, exprimer ses sentiments et son opinion.

On l'utilise aussi pour exprimer l'**habitude** et la **répétition**.

*Brode Gleeson **lives** with his mother in Cape Town.*
*He **seems** happy to live with her.*

Remarque : pour exprimer l'insistance dans une phrase déclarative, on peut ajouter *do* ou *does* devant le verbe.

*I **do feel** free.*

- Étant donné que le présent simple exprime une **habitude**, on le trouve souvent avec les adverbes de fréquence suivants : *sometimes*, *often*, *usually*, *always*, *never*.

She often flies to South Africa.

La proposition relative

- ***Who, which, that*** sont des pronoms relatifs. Ils peuvent être sujets ou compléments de verbe.

who → humain *which* ou *that* → non-humain

- ***Who, which, that*** introduisent une proposition relative qui détermine le nom qu'elle complète. Elle est alors indispensable. Il n'y a pas de virgule avant le pronom relatif.

*There is a reticence to tunes **that** sound like digital music.*

*Nadine Gordimer is the South-African writer **who** was awarded the literature Nobel Prize back in 1991.*

*The Cape Town bus **which** is not running today is being repaired.*

⚠ Ces pronoms peuvent être omis quand ils sont compléments d'objet.

*The new fashion trend **Ø** the youth follow is revolutionary. (Ø = that)*

- ***Who, which*** introduisent une proposition relative qui apporte une précision au nom qu'elle complète. Elle n'est pas indispensable et est séparée par une virgule.

*The album, **which** is still in process, will have four tracks.*

*The woman, **who** has just arrived, comes from Johannesburg.*

1 Identifiez la valeur du présent simple : caractérisation ou habitude / répétition.

a. Teenagers hope to have a better future.
b. I often travel to Durban because of my work.
c. More and more young people matriculate at university each year.
d. We prefer not to look at the past.
e. You look very disappointed.

2 Indiquez l'adverbe ou l'élément qui justifie le présent simple dans la phrase.

a. This guide organises package tours to Cape Town every six months.
b. Whenever people think of South Africa, they think of the films *Out of Africa* or *Cry Freedom*.
c. Some cinema-goers sometimes mention the films *Invictus* or *Mandela and de Klerk*.

3 Repérez la proposition relative et le nom qu'elle complète. Dites si elle détermine ou précise le nom.

a. Thabang Mabaso is the ballet dancer who grew up in Orange Farm.
b. His mother, who wanted him to do another job, never considered ballet as a proper career.
c. South Africa, which has enough diversity to develop like the US, has changed a lot since 1994.
d. Orange Farm is a township that is located outside Johannesburg.

4 Choisissez le bon pronom relatif : *that, who, which* ou Ø.

a. I am working on a project ... portrays the youth.
b. The ballet dancer ... has been successful is Thabang Mabaso.
c. The teen ... I met adores the Smarteez.
d. They are finishing the recording of a song, ... will be out in a month.

Improve your pronunciation

Précis de phonologie, p. 242

Les sons /ʊ/ et /uː/

Audio
CD1 piste 12
MP3 n° 17

Les sons /ʊ/, voyelle brève, et /uː/, voyelle longue, peuvent correspondre à plusieurs graphies, donc à des orthographes différentes.

- Le son /ʊ/ peut correspondre à la graphie :
  - **o** (*wolf*, *woman*)
  - **oo** (*book*, *foot*, *cook*)
  - **ou** (*could*, *would*, *should*)
  - **u** (*put*, *pull*, *push*, *butcher*)
- Le son /uː/ peut correspondre à la graphie :
  - **oeu** (*manœuvre*)
  - **ew** (*crew*, *new*)
  - **o** (*lose*, *move*, *two*, *do*)
  - **oe** (*canoe*, *shoe*)
  - **oo** (*shoot*, *cool*, *food*)
  - **ou** (*through*, *youth*)
  - **u** (*Luke*, *issue*, *glue*)
  - **ui** (*fruit*, *juice*, *bruise*)

5 Écoutez et classez les mots selon leur prononciation /ʊ/ ou /uː/.

Audio
CD1 piste 13
MP3 n° 18

a. full • fool
b. school • rule
c. could • cool
d. youth • truth
e. put • root

6 Écoutez et classez les mots selon leur prononciation /ʊ/ ou /uː/.

Audio
CD1 piste 14
MP3 n° 19

Zulu • book • student • queue • woman • look • move • foot • through • produce • would • opportunity • who • good • improve • lose

Work on your writing skills

Les majuscules

On utilise principalement les majuscules dans les cas suivants :

– en **début de phrase** ;
He gives ballet lessons in the townships.

– pour les **noms propres** (personnes, villes, pays, continents…) ;
Nelson Mandela, *Johannesburg*, *South Africa*

– dans les **titres** qui font référence à une personne précise ;
Miss Dutoit, *President Zuma*, *King Shaka*

– pour les **lieux** spécifiques ;
Ponte City Tower

– pour les **nationalités**, groupes ethniques et langues ;
South Africans, *Zulus*, *English*

– dans les titres d'**œuvres**, les noms d'**organisations** et les **marques** ;
Bayeza, *A Dry White Season*

– pour le **pronom** personnel sujet de la première personne du singulier : *I* ;

– dans les noms des **jours** de la semaine, **mois**, jours fériés et périodes historiques ;
Monday, *March*, *Easter*

– dans les **abréviations**.
ANC (African National Congress)

7 Rétablissez les majuscules aux bons endroits dans les phrases. Justifiez vos choix à l'oral.

a. the capital city in south africa is pretoria.
b. june 16 is now a public holiday named youth day.
c. do you know *black diamond*? it is a south african novel.
d. it is about a bodyguard who works at vip protection services and a woman who owns an old fiat uno.
e. one of the funniest replies is: "you are not dressed, mr naidoo."
f. i wish i could visit the carlton centre in johannesburg.

Build up your vocabulary

Audio
CD1 piste 15

South Africa's young generation
MP3 n°20

youth: youngsters
apartheid /əpɑːteɪt/
born-free
Mandela's generation
post-apartheid
Rainbow Nation
legacy: heritage
forgiveness
diversity
reconciliation
conscious: aware
trendy
audacious
enthusiastic
talented
thrive /θraɪv/: succeed
have potential
forgive

South Africa

Politics
MP3 n°23

freedom
democracy
democratic elections
activism
free expression
human rights
apolitical: without political opinion
defend
convey a message
reconstruct
denounce
raise awareness

Culture
MP3 n°21

a multicultural society
a means of expression
pop culture /kʌltʃə^{r}/
tradition
modern
vibrant
revolutionary
express your creativity
identify as

Struggles and successes
MP3 n°22

equality ≠ inequality
opportunities ≠ challenges
discrimination
disillusion: disappointment
education
issue: problem
(un)employment
segregation
potential
living conditions
optimistic ≠ pessimistic
happy ≠ dissatisfied
hopeful
fulfil one's hopes
dream
lose hope

Apprenez et révisez le vocabulaire !

Utilisez Quizlet pour vous entraîner en vous amusant.

Quizlet
hatier-clic.fr/lmu010

Utilisez le vocabulaire en contexte.

1 Replacez ces mots de la carte mentale au bon endroit.

legacy • unemployment • disappointment • democracy • youth • challenges • convey a message • apolitical • thrive • opportunities • segregation • multicultural.

a. Sadly geographical ... is still a reality in South Africa.
b. The ... rate among the ... is very high.
c. South Africans are facing a lot of ... and ... at the same time.
d. The economy can only ... if the government takes serious measures.
e. Nelson Mandela's ... is peace, hope and dignity.
f. Today the country is a young ... and is officially a ... society.
g. Do you think that ballet can ...?
h. ... towards politicians partly explains the ... behaviour of people.

2 Dites ce que la génération *born-free* représente pour vous en utilisant au moins deux mots de chaque catégorie de la carte mentale.

AUTO évaluation

Faites le quiz interactif en ligne et suivez les conseils pour vous préparer à l'évaluation.

Quiz
hatier-clic.fr/lmu011

Project #1

Make a portrait of a member of the born-free generation for a documentary.

1 Introduce your character.
- ✓ Choose your character's name, age, and family background.
- ✓ Decide on your character's occupation (student, young professional...).
- ✓ Select her or his interests.

2 Prepare her or his historical background.
- ✓ Explain how her or his family's life changed after apartheid.
- ✓ Use dates and real events to connect your character's story to the history of South Africa.
- ✓ Use the **preterite** to talk about the past.

3 Talk about your character's present situation.
- ✓ Talk about the impact of post-apartheid in your character's life today.
- ✓ State if your character is facing any difficulties (education, employment).
- ✓ Talk about her or his hopes for the future.

4 Prepare yourself and act it out!
- ✓ Rehearse your portrait to make it sound as natural as possible.
- ✓ Check your pronunciation on an online dictionary.
- ✓ End on a positive note or a slogan to show the potential of South Africa.

➤ Fiche de méthodologie N°20 p. 280

Project #2

Write an article showcasing the new face of post-apartheid South Africa.

1 Introduce the born-free generation.
- ✓ Give a definition of the born-free generation.
- ✓ Explain its link with Nelson Mandela.

2 Say what the end of apartheid means in people's lives.
- ✓ Express the feelings of joy that people felt. Use powerful **adjectives** and **superlatives**.
- ✓ Describe the opportunities and challenges for South Africans today.
- ✓ Explain how they relate to politics.

3 Talk about their life and culture.
- ✓ Say how they feel in today's South Africa.
- ✓ Give information about their lifestyle and culture.
- ✓ Use the **simple present** to talk about their life.

4 Conclude
- ✓ Write a short conclusion about the born-free generation.
- ✓ Underline their hopes.

➤ Fiche de méthodologie N°22 p. 284

Let's RECAP

Lisez les questions-clés et complétez la fiche bilan avec des exemples et des documents que vous avez étudiés ou découverts.

AXE 1 | Intergenerational relationships

SÉQUENCE 1 How is the Irish heritage passed on?

E-workbook
Bilan à compléter
hatier-clic.fr/lmu012

How are Irish traditions and history passed on to the next generations? How is the Irish culture spread across the world?

#traditions
How do Irish traditions establish a link between generations globally?

#generations
How do generations communicate and pass on their traditions?

#heritage
How is the Irish heritage celebrated? How does it reach people across the world?

#culturaldiversity
How culturally diverse are the Irish?

#irishness
What does it mean to be Irish today?

SÉQUENCE 2 How can the born-free generation build its future?

E-workbook
Bilan à compléter
hatier-clic.fr/lmu013

What are the opportunities and challenges for this South-African generation? How do they perceive their future?

#thinkdifferently
How have priorities and interests changed for the generation born after 1994?

#mandelaslegacy
What has changed since the end of apartheid? How far has it opened opportunities for new generations?

#intergenerational
How do new generations see themselves in comparison with their parents' generation?

#bornfreegeneration
What does it mean to be part of the born-free generation? What are this generation's ambitions?

GO4IT!

Lisez et écoutez de l'anglais en dehors de la salle de classe ! Voici quelques conseils en lien avec votre séquence.

SÉQUENCE 1

Books

Walk the Blue Fields,
CLAIRE KEEGAN, 2007

Scarlet Feather,
MAEVE BINCHY, 2000

The Commitments,
RODDY DOYLE, 1987

Films

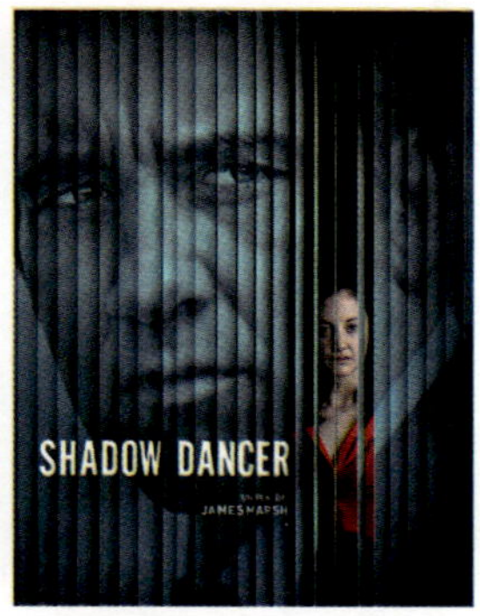

Music

THE DUBLINERS
THE POGUES
DE DANNAN
PLANXTY
ANDY IRVINE
U2
THE CORRS

Timeline

http://bbc.in/2EwJ7th

Country ID, p. 188

SÉQUENCE 2

Books

The Hidden Star, K. SELLO DUIKER, 2006

Coconut, KOPANO MATLWA, 2007

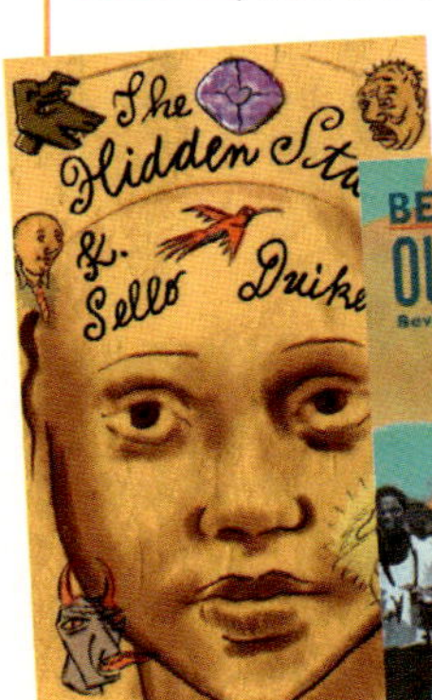

Out of Bounds: Seven Stories of Conflict and Hope,
BEVERLEY NAIDOO, 2001

Mama Africa!: How Miriam Makeba Spread Hope with Her Song,
KATHRYN ERSKINE, CHARLY PALMER, 2017

Films

Online portfolios

http://www.alexiawebster.com/this-generation/
http://www.chrissaunders.co
https://graemewilliams.co.za/as-the-grass-grows-2/

Timeline

Country ID, p. 190

AXE 2

Professional fields, the world of work

Les univers professionnels, le monde du travail

SÉQUENCE 1

Do gap years really prepare for work life?

Projects

Project #1: Take part in the competition: "Win a free gap year abroad!" Prepare a video to show you are the best candidate.

Project #2: Write an email to apply for an internship during your gap year abroad.

Tools

Grammaire la phrase simple, verbe + *to* + infinitif, l'impératif
Phonologie la diphtongue /eə/
Écriture l'e-mail formel
Vocabulaire la personnalité, le travail

SÉQUENCE 2

Is Canada a dream job country?

Projects

Project #1: Act out a phone conversation between a potential immigrant and a Canadian immigration advisor.

Project #2: Create a poster to encourage young people to move to Canada for a contest set up by the Canadian government.

Tools

Grammaire l'article indéfini (*a* / *an*), *can* et *may*
Phonologie la prononciation de *-ng*
Écriture la ponctuation du dialogue
Vocabulaire l'immigration, le travail

#careerchoice #volunteering #socialising #workingabroad #dreamjob

#opportunity #immigration #work #dream #younggeneration

Nathan Phillips Square, Toronto

SÉQUENCE 1

Do gap years really prepare for work life?

A Taking a gap year

GROUP WORK

GROUP A

"Make the world your classroom!" Vidéo DVD

✦ *Studying abroad – why you should do it!*
University of Adelaide, Australia, 2015

GROUP B

"A year off before College" Audio CD1 piste 16

Journalist Tanya Rivero and University of Michigan sociology professor Elizabeth Armstrong speak about taking a gap year in the TV program *Lunch Break* by *The Wall Street Journal*.

GROUP C "The best four months of my life"

I worked on a summer camp in the USA for four months a few years ago and it was without a doubt the best four months of my life. I couldn't afford to take a full year out so I went to camp, and then went to Australia to hang out with all my newfound friends for two months. If you even have the slightest inkling[1] that you'd like to go travelling I'd definitely say go for it. If you're nervous about going by yourself then join a project or experience like I did. I loved being away from home in the end and I strongly believe it has made me all the more employable and interesting in later life.

✦ Lucy Harper, author of *Secret Diary of a Camp Counselor*, 2011

1. vague idea

Pédagogie différenciée GROUP WORK

1. With your group, study your document and create a mind map with key words.
2. List the benefits of taking a gap year.
3. With your classmates, write a definition of a gap year and share it with the class.

Grammar Spot

Simple sentences Tools → p. 52

"Gap years have long been popular in Europe and Australia."

Verb + *to* + infinitive Tools → p. 52

"I couldn't afford **to** take a full year out."

Word Spot

- autonomy
- opportunity: chance
- career /kərɪəʳ/
- internship: work experience
- full-time ≠ part-time, half-time
- beneficial: profitable
- helpful
- volunteer: help
- work for a charity
- join a project: engage in a project
- achieve a goal
- grow up: mature
- fulfil oneself
- take some time off school

B The gap year trend

America's (small) new trend: taking a gap year

Gap years have long been popular in Europe and Australia. Now, a small but growing group of U.S. teens and their parents are jumping aboard the gap year trend.

When Hillary Billings' oldest son, Ted, was accepted at New York University (NYU), she was proud – but concerned. "We felt he needed another year to mature," Billings says. Before her son was "thrown into the deep end[1] in the Big Apple," she wanted him to take a gap year to mature a little so he'd be ready for the urban living, social life, and academics at NYU. […]

Gap years have long been popular in Europe and Australia. The concept originated in the grand tours enjoyed by aristocratic youth in the late 17th, 18th, and early 19th centuries. […]

Upper-class vagabonds traversed the continent and exotic corners of the British Empire, familiarizing themselves with foreign flavors, curious customs, and opposing perspectives. In the 1970s, soul-searching backpackers put their twist on[2] the tradition, which continues today. Due to economic conditions in 2012, only 12.5 percent of UK students took a gap year – it was the lowest number in a decade. In Australia, nearly a quarter of all students take gap years. In the U.S., though, the numbers are much smaller: an estimated 1.2 to 2 percent of students take a gap year. […] Celebrity endorsers[3] and media coverage help fuel the trend[4]. Malia Obama's gap year, before starting Harvard in fall 2017, is an internship at the U.S. Embassy in Spain. Benedict Cumberbatch spent his teaching English at a Tibetan Buddhist monastery, and Prince Harry helped build a clinic in Lesotho, Africa. […]

Gap year companies also play a role, motivating curious parents, particularly those who can afford the astronomical prices. (A three-month excursion to broaden your teen's perspective can cost upwards of $15,000 – and still leaves teens 3/4 of the year… for parents to pay for?)

✦ Hank Pellissier, greatschools.org, June 21, 2018

1. put into a new situation without preparation or introduction
2. interpreted it to suit their needs
3. supporters
4. make it popular

1 Look for dates and places. Show the origins and evolution of gap years.

2 Name three celebrities who took a gap year. Say what their gap years consisted in.

3 Pick out words related to money. Show how it can be a barrier to taking a gap year.

4 Explain to your school's careers officer why taking a gap year is a new trend in the USA.

Prepare your project

Prepare a one-minute audio for your school radio station to explain why people should take gap years and why it can be beneficial.

Grammar Tip Précis → p. 227

Use **should** to give advice.

Memory Challenge

Look at the picture above. You have two minutes to find as many words relating to the topic as possible.

C Living abroad

Classe inversée

Vidéo hatier-clic.fr/lmu014

E-workbook Classe inversée hatier-clic.fr/lmu015

1 Find out the three types of gap year Anne talks about.

2 Use the following words to explain what could be positive about taking a gap year.

skills - confidence - sell - volunteering - internship

3 ***PAIR WORK*** Play the "Yes, but..." game. Choose an idea and say it to your classmate. He or she needs to listen and give a counter argument.

It'll help you find the right career. · It can be dangerous! · It's expensive! · You'll be a year behind... · You'll have tons of stories! · It'll be an incredible adventure... · You'll have a great CV. · You'll feel homesick...

D Let's apply!

African Conservation Experience

info@conservationafrica.net
+44 (0) 1454 269182
www.conservationafrica.net

African Conservation Experience offer volunteering opportunities at wildlife conservation projects in southern Africa. You can count on our full support and more than 10 years experience. See our main advert in Conservation.

Flying Fish UK Ltd

mail@flyingfishonline.com
+44 (0)1983 280641
www.flyingfishonline.com

Flying Fish trains and recruits over 1000 people each year to work worldwide as yacht skippers and as sailing, diving, surfing, windsurfing, ski and snowboard instructors.

Adventure Alternative

office@adventurealternative.com
+44 (0) 28 708 31258
www.adventurealternative.com

Teaching and volunteering in needy schools and orphanages in Kenya and in schools in Kathmandu (includes Himalayan trek).

AmeriCamp

info@americamp.co.uk
0161 312 3640
www.americamp.co.uk

We offer people around the world the chance to work in the USA at a summer camp and become an AmeriCamper. We pay at least $1,500 per month and you make memories that last a lifetime! Join the AmeriCamp Revolution!

1 Read these ads. List the types of activities you can do during a gap year.

2 In the Word Spot, pick out words you find appropriate for each job. Use them to make one sentence per job.

3 Choose one of these ads and prepare your written application. Describe yourself using five adjectives and find three reasons why you would be perfect for the work or volunteer position.

Grammar Spot

Imperative Tools → p. 52
"Join the Americamp revolution!"

Word Spot

position: job
empathy: compassion
flexibility ≠ rigidity
self-assurance
kind: nice ≠ nasty
outgoing ≠ shy
energetic: dynamic
hardworking ≠ lazy
responsible ≠ irresponsible
sociable: easy-going
reliable ≠ unreliable
honest /ɒnɪst/
mature /mətʃʊəʳ/
look after: babysit: take care of
charity work

E The gap year quiz

You decide: is a gap year right for you?

A special quiz to help you make up your mind, by Professor Cary Cooper, professor of organisational psychology and health at Lancaster University Management School.

Circle the response that most applies to you.

1 In making a decision about most things, I usually:
[a] know my own mind and make decisions straight away
[b] take some time to make them
[c] try to avoid making a decision as long as I can

2 In my lifetime, I have travelled:
[a] a great deal in many countries
[b] to some countries with my parents in the summer
[c] hardly at all

3 While at school, I have:
[a] worked in a number of jobs whenever I had the time
[b] done some work but infrequently
[c] done little or no paid work

4 During my teenage years, I tend to:
[a] often get involved in volunteering work in the UK and abroad
[b] do some volunteer work at home and abroad but not a lot
[c] get on with my studies and do little or no volunteer work

5 My parents tend to:
[a] let me do as I please
[b] provide me with some space to do as I wish but create quite a few limits
[c] set very strict limits on my behaviour and provide me with little personal space

6 The expectations of my parents on my future career:
[a] are minimal and they leave it up to me
[b] are moderate, with subtle pressure to do some kinds of jobs
[c] are very heavy, wanting me to do only certain types of job

7 I really know what I want to do for a job and career:
[a] very much
[b] somewhat
[c] I don't actually have a clue

The Guardian

1 Take the quiz yourself.

2 ***PAIR WORK*** Ask your partner his or her score and compare your answers.

E-workbook
Fiche à imprimer
hatier-clic.fr/lmu016

3 Do you agree with the advice given based on your score? Speak for one minute to give your opinion about it.

Memory Challenge

Your partner gives you an internship field or a volunteering experience field. Say all the words that come to mind.

Prepare your project

Prepare a face-to-face interview. Choose a job and write five questions to ask a candidate.

Grammar Tip Précis → p. 214

To ask a question you need:
(question word) + auxiliary + subject + verb (+ object)?

Tools in the Spotlight

Entraînez-vous sur la plateforme *Let's Meet Up!*
reussirenlangues.fr

Practise your grammar

Précis grammatical, p.192

La phrase simple

• La phrase simple est une phrase déclarative qui suit le modèle **SVO** : **S**ujet + **V**erbe + **O**bjet.

He took a gap year.
S V O

• À cette base, il est possible d'ajouter des **compléments circonstanciels** (de temps, de lieu, de manière, etc.) ou un **adjectif** si l'on utilise un auxiliaire.

*Gap years have long been **popular** **in Europe and Australia**.*
S V adjectif complément de lieu

• La phrase simple peut être **coordonnée** (par ***and***), mais elle ne comporte pas de subordonnée (réservée à la phrase complexe).

*He took a gap year **and** spent 12 months in the UK.*

1 **Indiquez les phrases simples et les phrases complexes.**

a. She did an internship in Cape Town.
b. He took a gap year in India and studied Indian culture.
c. As she was interested in American culture, she preferred to go to the United States.
d. A gap year is usually a first step towards more independence.
e. They have saved money for their children's gap year, although they come from a poor background.
f. When you have finished filling in your gap year form, please contact the university dean directly.
g. They enjoyed their gap year in Australia.

Verbe + *to* + infinitif

• Certains verbes sont toujours suivis directement par un infinitif en ***to*** : *afford, consent, fail, hasten, hesitate, learn, manage, offer, prepare, refuse, tend, threaten, undertake, volunteer.*

*I couldn't afford **to** take a full year out.*

• D'autres verbes peuvent être suivis soit par un infinitif en ***to*** soit par une proposition introduite par ***that*** : *agree, arrange, claim, decide, demand, hope, pretend, promise, swear, pretend.*

*She hopes **to** spend a gap year in New Zealand.*
*She hopes **that** her parents will back up her project.*

2 **Complétez les phrases suivantes par l'infinitif en *to* ou par le gérondif.**

a. She is interested in (**to spend** / **spending**) a year in Canada.
b. But she doesn't know whether she can afford (**to spend** / **spending**) a whole year or only six months there.
c. They have volunteered (**to build** / **building**) a hospital in India.
d. After (**to arrive** / **arriving**) in South Africa, he managed (**to find** / **finding**) a studio flat in Cape Town.
e. He promised (**to visit** / **visiting**) his aunt, who lives in Cape Town.

L'impératif

• L'impératif est constitué de la base verbale seule à la **2e personne du singulier ou du pluriel**.

Join the Americamp revolution!

• À la **3e personne du singulier ou du pluriel**, il se construit avec ***Let*** + pronom complément + base verbale.

***Let her choose** Canada if she wants, why not?*
***Let them pack up!** They are flying soon.*

• À la **forme négative** de l'impératif, on utilise ***don't*** + base verbale.

***Don't waste** your time and apply immediately!*

3 **Écrivez des phrases à l'impératif à partir des expressions suivantes.**

a. Change your currency (**you**)
b. Forget your visa (**you + not**)
c. Invite them over to our farewell party (**us**)
d. Take your camera with you (**you**)
e. Speak your mother tongue (**you + not**)
f. Speak as much English as you can (**you**)
g. Go to the airport now (**us**)

Improve your pronunciation

Précis de phonologie, p. 242

La diphtongue /eə/

Audio CD1 piste 17 MP3 n° 24

- La diphtongue /eə/ est généralement **suivie de la lettre *r*.**
- Cette diphtongue peut correspondre à plusieurs graphies :
  - graphie ***ar*** (*dare, share, stare, bare, Mary, wary*)
  - graphie ***air*** (*pair, hair, fair, dairy, chair*)
  - graphie ***ear*** (*pear, bear, tear, wear*)
  - graphie ***eir*** (*their*)
  - graphie ***ere*** (*there*)

4 **Indiquez pour les mots suivants s'il s'agit du son /e/ ou /eə/, puis vérifiez avec l'enregistrement.**

Audio CD1 piste 18 MP3 n° 25

pear • pet • there • wear • vet • debt • dare • stare

5 **Indiquez le son /eə/ dans les phrases suivantes, puis vérifiez et répétez avec l'enregistrement.**

Audio CD1 piste 19 MP3 n° 26

a. They shared a flat in Maryland.
b. They wear a T-shirt and shorts when they go to a tropical place.
c. Beware of the sun and bring a pair of sunglasses!
d. If you tear your ticket, you can be fairly sure there will be a problem.

Work on your writing skills

L'e-mail formel

Pour écrire un e-mail formel à quelqu'un que l'on ne connaît pas, il faut suivre quelques règles.

Destinataire :
@nomdel'entreprise ou hébergeurdel'adresseemail

Émetteur·trice :
votre adresse e-mail

-Cc (*carbon copy*) :
destinataire qui recevra une copie de l'e-mail

To: liz.turner@cnn.com
From: jeff.guill@gmail.com
Cc: pamela.carfax@gmail.com
Subject: Gap year internship

Dear Mrs Turner

I would like to do an internship in your company during my gap year. [...]
You will find my CV attached.
I look forward to hearing from you very soon.
If you have any questions, do not hesitate to contact me.

Yours sincerely

Jeff Guill

Pièce jointe à l'e-mail :
CV (UK) = *resume* (US)

Autre formule possible :
I look forward to your reply.

Salutations
Si on connaît les destinataires :
Dear Mr / Mrs + NOM (sans virgule)
avec *Yours sincerely* (sans virgule)
ou *Kind regards*

Si on ne connaît pas les destinataires :
Dear Sir or Madam (sans virgule)
avec *Yours faithfully* (sans virgule)

6 **Écrivez un e-mail à Kate Toleafoa, directrice de Gap Year International en Nouvelle Zélande pour lui demander des informations sur les stages possibles dans les fermes néo-zélandaises. Vous mettez en copie votre professeur, Ronan Philips.**

Build up your vocabulary

Audio
CD1 piste 20

Personality MP3 n°27

empathy: compassion
flexibility ≠ rigidity
kind: nice ≠ nasty
responsible ≠ irresponsible
outgoing ≠ shy
energetic: dynamic
hardworking ≠ lazy
sociable: easy-going
reliable ≠ unreliable
honest /ɒnɪst/
mature /mətʃʊə^{r}/
confident

Skills MP3 n°28

listener /lɪs^{ə}nə^{r}/
teamwork
leadership
management
communication
creativity
interpersonal skills
IT /aɪti:/
social media
communicate
cooperate
coordinate
organise

Growing up MP3 n°31

autonomy
self-assurance
confidence
grow up: become mature
fulfil oneself
know who you really are
achieve a goal
take some time off school
travel

Gap year

Professional experience MP3 n°30

CV (*GB*): resume (*US*)
career /kərɪə^{r}/
position: job
full-time ≠ part-time, half-time
internship: work experience
volunteer work ≠ paid work
charity work
opportunity: chance
cashier
salesperson
dog walker
teacher
babysitter
look after children: babysit

Volunteering MP3 n°29

community
charity
fundraiser
beneficial: profitable
helpful
generous
engage in a project
volunteer: help for free
work for a charity

Apprenez et révisez le vocabulaire !

Utilisez Quizlet pour vous entraîner en vous amusant.

Quizlet
hatier-clic.fr/lmu017

Utilisez le vocabulaire en contexte.

1 Écrivez la fin des phrases suivantes en utilisant des mots de la carte mentale.

a. Taking a gap year is great because...
b. When on a gap year you can...
c. Doing charity work is a good way to be...
d. In order to get a job on a gap year you need to have...
e. You can learn about yourself whilst living abroad and...
f. Young people can develop their skills and show...

2 Vous expliquez à vos parents que vous allez apprendre beaucoup pendant votre année de césure à l'étranger. Écrivez un court dialogue en utilisant au moins 15 mots de la carte mentale.

AUTO évaluation

Faites le quiz interactif en ligne et suivez les conseils pour vous préparer à l'évaluation.

Quiz
hatier-clic.fr/lmu018

Project #1

Take part in the competition: "Win a free gap year abroad!" Prepare a video to show you are the best candidate.

1 Pick the type of gap year you would like to take.

- ✓ You could discover the world by travelling, do internships to find the right career, help the community by joining a charity...

2 Think about why you are the best candidate and how it would be beneficial for you.

- ✓ Find arguments based on your personal experience and the documents of the unit.
- ✓ Make a list of adjectives you can use to describe yourself.

3 Organise your act!

- ✓ Use linking words to present your arguments: **to start with, first of all, moreover, also, in addition, more importantly**; and to give examples: **for instance, for example...**

4 Be creative in the way you present your video.

- ✓ Use the **present tense** to introduce yourself.
- ✓ Find ways to stand out with a special setting, costume or music! Use humour :)

5 Practice... until you have the perfect shot!

- ✓ Check the pronunciation of difficult words on wordreference.com and repeat them over and over.
- ✓ Don't speak too quickly. Be clear.

Fiche de méthodologie N°12 p. 266

Project #2

Write an email to apply for an internship during your gap year abroad.

1 Imagine your dream internship.

- ✓ Think about what you would like to do: work in a large international company, try an unusual job in an amazing place...

2 Introduce yourself.

- ✓ Present your academic studies using the **preterite** with verbs such as **pass, get a degree in + year...**
- ✓ Put forward your sporting achievements and your cultural activities: music, art...
- ✓ Describe your community involvement using the **present perfect**: **I have already helped... I have taken part in...**

3 Convince your future employer.

- ✓ Indicate which internship you are applying for and why you chose it.
- ✓ Prove you are the best candidate using adjectives from the mind map p. 54.
- ✓ Use linking words to structure your email: **firstly, secondly, then, in addition...**

4 Present your email correctly.

- ✓ Use the correct salutations. Start with: **Dear + Mr / Mrs + family name**, and finish with: **Yours sincerely + your name**.
- ✓ Point out that your CV is attached to your email.

Fiche de méthodologie N°14 p. 270

SÉQUENCE 2

Is Canada a dream job country?

A Young Canadians' future jobs

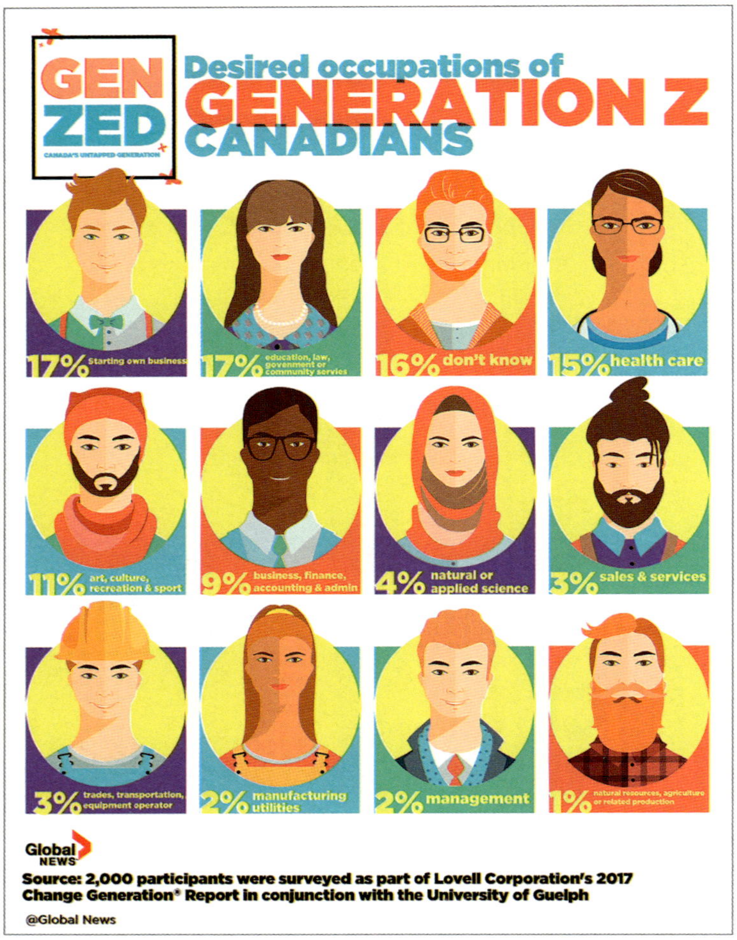

1 Read the Culture Tip and identify the type of document (topic, participants…).

2 Focus on the numbers and comment on the results.

3 Conduct this survey in your class. Discuss the results and compare them to the Canadian ones.

E-workbook
Fiche à imprimer
hatier-clic.fr/lmu019

Culture Tip

Generation Z or Gen Z is the generation born between the mid-1990s and 2015 approximately and came after the Millennials (Generation Y). They have also been called the Neo-Digital Natives and the Post-millennials. They are the most connected, educated and sophisticated generation ever.

B Preparing for the jobs of tomorrow

Vidéo
DVD

1 Watch the video and focus on repetitions. Use them to introduce the video (source, audience and general message).

2 Give as many elements as possible on the jobs of tomorrow.

3 Pick a job described in the ad and explain to a friend why you would like to do it.

Grammar Spot

The indefinite article (a / an) Tools → p. 60

"We need new skills for a completely new job force, but we're not prepared."

Word Spot

career
workplace
job market
engineering
research and development (R & D)
sustainable energy
innovation
field of interest
quality of life
high-tech: sophisticated
skilled: qualified
welcoming
promising ≠ hopeless
top-notch: excellent
design: create
empower: give power to

C The Canadian dream?

Classe inversée

E-workbook
Classe inversée
hatier-clic.fr/lmu020

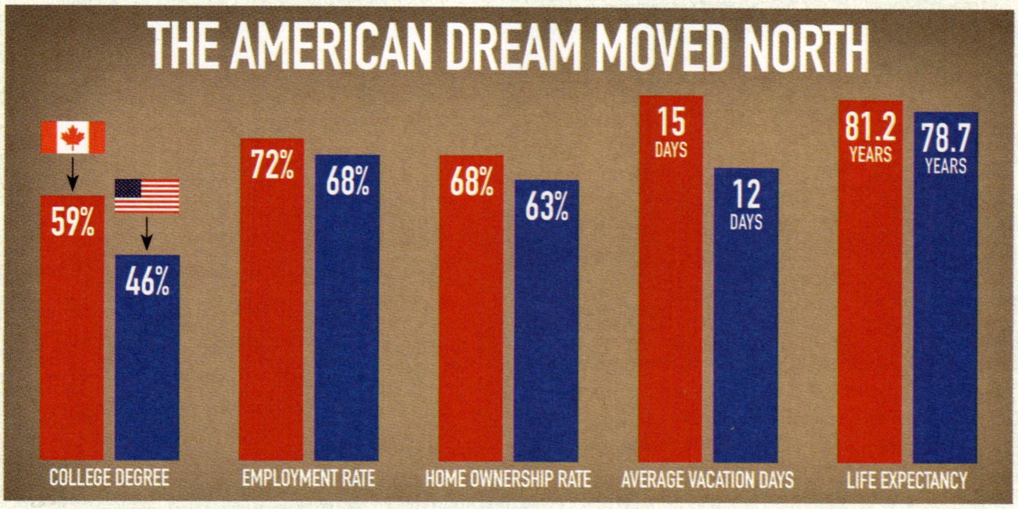

From the very moment of its creation, Americans have always imagined their country to be a beacon[1] of opportunity for the world. Thomas Jefferson lit that torch when he wrote in the Declaration of Independence that all men have the right to "life, liberty, and the pursuit of happiness". [...]

But where once America stood alone as the land of opportunity, there are now dozens of other countries that have surpassed the United States; chief[2] among these is its unassuming northern neighbour, Canada. Where do you go now for "Life, liberty, and the pursuit of happiness"? Canadians live 2.5 years longer than Americans. They are six times less likely to be incarcerated. And the World Economic Forum ranks Canadians as the 6th happiest people in the world, while Americans lag behind[3] at 13th.

Every aspect of the American dream is now more easily found in Canada. In the United States, 46 per cent of the population has been able to obtain a college degree—in Canada it's 59 per cent. After graduation, Canadians are more likely to find work, with an employment rate four points better. [...]

By virtually every measure, Canada has surpassed the United States as the shining city on the hill, where everyone is safe to reach their potential. And people around the world have begun to notice. From the United States, refugees and asylum seekers are now fleeing into Canada hoping for a fair immigration hearing and a better future. In Latin America, there are reports of economic migrants heading north, intending to cross the U.S. border and keep moving, into Canada. And, overseas, ESL[4] students are increasingly choosing Canada over the U.S.

✦ Scott Gilmore, *The American Dream has moved to Canada*, *Macleans.ca*, February 28, 2017

1. guiding light 2. leading 3. are far behind 4. English as a Second Language

1 Read from line 1 to 6 and present the American dream.

2 Compare life in the US and in Canada using the text and the chart.

3 Explain how this situation benefits Canada.

4 ***PAIR WORK*** Imagine a WhatsApp chat between an ESL student and his or her American friend.

Student A You are an ESL student living in Canada. Convince your American friend to come to study in Canada.

Student B You are an American student. You are thinking about moving to Canada to study.

Prepare your project

Create an ad for your school radio to attract young professionals to Canada.

Grammar Tip Précis → p. 217

Use the modals **will** to express the future and **can** to express possibility.

Memory Challenge

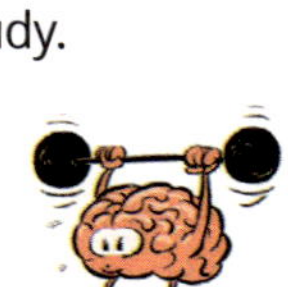

In one minute, find at least five words related to the world of work.

Is Canada a dream job country?

D A land of opportunity

✦ Rany Ibrahim won the RBC Top 25 Immigrant Award in 2013. This award, created by the magazine *Canadian Immigrant* is sponsored by the Royal Bank of Canada. It recognises the success and achievements of Canadian immigrants.

You came to Canada as an international student many years ago and stayed. Why did you choose Canada?

I came because of Canada's international reputation as a peaceful, safe and friendly country. It was a vague image at the time, more of a hope. At some level, you don't get to know what Canada is really like until you arrive. I was looking for a place to do a graduate degree[1] and Canada presented itself as a country where you could get a quality education in an interesting and accepting culture.

What did you expect before you arrived and how has your experience measured up to this?

I expected Canada to have more people — at least in the places I first went to. I had a hard time comprehending how massive the country is and how few people live here. [...] While the country's physical size surprised me, I remember being amazed by the scale of opportunities Canada has to offer for immigrants.

To me, Canada was, and still is, the land of opportunity. You can make it in Canada. It's an environment that allows people to create and innovate and I believe it brings out the best in people. Canada transformed me into someone who believes that dreams are possible and has the freedom to reach[2] for them. [...]

How does Canada do at marketing itself globally, how do people abroad view Canada and what's the biggest selling-feature you think Canada has to offer?

What Canada has is a great image; it is positive across the board[3]. I was doing extensive international travel years ago and it was clear that Canada has one of the best international reputations in the world. This is in terms of happiness, health, safety, friendliness and the stability of the economy. This is something Canadians should be proud of. The promise of economic opportunity and a safe place to settle is what makes Canada very attractive to people overseas[4].

✦ www.centuryinitiative.ca, 2016

1. university diploma 2. catch 3. globally 4. abroad

Pédagogie différenciée

TRAIL A

1 Pick out the reasons why Rany Ibrahim chose to move to Canada (l. 1-9).

2 Give three elements that make Canada a good place to immigrate to (l. 10-23).

3 Focus on positive words about Canada. Describe Canada's international reputation (l. 24-36).

TRAIL B

1 List the reasons why Rany Ibrahim came to Canada.

2 According to Rany indicate what makes Canada a great country to work in.

3 Explain the image Canada has overseas.

Meet up! ***PAIR WORK*** Discuss if Canada can be considered a land of opportunity and if you would like to move there. You can use arguments from the text.

Word Spot

- application: request (for a job)
- background: experience
- work permit: work authorisation
- eligibility: qualification
- opportunity
- process: series of actions to do
- residence: place of living
- self-explanatory: easily understandable
- supportive: helpful
- temporary ≠ permanent
- safe: secure
- switch: change
- apply for a job ≠ resign
- fill in (*UK*), fill out (*US*): complete a document
- submit: suggest
- require: demand
- book: reserve

Grammar Spot

Can and may Tools → p. 60

"you **can** make it in Canada"
"this **may** come in a few days weeks or even months"

E Easy entry for skilled workers?

E-workbook
Fiche à imprimer
hatier-clic.fr/lmu021

Culture Tip

Express Entry is a system used by the federal government, provincial governments and Canadian employers to recruit skilled workers. It is aimed at facilitating the immigration of qualified workers, that is to say people who have professional skills that are needed in Canada.

Student A Audio CD1 piste 21 **Student B** Audio CD1 piste 22

1. ***PAIR WORK*** Listen to your recording and find information about the interviewees.
2. Give the reasons why these professionals chose to live in Canada.
3. Describe the role of Express Entry in their experience.
4. ***PAIR WORK*** Act out a conversation between the two interviewees talking about their experience with Express Entry.

F International Experience Canada

Vidéo
DVD

E-workbook
Fiche à imprimer
hatier-clic.fr/lmu022

✦ *The IEC 2019 Season is open!*, Moving2Canada, 2019

1. Present the IEC programme (candidates, conditions and objectives).
2. Explain the popularity of the Working Holiday programme.
3. List the four steps to be accepted in this programme.
4. Draw a mind map to recap the IEC programme to a friend (in English or in French).

Prepare your project

Answer the following questions for a FAQ on a website dedicated to immigration in Canada.

- Why move to Canada?
- How to get a visa?

Grammar Tip

Précis → p. 219

Use the **simple present** to talk about a general situation.

Memory Challenge

In groups, you have two minutes to find three reasons why moving to Canada is a good idea.

Tools in the Spotlight

Entraînez-vous sur la plateforme *Let's Meet Up!*
reussirenlangues.fr

Practise your grammar

Précis grammatical, p. 192

L'article indéfini (*a / an*)

• L'article indéfini (*a / an*) s'emploie avec un nom **dénombrable**, c'est-à-dire qui peut être compté. On emploie ***a*** devant un son consonne et ***an*** devant un son voyelle.

*Montreal is **a** famous bilingual city.*

*The country has **an** employment rate which attracts a lot of foreign job-seekers.*

• Le choix de ***a*** ou ***an*** dépend du son et non pas de la graphie : *university*, dont la syllabe initiale commence par la voyelle *u à* l'écrit, est bien le son consonne /j/.

*McGill is **a** university.*

• De même, on emploie ***a*** devant un *h* aspiré, et ***an*** si le *h* n'est pas prononcé.

*They stayed at **a** hotel in Toronto.*

*It is **an** honour for this player to have been selected by this Canadian soccer team.*

⚠ Lorsque l'on parle de métier, l'anglais emploie l'article indéfini, contrairement au français.

*This Quebecker is **an** engineer.* Ce Québécois est ingénieur.

1 Complétez par *a* ou *an*.

a. This Generation Z young Canadian man is looking for ... job.
b. However, he wants to have ... inspiring job in the IT sector.
c. According to ... survey, 16% of young Canadians don't know what they want to do later.
d. The positive image of the country has ... huge impact on immigrants.
e. Americans have always considered their country as ... attractive beacon of opportunity for the world.

2 Choisissez la bonne réponse.

a. Every immigrant wants to fulfil (**a** / **an**) dream.
b. Canada is (**a** / **an**) amazing country.
c. Canada is (**a** / **an**) young nation.
d. Canadians can expect to reach (**a** / **an**) average life expectancy of more than 81 years.
e. That's why refugees and asylum seekers hope for (**a** / **an**) better future in Canada.

Can et *may*

• Le modal ***can*** peut exprimer la **capacité** ou la **possibilité**. Comme tout modal, il est invariable et suivi d'une base verbale.

*You **can** make it in Canada.*
Tu peux réussir au Canada. → possibilité

*This Canadian girl **can** speak both French and English.*
Cette jeune fille canadienne sait parler le français et l'anglais. → capacité

• Le modal ***may*** exprime la **probabilité** qu'un événement ait lieu. La probabilité que cet événement se produise est de 50%.

*This **may** come in a few days.*
Il est possible que cela arrive dans quelques jours.

• Parmi les autres valeurs de ***may***, on trouve aussi la **permission, l'autorisation** de pouvoir faire quelque chose.

*You **may** work in Canada if you have a visa.*
Tu peux (= as le droit de) travailler au Canada si tu as un visa.

3 Complétez par *can* ou *may*.

a. If you like the cold, you ... go to Canada in winter.
b. You ... speak both English and French in Montreal.
c. Canada ... be a land of opportunity for a lot of immigrants.
d. I don't know yet where I would like to work later, but I ... go to Ottawa.
e. If I ... do so in compliance with immigration laws, I will do a six-month internship in Vancouver.

4 Indiquez si *can* exprime la possibilité ou la capacité, et si *may* désigne la probabilité ou la permission.

a. You **can** learn English in Toronto.
b. You **may** use my Canada travel guidebook.
c. Sue **can** speak both English and French fluently.
d. She **may** go to Quebec for her gap year, but she doesn't know yet.
e. In 1931 James Truslow Adams first defined "the American dream" as the dream of a land where immigrants **can** enjoy a "better and richer and fuller" life.

Improve your pronunciation

Précis de phonologie, p. 242

La prononciation de *-ng*

Audio CD1 piste 23 MP3 n° 32

La prononciation de *-ng* dépend de la place occupée par celui-ci au sein du mot.

- Si *-ng* fait partie d'une **syllabe finale**, il se prononce **/ŋ/**. La graphie *-ng* est alors à la fin du mot et est précédée d'un son voyelle.

working /wɜːkɪŋ/, *young* /jʌŋ/, *song* /sɒŋ/, *hang* /hæŋ/, *among* /əmʌŋ/, *thing* /θɪŋ/

- Ce son **/ŋ/** de la graphie *-ng* est le même son que l'on trouve pour la graphie *-nk*, dans les mots comme :

think /θɪŋk/, *thinker* /θɪŋkəʳ/.

- Si *-ng* se trouve au **milieu d'un mot** et qu'il est précédé d'une voyelle, la voyelle et le *-n* forment alors une syllabe à part entière et le *-g* appartient à la syllabe suivante. ***-g* + *a*, *o*** ou ***u*** sera prononcé **/g/**, alors que ***-g* + *e*** ou ***i*** se prononcera /dʒ/.

engage /ɪngeɪdʒ/

ingenious /ɪndʒiːniəs/, *engineer* /endʒɪnɪəʳ/

5 **Indiquez si les *-ng* des mots suivants se prononcent /ŋ/, /g/ ou /dʒ/, puis vérifiez avec l'enregistrement.**

Audio CD1 piste 24 MP3 n° 33

engagement • parking • bring • engineer • along • language • length

6 **Indiquez la prononciation des graphies *-ng* soulignées, puis vérifiez avec l'enregistrement.**

Audio CD1 piste 25 MP3 n° 34

a. They met Jenny at the *Day of Languages* among the participants.
b. She is now engaged to a young Canadian man.
c. She greeted us with a pleasing smile and told us that her fiancé was an engine driver.
d. If you look at the situation from another angle, English is definitely an advantage.
e. Open-mindedness and willingness to change are some of the ingredients necessary for a successful life abroad.

Work on your writing skills

Le dialogue

- Pour insérer un dialogue dans un récit, il faut :
  - utiliser des guillemets d'ouverture et de fermeture de dialogue " ".
  - introduire directement les répliques sans tiret (à l'inverse du français !).
  - aller à la ligne à chaque changement d'interlocuteur·rice.
  - ajouter une virgule avant de fermer les guillemets quand la phrase est affirmative.
  - employer des verbes introducteurs de parole précédés du sujet, au prétérit simple généralement. Ils donnent des précisions sur la personne qui parle, la manière, la voix (*say*, *admit*, *exclaim*, *snap*, *pretend*...), etc.
  - ajouter un adverbe ou un verbe en *-ing* pour expliquer de quelle façon la personne parle.

*"Which job are you talking about?" Martin **asked** Emily.*

"You know. The one that is based in Toronto."

*"Oh, yes, I remember now," he **replied rapidly**.*

7 **Réécrivez ce texte en respectant les règles de présentation du dialogue en anglais.**

Emily began smiling: I will start working as an IT designer next month. I will work in a small team. Two of my colleagues are from England... When will you leave? Oscar interrupted her suddenly. Well, I will leave the country next week if I have my visa on time. There was a strange feeling all over the lounge. Emily's friends were perplexed, they didn't know what to say and how to react. That's great news. Congratulations! I finally said, happy for her but also sad. I knew I would miss her.

8 **Inventez la suite du dialogue en utilisant au moins cinq des verbes introducteurs.**

admit • add • exclaim • agree • announce • insist • declare • repeat • ask

Build up your vocabulary

Audio
CD1 piste 26

Immigrating to Canada

Reputation — MP3 n°35

opportunity /ɒpətʃuːnəti/
landscape
wilderness
accepting culture
promising ≠ hopeless
welcoming
supportive: helpful
safe: secure
beautiful
top-notch: excellent

Immigrate — MP3 n°36

application: request (for a job)
work permit: work authorisation
background: experience /ɪkspɪəriəns/
eligibility: qualification
temporary ≠ permanent
self-explanatory: easily understandable
process: series of actions to do
fill in (*UK*), fill out (*US*): complete a document
submit: suggest
switch: change
book: reserve
require /rɪkwaɪər/: demand

Work — MP3 n°39

job market
workplace
career /kərɪəʳ/
professionals
high-tech: sophisticated
skilled: qualified
apply for a job ≠ resign
make a dream job a reality

Life — MP3 n°38

residence: place of living
quality of life
life expectancy
happiness
health care
home ownership
economy
vacation
stress level
freedom
well-being
stable
stressful ≠ laid-back
empower: give power to

Study — MP3 n°37

engineering
research and development
artificial intelligence
field of interest
innovation
degree
sustainable /səsteɪnəbᵊl/ energy
design: create

Apprenez et révisez le vocabulaire !

Utilisez Quizlet pour vous entraîner en vous amusant.

Quizlet
hatier-clic.fr/lmu023

Utilisez le vocabulaire en contexte.

1 Complétez les phrases suivantes avec des mots de la carte mentale.

a. Canada is a welcoming and pleasant country for tourists and … .
b. Canada offers a great … for immigrants looking for a new life.
c. If you need a permanent visa you must … … several documents.
d. Canadian companies can also offer … jobs to students and workers who do not intend to settle in Canada for the rest of their lives.
e. Immigrants move to Canada to enjoy the … … … .
f. Canada is also famous for its beautiful … and snowy winters.

2 En utilisant les mots suivants, écrivez les conseils qu'un·e immigrant·e arrivé·e il y a quelques années donnerait pour réussir son installation au Canada.

working — visa — apply for a job — high-tech — design — qualification — temporary

AUTO évaluation

Faites le quiz interactif en ligne et suivez les conseils pour vous préparer à l'évaluation.

Quiz
hatier-clic.fr/lmu024

Project #1

Act out a phone conversation between a potential immigrant and a Canadian immigration advisor.

1 Choose your role.

- ✓ Create your character.

  Immigration advisor: name and surname, location, missions...

  Potential immigrant: identity, age, nationality, skills, professional experience, aspirations in Canada...
- ✓ Put yourself in the shoes of your character.

2 Think about your questions, answers and arguments.

- ✓ **Immigration advisor:** Find information about Canada and the application processes in the unit. Be prepared to answer the candidate's questions.
- ✓ **Potential immigrant:** Prepare your questions (employment opportunities, country's reputation, application process).

3 Prepare yourself for the discussion.

- ✓ **Immigration advisor:** be professional, use expressions like **how can I help you?, Is there anything else I can do for you?**
- ✓ **Potential immigrant:** be very polite and use expressions like **I would like to know if, I would appreciate if you could, I was wondering if...**
- ✓ Note down key words and check the pronunciation of difficult words on an online dictionnary.

4 Act out the conversation.

- ✓ Use gap fillers: **so, well, in fact, let me think...**
- ✓ Add comments and reactions to sound more natural: **that's wonderful... Yes, I would love to... Great! I see!... As I said...**

Fiche de méthodologie N°19 p. 278

Project #2

Create a poster to encourage young people to move to Canada for a contest set up by the Canadian government.

1 Gather arguments for your poster.

- ✓ Find reasons why people would want to live in Canada.
- ✓ Note down the arguments and organise them in order of importance. Think about your target audience!

2 Focus on the message.

- ✓ Give examples showing that Canada has a lot to offer.
- ✓ Find a powerful and convincing slogan.

3 Think about visual elements.

- ✓ Look for pictures to promote Canada.
- ✓ You can add quotes of people who already have a Canadian experience.
- ✓ Draft your poster and organise the elements to make the poster easy to understand.

4 Create the poster!

- ✓ Use online tools to make your poster look graphic and attractive.
- ✓ Use various text sizes according to the information. Your slogan must be bigger.

Fiche de méthodologie N°9 p. 261

Let's RECAP

Lisez les questions-clés et complétez la fiche bilan avec des exemples et des documents que vous avez étudiés ou découverts.

AXE 2 | Professional fields, the world of work

SÉQUENCE 1 Do gap years really prepare for work life?

E-workbook
Bilan à compléter
hatier-clic.fr/lmu025

What are the pros and cons of a gap year? How can a gap year boost your future career?

#careerchoice
To what extent can gap years help students choose a career path?

#volunteering
How can volunteering during a gap year help choose a future career?

#socialising
Do gap years enable students to socialise with people from other cultures and backgrounds?

#workingabroad
What are the opportunities available for young people enjoying a gap year? How do you find a job abroad?

#dreamjob
How can a gap year help students find their dream job?

SÉQUENCE 2 Is Canada a dream job country?

E-workbook
Bilan à compléter
hatier-clic.fr/lmu026

What makes Canada an attractive country for students and young professionals? What are the different ways to emigrate to Canada?

#dream
What is the Canadian dream?

#younggeneration
What are the professional aspirations of the younger generation in Canada?

#work
Why do professionals enjoy working in Canada?

#immigration
How to apply to travel, study or work in Canada?

#opportunity
To what extent is Canada a land of professional opportunities?

Lisez et écoutez de l'anglais en dehors de la salle de classe ! Voici quelques conseils en lien avec votre séquence.

SÉQUENCE 1

Novels and short stories

Down Under, Bill Bryson, 2000

Amazing Gap Year Adventures, Tammy Cohen, 2007

The Secret Life of Backpackers, Barry Divola, 2008

Tales from Nowhere, Simon Winchester, Tim Cahill, Pico Iyer, 2017

Books

Gap Year Adventures: An Essential Pocket Guide to Making It Count, Tamsin King, 2016

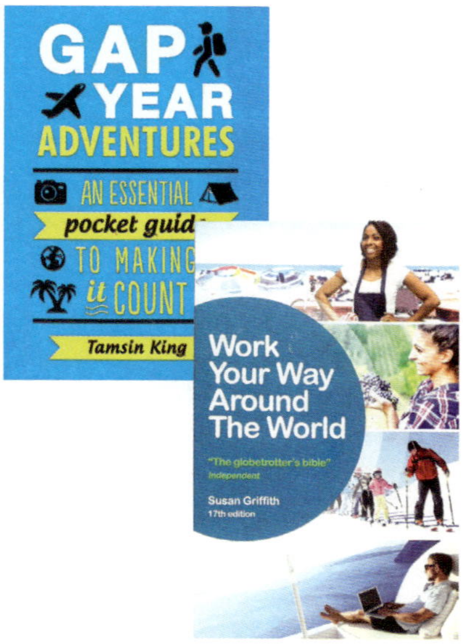

Work Your Way Around the World, Susan Griffith, 2017

TV series

Websites

Advice on gap years
gapyearassociation.org (USA)

Information about gap years
gapyear.com (UK)

Blog about gap year activities
productivegapyear.com

SÉQUENCE 2

Books

Lives of Girls and Women, Alice Munro, 1971

Green Grass, Running Water, Thomas King, 1993

Souvenir of Canada, Douglas Coupland, 2002

Essex County, Jeff Lemire, 2009

The Great Canadian Bucket List, Robin Esrock, 2017

Films

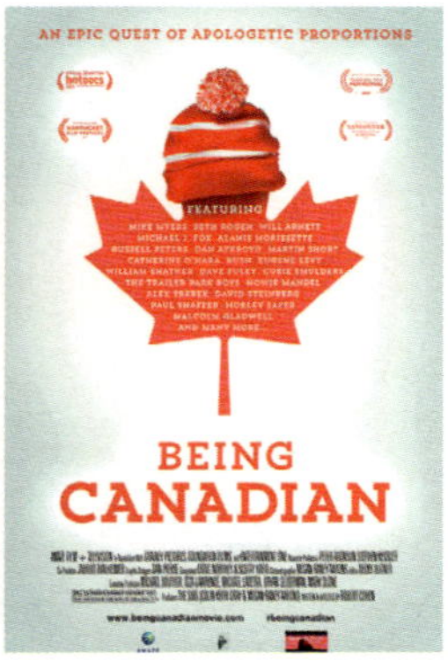

Music

Leonard Cohen	Alanis Morissette
Joni Mitchell	Arcade Fire
Neil Young	Avril Lavigne
Bryan Adams	Justin Bieber

Websites

Tips for studying and working in Canada
http://bit.ly/2tModMC

Information about travelling in Canada
http://bit.ly/2SJGPd7

Timeline

Country ID, p. 189

AXE 3

Village, neighbour-hood, city

Le village, le quartier, la ville

SÉQUENCE 1 How does gentrification impact US cities?

Projects

Project #1: Participate in a town meeting about the construction of a new block of flats in your neighbourhood.

Project #2: Create a poster for your residents' association to raise awareness on the dangers of gentrification.

Tools

Grammaire	le révolu avec *used to, for, since, ago*
Phonologie	l'accent tonique
Écriture	le doublement des consonnes
Vocabulaire	le quartier, le logement

SÉQUENCE 2 What are the challenges facing Indian cities?

Projects

Project #1: Give an inauguration speech as the mayor of a new suburban city near Mumbai.

Project #2: Write a post on your travel blog. Explain the specificities of Indian cities to your internatio-nal readers.

Tools

Grammaire	le comparatif, *some, any* et *no*
Phonologie	la lettre *r*
Écriture	le billet de blog
Vocabulaire	les villes, l'architecture

#neighbourhood #communitylife #transformation

#cosmopolitan #displacement

Second Avenue and East 1st Street, New York in 2005 and 2014

#culturalcodes #metropolis

#mutation #technology

#tradition #urbanisation

Main Bazar, Paharganj, New Delhi

SÉQUENCE 1

How does gentrification impact US cities?

A Diagnosing gentrification

✦ Crown Heights, Brooklyn, New York City

To the residents at 1030 Carroll Street in the Crown Heights[1] neighborhood of Brooklyn, a new bank of Citi Bikes — the bike sharing program typically found in wealthier neighborhoods — isn't a sign that city officials are investing in their health and wellness. Instead, it's a signal to longtime residents that their area has entered late-stage gentrification.

"As people move out, new people move in and their rents are going sky high," said Clentine Fenner, 68, who has lived at 1030 Carroll Street since 1976. Fenner, a retired educator and childcare advocate, has spent the bulk of her adult life in her first floor apartment. Over the past century, Crown Heights has been a neighborhood that includes communities of Hasidic Jews, African-Americans who migrated from the South and Caribbean immigrants.

In the early 2000s, affluent white residents started moving in from Manhattan, attracted by historic brownstones[2], easy access to the borough's cultural institutions and subway, and close proximity to the 526-acre Prospect Park. Fenner appreciates some of the perks that investment in Crown Heights has accrued, like new cafes and restaurants, and trees that the city planted on her block. She's less enthusiastic about her building's ongoing construction, noise from which wakes her up early and coats her building's hallways and stairwells in a fine layer of dust. When workers were demolishing the unit adjacent to hers to upgrade it with luxury fixtures, Fenner woke up coughing and said she couldn't get the dusty grit out of her eyes. "It really had gotten bad," she said. "But I still refuse to move."

✦ Erin Schumaker, *Diagnosing Gentrification, HuffPost*, February 12, 2018

1. affluent residential neighbourhood in Brooklyn. 2. brick townhouse, very common in Brooklyn.

Pédagogie différenciée

TRAIL A

1 Look at the photo. Read the first paragraph and the Culture Tip. Describe this neighbourhood.

2 Read the rest of the article and pick out the three main drawbacks of gentrification.

3 Find elements that make Crown Heights so attractive to new inhabitants.

TRAIL B

1 Read the Culture Tip and find elements in the text to show the area is gentrified.

2 Explain why long-time residents aren't satisfied with the changes in their neighbourhood.

3 Show how Crown Heights has become a better place to live.

Meet up! Post a comment from Clentine Fenner on the Facebook page of the town hall to complain about gentrification in Carroll Street.

Culture Tip

Gentrification is the restoration of a broken-down urban area. Buildings are modernised, new businesses open and many people who have always lived there must leave because everything gets more expensive.

Grammar Spot

Used to Tools → p. 72

"It was a place I **used to** call home"

Word Spot

loss ≠ gain
rent: payment for a flat (*UK*) / an apartment (*US*)
landlord: owner
tenant: occupant of a place
housing: residence
amenities: conveniences
eviction
drawback: disadvantage
affordable: cheap
global: universal
displace: move sbdy from their place
evict: expel
improve: make better
own: possess

B The Gentrification Song

Classe inversée

Audio
CD1 piste 27
MP3 n° 40

E-workbook
Classe inversée
hatier-clic.fr/lmu027

1 Read the title and listen to the chorus of the song. What has changed in the singer's neighbourhood?

2 Pick out the difficulties residents have to face.

3 Name what the singer misses most. What does he denounce in his song?

4 Use the following words to sum up the song.

gentrified - regret - move out - neighbourhood - unaffordable

C Hipster-mites

✦ Mural by Alberto Serrano and The Royal Kingbee on Walton Avenue, The Bronx, New York City, 2015

1. when members of the dominant culture adopt elements of a minority culture 2. flats 3. American supermarket chain with only healthy and organic foods

1 Find out which insect in the mural represents long-time residents and which one represents newcomers.

2 Explain the consequences of gentrification for the area represented in the mural.

3 Send a message to the artists on their Twitter account to give them your opinion about the mural.

Prepare your project

You are a member of an anti-gentrification association. Try to convince somebody to attend the next meeting.

Grammar Tip Précis → p. 227-228

Use **should** and the **imperative** to convince people:
You should come and see! Don't think twice!

Memory Challenge

Look at p. 68-69 then close your book. Write the letters of the alphabet, for each letter try to note down at least one word linked to gentrification.

D Ways to fight back

✦ Poster in a street of Cincinnati, Ohio

1 Describe the poster and explain why it was put up in the street.

2 Use the following words to sum up the demands expressed in this poster.

affordable - displacement - renters

3 You are handing out this poster in the street. Imagine what you say to the passers-by.

E My hood is not for sale

Audio
CD1 piste 28

Guadalis Del Carmen is an American playwright and actress. She was born and raised in Chicago by Dominican parents. She wrote a play entitled *Not for Sale*, set in Humboldt Park.

1 Listen to the interview and explain how gentrification is described in the play.

2 List the three sides of gentrification evoked by the playwright.

3 Pick out the reasons why the UrbanTheater Company was the perfect place for the play.

4 ***PAIR WORK*** Act out the meeting of a victim of gentrification who comes across Guadalis Del Carmen at the market and tells her what he or she thinks of her work.

Culture Tip

Boricua means a Puerto Rican or a person of Puerto Rican descent. It comes from *Borinquen*, the original name of the island of Puerto Rico.

Grammar Spot

For, since, ago Tools → p. 72

"Cities **for** generations have been a place for the refugees, the immigrants..."

Word Spot

union
perk: advantage
rally: mass meeting
expenses: costs
local: sbdy who lives in the area
affluent: well-off: rich
unaffordable: high-priced
unfair: unjust
attend a meeting
join an event
make oneself heard
stand up for oneself: defend oneself
move out: pack up ≠ stay
upgrade: ameliorate

F An economic apartheid

Vidéo
DVD

E-workbook
Fiche à imprimer
hatier-clic.fr/lmu028

✦ *Gentrification in San Francisco*, CNN, 2016

1 Use the following words to explain what Cleve Jones means by "economic apartheid".

`wealthy - area - leave`

2 Pick out the words referring to the long-time population of the neighbourhood.

3 Name the three advantages of gentrification.

4 You are the journalist, write a short article to sum up your encounter with Cleve Jones.

G "An invasion of sorts"

The scene takes place in Atlanta, Georgia. Barlowe Reed rents a house near the historic birth home of Dr. Martin Luther King Jr., in a neighbourhood called Old Fourth Ward. He is in a Baptist church, attending the meeting of the Old Fourth Ward Civic League[1]. After dealing with civic questions, the pastor announces that City Councilman Clifford Barnes is about to make a speech and meet the citizens.

Standing there in a pin-striped suit[2], Barnes looked like a displaced king among commoners. Speaking in measured tones, he told the crowd the meeting was to discuss a neighborhood problem, which he described as an "invasion of sorts."

"In recent months we've seen people moving into the Old Fourth Ward at a shocking rate. Some of the new-comers are black professionals, like myself." (He could barely contain his pride in the comparison.) "Most of the new people, though, you could classify as 'other'."

That jab[3] drew scattered[4] laughter. Barlowe shifted uncomfortably in his seat.

"We certainly don't mind people fusing[5] new blood into our neighborhoods," Barnes declared. "We're all God's children, for sure. But as we look around the city, we see a curious pattern taking shape. It's happened in Summerhill. It's happened in Oakhurst. It's happening in Kirkwood. It's spreading to East Point, and now we're seeing it with our own eyes, right here in the ward."

✦ Nathan McCall, *Them*, 2007

1. association whose goal is to improve the quality of life of a neighbourhood. It allows citizens to find a voice in local government. 2. suit with parallel lines on the fabric 3. (here) attack 4. (here) a lot of 5. bringing, injecting

1 Read the introduction and the first paragraph and explain the main topic of the meeting.

2 Explain how the new inhabitants of the neighbourhood are perceived.

3 Describe how gentrification is presented in the extract.

Prepare your project

You attend a council meeting about gentrification and decide to send a short e-mail to the town hall to express your fears and worries about the future of your neighbourhood.

Grammar Tip Précis → p. 226

Use **if** followed by the **present + future**, to express how the situation is now and how you believe it will become.

Memory Challenge

Close your book and challenge a classmate. Each of you has to name as many advantages or disadvantages of gentrification as possible.

Tools in the Spotlight

Entraînez-vous sur la plateforme *Let's Meet Up!*
reussirenlangues.fr

Practise your grammar

Précis grammatical, p.192

Le révolu avec *used to*

- ***Used to*** exprime un **passé révolu**. Contrairement au prétérit qui ne fait que situer l'événement dans le passé, ***used to*** indique aussi que dans le présent, la situation est changée. Entre-temps, il y a donc eu une modification.

Used to est suivi de la base verbale.

*There **used to be** old red-brick buildings in Brooklyn.*

→ On exprime le fait que ces bâtiments ne sont plus là, qu'ils ont été détruits ou remplacés.

*There **were** old red-brick buildings in Brooklyn when I last visited New York.*

→ On exprime la présence de bâtiments anciens en brique rouge à Brooklyn dans le passé. On ne dit pas si ces bâtiments sont encore là ou pas.

1 Transformez ces phrases pour exprimer le révolu avec *used to*.

a. The library was next to the town hall in the past. Now, they've knocked it down.
b. Working-class people lived in this area. Gentrification forced them to move.
c. Rents were much cheaper in this city. Things changed a lot since then!
d. This place was unpopular. Now, it keeps attracting middle-class people.

2 Choisissez la forme qui convient.

ALISON: Do you remember when there (**used to be / was**) that fancy pizza place in Brooklyn?
JIMMY: Yes, we (**used to go / went**) there every Sunday evening.
ALISON: Yeah, it (**used to be / was**) brilliant! Mike owns it now.
JIMMY: I think it (**used to be / was**) his father who (**used to run / ran**) the place back then.

For, since, ago

- ***For*** et ***since***, accompagnés de l'aspect ***have + en*** (*present perfect* ou *past perfect*) signifient « **depuis** ».
  - ***For*** est utilisé avec une expression de **durée** (*for twenty minutes, for centuries*...).

*Cities **for** generations have been a place for the refugees, the immigrants...*

⚠ Accompagné d'un prétérit, ***for*** veut dire « pendant ».

*The major US cities were hit by gentrification between 2000 and 2010, **for** ten years.*

  - ***Since*** est employé pour un **point de départ** (*since last year, since gentrification hit US cities*...).

*Clentine Fenner, 68, who has lived at 1030 Carroll Street **since** 1976.*

- ***Ago*** est toujours accompagné du prétérit. Il se place après un complément de temps et correspond à « **il y a** + complément de temps » (*three hours ago, two minutes ago*).

*Gentrification became a middle-class phenomenon twenty years **ago**.*

3 Complétez ces phrases par *for, since* ou *ago*.

a. Hipsters didn't come to this restaurant four years ... .
b. Rents have been increasing ... a couple of years.
c. They have been living in this condo ... 2018.
d. This city has been one of the most artistic places ... three years.
e. I visited Brooklyn and its suburban districts two years ... .

4 Terminez les amorces en *for* ou *since* par les expressions suivantes.

last year • three days • two hours • 2018 • four centuries

a. for...
b. since...
c. for...
d. for...
e. since...

Improve your pronunciation

Précis de phonologie, p. 242

L'accent tonique

Audio
CD1 piste 29
MP3 n° 41

• C'est l'accent qui porte sur l'une des syllabes d'un mot. En phonétique, il est graphiquement représenté par le signe ' avant la syllabe.

• On peut dégager les règles d'accentuation suivantes :

– Pour les **adjectifs et les noms de deux syllabes**, l'accent tonique porte généralement sur la **première syllabe** : *'ticket, 'brother, 'perfect...*

– Pour les **verbes de deux syllabes**, l'accent tonique est en général sur la **dernière syllabe** : *for'bid, co'llect, be'gin...*

– Pour les **mots terminés en *-ion***, l'accent tonique porte sur la **syllabe précédant *-ion*** : *infor'mation, communi'cation, ad'mission...*

Exception : *'television*

– Pour les **mots terminés en *-ic***, l'accent tonique porte sur la **syllabe précédant *-ic*** : *dra'matic, me'chanic, fan'tastic...*

Exceptions : *'Catholic, 'Arabic, a'rithmetic, 'politics*

– Pour les **mots terminés en *-ee* et *-oo***, l'accent porte sur cette **dernière syllabe** : *employ'ee, trai'nee, ta'boo, ta'ttoo, sham'poo...*

Exceptions : *co'mmittee, 'coffee*

5 **Indiquez l'accent tonique dans ces mots de deux syllabes, puis vérifiez vos réponses avec l'enregistrement.**

Audio
CD1 piste 30
MP3 n° 42

forget • remove • ticket • sister • neighbour • district • packet • station

6 **Indiquez l'accent tonique dans ces mots de plus de deux syllabes, puis vérifiez vos réponses avec l'enregistrement.**

Audio
CD1 piste 31
MP3 n° 43

gentrification • optimistic • renovation • artistic • dynamic • employee • kangaroo

Work on your writing skills

Le doublement des consonnes

• En anglais, lorsqu'un verbe ou un adjectif se termine par une **voyelle écrite entre deux consonnes** (Consonne Voyelle Consonne), on **double** la consonne finale si la syllabe est accentuée.

– Verbes d'une syllabe : *stop* → *stopped*

– Adjectifs d'une syllabe : *hot* → *hotter*

– Verbes de deux syllabes ou plus : *forget* → *forgetting*

• En anglais britannique, lorsque le verbe se termine par une voyelle suivie de la lettre *l*, on double le *l*.

travel → *travelling* *cancel* → *cancelled*

7 **Écrivez les verbes entre parenthèses à la forme qui convient.**

a. Smoking in this area was ... (ban) two years ago. People ... (stop) throwing their cigarette butts in the street, which made the area cleaner.

b. She was ... (jog) in the park and saw a man who was ... (cut) roses illegally.

c. This street artist keeps ... (travel) around the world to spread his message.

8 **Utilisez l'amorce et les verbes suivants pour écrire un court article de journal.**

stop • admit • forget • travel • prefer • plan • occur

Last week, the inhabitants of Brooklyn Heights demonstrated against gentrification...

Build up your vocabulary

Audio
CD1 piste 32

Gentrification

Demonstrate
MP3 n°50

- union
- protest: demonstration
- rally: mass meeting
- banners: signs
- attend a meeting
- join an event
- stand up for oneself: defend oneself

Negative consequences
MP3 n°44

- loss ≠ gain
- expenses: costs: charges
- drawback: disadvantage
- eviction
- unaffordable: high-priced
- unfair: unjust
- displace /dɪspleɪs/
- move sbdy from their place
- evict: expel
- move out: pack up ≠ stay
- wreck: destroy

Housing
MP3 n°45

- building
- rent: payment for an apartment (*US*) / flat (*UK*)
- landlord: owner
- tenant: occupant of a place
- housing: residence

New neighbourhoods
MP3 n°46

- bike-sharing system
- hipster culture
- tourist: sightseer
- organic food
- local markets
- barbershop
- art-loving crowd /kraʊd/
- vibrant
- minimalist
- affluent: well-off: rich

Positive change
MP3 n°49

- perk: advantage
- amenities /əmiːnətiz/: conveniences
- store (*US*): shop (*UK*)
- ecological: eco-friendly
- attractive
- welcoming
- regenerate: renew
- rehabilitate: revamp
- upgrade: improve: make better
- cycle to work

Economic situation
MP3 n°48

- economic boom
- growth: development
- house value: price of a house
- real estate: house market
- property prices
- own: possess
- increase: go up: soar

Old neighbourhoods
MP3 n°47

- district: neighbourhood
- local community
- inhabitant
- derelict: in bad condition
- affordable: cheap
- global: universal /juːnɪvɜːsəl/
- strong
- run-down: neglected
- tag a wall

Apprenez et révisez le vocabulaire !

Utilisez Quizlet pour vous entraîner en vous amusant.

Quizlet
hatier-clic.fr/lmu029

Utilisez le vocabulaire en contexte.

1 Complétez les phrases suivantes avec des mots de la carte mentale.

a. I have been living in this ... for years and I won't move out!
b. This building has just been ... , it is much more modern now.
c. Yesterday, the residents ... ... which was about the opening of a new vegan restaurant.
d. The rent of this apartment has increased so much it is now ... for the tenants.
e. Thanks to the ... ... , the inhabitants use less their cars to go to work.
f. One of the main drawbacks of gentrification is the ... of the poorer inhabitants.

2 Trouvez les mots qui correspondent à ces définitions dans la carte mentale puis écrivez un court paragraphe sur les avantages et inconvénients de la gentrification.

a. an increase in economic activity
b. benefit
c. a situation that does not give equal treatment to everyone
d. a large public meeting

AUTO évaluation

Faites le quiz interactif en ligne et suivez les conseils pour vous préparer à l'évaluation.

Quiz
hatier-clic.fr/lmu030

Project #1

Participate in a town meeting about the construction of a new block of flats in your neighbourhood.

1 **Choose your character: a US city official or an inhabitant of the area. Imagine what his or her opinion is.**

- ✓ Put yourself in your character's shoes. Choose his or her identity (name, age, occupation).
- ✓ Think about your character's opinion on gentrification.
- ✓ Expose the situation: **here are the facts...**

2 **List three arguments and illustrate them with precise examples or anecdotes.**

- ✓ List your arguments and articulate them: **first**, **then**, **finally**...
- ✓ Use examples: **for instance**, **for example**...

3 **Listen to your interlocutor and react to what he or she says.**

- ✓ You can express your agreement (**I agree**, **absolutely**, **you're right**) or your disagreement (**I disagree**, **this is not true**).
- ✓ Prepare your counter arguments (**on the other hand**...).
- ✓ Use gap fillers (**er**, **hum**, **well**, **so**...) when you need time to think.

4 **Be convincing!**

- ✓ Use short and catchy sentences.
- ✓ Pay attention to your body language. Look at your partners.
- ✓ Stress the right syllable on the key words. You can check on an online dictionary.

➤ Fiche de méthodologie N°19 p. 278

Project #2

Create a poster for your residents' association to raise awareness on the dangers of gentrification.

1 **Find the name of your association.**

- ✓ Invent a name according to the city in which your association is. You can look for cities in the unit or other US cities.
- ✓ Try to find an acronym for it, like The Brooklyn Anti-gentrification Network (BAN)!

2 **Create one or two catchy slogans.**

- ✓ Catch the viewers' attention with a pun or a short sentence:
  "Diversity not displacement"
  "Gentrification in progess"
- ✓ In order to make people feel involved, use the imperative and direct questions.

3 **List the main dangers of gentrification.**

- ✓ Find the major drawbacks of gentrification in the unit.
- ✓ Use the comparative to show it was better in the past.

4 **Use a software for the layout of your poster and add appropriate illustrations.**

- ✓ Search the internet and find images that represent gentrification.
- ✓ It can be helpful to have a nice lay out. You can use websites like canva.com or genial.ly.

➤ Fiche de méthodologie N°9 p. 261

SÉQUENCE 2

What are the challenges facing Indian cities?

A From villages to cities

Classe inversée

✦ *India: Crowded Cities, UN Stories*, United Nations, 2015

Vidéo hatier-clic.fr/lmu031

E-workbook Classe inversée hatier-clic.fr/lmu032

1 Pick out the numbers, say what they show about the Indian population.

2 Give the reasons why Ranjit Kumar Singh and many other people decided to live in Delhi.

3 Explain the consequences of this shift on large cities.

4 Write the YouTube caption accompanying this video on the United Nation's channel.

B Architects' views on Indian cities

Vidéo DVD

E-workbook Fiche à imprimer hatier-clic.fr/lmu033

✦ *Mumbai: Maximum City under Pressure*, Urban-Think Tank (U-TT), 2014

1 Pick out words related to the work of architects and their role in the city.

2 Give the percentage of people living in poor or informal conditions. Explain why Prasad Shetty says "that's the city!"

3 Define the expression "maximum city" with words and figures from the video.

4 Imagine the reaction of an architect who sees this screenshot.

Grammar Spot

Comparatives Tools → p. 80

"his dream life is bigger than his squalid quarters"
"a collective larger than himself"

Word Spot

district: area or zone with fixed borders
housing: accommodation
slum: very poor living place
settlement: informal place to live
suburb: area near a large city
traffic congestion: traffic jams
public facilities: public equipment
crammed: full of people
rural ≠ urban
safe: secure
crowded: populated
filthy: very dirty
build: construct
erase: demolish
develop: create new housing
plan: organise

C Living in a mega city

Culture Tip

Mumbai is the financial and commercial capital of India. Mumbai became the official name of the city in 1996.
It is still quite often called Bombay which was its name during the colonial period.

Returning to the city after a 21-year absence, the narrator tells the story of the many changes that happened in Bombay, his hometown. He meets new friends: Mona Lisa who is a bar dancer, Ajay, a perfect policeman and Girish, a computer entrepreneur who grew up in slums.

The Battle of Bombay is the battle of the self against the crowd. In a city of fourteen million people, how much value is associated with the number one? The battle is man against the Metropolis; which is only the infinite extension of Man and the demon against which he must constantly strive[1] to establish himself or be annihilated[2].

A city is an agglomeration of individual dreams, a mass dream of the crowd. In order for the dream life of a city to stay vital each individual dream has to stay vital. Mona Lisa needs to believe she will be Miss India. Ajay needs to believe he will escape the police force. Girish needs to believe he will be a computer magnate[3]. The reason a human being can live in a Bombay slum and not lose his sanity is that his dream life is bigger than his squalid[4] quarters. It occupies a palace. But what every Indian also desires secretly is to devote his life to a collective larger than himself.

✦ Suketu Mehta, *Maximum City: Bombay Lost and Found*, 2004

1. struggle 2. erased, destroyed 3. very rich business person
4. very dirty

Pédagogie différenciée

TRAIL A

1. In the first paragraph, find words showing that living in a big city is like fighting a war.
2. Pick out words and expressions showing the opposition between the individual and the crowd in the first paragraph.
3. Give three examples of dreams from line 10 to 15.
4. Explain why dreaming is important in Mumbai.

TRAIL B

1. Explain the sentence "The battle is man against the Metropolis".
2. Use words and expressions from the first paragraph to identify the "man" and the "demon".
3. Pick out examples of dreams in the second paragraph.
4. Explain the role of dreams in a city like Mumbai.

Meet up! For your book club, explain how Suketu Mehta portrays life in Mumbai.

Prepare your project

PAIR WORK Discuss the pros and cons of living in a megacity like Mumbai. Decide whether you would like to live in such a city.

Grammar Tip

Précis → p. 209

Use **percentages**, **figures** and **numbers** to illustrate your arguments.

Memory Challenge

Work in pairs. Find as many words as you can about Mumbai in 30 seconds. Have you found more than your partner?

D The caste system in Indian villages

✦ *Sujatha Gidla (left), with her family*, Andhra Pradesh, India, 1966.

I was born in south India, in a town called Khazipet in the state of Andhra Pradesh.

I was born into a lower-middle-class family. My parents were college lecturers.

I was born an untouchable.

When people in this country ask me what it means to be an untouchable, I explain that caste is like racism against blacks here. But then they ask, "How does anyone know what your caste is?" They know caste isn't visible, like skin colour.

I explain it like this. In Indian villages and towns, everyone knows everyone else. Each caste has its own special role and its own place to live. The brahmins (who perform priestly functions), the potters, the blacksmiths, the carpenters, the washer people, and so on — they each have their own separate place to live within the village. The untouchables, whose special role — whose hereditary duty — is to labour in the fields of others or to do other work that Hindu society considers filthy, are not allowed to live in the village at all. They must live outside the boundaries of the village proper. They are not allowed to enter temples. Not allowed to come near sources of drinking water used by other castes. Not allowed to eat sitting next to a caste Hindu or to use the same utensils. There are thousands of other such restrictions and indignities that vary from place to place. Every day in an Indian newspaper you can read of an untouchable beaten or killed for wearing sandals, for riding a bicycle.

In your own town or village, everyone already knows your caste; there is no escaping it. But how do people know your caste when you go elsewhere, to a place where no one knows you? There they will ask you, "What caste are you?" You cannot avoid this question. And you cannot refuse to answer. By tradition, everyone has the right to know.

✦ Sujatha Gidla, *Ants Among Elephants*, 2017

Culture Tip

The **caste system** is a system in India that was mainly used by Hindus. It started as a job system but later became a social class system that organised the Indian society. Whereas the caste system tends to become less important in Indian cities, it remains strong in villages and towns.

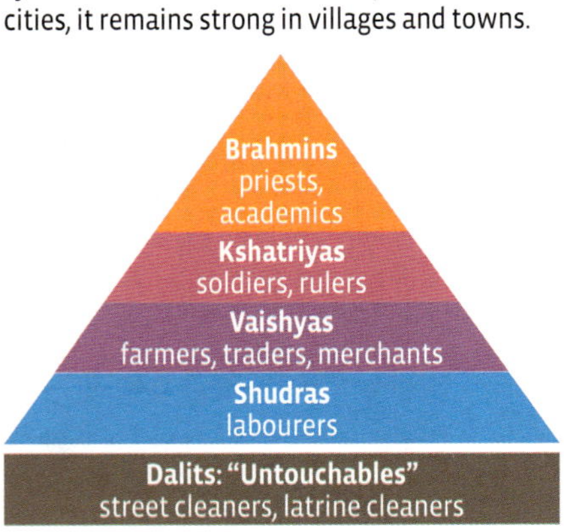

1 Pick out information about the narrator.

2 Identify the different jobs and use the Culture Tip to name their caste. Give details about where they live in Indian villages and towns.

3 List all the places in villages and towns where the "untouchables" are not allowed.

4 Draw a sketch to explain to a friend how Indian villages are organised and ruled by the caste system.

Grammar Spot

Some, any, no Tools → p. 80

"I do hope that it's not just a hype and that **some** of it comes to fruition."

Word Spot

city council: local city government
housing development: estate projects
social segregation
boundaries: limits
amenities /əmiːnətiz/: equipment
infrastructures: installations
investor: sbdy who finances projects
hierarchical (system) /haɪərɑːkɪkəl/
poor: deprived /dɪpraɪvd/
be excluded: be barred from
evolve: develop
value: promote
face challenges
provide: offer

E Bangalore: an Indian tech hub

Vidéo DVD

✦ Bagmane IT Park in Bangalore

Culture Tip

Bangalore (pictured left), officially known as Bengaluru is a megacity and the third most populous city in India. It is the country's leading Information Technology exporter, that's why it is also nicknamed the "Silicon Valley of India". It is a tech hub, a place that is created to help technology start-ups succeed.

✦ *Journey Through India*, CNBC International, 2018

1. Read the Culture Tip and watch the video. Present Bangalore in a few sentences.
2. Pick out two drawbacks linked to its rapid development.
3. Explain why Divya Hegde's project is interesting.
4. For your English class blog, record a short presentation about Bangalore showing why it is an interesting place to live in.

F Smart cities

Vidéo DVD

✦ *India's smart city plan and what it means for Indians*, ORF, 2017

1. Pick out numbers and introduce Magarpatta city.
2. Explain what is special about this city.
3. Give information on Shankar Magar (job, place of living) and explain what has changed for him and his family.
4. Write the definition of a smart city (role, investors and priorities).

Prepare your project

You have visited an Indian city. Write a message on a travel forum about the discoveries you have made there.

Grammar Tip

Précis → p. 207

Use **comparative** and **superlative** forms to express your surprise!

Memory Challenge

In pairs, play Hangman, each of you chooses three words to talk about Indian cities and your partner has to find them.

Tools in the Spotlight

Entraînez-vous sur la plateforme *Let's Meet Up!*
reussirenlangues.fr

Practise your grammar

Précis grammatical, p.192

Les comparatifs

- **Le comparatif** de **supériorité** des adjectifs courts se forme par l'ajout de ***-er***, suivi de ***than*** si le deuxième élément comparé est mentionné.
*a collective larger **than** himself*

⚠ *big → **bigger*** *thin → **thinner***
*good → **better*** *bad → **worse***

Le comparatif de supériorité des adjectifs longs se forme à l'aide de ***more*** + adjectif (+ ***than***).
*A bike is **more** convenient **than** a car in some Indian areas.*

- Le **comparatif d'infériorité** se forme à l'aide de ***less*** + adjectif court ou long (+ ***than***).
*Mumbai is **less** populated **than** New Delhi.*

- Le **comparatif d'égalité** s'exprime par ***as*** + adjectif court ou long + ***as***.
*Mumbai is **as** crowded **as** New Delhi.*

1 **Mettez les phrases au comparatif indiqué entre parenthèses.**

a. Urban architects in Mumbai are ... (determined) ... city dwellers. (=)
b. New Delhi is (big) ... ... Mumbai. (+)
c. Kolkata in West Bengal is ... (populated) ... Mumbai. (-)
d. The roads in Mumbai are ... (congested) ... in New Delhi. (=)
e. This place is ... (crowded) ... Chennai, the biggest economic centre of South India. (-)

2 **Complétez par *as*, *less*, *more* et *than*.**

a. I found this Bollywood film as interesting ... any Hollywood film.
b. Bangalore is ... modern ... Chennai.
c. Bangalore is larger ... Kolkata.
d. Life in India is ... expensive than in London.

Some, any, no, every

- ***Some*** désigne une **quantité indéfinie**. Il peut être suivi d'un nom.
*There are **some** homeless people in the city.*

- ***Any*** veut dire « **n'importe quel·le** » dans une phrase affirmative.
***Any** visitor to India needs to have a visa.*

Dans une phrase négative, ***any*** est précédé de ***not*** et il exprime une **quantité nulle** (en soulignant l'absence d'éléments en question).
*There **aren't any** tourists in this remote Indian area.*

- Une **quantité nulle** peut aussi s'exprimer directement par ***no***, suivi du nom.
*There are **no** tourists in this remote Indian area.*

- ***Every***, suivi d'un nom au singulier, permet d'exprimer un ensemble d'éléments. Il correspond à « **tou·te·s les** ».
***Every** day in India is different.*

- ***Some***, ***any***, ***no*** et ***every*** ont des pronoms indéfinis composés en ***-where*** pour le lieu (*anywhere*), ***-one*** pour une personne (*anyone*) et ***-thing*** pour une chose (*anything*).

3 **Complétez par *some*, *any*, *no* ou *every*.**

a. ... visitor should avoid drinking tap water in developing countries. ... unwary tourists do so, but they run the risk of suffering from a stomach ache.
b. There is almost ... future in rural areas, so a lot of people move to the main Indian cities.
c. There are ... interesting traditions in India.
d. I haven't taken ... pictures of the Taj Mahal yet.

4 **Complétez par les pronoms indéfinis : *anything*, *everywhere*, *something*, *everyone*, *someone*.**

a. She wants to go ... when she visits India.
b. ... has heard of the Taj Mahal.
c. ... funny happened! The guide got lost in the city!
d. I don't want to visit ... in particular today. Let's go to the local Indian market!
e. Is this ... you know?

Improve your pronunciation

Précis de phonologie, p. 242

La lettre r

Audio
CD1 piste 33
MP3 n° 51

La lettre *r* se prononce différemment selon la place de la graphie *r* au sein du mot.

• Si la lettre *r* est placée **après un son voyelle** : en anglais britannique, le *r* ne sera **pas prononcé**, mais le son voyelle qui le précède sera toujours un **son allongé**.

according /əkɔːdɪŋ/ *transport* /trænspɔːt/

Notez qu'en anglais américain, le *r* sera prononcé après le son /ɔː/ et /ɑː/ : /əkɔːrdɪŋ/, /trænspɔːrt/.

• Si la lettre *r* est placée au **début du mot** ou **après un son consonne** : le *r* sera alors prononcé /r/.

rank /ræŋk/ *resident* /rezɪdənt/

• Si la lettre *r* est placée **après un son voyelle à la fin d'un mot** : *r* n'est **pas prononcé**, mais il peut y avoir une liaison si le mot qui suit commence par un son voyelle.

The investor is Indian.
/ɪnvestəriz/

5 **Indiquez si la graphie *r* correspond à une voyelle allongée, ou si elle est prononcée /r/, puis vérifiez avec l'enregistrement.**

Audio
CD1 piste 34
MP3 n° 52

rural • traveller • internal • revolution • country • return • part • corner

6 **Indiquez la prononciation des *r* soulignés (non prononcé, voyelle allongée ou /r/), puis vérifiez et répétez après l'enregistrement.**

Audio
CD1 piste 35
MP3 n° 53

a. Smart City Mission is an urban renewal programme set up by the Indian government.
b. The idea is to develop and renovate 100 cities across the country.
c. Travellers will be happy to discover this urban revolution in every corner of various cities.
d. The renovated cities will become greener and more citizen-friendly.

Work on your writing skills

Le billet de blog

• Le billet ou article de blog est toujours rédigé à la **1re personne du singulier**. Il reflète l'opinion, la prise de position, les sentiments ou les impressions du ou de la bloggeur·euse.

• Les temps sont généralement le **prétérit simple** ou **en *be* + V-*ing***, le ***present perfect*** et le ***past perfect*** pour raconter des événements qui ont déjà eu lieu et sur lesquels la personne souhaite s'exprimer.

• Les faits relatés sont chronologiques et on leur associe souvent des **marqueurs de temps** du passé.
Two days ago, I was in Mumbai.

• Le registre de langue est **informel sans être familier**. Le contenu est structuré, les phrases sont simples avec des connecteurs logiques pour montrer le lien entre les lieux et les actions.

TIP Avant de rédiger, prenez en note les éléments les plus importants que vous souhaitez mentionner. Choisissez une organisation chronologique et utilisez des connecteurs (*first, then, next, afterwards, as soon as*…).

7 **Parmi les éléments suivants, identifiez ceux qui pourraient figurer dans un billet de blog.**

a. *Dear Sir or Madam*
b. *Hello everyone, it's a real pleasure to present…*
c. *Kind regards,*
d. *All the best*
e. *See you everyone!*
f. *To whom it may concern*
g. *Sincerely*
h. *I am writing to draw your attention to…*
i. a text of 5 to 10 lines
j. a compact text of three pages
k. no illustration
l. some illustrations

8 **Vous revenez d'un séjour dans une *smart city* ou à Bangalore, écrivez l'introduction du billet pour votre blog.**

Build up your vocabulary

Audio
CD1 piste 36

Indian cities challenges

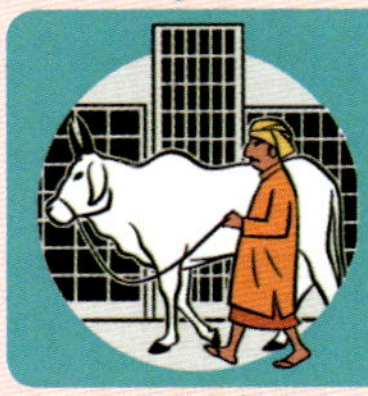

Architecture MP3 n°54

plan: organise
evolve: develop
housing development /haʊzɪŋ/: real estate projects
build: construct
erase, demolish
leverage /liːvərɪdʒ/: mobilise

Cities MP3 n°55

boundaries: limits: borders
district: area or zone with fixed borders
housing: accommodation
public facilities, community facilities
provide: offer
amenities /əmiːnəti/: equipment
infrastructure /ɪnfrəstrʌktʃəʳ/: installations
city council: local city government
spreading: developing rapidly

New cities MP3 n°58

investor: sbdy who finances projects
tech start-ups: small new high technology companies
tech hub /hʌb/: high technology centre with high tech businesses
develop: create new housing
value: promote

Challenges MP3 n°57

population
migration
motor vehicle: car, bus, scooter
crowded: populated
jammed: crammed: full of people
filthy: very dirty
rural ≠ urban
safe: secure
suburb: area near a large city
traffic congestion: traffic- jams
face challenges

Poverty MP3 n°56

caste system: hierarchical system /haɪərɑːkɪkəl/
social segregation
poor: deprived /dɪpraɪvd/
needy ≠ rich
settlement: informal place to live
slum: very poor living place
be excluded: be barred from

Apprenez et révisez le vocabulaire !

Utilisez Quizlet pour vous entraîner en vous amusant.

Quizlet
hatier-clic.fr/lmu034

Utilisez le vocabulaire en contexte.

1 Complétez les phrases suivantes avec des mots de la carte mentale.

a. Because of the combination of population growth and rapid urbanisation, Indian cities have to ... urgently.
b. Poor housing such as ... are ... .
c. As a consequence, public ... must be created, as well as ... ...
d. In Indian villages, the ... ... still exists nowadays. It is a major cause of ... .
e. New types of cities are created: smart cities. They provide infrastructures for ... ... thanks to the money of ... .

2 À partir des documents étudiés dans la séquence et des mots suivants, écrivez un court article pour expliquer les défis que les grandes villes indiennes doivent affronter de nos jours.

migration | population | traffic-jams | slum

AUTO évaluation

Faites le quiz interactif en ligne et suivez les conseils pour vous préparer à l'évaluation.

Quiz
hatier-clic.fr/lmu035

Project #1

Give an inauguration speech as the mayor of a new suburban city near Mumbai.

1 **Search for information about challenges in big Indian cities.**
- ✓ You can have a look in the unit or in your notes.
- ✓ List the different challenges: **density of population**, **poor housing**, **caste system**, **gender inequalities**, **traffic congestion**, **pollution**...

2 **Make a draft version of your speech.**
- ✓ Choose three priorities.
- ✓ List your projects and show what the situation was and how it will change.
- ✓ Use linking words to connect your ideas: **first**, **then**, **because**, **as a result**, **as a consequence**...

3 **Prepare yourself.**
- ✓ Create a mind map to remember the important information.
- ✓ Classify your projects using ordinal numbers: **first**, **second**...
- ✓ Don't forget to prepare an introduction and a conclusion!

4 **Deliver your speech!**
- ✓ Use the present tense to say your name and welcome your audience.
- ✓ Speak slowly, loud and clear... smile!
- ✓ Thank the audience for their attention!

➤ Fiche de méthodologie N°20 p. 280

Project #2

Write a post on your travel blog. Explain the specificities of Indian cities to your international readers.

1 **Look for information on the specificities of Indian cities.**
- ✓ Make a list of elements you want to mention on your blog post.
- ✓ Look on the internet or in your notes.

2 **Prepare a draft version of your post.**
- ✓ Organise your post and write down the information you want to give.
- ✓ Give examples with accurate figures and percentages to illustrate your point.
- ✓ Use the preterite to share your experience.

3 **Write your post.**
- ✓ Express your personal point of view: **from my point of view**, **I believe**, **to my mind**, **I feel**...
- ✓ Use the comparative to show differences between traditional and modern Indian cities.
- ✓ Use linking words to connect your ideas.

4 **Add images and check your blog post!**
- ✓ Insert sketches or photographs to illustrate your ideas.
- ✓ Make sure that you have an introduction and a conclusion.
- ✓ Before posting, proofread your text using an online dictionary like wordreference.com.

➤ Fiche de méthodologie N°22 p. 284

Let's RECAP

Lisez les questions-clés et complétez la fiche bilan avec des exemples et des documents que vous avez étudiés ou découverts.

E-workbook
Bilan à compléter
hatier-clic.fr/lmu036

SÉQUENCE 1 — How does gentrification impact US cities?

How have urban areas evolved with gentrification in the USA?
What are the economic and social consequences of gentrification in American neighbourhoods?

#neighbourhood
How does gentrification change US neighbourhoods?

#communitylife
How do communities come together to fight gentrification?

#transformation
Does gentrification help improve urban areas?

#displacement
What are the consequences of gentrification?

#cosmopolitan
Does gentrification have an impact on the diversity of the population?

AXE 3 | Village, neighbourhood, city

E-workbook
Bilan à compléter
hatier-clic.fr/lmu037

SÉQUENCE 2 — What are the challenges faced by Indian cities?

How is the migration from rural areas to cities affecting the way the cities are built?
What are the new Indian cities like?

#technology
How is the construction of tech hubs changing India?

#urbanisation
How do megacities deal with the growing density of the population?

#metropolis
What social challenges are faced by Indian megacities?

#culturalcodes
How do historical and cultural codes still affect the way people live in India?

#mutation
How is urbanisation changing India?

#tradition
What are the main impacts of the caste system in towns and villages?

Lisez et écoutez de l'anglais en dehors de la salle de classe ! Voici quelques conseils en lien avec votre séquence.

SÉQUENCE 1

Books

This Side of Home, RENÉE WATSON, 2015

How to Kill a City: Gentrification, Inequality, and the Fight for the Neighborhood, PETER MOSKOWITZ, 2017

Film, documentary, Web series

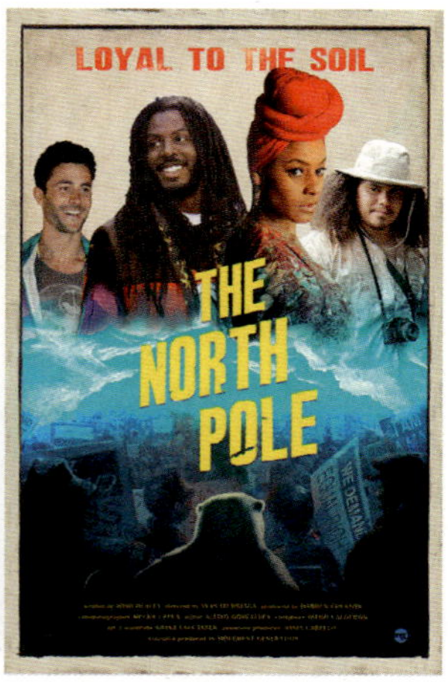

Videos

WEB SERIES *The North Pole*, 2017
http://bit.ly/2H2jRg9

REPORT *10 years After Katrina, Has New Orleans Been Rebuilt, or Just Gentrified?*, 2015
http://bit.ly/2tUjPhG

Songs

My City Was Gone, THE PRETENDERS, 1984
http://bit.ly/1Fpulu2

Four Out of Five, ARCTIC MONKEYS, 2018
http://bit.ly/2wz8gAy

Websites

Extract from *No Small Plan*, a graphic novel about Chicago
http://bit.ly/2vb62Wn

Cartoons about gentrification
http://bit.ly/2VKPMF7

SÉQUENCE 2

Books

City of Djinns: A Year in Delhi, WILLIAM DALRYMPLE, 1993

The God of Small Things, ARUNDHATI ROY, 1997

Q&A, VIKAS SWARUP, 2005

The White Tiger, ARAVIND ADIGA, 2008

The Ministry of Utmost Happiness, ARUNDHATI ROY, 2017

Films and documentary

Mother India, DIR. BY MEHBOOB KHAN, 1957

Salaam Bombay!, DIR. BY MIRA NAIR, 1988

Bombay, DIR. BY MANI RATNAM, 1995

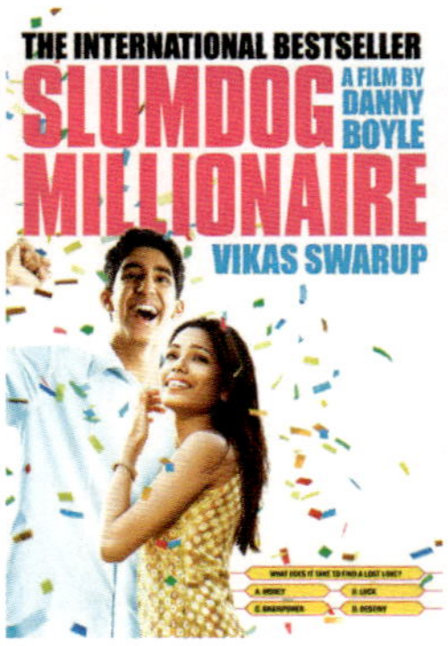

Songs

RAVI SHANKAR http://bit.ly/2ESYECX

Brimful of Asha, CORNERSHOP, 1997
http://bit.ly/1ngrcrP

Rebel Warrior, ASIAN DUB FOUNDATION, 1995
http://bit.ly/2XHbrjf

Timeline

Country ID, p. 191

AXE 4

Self-representation and relationship to others

Représentation de soi et rapport à autrui

SÉQUENCE 1 How do stereotypes impact women's empowerment?

Projects

Project #1: Convince the producers of your TV show to invite a celebrity who is trying to end stereotypes on women.

Project #2: For International Women's Day, create a leaflet to denounce stereotypes and encourage women's empowerment.

Tools

Grammaire	les verbes à particule, le discours indirect
Phonologie	l'accent contrastif
Écriture	le tiret et le trait d'union
Vocabulaire	la représentation des femmes, les médias

SÉQUENCE 2 How are Native Americans represented in the USA?

Projects

Project #1: Choose a misconception about Native Americans and explain why it is wrong in a 90-second speech.

Project #2: Write a blog post describing how Native American culture has been represented in the USA.

Tools

Grammaire	l'adverbe, le gérondif
Phonologie	les sons /ð/ et /θ/
Écriture	l'utilisation du *y* et du *i*
Vocabulaire	les clichés, les traditions

#fashion #stigmatisation
#empowerment
#socialnetworks #bodyimage

New H&M store, New York City, 2015

#customs #representation
#history
#clichés #fashionandtensions

Watching the Colonists Construct James Fort (1607), Sidney E. King, 1956-57

SÉQUENCE 1

How do stereotypes impact women's empowerment?

A Cover girls

GROUP WORK

GROUP A

✦ *Seventeen magazine*, April 1956 issue

GROUP B

✦ *Seventeen magazine*, December 2018 - January 2019 issue

1 Describe your group's cover (colours, picture, headlines, topics).

2 Say how women are represented on your cover.

3 Compare your covers. Discuss how the pressure put on women has evolved.

B Gender stereotypes in advertising

Vidéo hatier-clic.fr/lmu038

1 Say how women are usually represented on TV ads.

2 List as many problems about women's representation in advertisements as you can.

3 Show why there are differences between advertising and reality.

4 Explain the goal of this ad and the meaning of the word "adpology" to your English friend.

Grammar Spot

Phrasal verbs Tools → p. 92

"... while **growing up**."
"... we **start off** with men as the standard ..."

Word Spot

headline
magazine issue
commercial: advert, ad, advertisement
stereotype: cliché
sexism
role model: example
manifesto: written statement
empowerment: gaining power or freedom
emancipation
voluptuous body
body-shaming
curvy ≠ skinny
appealing: attractive
superficial
expect sbdy to
be expected to
be sorry for: apologise for
remember: recall

C Representation and gender expectations

"I am trying to unlearn many lessons of gender I internalized while growing up. But I sometimes still feel vulnerable in the face of gender expectations.

The first time I taught a writing class in graduate school, I was worried. Not about the teaching material, because I was well prepared and I was teaching what I enjoyed. Instead I was worried about what to wear. I wanted to be taken seriously.

I knew that because I was female, I would automatically have to prove my worth[1]. And I was worried that if I looked too feminine, I would not be taken seriously. I really wanted to wear my shiny lip gloss and my girly skirt, but I decided not to. I wore a very serious, very manly and very ugly suit.

The sad truth of the matter is that when it comes to appearance, we start off with men as the standard, as the norm. Many of us think that the less feminine a woman appears, the more likely she is to be taken seriously. A man going to a business meeting doesn't wonder about being taken seriously based on what he is wearing – but a woman does.

I wish I had not worn that ugly suit that day. Had I then the confidence I have now to be myself, my students would have benefited even more from my teaching. Because I would have been more comfortable and more fully and truly myself.

I have chosen to no longer be apologetic for my femininity. And I want to be respected in all my femaleness. Because I deserve to be. I like politics and history and am happiest when having a good argument about ideas. I am girly. I am happily girly. I like high heels and trying on lipsticks. It's nice to be complimented by both men and women (although I have to be honest and say that I prefer the compliments of stylish women), but I often wear clothes that men don't like or don't 'understand'. I wear them because I like them and because I feel good in them.

The 'male gaze', as a shaper[2] of my life's choices, is largely incidental[3]."

✦ Chimamanda Ngozi Adichie, *We Should All Be Feminists*, 2014

1. value 2. a decider 3. of minor importance

Pédagogie différenciée

TRAIL A

1 Tell whether these adjectives are related to females or males in the text.

vulnerable - worried - shiny - girly - serious - manly - ugly - respected - stylish

2 Find who is considered the norm regarding clothes at work.

3 Compare the author's style when she started teaching with her style now. Use these adjectives.

stylish - unsure - worried - feminine

TRAIL B

1 Build a two-column chart. In the 1st column, pick out adjectives related to females. In the 2nd, pick out adjectives related to males.

2 Find sentences that illustrate how men and women are supposed to act regarding clothes.

3 In your own words, compare the author's style when she started teaching with her style now.

Meet up! Write a few sentences to explain how clothing is imposed on women.

Prepare your project

You work for a women's magazine and you want the next cover to break gender stereotypes. Present it to the editorial board and be convincing when you describe it.

Grammar Tip Précis → p. 220

Use the **present *be* + V-*ing*** when you describe a picture or a magazine cover.

Memory Challenge

In pairs, write down as many stereotypes on women as you can in one minute and oppose them to reality. It's a competition!

D Self-esteem and insecurity

Essena O'Neill, an Australian teenager, quit Instagram and called it 'contrived[1] perfection'. We asked several young women about the pressure of the social media platform and how it affects their digital and personal lives.

This week, Essena O'Neill, an Australian teenager with more than half a million followers on Instagram, made headlines after announcing that she was quitting the platform because it is "contrived perfection made to get attention".

"I remember I obsessively checked the like count for a full week since uploading it," she wrote of her first-ever post on Instagram, a selfie that now has close to 2,500 likes. "It got 5 likes. This was when I was so hungry for social media validation ... Now marks the day I quit all social media and focus on real life projects."

We wondered: how many young women share O'Neill's experience? So we asked several others about whether they feel pressured to appear a certain way on Instagram, and how the platform affects their self-esteem.

Michelle Linker, 24: 'I absolutely feel insecure'

"I get serious Fomo (fear of missing out) with Instagram, and with all social media. People are publicizing usually something really cool or fun that they're doing, or at least they make it appear that way. I absolutely feel insecure.

I'm 24, I'm a young professional in Toronto, but I have had Instagram since I was in university. I do feel a pressure to look particularly good. I would never post a photo that wasn't flattering[2] of me.

I feel anxiety over how many likes I get after I post a picture. If I get two likes, I feel like, what's wrong with me? Some people judge Instagram by deleting photos that don't get enough likes. I wouldn't do that, but I would definitely second-guess[3] my intentions with posting them."

✦ Mahita Gajanan, *Young women on Instagram and self-esteem: 'I absolutely feel insecure'*, *The Guardian*, November 3, 2015

1. arranged 2. complimentary 3. think again

✦ Instagram post by Essena O'Neill, 2015

1 Observe the Instagram post. Explain what is special about the caption.

2 Read the article. Pick out elements indicating that Essena O'Neill was obsessed by her representation on social media.

3 Describe Michelle Linker's relationship with Instagram, and how it affects her daily life.

4 Search the internet for a perfect picture posted by a celebrity. Write a real caption in the style of Essena O'Neill to denounce the pressure of social media on women.

Grammar Spot

Indirect speech TOOLS → p. 92

"Essena O'Neill [...] made headlines after **announcing that she was quitting the platform...**"

Word Spot

- illusions: lies /laɪz/
- pride: high opinion of sbdy
- assured ≠ uncertain
- self-confident ≠ insecure
- daring: bold: courageous
- determined: tenacious
- unapologetic ≠ sorry
- epic: legendary: mythic
- iconic /aɪkɒnɪk/: emblematic
- obsessive: fixated
- take in sthg: consider true
- take sbdy seriously
- encourage: support
- discriminate
- pretend

E An inspirational message

✦ Instagram post by Beyoncé, July 22, 2014

Culture Tip

Rosie the Riveter was invented during WWII to embody women and inspire them to contribute to the war effort by working hard in factories. Feminists then used this representation to fight back patriarchal society with its message.

1. Identify the document and say what you know about Beyoncé.
2. Read the Culture Tip and comment on Beyoncé's attitude.
3. Imagine whom the message "We can do it!" is addressed to.
4. ***PAIR WORK*** Comment Beyoncé's post on Instagram. Discuss her message about women's representation with another fan.

F RBG: an icon

Classe inversée

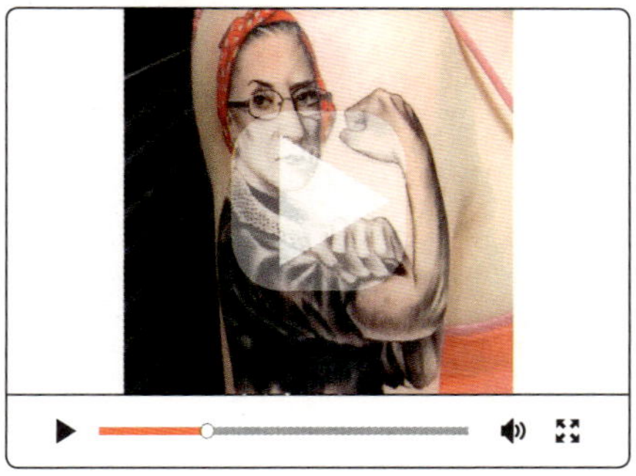

✦ *RBG*, dir. by Julie Cohen and Betsy West, 2018

Vidéo
DVD
hatier-clic.fr/lmu039

E-workbook
Classe inversée
hatier-clic.fr/lmu040

1. Find elements about the woman in the trailer (occupation, nationality, name).
2. Explain what type of person she is.
3. Find elements in the video showing that this woman is considered an icon. Focus on nicknames and adjectives.
4. Explain why RBG is important for the representation of women and why it is essential to see more women like her in the media.

Culture Tip

The Supreme Court is the most important law court in the USA. It has the right to change the decisions of all the other courts. Its 9 members (or less) are appointed by the President for life, but their nomination must be approved by the Senate.

Prepare your project

You are inspired by a famous woman. Prepare a post for your followers. Explain the positive sides and the dangers linked to women's representation online.

Grammar Tip

Précis → p. 223

Use the **present perfect** (have + past participle) to make an assessment on women's representation.

Memory Challenge

Look at any document you have studied in class for two minutes. Close your book and explain to a classmate everything you remember about it. Your classmate must guess which document you are talking about.

Tools in the Spotlight

Entraînez-vous sur la plateforme *Let's Meet Up!*
reussirenlangues.fr

Practise your grammar

Précis grammatical, p.192

Les verbes à particule

- Les verbes à particule sont des verbes suivis d'une particule adverbiale. Le verbe à particule peut avoir un **sens complètement différent** du verbe dont il est issu.

give (donner) ≠ *give up* (renoncer)

- Contrairement aux verbes prépositionnels qui sont suivis d'une préposition obligatoirement accompagnée d'un nom ou pronom, les verbes à particule peuvent être **employés seuls**, sans nom après la particule.

*I am trying to unlearn many lessons of gender I internalized while **growing up**.* → *She **grew up**.*

*We **start off** with men as the standard.* → *Let's **start off**!*

⚠ Quand le verbe à particule est suivi d'un pronom, la particule doit se placer **après** le pronom.

*He **gave up** the project.* → *He **gave** it **up**.* (particule *up* placée après le pronom *it*)

*She **took off** her cap.* → *She **took** it **off**.* (particule *off* placée après le pronom *it*)

1 Remplacez les éléments soulignés par l'un des verbes à particule suivants : ***grow up, give up, watch out, start off, sum up.***

a. She spent her childhood in California.
b. So let's recap! Who is coming to this TED Talk conference on women's rights?
c. To begin with, she would like to sign this petition in favour of equal pay.
d. Be careful! Some of them will not come to the meeting.
e. She wanted to join this organisation, then she changed her mind.

2 Remplacez les mots soulignés par un pronom.

a. They gave up the idea of signing up this petition.
b. They turned down the offers.
c. He woke up his father.
d. She put down her cup of tea and started to make a speech.

Le discours indirect

- Le discours indirect permet de **rapporter des paroles** prononcées au discours direct.
- En général, le discours indirect est introduit par un **verbe introducteur** (*say, tell, mention, claim, announce, declare, add*...).

*Essena O'Neill made headlines after **announcing that** she was quitting the platform.*

- Pour passer du discours direct au discours indirect, il faut ajuster la **concordance des temps** et modifier les pronoms ainsi que les marqueurs temporels.

Discours direct :

"I 'm quitting the platform tomorrow," she said.

(I : pronom ; 'm quitting : présent en *be* + V-*ing* ; tomorrow : marqueur temporel ; said : verbe introducteur au prétérit)

Discours indirect :

She said that she was quitting the platform the following day.

(said : verbe introducteur au prétérit ; she : pronom ; was quitting : prétérit en *be* + V-*ing* ; the following day : marqueur temporel)

3 Mettez au discours indirect.

a. "I will do an internship in a women's organisation," she said.
b. "Women are paid the same wages as men in this firm," he announced.
c. "I want to decorate my office for the celebrations tomorrow," she said.
d. "People stood up for such noble causes yesterday," he mentioned.

4 Mettez au discours direct.

a. Beyoncé announced that she would always back up women's organisations.
b. She said that she had used a Nigerian feminist writer's speeches for her video clip.
c. She added that she was going to post a recommendation on her Instagram account.
d. She said that her video clip had been watched by millions of fans.

Improve your pronunciation

Précis de phonologie, p. 242

L'accent contrastif

Audio
CD1 piste 37
MP3 n° 59

L'accent contrastif met en opposition deux mots ou propositions, afin d'attirer l'attention de l'interlocuteur sur le **contraste**, l'**ajout** ou le **caractère inattendu**.

*Sorry advertising suggested you should rollerskate on your period, and that only **certain** bodies were ready for the beach. Sorry for shaving **already** shaved legs.*

*Thousands of State **and** Federal laws discriminated on the basis of gender.*

Certain /'sɜːtᵊn/, qui porte l'accent contrastif, est opposé implicitement à *all bodies* : *only certain bodies – not all of them!*

Already /ɔːl'redi/, fortement accentué, marque l'inattendu: raser des jambes déjà rasées. On insiste sur cette surprise.

And /'ænd/, sous sa forme accentuée, insiste sur les deux types de lois : nationales et fédérales.

5 Indiquez l'accent contrastif, puis vérifiez avec l'enregistrement.

Audio
CD1 piste 38
MP3 n° 60

a. She is taking part in today's march and tomorrow's rally.
b. Sorry for signing up an already signed document again!
c. Sarah, Jane, Janet, Sue... and Tom stood up for this cause!
d. Only certain activists approved of this measure – not all of them!
e. Sheryl Sandberg says that all women should lean in – not lean back.
f. Yet, Michelle Obama declares that only certain women will make it to the top.
g. The gender parity petition is available online, and surprisingly enough, even in all the local newspapers.

Work on your writing skills

Le tiret et le trait d'union

- Il ne faut pas confondre le **tiret** et le **trait d'union**.

A man going to a business meeting doesn't wonder about being taken seriously based on what he is wearing – but a woman does.

*She wrote of her **first-ever** post on Instagram, a selfie that now has close to 2,500 likes.*

- Le tiret est utilisé pour faire une **précision** (*"A man doesn't wonder – but a woman does"*). Il peut contribuer à **accentuer** une phrase et mettre en valeur l'information.

TIP N'utilisez les **tirets** que si votre propos vient véritablement préciser quelque chose que vous jugez important, sinon utilisez des parenthèses.

- Le trait d'union sert le plus souvent à **relier** deux mots (*her first-ever post*) ou bien un mot avec sa particule (*up-to-date*). Le trait d'union est également nécessaire pour écrire les **nombres composés de 21 à 99** (*twenty-two*).

TIP Vérifiez dans un dictionnaire récent si vous avez besoin d'un **trait d'union** lorsque vous hésitez sur un mot qui vous semble composé.

6 Les tirets et les traits d'union ont disparu dans ce texte. Copiez-le en replaçant les tirets et traits d'union qui manquent.

Ruth Bader Ginsburg is an important figure for women's representation. She celebrated her eighty fifth birthday in two thousand eighteen. She is a dedicated and decisive judge being a Supreme Court judge. She has become a well known popular icon.

7 Replacez les informations suivantes dans le texte en utilisant des tirets.

a well-known Nigerian writer | more than 78 million views on YouTube | recreating Rosie the Riveter | a famous American singer

Beyoncé is thought to be a feminist because of her messages. For example, she posted a picture on her Instagram account. She invited Chimamanda Ngozi Adichie to participate in one of her video clips. The video clip met a huge success.

Build up your vocabulary

Audio
CD1 piste 39

Women's representation

Diversity MP3 n°61

multiculturalism
ethnicity
skin colour
sexual orientation
disability
body positivity ≠ body-shaming
(body) curves
voluptuous body
curvy ≠ skinny
all shapes and sizes

Positive image MP3 n°62

pride: high opinion of sbdy
empowerment: gaining power or freedom
emancipation
appealing: attractive
role model: example (to follow)
body image: self-perception
confidence: self-assurance
self-confident ≠ insecure
assured ≠ uncertain
daring: bold: courageous
tenacious: determined
unapologetic ≠ sorry
epic: legendary: mythic

Discrimination MP3 n°63

stereotype: cliché
gender gap
sexism
racism
stigma
stigmatisation
prejudice
obsessive: fixated
be expected to
expect sbdy to
bully sbdy
discriminate

Appearance MP3 n°66

fashion
clothing
collection: range of clothes
dress
skirt
suit
high heels ≠ flat shoes
make-up: cosmetics
hairstyle
models
iconic /aɪkɒnɪk/: emblematic
girly ≠ manly
wear

Media MP3 n°65

headline
magazine issue
commercial: advert, ad, advertisement
mass media
representation
manifesto: written statement
remember: recall
give visibility
encourage: support
challenge sbdy: dare sbdy
demand: request

Social networks MP3 n°64

social media
pressure
illusions: lies /laɪz/
superficial
take sbdy seriously
take in sthg: consider true
be sorry: apologise for
advertise
perpetuate an image
pretend

Apprenez et révisez le vocabulaire !

Utilisez Quizlet pour vous entraîner en vous amusant.

Quizlet
hatier-clic.fr/lmu041

Utilisez le vocabulaire en contexte.

1 Complétez les phrases suivantes avec des mots de la carte mentale.

All that women can see on television are images of how a perfect woman is ... to look. The bodies of women come in ... ... and we should see more of them on magazine covers. But there is still a huge ... against women. This proves to be even worse for women with different ... . They are facing both stereotypes and ... . Fortunately, the media are giving them more ... nowadays.

2 Écrivez deux ou trois phrases pour dénoncer les stéréotypes auxquels font face les femmes. Utilisez les synonymes des mots suivants, que vous trouverez dans la carte mentale.

preserve an image | commercial | cosmetics | masculine | body image

AUTO évaluation

Faites le quiz interactif en ligne et suivez les conseils pour vous préparer à l'évaluation.

Quiz
hatier-clic.fr/lmu042

Project #1

Convince the producers of your TV show to invite a celebrity who is trying to end stereotypes on women.

1 **Choose a celebrity who is famous for his or her work against stereotypes on women.**

- ✔ Find information about him or her (identity, occupation, famous for, etc.).
- ✔ Find information about his or her involvement concerning gender stereotypes.

2 **Take a few notes on the topic of women's representation.**

- ✔ List the different gender stereotypes your show is going to deal with: **first**, **second**, **third**...
- ✔ Explain how they can be broken.
- ✔ Illustrate with precise examples using: **for example, such as, to illustrate this idea**...

3 **Organise your notes and prepare for d-day.**

- ✔ Check the pronunciation of difficult words using wordreference.com.
- ✔ Repeat some words to know how to pronounce them and how to stress them properly.
- ✔ Organise your notes: create a mind map or a word cloud to memorise your arguments and examples.

4 **Time to convince your producers!**

- ✔ Use expressions to give your opinion: **In my opinion... To me... I believe... I am convinced... I have no doubt...**

➤ Fiche de méthodologie N°20 p. 280

Project #2

For International Women's Day, create a leaflet to denounce stereotypes and encourage women's empowerment.

1 **Prepare your leaflet.**

- ✔ Look up on the internet to find information about International Women's Day: internationalwomensday.com.
- ✔ In your copybook, identify the type of discrimination you want to write about: body, clothing...
- ✔ You can find examples in the unit.

2 **Gather and organise your ideas.**

- ✔ Prepare a list of examples of discriminations you want to include in your leaflet.
- ✔ List your arguments to show why it is important to encourage women's empowerment.
- ✔ You can think about a slogan.

3 **Write your leaflet.**

- ✔ Use the **simple present** to speak about gender stereotypes. Don't forget to add **s** to 3rd person singular verbs!
- ✔ Use the **imperative** to express emergency: **Let's put an end to gender stereotypes!**
- ✔ Use the **present perfect** to show the lack of evolution: **Women have been diminished for too long!**

4 **Customize your leaflet.**

- ✔ Check your production for grammar and spelling mistakes.
- ✔ You may use canva.com to fashion your leaflet.
- ✔ You can create it with genial.ly to make it interactive.

➤ Fiche de méthodologie N°9 p. 261

SÉQUENCE 2

How are Native Americans represented in the USA?

A Portraying Native Americans

GROUP WORK

GROUP A Photographs by Edward Curtis (1868-1952) *"I want to make them live forever. It's such a big dream, I can't see it all."*

Chief Joseph, Nez Percé, 1903

Hupa woman, c. 1924

Little Hawk, 1907

Medicine Crow, c. 1908

GROUP B Indian memes*

* a video, an image, a text, that is copied and spread very quickly on the internet

1 Describe your group's pictures and give your impressions about these Native Americans: mood, setting, and facial expressions.

2 Indicate if this type of representation is a typical way of portraying Native Americans. Give your opinion about its impact on the viewer.

3 Explain what the goals of the artist or the meme creator might have been.

4 Explain the double meaning of "dream" in Curtis's quote (***GROUP A***) and of "popular" in the first meme (***GROUP B***).

Grammar Spot

The gerund Tools → p. 100
"Quit grinning"

Word Spot

- makeover: the change of someone's appearance
- tribe /traɪb/
- headdress: war bonnet
- regalia /rɪgeɪliə/: traditional costume
- feather /feðə^{r}/
- breastplate: a piece worn on your torso
- self-humour
- austere: stern, severe, serious
- see the bright side of life

B Indian humour

It has always been a great disappointment to Indian people that the humorous side of Indian life has not been mentioned by professed experts on Indian Affairs. Rather the image of the granite-faced grunting[1] redskin has been perpetuated by American mythology. [...]

The Indian people are exactly opposite of the popular stereotype. [...] Indians have found a humorous side of nearly every problem and the experiences of life have generally been so well defined through jokes and stories that they have become a thing in themselves.

For centuries before the white invasion, teasing[2] was a method of control of social situations by Indian people. Rather than embarrass[3] members of the tribe publicly, people used to tease individuals they considered out of step[4] with the consensus of tribal opinion.

In this way egos were preserved and disputes within the tribe of a personal nature were held to a minimum.

✦ Vine Deloria Jr., *Custer Died for Your Sins: An Indian Manifesto*, 1969

1. making a low sound instead of speaking 2. mocking
3. instead of embarrassing 4. in disagreement

1 Read the text and say which illustrations on the opposite page correspond to the "popular stereotype".

2 Explain what is meant by "the granite-faced grunting redskin" (l. 5).

3 Pick out the elements showing how important humour is in Native Americans' day-to-day lives.

4 ***PAIR WORK*** Using the text, discuss how Curtis's photographs misrepresented Native Americans.

Culture Tip

Vine Deloria Jr. (1933-2005) was an American Indian author, historian, and activist. His books raised awareness about American Indian issues. He is also known for his academic career at the University of Arizona. He created the first master's degree programme in American Indian Studies in the USA.

C How to be a "real" Indian?

Vidéo DVD

✦ *Smoke Signals*, dir. by Sherman Alexie, 1998

1 Describe the Native American in the screenshot and compare it with the pictures on the left page.

2 List the guidelines Thomas is supposed to follow to look "Indian".

3 Transform one of Edward Curtis's photographs into a meme that could sum up the point of view developed in the video.

Prepare your project

IN GROUPS OF FOUR, debate the stereotypes commonly associated with Native Americans.

Grammar Tip

Précis → p. 219

Use the **simple present** to express caracteristics or stereotypes.

Memory Challenge

Taboo! Talk about Indian humour without using the following words: humour, Indian, American.

D Facts and myths about Pocahontas

Historian Camilla Townsend gives her point of view about the American Indian princess.

Pocahontas might be a household name[1], but the true story of her short but powerful life has been buried in myths that have persisted since the 17th century.

To start with, Pocahontas wasn't even her actual name. Born about 1596, her real name was Amonute, and she also had the more private name Matoaka. Pocahontas was her nickname, which depending on who you ask means "playful one" or "ill-behaved[2] child."

Pocahontas was the favorite daughter of Powhatan, the formidable ruler[3] of the more than 30 Algonquian-speaking tribes in and around the area that the early English settlers would claim as Jamestown, Virginia.

Years later – after no one was able to dispute the facts – John Smith wrote about how she, the beautiful daughter of a powerful native leader, rescued him, an English adventurer, from being executed by her father.

This narrative of Pocahontas turning her back on her own people and allying with the English, thereby[4] finding common ground between the two cultures, has endured for centuries. But in actuality, Pocahontas's life was much different than how Smith or mainstream[5] culture tells it. It's even disputed whether or not Pocahontas, age 11 or 12, even rescued the mercantile[6] soldier and explorer at all, as Smith might have misinterpreted what was actually a ritual ceremony or even just lifted the tale from a popular Scottish ballad.

✦ www.smithsonian.com, March 23, 2017

1. a famous name worldwide 2. undisciplined 3. leader 4. and so 5. conventional 6. who did commerce

✦ Coloured lithograph, c. 1870

1 Look at the lithograph and describe the scene in detail (characters, age, situation, eye contact...).

2 Read the text and explain the different names given to Pocahontas.

3 Pick out elements mentioning the different sources of information. Say if the story of Pocahontas is historically true.

4 Create an audio guide of this picture and explain the true story of Pocahontas.

Culture Tip

John Smith was an English soldier, explorer, and colonial governor who played an important role in the establishement of Jamestown, the first English colony in North America, in the early 17th century.

Grammar Spot

Adverbs Tools → p. 100

"what was **actually** a ritual ceremony"

Word Spot

tepee: American Indian tent
traditional apparel: traditional clothing /kləʊðɪŋ/
fallacy: false or mistaken idea
enduring stereotype: stereotype that still exists
backlash
bold: courageous, brave /breɪv/
ambiguous
misleading: causing sbdy to believe sthg is not true
unlikely: improbable
accurate /ækjərət/: conforming exactly to truth
prevent sthg from happening: stop sthg from happening
be hurtful
cause a controversy
honour ≠ dishonour
disrespect: be off-limits

E Wearing a headdress

Amy Stretten* @amystretten — Suivre

A Native American headdress is not a hat. Try again, @Pharrell. #NotHappy @ELLEMagUK @ELLEmagazine

18:20 - 3 juin 2014

* Amy Stretten is a Native American journalist.

Culture Tip

Cultural appropriation is the adoption of some elements of a culture by another more dominant culture without proper context. Examples of cultural appropriation are numerous in the fashion industry or in American football with team names or mascots.

1 Describe the cover of *Elle Magazine* and what Pharrell Williams is wearing.

2 Read the Culture Tip and explain why the tweet criticises Pharrel Williams's choice.

3 Imagine the video message left by Amy Stretten on her YouTube channel to explain her tweet.

F Misconceptions explained

Classe inversée

✦ *Teen Vogue*, 2016

Vidéo hatier-clic.fr/lmu043

E-workbook Classe inversée hatier-clic.fr/lmu044

1 Use the following words to introduce the video:

headdress - tribe - wear

2 Explain what the headdress symbolises.

3 Explain this sentence: "If you were to buy a headdress that would be disrespectful."

Prepare your project

Write a tweet denouncing the misconceptions people had of Native Americans in the past and still have today.

Grammar Tip

Précis → p. 201-203

Don't forget to use **quantifiers** to avoid making generalities.

Memory Challenge

Split up into two groups. Challenge the other group with questions about the representations of Native Americans. The group with the most correct answers wins.

Entraînez-vous sur la plateforme *Let's Meet Up!*
reussirenlangues.fr

Tools in the Spotlight

Practise your grammar

Précis grammatical, p. 192

L'adverbe

- L'adverbe permet d'**insister sur un aspect** de l'action et donc de **préciser la manière** dont l'action est effectuée. Il est en général placé avant le verbe principal de la phrase dans laquelle il se trouve, sauf quand il est utilisé avec l'auxiliaire *be*.

*"what was **actually** a ritual ceremony"*

- Les adverbes peuvent préciser :
  - le **lieu** (*here, there, above…*) ;
  - le **temps** (*today, yesterday…*) ;
  - la **manière** (*quickly, angrily…*) ;
  - le **degré** (*quite, too…*) ;
  - la **modalité** (*probably, almost, certainly…*) ;
  - la **fréquence** (*always, rarely, usually…*).

1 **Complétez les phrases suivantes en plaçant l'adverbe entre parenthèses au bon endroit.**

a. The family admitted that the woman was right. (finally)
b. According to the speaker, history books tell the truth. (rarely)
c. Most people have heard of Pocahontas, the American Indian princess. (undeniably)
d. Native Americans are opposite of the popular stereotype. (exactly)
e. Teasing was a method of control. (often)
f. It has been a great disappointment to a lot of historians. (always)
g. Numerous stereotypes are associated with Native Americans. (commonly)

Le gérondif

- Le **gérondif** est un **verbe** transformé en **nom** avec l'ajout de *-ing*. Il permet à la personne qui s'exprime de faire référence à une expérience déjà vécue, une action déjà commencée ou un projet déjà envisagé.
- On le trouve dans les cas suivants :

Expression des préférences, des sentiments	*hate, enjoy, like, can't bear, can't stand, look forward to…*
Action déjà commencée	*finish, keep (on), stop, quit, give up, resume, continue…*
Projet déjà envisagé	*imagine, mind, consider, risk…*
Quand le verbe occupe la place du sujet	*Laughing was used to solve problems.* *Buying a headdress is disrespectful.*

2 **Précisez dans quel cas le gérondif est utilisé dans les phrases suivantes.**

expression des préférences, des sentiments — action déjà commencée — projet déjà envisagé — quand le verbe occupe la place du sujet

a. Settling in America was tough.
b. People should stop making fun of Indians.
c. Hollywood has kept on portraying Native Americans in movies.
d. Pocahontas could not help standing between her father and John Smith.
e. Finding a humourous side of every problem is quite courageous.

3 **Complétez ces phrases avec un gérondif ou un infinitif.**

a. … a headdress is highly symbolic. (wear)
b. Indians prefer … off problems. (laugh)
c. Settlers forced Indians … their territories. (leave)
d. Americans should stop … Pocahontas as a Walt Disney character. (present)

Improve your pronunciation

Précis de phonologie, p. 242

Les sons /ð/ et /θ/

Audio
CD1 piste 40
MP3 n° 67

- Les sons /ð/ et /θ/ correspondent toujours à la graphie ***th***, mais toutes les graphies ***th*** ne correspondent pas systématiquement à ces sons.

- Le son /ð/ crée une vibration des cordes vocales si l'on met sa main sur sa gorge. Il est proche du son /v/ en français. Le son /ð/ correspond à un *hard sound*.

Graphie	Son /ð/
th	*this*, *these*, *those*, *brother*, *other*, *breathe*

- À l'inverse, le son /θ/ est sourd (pas de vibration des cordes vocales si l'on met sa main sur sa gorge). Il est proche du son /f/ en français. Le son /θ/ correspond à un *soft sound*.

Graphie	Son /θ/
th	*think*, *three*, *month*, *seventh*, *youth*, *path*

Exceptions : graphie *th* prononcée /t/ : *thyme*, *the Thames*, *Thomas*, *Thailand*.

4 **Écoutez la phrase suivante et classez les mots dans un tableau à deux entrées selon la prononciation du « th » que vous identifiez.**

Audio
CD1 piste 41
MP3 n° 68

This year, they think they won't celebrate Thanksgiving since their best friends said they wouldn't either.

5 **Complétez les phrases suivantes avec l'expression *soft sound* ou *hard sound*.**

« th » dans *the*, *this*, *that*, *there* et *then* est un ... . Il se prononce /ð/.
« th » à la fin d'un mot comme dans *both*, *math*, *north* correspond à un ... . Il en va de même pour *think*, *through*, *threatened*. Il se prononce /θ/.

6 **Lisez les phrases suivantes à haute voix et classez les mots selon la prononciation du « th ». Puis vérifiez avec l'enregistrement.**

Audio
CD1 piste 42
MP3 n° 69

Both their kids were disappointed with the truth about Pocahontas.
There's another reason, they thought they were threatened.

Work on your writing skills

L'utilisation du *y* et du *i*

Le ***y*** se transforme en ***i*** dans certains mots.

- C'est le cas pour les **noms** singuliers terminés en ***y*** lorsqu'on les met au **pluriel**.

a party → *parties* *a baby* → *babies*

- Pour les **adjectifs** terminés en ***y***, le ***i*** apparaît au **comparatif**.

pretty → *prettier* *happy* → *happier* *lucky* → *luckier*

- Pour les **verbes** dont l'infinitif est terminé en ***y***, le ***i*** apparaît dans les verbes **conjugués**.

apply → *applies* (3e personne du présent simple), *applied* (prétérit)

⚠ Les verbes terminés en ***ay***, ***ey*** et ***oy*** gardent leur ***y***.

it betrays, *it conveys*, *it destroys*

- Pour former les **adverbes** : les adjectifs en ***y*** voient leur ***y*** devenir ***i***, auquel on ajoute ***ly*** pour constituer l'adverbe.

pretty → *prettily* *happy* → *happily* *lucky* → *luckily*

7 **Écrivez le pluriel de ces mots.**

city • ancestry • ally • family • infamy • controversy

8 **Écrivez les verbes suivants à la troisième personne du présent simple.**

to destroy • to try • to convey • to envy • to magnify • to play • to exemplify • to cry

9 **Écrivez le discours d'un jeune Amérindien à l'occasion du *Zero Discrimination Day*. Utilisez un maximum de mots de la liste suivante en appliquant les instructions entre parenthèses.**

mighty (comparative of superiority) • ally (plural) • corny (comparative of superiority) • family (plural) • destroy (3rd person present) • ancestry (plural) • magnify (3rd person present) • creepy (comparative of superiority) • infamy (plural) • cry (3rd person) • shy (comparative of superiority) • personify (3rd person present) • sneaky (comparative of superiority)

Build up your vocabulary

Audio
CD1 piste 43

Native Americans

Truth ≠ lies (MP3 n°70)

ambiguous
misleading: causing sbdy to believe sthg not true
true ≠ false
lie: tell false stories
play tricks on sbdy
prevent sthg from happening: stop sthg from happening

Clichés (MP3 n°73)

cliché ≠ accurate fact
backlash
fallacy: false or mistaken idea
enduring stereotype: stereotype that still exists
austere: stern, severe, serious
unlikely: improbable
accurate /ækjərət/: conforming exactly to truth
be hurtful
cause a controversy
honour ≠ dishonour
disrespect: be off-limits

Mood (MP3 n°71)

makeover: the change of someone's appearance
self-mockery: capacity to make fun of oneself
self-humour
bold: courageous, brave /breɪv/
see the bright side of life

Customs (MP3 n°72)

tribe /traɪb/
garments: clothing
tepee: American Indian tent
traditional apparel: traditional clothing /kləʊðɪŋ/
headdress: war bonnet
regalia /rɪgeɪliə/: traditional costume
feather /feðəʳ/
breastplate: a piece worn on your torso

Apprenez et révisez le vocabulaire !

Utilisez Quizlet pour vous entraîner en vous amusant.

Quizlet
hatier-clic.fr/lmu045

Utilisez le vocabulaire en contexte.

1 Complétez les phrases suivantes avec des mots de la carte mentale.

A lot of ... legends exist about Native Americans. Most people believe they are ... and bizarre, living in ... and always wearing their ... . In fact, this ... stereotype is not true, it's a ... . On the contrary they are ... , and love ...-... probably to avoid a ... . A lot of facts are still ... which causes one of the biggest ... in American History.

2 Écrivez un disours dénonçant les stéréotypes dont sont victimes les Amérindiens. Utilisez la traduction anglaise des mots suivants que vous trouverez dans la carte mentale.

trompeur — austère — autodérision — être irrespectueux — provoquer une controverse

AUTO évaluation

Faites le quiz interactif en ligne et suivez les conseils pour vous préparer à l'évaluation.

Quiz
hatier-clic.fr/lmu046

Project #1

Choose a misconception about Native Americans and explain why it is wrong in a 90-second speech.

1 Select the topic of your speech.

- ✓ Choose the misconception you want to talk about: Pocahontas, humour, wearing a headress for example.
- ✓ Note down your ideas and organise them.

2 Find convincing arguments.

- ✓ Each argument has to stand for an idea.
- ✓ Explain each argument and illustrate it with a concrete example (it can be a film, a comic strip, a video...).

3 Organise your story.

- ✓ Use linking words: **firstly**, **secondly**, **furthermore**, **finally**, **to conclude**...
- ✓ Prepare a short introduction and a conclusion.

4 Rehearse.

- ✓ Make a list of 15 words.
- ✓ The more you practise, the less you will need your list!
- ✓ You can practise in front of a mirror or friends.

5 Action!

- ✓ Don't read your notes. Speak at least for 90 seconds and be convincing!

➤ Fiche de méthodologie N°20 p. 280

Project #2

For Native American Day, write a blog post describing how Native American culture has been represented in the USA.

1 Choose elements of the Native American culture.

- ✓ Use documents from the unit or elements you are familiar with.
- ✓ Collect information online.

2 Criticise how they are represented.

- ✓ Add historical information to explain your choice.
- ✓ Structure your paragraph.

3 Add a warning at the end.

- ✓ Make your readers aware of how dangerous cultural appropriation and stereotypes can be.
- ✓ Use expressions of contrast (**whereas**, **on the contrary**...) and consequence (**as a result**, **as a consequence**...).

4 Check your blog post.

- ✓ Look for spelling mistakes.
- ✓ Look for grammatical errors.

➤ Fiche de méthodologie N°7 p. 258 N°22 p. 284

Let's RECAP

Lisez les questions-clés et complétez la fiche bilan avec des exemples et des documents que vous avez étudiés ou découverts.

AXE 4 | Self-representation and relationship to others

SÉQUENCE 1 — How do stereotypes impact women's empowerment?

How are women represented in the media?
Can all women relate to this representation?

E-workbook
Bilan à compléter
hatier-clic.fr/lmu047

#fashion
How does fashion represent women? Can women use fashion to express themselves?

#stigmatisation
How can gender stereotypes be fought?

#socialnetworks
What impact can social media have on women's representation? Can social networks be used to convey a positive and inclusive representation of the woman's body?

#empowerment
How can women become more empowered? To what extent is women's empowerment slowed down?

#bodyimage
How are women's images of their bodies influenced by the media?

SÉQUENCE 2 — How are Native Americans represented in the USA?

What is the image of Native Americans in history and popular culture?
How accurate is this representation?
What do Native Americans think about this representation?

E-workbook
Bilan à compléter
hatier-clic.fr/lmu048

#fashionandtensions
How does fashion use Native American apparel? What is cultural appropriation?

#representation
How has popular culture been portraying Native Americans?

#customs
How have Native American customs and traditions been represented historically? What part does humour play in Native American culture?

#history
How have Native Americans been portrayed in history?

#clichés
What clichés do Native Americans face? How do they react to them?

GO4IT!

Lisez et écoutez de l'anglais en dehors de la salle de classe ! Voici quelques conseils en lien avec votre séquence.

SÉQUENCE 1

Books

The Yellow Wallpaper,
Charlotte Perkins Gilman, 1892

A Room of One's Own,
Virginia Woolf, 1929

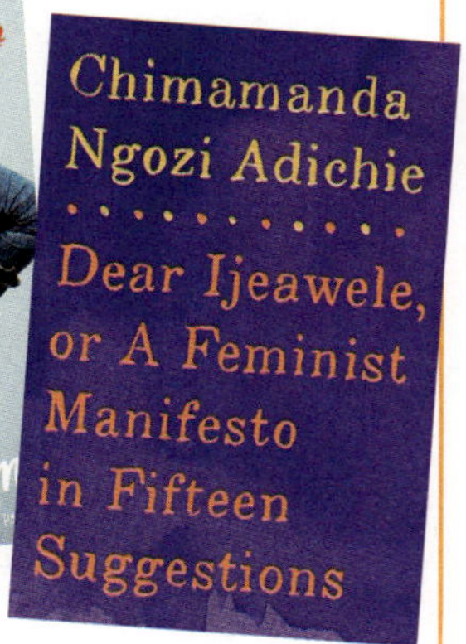

A New Model,
Ashley Graham, 2017

Dear Ijeawele, or A Feminist Manifesto in Fifteen Suggestions,
Chimamanda Ngozi Adichie, 2017

Films

Speeches

Cameron Russell: *Looks Aren't Everything. Believe Me, I'm a Model.*
http://bit.ly/2TysB39

Lindsay Kite: *Body Positivity or Body Obsession? Learning to See More & Be More*
http://bit.ly/2SOlPlF

Emma Watson: HeForShe UN campaign
http://bit.ly/1qpJRgG

Videos

Always #LikeAGirl campaign
http://bit.ly/2wEtZSA

Ban Bossy campaign
http://bit.ly/1geyVlq

Songs

Try, Colbie Caillat, 2014
http://bit.ly/1xVYLIA

Girl on Fire, Alicia Keys, 2012
http://bit.ly/L9dyX2

SÉQUENCE 2

Books and articles

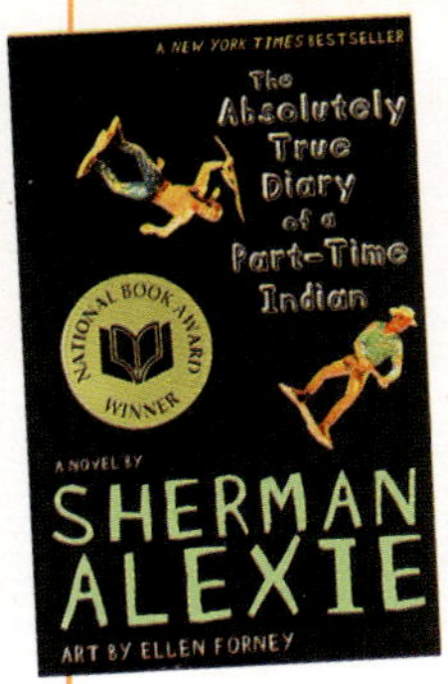

The Absolutely True Diary of a Part-Time Indian,
Sherman Alexie, 2007

Indian Shoes,
Cynthia Leitich Smith, 2002

Everything You Need to Know About Indigenous Peoples Day,
time.com, 2017
http://ti.me/2goNzMw

Native American photographers respond to Edward Curtis' images 100 years later,
theguardian.com
http://bit.ly/2m8G3rR

Edward Curtis' Epic Project to Photograph Native Americans,
smithsonianmag.com, 2012
http://bit.ly/2qDUSZ8

Films

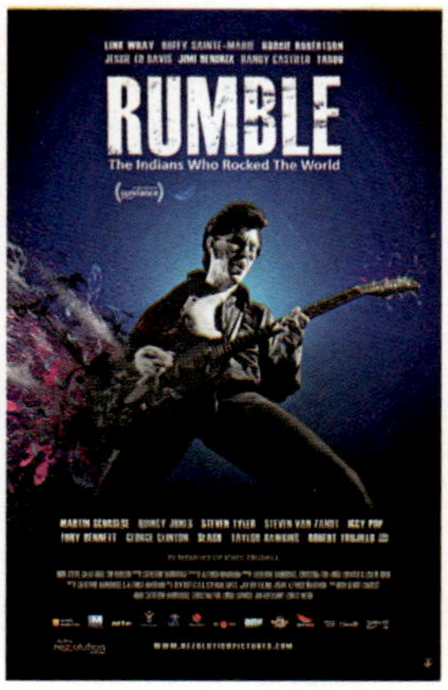

Videos

Redskin – Native Americans – One Word,
Cut
http://bit.ly/2maMGds

6 misconceptions About Native American People, Teen Vogue
http://bit.ly/2jKyPXU

Website

Native American Heritage,
National Archives
http://bit.ly/2qFgC6H

AXE 5

Sports and society

Sports et société

SÉQUENCE 1 Does American football bring people together?

Projects

Project #1: Record the video that a football player who took a knee, posted for his fans on his Facebook page.

Project #2: Take part in a discussion on an NFL online forum about whether the Super Bowl brings Americans together.

Tools

Grammaire le présent en *be* + V-*ing*, le pluriel des noms
Phonologie les consonnes muettes
Écriture les faux amis
Vocabulaire le sport, l'identité nationale

SÉQUENCE 2 Is football a medium of social inclusion in the UK?

Projects

Project #1: Act out the interview of a British football player. Discuss the values and role of football in the UK.

Project #2: Create a brochure for a British football club presenting its history and values.

Tools

Grammaire le prétérit, le *past perfect*
Phonologie les paires minimales
Écriture les homophones
Vocabulaire le football, la société

#hypermediatised #teamsport #nationalpride
#socialevent #politicalstatement

The Atlanta Falcons entering the field at Super Bowl LI at the NRG Stadium in Houston, Texas, 2017

#socialisation #senseofbelonging #nationalunity
#supporters #discrimination

England fans in Moscow, Russia, World Cup 2018

SÉQUENCE 1

Does American football bring people together?

A What is the Super Bowl?

1 **What's So Super About Super Bowl Sunday?**

2 **Super Bowl Makes 'Heroic' Play To Unify America**

3 **2018 Super Bowl: Trump brings up national anthem debate in pregame statement**

4 **The Power of Super Bowl Advertising**

A For the first time in a decade, there was no presidential interview on Super Bowl Sunday but Donald Trump, who is spending the weekend at his Mar-a-Lago estate, did release a statement hours before the Patriots and Eagles face off in Super Bowl LII and it included a familiar theme: The importance of standing for the national anthem.

✦ Ryan Wilson, cbssports.com, 2018

B Super Bowl LII — through the NFL-controlled moments and many top ads — made a Herculean effort to re-inspire and unify Americans feeling battered by divisive politics and polarizing public discourse. The NFL memo: This Super Bowl must deliver the warm and fuzzies by celebrating heroes and our common humanity.

✦ Anne Zeiser, mediapost.com, 2018

C Each winter, millions of Americans gather around their televisions for Super Bowl Sunday. The Super Bowl is the championship game of the National Football League (NFL). NFL teams compete throughout the fall for the honor of being one of the top two teams who get to play in the biggest game of the year: the Super Bowl. Though you may not find it listed on any calendar, Super Bowl Sunday is considered an unofficial holiday in the United States. In fact, after Thanksgiving, more food is eaten on Super Bowl Sunday than any other day of the year.

✦ wonderopolis.org

D In my estimation, the Super Bowl features three big events: the game, half-time show and commercials. The importance of the game goes without saying. The winner earns the glory, the ticker tape parade and the ring. The half-time show is filled with hype, lights, bling and big names. The commercials bring entertainment and an opportunity to sell to the largest television audience of the year.

✦ Marianne Bickle, forbes.com, 2012

Culture Tip

The **half-time show** takes place every Super Bowl during the break midway through the game. Concerts are organised and stars perform in the middle of the stadium.

1 Match each newspaper title with its corresponding article.

2 Create a mind map on the Super Bowl with words and expressions from the texts.

3 Use your mind map to explain what the Super Bowl is.

Grammar Spot

Present be + V-ing Tools → p. 112

"Donald Trump who **is spending**"

"**Are** you **kidding**?"

Word Spot

- bank holiday
- game
- cheerleaders
- pride
- celebration
- happiness: joyfulness
- unity
- unifying factor
- spend time with friends
- have fun: enjoy oneself
- cheer: yell supportingly
- eat together
- come together: unify
- share values
- unite: bring together
- different background: different cultural baggage

B Game day

Vidéo
hatier-clic.fr/lmu049

✦ *Super Bowl: What does it mean to Americans?*, BBC News, 2015

1 Watch the video and comment on the public: clothes, behaviour and mood.

2 ***PAIR WORK*** Create a word cloud with the different meanings the Super Bowl has and compare it with the rest of the class.

3 You are the BBC journalist who interviewed these people. Write a short caption for your video post on Twitter to report what supporters think of the Super Bowl.

C National pride

✦ Idina Menzel sings the national anthem prior to Super Bowl XLIX between the New England Patriots and the Seattle Seahawks at University of Phoenix Stadium in Glendale, Arizona, February 1, 2015.

1 Look at the photograph and list as many elements linked to the USA and sports as you can.

2 Explain in your own words what the people in the photograph are doing and why.

3 Interview three people in the class to have their opinion about the importance of singing the national anthem before a game.

Prepare your project

Make a one-minute speech to explain what the Super Bowl means to Americans.

Grammar Tip Précis → p. 193

Pay attention to the use of **articles**.
the USA – **Ø** Americans

Memory Challenge

Work in pairs. Each of you needs to give a new word learnt p. 108 and 109. The last one to speak wins.

Does American football bring people together?

D The national anthem in sports

How "The Star-Spangled Banner" became a part of American sports culture

"Ladies and gentlemen, please rise for our national anthem."

You'll hear some version of this announcement at the start of most sporting events, whether they be professional, college or youth-level. The performance of the national anthem is a well-established part of American athletic competitions. Yet "The Star-Spangled Banner" typically doesn't make an appearance at many other public gatherings. We don't sing or listen to it before concerts, Broadway shows, operas or lectures. So why do we do this for sports? The answer goes back to America's pastime: baseball. [...]

✦ Whitney Houston, 1991

During World War II, playing the national anthem before regular baseball games became the norm, thanks to an upswing[1] in patriotic sentiment and technological developments in sound systems that allowed for the playing of the song without the added expense of hiring a band.

The practice spread to other sports as well. After the war ended in 1945, NFL Commissioner Elmer Layden stated his intention to make "The Star-Spangled Banner" a permanent part of every football game. "We must not drop[2] it simply because the war is over. We should never forget what it stands for," Layden declared. [...] With its evocations of warfare[3] and patriotism, "The Star-Spangled Banner" has become a seemingly inextricable part of American sports culture — and even pop culture, thanks to iconic moments like Whitney Houston's powerful 1991 Super Bowl performance during the Gulf War. [...] Over the years, the anthem has certainly played a part in cultural wars. Most recently, quarterback Colin Kaepernick's decision to protest racial injustice by kneeling during "The Star-Spangled Banner" has been the subject of heated debate.

In 1968, Olympic athletes Tommie Smith and John Carlos were thrown out of Olympic Stadium in Mexico City after raising their fists in a Black Power salute as they stood on the medal podium during "The Star-Spangled Banner."

✦ Caroline Bologna, *The History Of The National Anthem In Sports*, *HuffPost*, May 19, 2018

1. a boom, a rise 2. stop 3. fights

Pédagogie différenciée

TRAIL A

1 Give the name of the American national anthem. Was it first sung in 1991, 1968 or 1945?

2 Give the name of the sport which played the national anthem first.

3 Use these words in a sentence to create a definition of the American hymn.

national - patriotic sentiment - warfare

4 Spot the names of three people who have shown signs of protests during the national anthem.

TRAIL B

1 Highlight the different dates or time periods in the text. Pick up the period of time when the anthem was first played during a sport competition.

2 Find the sport that first played the national anthem before a game.

3 Explain how the American hymn is linked to patriotism.

4 From line 34 to the end, pick out the different people mentioned by the author. Explain the link between the people and the national anthem.

Meet up! Explain the importance of the national anthem in American sports.

Grammar Spot

Plural of nouns Tools → p. 112

"Ladies and gentlemen"
"most sporting events"
"American athletic competitions"

Word Spot

coach
values: ideas
dignity
privileged
injustice
pride

patriotism
respectful ≠ disrespectful
different ≠ same
kneeling ≠ standing
oppress: torment

refuse ≠ accept
defend ≠ attack
stand up for your rights

E Conflicting views

✦ *Time Magazine*, October 03, 2016 (Time Inc. Used under license)

Culture Tip

Colin Kaepernick refused to stand up during the national anthem before an NFL game in 2016. He said "I am not going to stand up to show pride in a flag for a country that oppresses black people and people of color". He lost his job in the process.

1 Analyse the document and comment on the picture.

2 Read the cover and the Culture Tip. Explain why the fight is perilous.

3 ***GROUP WORK*** Kaepernick's gesture is "fueling a debate about privilege, pride and patriotism". Explain what the debate is about in your own words.

F The power of football

Classe inversée

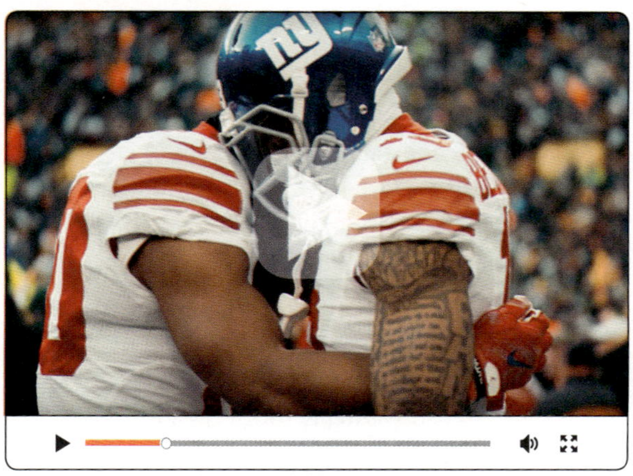

✦ *Inside These Lines*, National Football League, 2017

Vidéo
DVD
hatier-clic.fr/lmu050

E-workbook
Classe inversée
hatier-clic.fr/lmu051

1 Pick out the expression that is repeated. Explain what it evokes.

2 Say what values are expressed in the ad.

3 ***PAIR WORK*** Discuss the reasons why the NFL made this ad.

Prepare your project

The NFL's new policy requires players to stand for the national anthem on the field or wait in the locker room. Write a letter to the NFL in reaction to the new policy.

Grammar Tip

Précis → p. 217

Use **modals** to express your opinion.

Memory Challenge

In groups, choose one person mentioned p. 110-111 and make your group guess using only mimes and sounds!

Tools in the Spotlight

Entraînez-vous sur la plateforme *Let's Meet Up!*
reussirenlangues.fr

Practise your grammar

Précis grammatical, p.192

Le présent en *be* + V-*ing*

- Il indique que l'action est **en cours** au moment où l'on parle.

*Donald Trump, who **is spending** the weekend at his Mar-a-Lago estate...*

- Il convient aussi pour **commenter** quelque chose qui vient d'être dit.

*Oh my God! Are you **kidding**?*

- On l'utilise pour les **descriptions** d'images ou de tableaux.

*In this picture a football player **is standing** up for the national anthem.*

- Il sert aussi à faire référence à **l'avenir** avec un marqueur de temps du futur.

*This player **is taking** part in the Super Bowl next year.*

- On le trouve parfois avec l'adverbe ***always*** fortement accentué pour traduire l'**irritation** ou la **désapprobation** de celui qui parle.

*You're **always criticising** the Super Bowl!*

1 Choisissez entre le présent en *be* + V-*ing* ou le présent simple.

a. Look! This football player (**is taking / takes**) a knee.
b. (**Are you joking / do you joke**) when you say that you've never heard of the Super Bowl?
c. In this picture the football players (**are signing / sign**) autographs.
d. (**Are you watching / do you watch**) the Super Bowl every year?

2 Indiquez la valeur du présent en *be* + V-*ing* : action en cours, description, futur proche, désapprobation.

a. You're always disturbing me whenever I watch a match on TV.
b. I'm attending the championship tomorrow afternoon.
c. In this photograph the coach is speaking to the players.
d. Where are the children? Are they watching the match?
e. The players are training at the stadium at the moment.

Le pluriel des noms

Le **pluriel régulier** des noms se forme en ajoutant un ***s*** au nom au singulier.

most sporting events, American athletic competitions

- Certaines **terminaisons** sont **modifiées** au pluriel, notamment pour les noms se terminant par ***f*** ou ***fe***, ***ch***, ***sh***, ***ss***, ***x*** et ***y***.

leaf → *leaves* /z/ — *wife* → *wives* /z/
branch → *branches* /iz/ — *brush* → *brushes* /iz/
pass → *passes* /iz/ — *box* → *boxes* /iz/
lady → *ladies* /iz/

- Il existe des **formes irrégulières** de pluriel.

woman → *women* — *man* → *men* — *child* → *children*
tooth → *teeth* — *foot* → *feet*

⚠ En anglais, les **noms de famille** prennent la marque **+ *s*** au pluriel, contrairement au français.

the Smiths (les Smith)

3 Mettez au pluriel en faisant les modifications nécessaires.

a. A woman and a man can take part in any sporting event.
b. My child likes watching the Super Bowl.
c. You will receive an invitation to the Super Bowl in your in-box.
d. This lady doesn't feel like attending the tournament this month.
e. My foot is sore and my tooth is painful. I won't go and see the match today.

4 Soulignez les pluriels dans les phrases suivantes, puis indiquez leur singulier.

a. Most children like playing games of all kinds.
b. Both men and women usually watch the Super Bowl.
c. Sporting events and festivals attract a lot of amateurs.
d. Coaches use boxes to store their T-shirts.
e. These are the passes you need for your groups of fans.

Improve your pronunciation

Précis de phonologie, p. 242

Les consonnes muettes

Audio
CD1 piste 44
MP3 n° 74

Dans certains cas les consonnes initiales, intermédiaires et finales sont muettes : elles ne sont pas prononcées.

- Consonnes **initiales** muettes
  - ***k*** lorsqu'il est suivi de ***n*** : *knee, knife, knit, know*
  - ***h*** non aspiré : *heir, honest, honour, hour*
  - ***p*** dans les mots d'origine grecque : *psychology, psychiatry*
- Consonnes **intermédiaires** muettes
  - ***gh*** dans : *tonight, eight, daughter, bought, thought, although*
  - ***l*** dans : *could, would, should, walk, talk*
  - ***t*** dans : *listen, fasten, castle*
- Consonnes **finales** muettes
  - ***b*** dans : *climb, comb, thumb, lamb*
  - ***n*** lorsqu'il est placé après ***m*** : *autumn, condemn, solemn, column, hymn*

5 **Indiquez si la consonne initiale *k*, *h* et *p* est prononcée, puis vérifiez vos réponses avec l'enregistrement.**

Audio
CD1 piste 45
MP3 n° 75

kick • knit • kill • knee • hotel • hour • honourable • pastry • psychiatrist

6 **Prononcez les mots suivants, puis vérifiez votre prononciation avec l'enregistrement.**

Audio
CD1 piste 46
MP3 n° 76

although • half • muscle • sandwich • unknown • island • castle • sword

7 **Indiquez si la consonne finale *b* est prononcée, puis vérifiez vos réponses avec l'enregistrement.**

Audio
CD1 piste 47
MP3 n° 77

rob • knob • climb • rib • thumb • pub • lamb • lab

Work on your writing skills

Les faux amis

- La graphie de certains mots anglais est trompeuse. Elle rappelle un mot français existant mais signifie un mot complètement différent en français. Par exemple, ***library*** en anglais ne veut pas dire « librairie » en français, mais « bibliothèque ». On appelle ce type de mots des **faux amis**.
- Voici 10 faux amis très courants :

faux ami	traduction	et non	qui se dit
car	voiture	car	*bus*
coin	pièce de monnaie	coin	*corner*
pain	douleur	pain	*bread*
grave	tombe	grave	*serious*
figure	chiffre	figure	*face*
lecture	conférence	lecture	*reading*
achieve	réaliser, réussir	achever	*complete*
cry	pleurer	crier	*shout*
deceive	tromper, duper	décevoir	*disappoint*
novel	roman	nouvelle	*short story*

8 **Repérez les faux amis dans cette liste.**

car • achievement • cry • bus • pain

9 **Associez chaque mot à sa définition.**

lecture • eventually • bookshop • issue • library • pain • potentially • bread • reading • way out

a. place where you can buy books
b. exit
c. place where you can borrow books
d. in the end
e. what you feel when you have a toothache
f. speech made by an expert
g. you can spread butter and marmalade on it
h. favourite hobby for literature lovers
i. problem
j. possibly

10 **Utilisez cinq faux amis du tableau ci-contre dans des phrases.**

Build up your vocabulary

Audio CD1 piste 48

American football

Political statement — MP3 n°78

dignity
injustice
oppression
racism /reɪsɪzᵊm/
discrimination
different ≠ same
respectful ≠ disrespectful
privileged
stand up for one's rights
defend ≠ attack
oppress: torment
refuse ≠ accept
kneel /niːl/ ≠ stand
different background:
different cultural /kʌltʃᵊrᵊl/ baggage

Patriotism — MP3 n°82

national anthem /ænθəm/
bank holiday
values: ideas
national unity
pride
celebration
unifying factor: unifying force
unite: unify: bring together
share values

Sporting event — MP3 n°79

stadium
scoreboard
seats
front-row ≠ back-row seats
kick-off: start of the game
half-time
show
commercial: advert: ad
advertise
broadcast on TV / the radio
attend a game

Football — MP3 n°81

coach /kəʊtʃ/
team
players
cheerleaders
game
competition
finalist
nationwide
qualify
compete

Fans — MP3 n°80

fandom
jersey /dʒɜːzi/
cap
team apparel
emotions: feelings
happiness: joyfulness
cheer: yell supportingly
forget your problems ≠ have your problems in mind
eat together: share a dinner
spend time with friends or family
have fun: enjoy oneself
support a team

Apprenez et révisez le vocabulaire !

Utilisez Quizlet pour vous entraîner en vous amusant.

Quizlet hatier-clic.fr/lmu052

Utilisez le vocabulaire en contexte.

1 Complétez les phrases suivantes avec des mots de la carte mentale.

a. American football is an important … in the USA. Before the Super Bowl, famous artists sing the … … in the … . At … … in the middle of the game, there is a real … and there are many original … on TV.

b. Lately, some players have decided to … in order to denounce … , … and … . American football can be a symbol of … … but it is also the opportunity for certain players to … … for their … .

2 Décrivez un match du Super Bowl où un joueur s'agenouille à un·e ami·e qui ne connait pas du tout cette compétition. Trouvez les mots suivants dans la carte mentale et utilisez-les.

fierté | passer du bon temps avec sa famille | à travers le pays | s'agenouiller | partager des valeurs

AUTO évaluation

Faites le quiz interactif en ligne et suivez les conseils pour vous préparer à l'évaluation.

Quiz hatier-clic.fr/lmu053

Project #1

Record the video that a football player who took a knee, posted for his fans on his Facebook page.

1 Create your character.

- ✓ Be ready to introduce yourself (name, age, city, team).
- ✓ Talk about your love for football and what it symbolises for you.
- ✓ Choose a personality who inspires you.

2 Explain why you took a knee.

- ✓ Think of arguments that can illustrate your point of view.
- ✓ Use expressions to share your opinion: **I think... In my opinion... As far as I'm concerned... I agree with...**
- ✓ To structure your argument use linking words such as: **first**, **moreover**, **however**, **finally**.

3 Record yourself!

- ✓ Don't read your text, just write down 10-15 key words.
- ✓ Check the pronunciation of the words you are unsure about. You can use an online dictionary.
  bowl /bəʊl/, **an**them /æn.θəm/, **nat**ional /næʃ.ᵊnᵊl/

➤ Fiche de méthodologie N°12 p. 266

Project #2

Take part in a discussion on an NFL online forum about whether the Super Bowl brings Americans together.

1 Gather information from the unit.

- ✓ Look at the documents you studied and use the Culture Tip to find arguments.
- ✓ Find other texts and videos online.
- ✓ Take notes or draw a mind map with key words.

2 In pairs, imagine the online conversation.

- ✓ People will give their opinion about:
  – what the Super Bowl represents;
  – the unifying power it has in America;
  – the pregame and half-time shows.

3 Start the conversation.

- ✓ Your arguments should be structured: 1 idea = 1 example.
- ✓ Include photos, GIFs and memes to illustrate your arguments.
- ✓ Pay attention to spelling and the use of articles: **the** USA, **Ø** Americans, **the** Super Bowl.

4 Follow the rules of online writing.

- ✓ Forums have a set of rules you must respect. Think about what you write and stay polite.
- ✓ React to the other messages, remember it is a conversation.

➤ Fiche de méthodologie N°21 p. 282

SÉQUENCE 2

Is football a medium of social inclusion in the UK?

A A national pride

✦ England captain Bobby Moore accepts the World Cup from the Queen after winning over West Germany at Wembley Stadium in 1966.

1 Identify the people and the place. Describe the people in the foreground (attitude and expression).

2 Imagine a short dialogue between Queen Elizabeth II and Bobby Moore. She congratulates him for having won the World Cup and he thanks her for the prize.

B The secret story of football

PAIR WORK

E-workbook
Fiche à imprimer
hatier-clic.fr/lmu054

Student A

Audio
CD1 piste 49

1 Show that football is more than a sport.

2 Describe the challenge women's football faced in the 20th century.

Student B

Audio
CD1 piste 50

1 Sum up the opinion of the English about sports and politics. Illustrate it with the given example.

2 Show that football has an important role in communities in Britain.

Students A and B

3 Share your findings. List three facts people should know about football in Britain and present them to the class.

Grammar Spot

Past perfect Tools → p. 120
"What women **had achieved** during the war years was astonishing."

Word Spot

professional ≠ amateur
hobby: pastime
attraction
reputation: fame
national pride
roots: origins
progress: evolution: improvement
emancipation
legendary: memorable
historic
attract
gain popularity
support: encourage ≠ restrain: discourage
establish: take place
evolve: change
develop: grow
break down barriers

C Football and social classes

Football in Britain has historically been the bastion of male working-class culture. The professional sport has its roots in factory towns and cities of the north of England. Some of the UK's most successful football clubs were the product of industrial communities such as Manchester, Liverpool, Sheffield, Glasgow, and Newcastle, with some formed from works teams[1]. [...] For many male workers, watching their football club – or their country – was the cornerstone[2] of social life. But that has changed drastically over the last thirty years, because ticket prices have made regular attendance something that only a certain strata[3] of society can afford.

We shouldn't be overly nostalgic about this, since some positive changes have occurred in the British game over the past three decades. Stadia[4], once little more than tin sheds[5] with wooden planks for seats, have been transformed into safe and accessible spaces for supporters. A number of fatal disasters demonstrated that cramming[6] tens of thousands of fans into cramped[7], poorly policed terraces could not continue. Hooliganism – once rife[8] at football grounds across the UK – has been largely eradicated from within grounds due to regulations on design and security. The image of British football as a dangerous environment, associated with violence and shocking levels of racism, has been largely transformed (although instances still occur).

✦ Dr Andy Clark, *Working-Class Perspectives*, April 13, 2015

1. teams financed by a factory 2. foundation 3. class
4. stadiums 5. simple metal buildings 6. squeezing
7. small and crowded 8. frequent

Culture Tip

Football hooliganism is an aggressive and violent behaviour from supporters. From the 1960s onwards, it became a major problem in England, resulting in numerous deaths. Some laws have been enforced since the 1980s to tackle the issue.

Pédagogie différenciée

TRAIL A

1. Pick out information about the origins of football. Present the historical place of football in British society.
2. Spot two words related to money. Explain how ticketing impacted football fans.
3. Find words related to the design and security of stadiums. Explain the change which took place.

TRAIL B

1. Show how football is historically rooted in British society.
2. Explain the link between financial and social changes in football.
3. Recap the changes that are described in lines 13-27 and their impact on the image of the game.

Meet up! Tell a football fan what you understood about the importance of football in British society. You can do it in French or in English.

D Women, war and football

Vidéo DVD

E-workbook — Fiche à imprimer hatier-clic.fr/lmu055

✦ *No Game for Girls*, Eyefull Productions, 2015

1. Focus on the historical context. Present the munitionettes.
2. Explain the place of football in the munitionettes' lives.
3. Spot the obstacle faced by female football teams and explain its consequence.
4. Imagine the speech given by a munitionette in 1921 to persuade the Football Association to reconsider their decision.

Memory Challenge

Ask your partner to spell three words related to football. Give him or her a mark from 0 to 3.

Prepare your project

You are a journalist for BBC Sport. Write a three-fact article about football in British society.

Grammar Tip

Précis → p. 214

Introduce each fact with a question:
Wh-word / How + auxiliary + subject + verb (+ object)?

Is football a medium of social inclusion in the UK?

E "The fight is not over"

✦ England women's national football team, 2018

For those who have dedicated themselves to the success of women's football, the most important battle has already been won. The social stigma attached to girls playing the game, the discrimination, the derision, was removed years ago. But the fight is not over and here comes the even harder bit.

For all the advances made, the success of the England team in reaching the semi-finals of both the World Cup and the European Championships, the leap[1] in participation numbers and steady growth of a supporter base, women's football remains, in many ways, a minority sport. That needs to change and Kelly Simmons, the Football Association's new Director of Women's Football, is leading the charge to break into the mainstream[2]. [...]

While football is the fastest growing participation sport among girls in the UK, there is an unquenchable thirst[3] to expand.

"I genuinely believe that women's football can be the first female team sport to break through into the mainstream," said Simmons. [...]

"With the clubs we have and the investment that is taking place, we can be that breakthrough sport where the players are households names[4] playing in front of larger crowds at sustainable[5] clubs. [...]

We have all the major clubs in England represented by a women's team and if you look at Manchester United, they got more than 5,000 people watching their first game. With their huge fanbase, it's a big positive they are part of it. [...]

The FA has an ambition to make sure the clubs have everything they need to be the best they can be and there is a talent pathway for young players through the Academy programme."

✦ Luke Edwards, *Women's football can be the first female team sport to break through into the mainstream*, *The Telegraph*, September 7, 2018

1. jump 2. make women's football more mediatised 3. unstoppable wish 4. well-known players 5. viable

1 Identify the expressions linked to progress and victory (l. 1-10). Show that the situation of women's football has improved.

2 Find what the obstacle is and explain the sentence "But the fight is not over".

3 Say how the Football Association can help develop women's football.

4 Write three questions to interview Kelly Simmons on the current situation of women's football.

F Show Racism the Red Card

Vidéo DVD

✦ "Show Racism the Red Card" event, Sunderland Association Football Club, 2018

1 Explain who Gary Bennett is.

2 Pick out the actions young people can participate in and why they are important.

3 Focus on Gary Benett's description of football teams now. Show the link with the "Show Racism The Red Card" project.

4 Write a tweet showing your support for the "Show Racism The Red Card" project.

Grammar Spot

Preterite Tools → p. 120

"They all **created** their own newspapers."

Word Spot

opponent: rival	dignity	stigma
gender equality	moral responsibility	discrimination
key principles	zero tolerance against sthg	preserve the true spirit of the game
rules: laws	disability	transcend differences
fair play	disadvantage	set an / the example
integrity		

G Against discriminations

Classe inversée

Vidéo
DVD
hatier-clic.fr/lmu056

E-workbook
Classe inversée
hatier-clic.fr/lmu057

1 Give an example of supporters' positive behaviour and show its impact.

2 Show the type of discrimination the LGBT community can face in football stadiums.

3 Explain what fans should do if they witness discrimination.

4 Act as a coach briefing his or her young team on the main rules of conduct before attending a football game.

H Football for UNITED values

Club Charter

Our vision is to be the best football club in the world both on and off the pitch, and to help us achieve[1] this we live by the UNITED values:

- **U**nited
- **N**on-discriminatory
- **T**eam-orientated
- **I**nnovative
- **E**xcelling
- **D**etermined

Section 9, Manchester United Foundation

Manchester United Foundation works in some of the most disadvantaged[2] areas across Greater Manchester and uses the passion for Manchester United to educate, motivate and inspire young people. **Manchester United Foundation** delivers football coaching, educational programmes and personal development, providing young people with opportunities to change their lives for the better.

GOAL

To educate, motivate and inspire future generations to build better communities for all. Manchester United Foundation aims to achieve this goal by delivering in five areas:

Football
Provide football opportunities for school children and those with physical or mental disabilities, and also deliver girls only sessions and manage an FA Girls' Centre of Excellence.

Community Cohesion
Aim to engage some of the most hard-to-reach young people in the community by delivering football coaching and a range of alternative activity sessions at times when they could otherwise become engaged in anti-social behaviour.

Health
Use football, and other sports, to deliver a range of programmes to improve the health and well-being of local communities.

Education
Develop partnerships with schools to create community hubs[3] and also deliver a range of educational programmes to primary and secondary schools, using Manchester United as a hook to engage students.

Charities
Manage the Club's charity partnership with UNICEF, the longest standing relationship of its kind between a sports organisation and a global children's charity[4] and the distribution of signed merchandise for charitable purposes.

✦ Manchester United Football Club, 2018

1. accomplish 2. underprivileged 3. centres of activity 4. not-for-profit organisation

1 Focus on the paratext and explain what type of document this is.

2 Spot the words that refer to places, people and institutions. Say who Manchester United Foundation works with.

3 Pick out some verbs to define Manchester United Foundation's goal and actions.

4 Write a message on Manchester United Foundation's Facebook page asking them to launch a campaign in your school.

Prepare your project

PAIR WORK It is World Football Day!
Liverpool Football Club holds a stand in a school promoting official membership to the club.

Student A You are a member of Liverpool FC. Give information about the values and actions of the club.

Student B You are a student. Ask questions and give your views on the goals and values of the club.

Grammar Tip Précis → p. 217
Use the right modals: you **must** subscribe... You **can** attend... **Could** you explain...? You **would** become...

Memory Challenge

In teams, list three good behaviours from football fans. The team who finds them first wins.

Entraînez-vous sur la plateforme *Let's Meet Up!*
reussirenlangues.fr

Tools in the Spotlight

Practise your grammar

Précis grammatical, p.192

Le prétérit

- Le prétérit est un temps du passé, qui indique que l'événement a eu lieu dans un **passé** sans lien avec le présent de la personne qui parle.
- Il se forme avec **-ed** pour les verbes réguliers. Il existe une liste de verbes irréguliers qu'il faut connaître par cœur (voir p. 231).

*They all **created** their own newspapers.*

- Comme le prétérit est un temps qui situe l'événement dans le passé, il est souvent accompagné d'un **marqueur de temps** indiquant le passé, tel que *yesterday*, *two weeks ago*, *last month*, *in 2010*, *in the twentieth century*.

*The social stigma attached to girls playing the game **was** removed **years ago**.*

Le *past perfect*

- Le *past perfect*, appelé aussi *pluperfect*, est un temps du **passé** qui correspond, en général, au plus-que-parfait français.
- Il est composé de l'auxiliaire ***have* au passé** (*had*), suivi du **participe passé** du verbe.
- Le *past perfect* situe l'événement au **passé** par rapport à un **autre événement** lui-même au **passé** et indique que l'événement au ***past perfect*** est **antérieur** à celui au prétérit.

*They won the football match in 2017. They **had lost** in 2010.*

- À la manière du ***present perfect*** qui sert à faire un bilan dans le présent, le *past perfect* sert à faire un **bilan dans le passé.**

Le repère du bilan est un ***prétérit*** et on évalue tout ce qui a pu être fait jusqu'à ce repère passé.

Ce laps de temps particulier du passé peut être précisé par *at the time, during that period*...

*What women **had achieved** during the war years **was** astonishing.*

1 Mettez les verbes entre parenthèses au prétérit.

a. England (**beat**) West Germany in 1966.
b. The English team (**win**) the World Cup Final.
c. The English (**celebrate**) with cakes and party hats.
d. They (**be**) proud of their team.
e. Lily Parr (**be**) the first woman to be admitted into the English Football Hall of Fame.

2 Mettez les verbes entre parenthèses au prétérit ou au *present perfect*.

a. Look! I just (**buy**) tickets for the football match!
b. The last time I (**go**) to a football match was a long time ago.
c. I never (**go**) to Manchester but I (**hear**) about Manchester United of course!
d. Sue (**visit**) Liverpool three years ago?
e. Her husband (**not - spend**) his childhood in this city in the 1980s.

3 Choisissez la bonne réponse.

a. What Manchester United (**achieved / had achieved**) for many years was brilliant!
b. The previous week the P.E. teacher (**told us / had told us**) to bring our sports gear.
c. Rugby (**originated / had originated**) in the aristocratic public school called Rugby.
d. The term "soccer" (**was used / had been used**) in the United States, New Zealand and Australia for so many years.
e. Last year his team (**lost / had lost**) the tournament, but his former team (**won / had won**) four years before.

4 Complétez par le prétérit ou le *past perfect*.

a. In his free time, he always (**do**) some kind of sport when he was a boy.
b. In 2010 he (**play**) football. Three years earlier he (**start**) to play tennis.
c. They already (**prepare**) their sports bags when I (**arrive**).
d. She (**train**) a lot this year, that's why she (**win**) the competition.
e. He (**be**) there for half an hour when his coach (**invite**) him to join the team.

Improve your pronunciation

Précis de phonologie, p. 242

Les paires minimales

Audio
CD1 piste 51
MP3 n° 83

- Une paire minimale désigne deux mots qui diffèrent sur un seul **phonème**, c'est-à-dire un seul **son** en phonétique.

Par exemple : *pot* et *put* partagent les mêmes sons /p/, et /t/, mais le son voyelle est différent, /ɒ/ pour *pot* et /ʊ/ pour *put*.

- Il existe des **séries de mots** qui forment des paires minimales.

bug /bʌg/ *big* /bɪg/ *bag* /bæg/ *beg* /beg/

- Il arrive que la paire minimale se distingue uniquement par rapport à la longueur de la voyelle. La différence porte alors sur une voyelle **brève** et une voyelle **longue**.

bit /bɪt/ *beat* /biːt/ *live* /lɪv/ *leave* /liːv/
ship /ʃɪp/ *sheep* /ʃiːp/ *fit* /fɪt/ *feet* /fiːt/

5 **Indiquez si les paires de mots suivantes forment des paires minimales, puis vérifiez avec l'enregistrement.**

Audio
CD1 piste 52
MP3 n° 84

a. cheap - sheep
b. cheap - ship
c. beg - bet
d. bag - bet
e. bird - board
f. bull - bill
g. pass - part
h. boy - toy

6 **Indiquez les paires minimales. Répétez les phrases suivantes en les distinguant clairement, puis vérifiez avec l'enregistrement.**

Audio
CD1 piste 53
MP3 n° 85

a. The boy bought a toy – it was a small boat!
b. Could you pass me the ball, please? The bell is going to ring. Game over!
c. Watch out! There's some mud! Otherwise, you'll have to wash your shorts.
d. I can't live like that anymore, I need to leave the team!

Work on your writing skills

Les homophones

- Comme en français, il y a de nombreux mots anglais qui ont la **même prononciation** mais qui n'ont **pas le même sens** : c'est ce que l'on appelle des **homophones**.

*You're very lucky to go and **watch** a football game.*

*Don't forget to set the alarm on **your watch** for the football game!*

- Certains, comme ***you're*** et ***your***, ont la même prononciation mais n'ont **pas la même orthographe**.

he's ≠ *his* *whose* ≠ *who's* *they're* ≠ *their* ≠ *there*
ate ≠ *eight* *hear* ≠ *here* *buy* ≠ *by* ≠ *bye*

- D'autres en revanche, comme ***watch*** (regarder) et ***watch*** (montre), ont la même prononciation et la **même orthographe**.

bear (porter) ≠ *bear* (ours)
lie (être couché.e) ≠ *lie* (mentir)
right (droit) ≠ *right* (bon)

- Repérer les homophones permet d'éviter les incompréhensions à l'écrit comme à l'oral !

7 **Complétez les phrases suivantes en choisissant le mot qui convient.**

a. I … … cookies before the game! (**eight / ate**)
b. … be honest, you can't buy … tickets. It's … expensive! (**too / to / two**)
c. You should … the latest book … Sir Alexander Ferguson. (**by / buy**)
d. You can … the supporters sing from … ! (**hear / here**)
e. In one … we will be champion because this is … time to win! (**our / hour**)
f. During the … women football players also … shorts to play. (**wore / war**)

8 **Utilisez les mots suivants dans des phrases qui explicitent leur sens.**

a. their - there - they're
b. one - won
c. wait - weight
d. wear - where
e. it's - its
f. see - sea

Build up your vocabulary

Audio
CD1 piste 54

Football and society

Discrimination
MP3 n°86

- hooliganism /huːlɪgənɪzəm/
- violence /vaɪələns/
- insult
- banter: joke
- fight: battle: struggle
- racism ≠ anti-racism
- stigma
- stereotype
- abusive: insulting
- disadvantaged: underprivileged
- stigmatise
- be excluded
- be discriminated against

Inclusion
MP3 n°87

- moral responsibility
- integrity
- dignity
- gender equality
- disability
- LGBT (lesbian, gay, bisexual, and transgender)
- women's football
- zero tolerance against sthg
- charity: not-for-profit organisation
- key principles
- emancipation
- progress: evolution: improvement
- set an / the example
- transcend differences
- break down barriers

Competition
MP3 n°90

- professional ≠ amateur /æmətər/
- football club
- match: game
- derby /dɑːbi/: local competition
- opponent: rival
- rules: laws /lɔːz/
- fair play
- national pride
- reputation: fame
- preserve the true spirit of the game
- score a goal

Tradition
MP3 n°88

- legend
- roots: origins
- working class ≠ upper class
- pioneer
- legendary
- memorable
- historic
- evolve: change
- develop: grow
- establish: put in place

Fans
MP3 n°89

- fandom: a group of fans
- supporters
- hobby: pastime
- entertainment
- attraction
- chant
- applause
- stadium
- loyal /lɔɪəl/
- cheer: give loud encouragement
- support ≠ restrain
- encourage ≠ discourage
- gain popularity

Apprenez et révisez le vocabulaire !

Utilisez Quizlet pour vous entraîner en vous amusant.

Quizlet
hatier-clic.fr/lmu058

Utilisez le vocabulaire en contexte.

1 Complétez les phrases suivantes avec des mots de la carte mentale.

a. English ... were known for their violent behaviour in the 1960s.
b. Fans usually ... in the stadiums to ... their teams.
c. The ... of football date back to the Middle Ages in England.
d. Football ... ... in the 19th century in Britain.
e. Football is a sport that can ... racial, social and cultural differences.
f. Each club has the ... ... to ensure there is no discrimination during games.
g. There will be ... ... against perpetrators of violence in stadiums.

2 Écrivez cinq phrases sur le rôle du football au Royaume-Uni. Pour chaque phrase, choisissez deux mots de l'une des catégories de la carte mentale.

AUTO évaluation

Faites le quiz interactif en ligne et suivez les conseils pour vous préparer à l'évaluation.

Quiz
hatier-clic.fr/lmu059

Project #1

Act out the interview of a British football player. Discuss the values and role of football in the UK.

1 Choose your role.

- **Journalist:** Invent your name and decide which British TV channel you work for (BBC News, Sky Sports, BT Sport, ITV...).
- **Player:** Choose a famous British football player: female or male, young or old... Be original in your choice!

2 Collect information and ideas.

- **Journalist:** Find some information about the player's personal life and football career, his or her club and its values.
- **Player:** Find some information about your character's career and life. Think about the values that are important to you.

3 Get ready to speak!

- **Journalist** + **Player:** Create a mind map to recap the information you will need.
- **Journalist:** Review how to form questions: **(Wh-word / How +) auxiliary + subject + verb (+ object)?**
- **Player:** Remember how to give your views: **I really think that... To be honest...**

4 Act out the interview.

- **Journalist:** Put the correct intonation depending on the type of questions you ask.
- **Player:** Make sure that your answers are understood: **Do you see what I mean? Am I answering your question?**

Fiche de méthodologie N°19 p. 278

Project #2

Create a brochure for a British football club presenting its history and values.

1 Choose a club.

- Pick a British football club or invent one.

2 Write the "About us" section.

- Present the club: name, location, players, staff...
- Tell or imagine its history and evolution using past tenses: **preterite**, **present perfect**, **past perfect**.

3 Create the "Charter" section.

- Introduce the general vision of the club.
- Present the aims, fields of intervention, actions, partners...
- Use verbs and concrete examples to talk about engagement: **build**, **educate**, **work**...
- Use words linked to "Inclusion" from the mind map p. 122.

4 Customize your brochure.

- You can use a word processor or online tools such as desygner.com to create your brochure.
- Add a logo: you can draw it or find one on the internet.
- Add relevant pictures to illustrate your brochure (players, stadium...) but not too many!

Fiche de méthodologie N°9 p. 261

Let's RECAP

Lisez les questions-clés et complétez la fiche bilan avec des exemples et des documents que vous avez étudiés ou découverts.

AXE 5 | Sports and society

SÉQUENCE 1 Does American football bring people together?

E-workbook
Bilan à compléter
hatier-clic.fr/lmu060

How central is American football in US culture?
How strong is the link between Americans and the Super Bowl?

#hypermediatised
How big is the Super Bowl in American media (TV, social networks...)?

#socialevent
Why is the Super Bowl such an important social event? What are the big moments of a Super Bowl game?

#nationalpride
To what extent are American football games opportunities to show national pride?

#politicalstatement
How has the stadium been used as a platform for political statements?

#teamsport
Which values does American football carry as a team sport?

SÉQUENCE 2 Is football a medium of social inclusion in the UK?

E-workbook
Bilan à compléter
hatier-clic.fr/lmu061

How does football unite the British?
To what extent is football a sport for everyone?

#discrimination
How does football fight discrimination?

#nationalunity
To what extent does football symbolise national unity in the UK?

#senseofbelonging
How does football make people feel they belong to the same group no matter who they are and where they come from?

#socialisation
To what extent does football bring people from different social backgrounds together?

#supporters
How has supporting football teams evolved in the UK over time?

GO4IT!

Lisez et écoutez de l'anglais en dehors de la salle de classe ! Voici quelques conseils en lien avec votre séquence.

SÉQUENCE 1

Books

The Blind Side: Evolution of a Game, MICHAEL LEWIS, 2006

Football Genius, TIM GREEN, 2007

QB1, MIKE LUPICA, 2013

Songs

The Star-Spangled Banner, SUNG BY WHITNEY HOUSTON, 1991
http://bit.ly/1qNDG9z

All My Rowdy Friends Are Coming Over Tonight, HANK WILLIAMS JR., 1984
http://bit.ly/1NkAzB9

TV series

Films

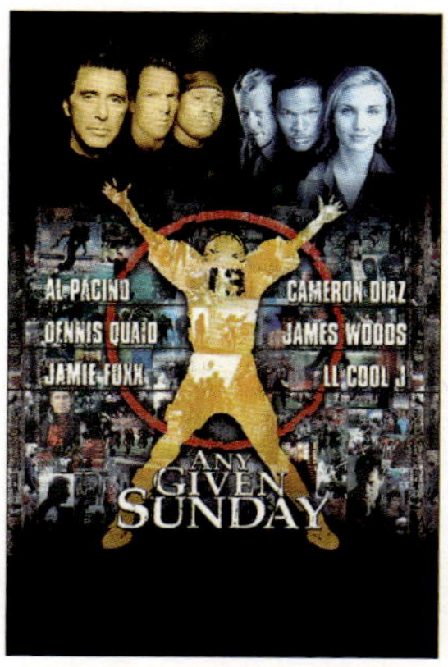

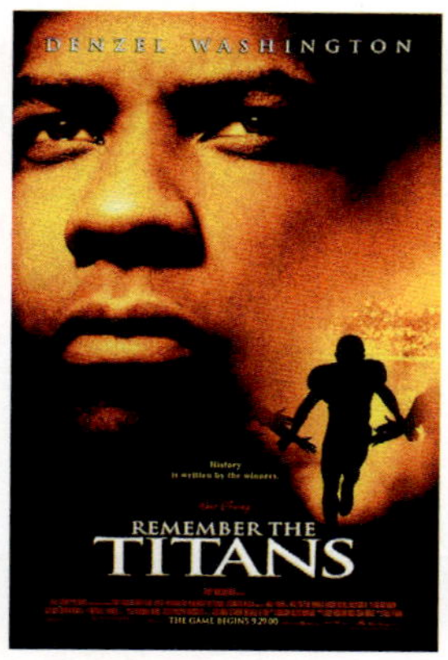

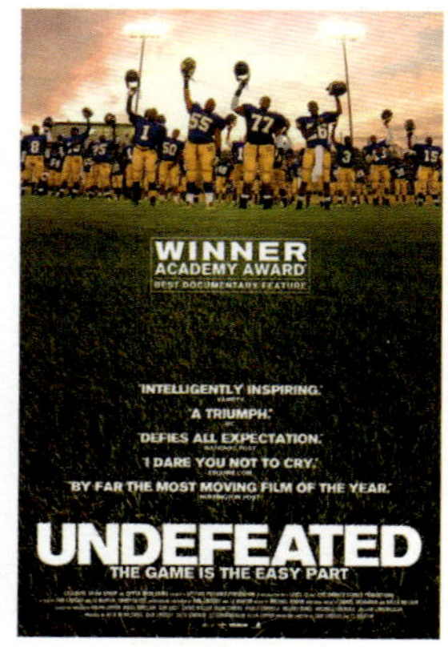

SÉQUENCE 2

Books

Fever Pitch, NICK HORNBY, 1992

The Damned Utd, DAVID PEACE, 2006

The Ball is Round: A Global History of Football, DAVID GOLDBLATT, 2008

Red Men: Liverpool Football Club - The Biography, JOHN WILLIAMS, 2010

Comics

Liverpool: The Comic Strip History, BOB BOND, 2013

Manchester United - Tales from History, PHILIPPE GLOGOWSKI, 2014

The Illustrated History of Football, DAVID SQUIRES, 2016

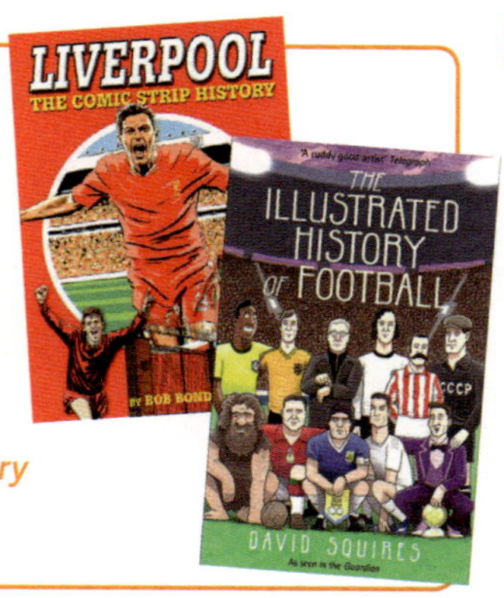

Songs

World in Motion, NEW ORDER, 1990
http://bit.ly/2H521J8

Three Lions, THE LIGHTNING SEEDS, 1996
http://bit.ly/ON3tAG

World at Your Feet, EMBRACE, 2006
http://bit.ly/2EEOgxe

Films

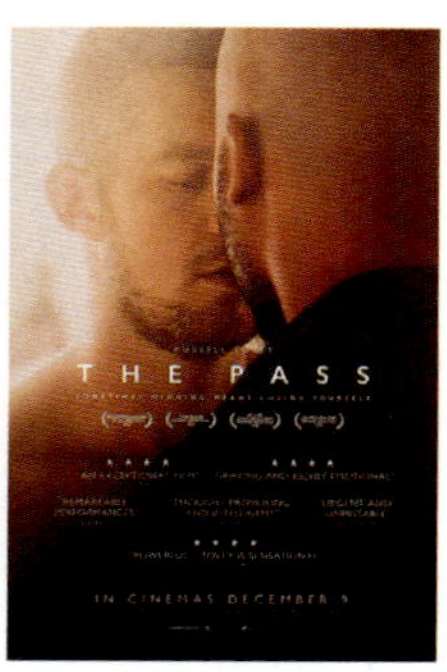

AXE 6

Creation and relation to arts

La création et le rapport aux arts

SÉQUENCE 1 Does rap rhyme with poetry?

Projects

Project #1: Record a speech to convince your teacher to include a rap artist in a poetry project.

Project #2: Create a poster for the rappers' Hall of Fame. Show the link between rap and poetry.

Tools

Grammaire	l'expression du but, les mots de liaison
Phonologie	les diphtongues /eɪ/ et /aɪ/
Écriture	l'apostrophe
Vocabulaire	le rap, les figures de style

SÉQUENCE 2 How do musicals reflect the English-speaking world?

Projects

Project #1: Become a YouTube influencer. Record a video to push tourists to see a live musical.

Project #2: Write a blog entry to recommend a musical reflecting the American or British society.

Tools

Grammaire	le superlatif, l'expression du contraste
Phonologie	les énoncés emphatiques
Écriture	le point final, d'interrogation et d'exclamation
Vocabulaire	les comédies musicales

#poetry #communicateemotions

#literarydevices #artisticexpression

Mural on Clink Street, London, by graffiti artist Jimmy C

#singanddance #defendacause

#emotion #thewestend

#socialissues #broadway

Broadway theatres near Times Square, New York City

SÉQUENCE 1

Does rap rhyme with poetry?

A What does rap mean?

Vidéo DVD

E-workbook
Fiche à imprimer
hatier-clic.fr/lmu062

1 Guess what the letters R, A, and P could stand for. Justify your choice.

Rapid Artistic Performance - Rhythm And Poetry - Real Angry Poet - Revolution And Power

2 Watch the video and say what you learned about the word "rap".

3 Leave a comment on Smart Rapper's video on YouTube and write what R, A, and P could stand for if it was an acronym.

B Rap or poetry?

GROUP WORK

GROUP A

There are words like Freedom
Sweet and wonderful to say,
On my heartstrings[1] freedom sings
All day everyday.

GROUP B

Now I may have faith[2] to make mountains fall
But if I lack love then I am nothin' at all
I can give away everything I possess
But left without love then I have no happiness

GROUP C

I start to think, and then I sink[3]
Into the paper like I was ink[4]
When I'm writing, I'm trapped in between the lines
I escape when I finish the rhyme.

GROUP D

I'm nobody! Who are you?
Are you nobody, too?
Then there's a pair of us – don't tell!
They'd banish us, you know.

1. strong feelings of love or sympathy 2. confidence 3. move to a lower level 4. fluid used for writing

1 Read out loud or even sing your group's lines. Say what creates musicality in the verse (use the Word Spot).

2 Focus on the syllables of each line and on the punctuation. Comment on the rhythm of your verse.

3 Convince your classmates about the genre of your verse: rap or poetry. Argue using your previous answers.

4 Show that rap and poetry are all about rhythm.

Grammar Spot

Expression of purpose TOOLS → p. 132

"Now I may have faith **to** make mountains fall."

Word Spot

- musical effect
- quick speech
- flow: the rhythm and the rhymes /raɪms/
- delivery: tone
- cadence /keɪdəns/: the beat
- rhythmic speech
- meaning
- metaphor
- meter: rhythm that repeats a pattern
- stanza: a series of lines

C It's all about emotion

Audio
CD2 piste 01

1 Match the words with their equivalents.

crack - concrete - feet -
grow - funny

strange - fissure - end of the legs -
flourish - cement

2 Listen to the poem and focus on the reader's intonation. Describe the emotions communicated.

3 Read the Culture Tip and listen to the poem again. Explain how "the rose that grew from concrete" could be an illustration of Tupac Shakur's life.

4 Rewrite the poem in form of a fairytale: Once upon a time... Give it a new title.

Culture Tip

Tupac Shakur (1971-1996) is regarded as one of the best hip-hop artists of all times. He was born in New York City but moved to Los Angeles and was considered a West Coast-based rapper. His lyrics were about rap, race relations, and young black men in America. He was murdered in a shooting in Las Vegas.

D Rap IS poetry!

Pédagogie différenciée **GROUP WORK**

1 Listen to your recording and list the words linked to poetry.

2 Explain what vision of rap is described in your recording.

3 Sum up the speaker's opinion about rap.

4 Write a short speech defending the idea that rap is poetry.

GROUP A

Audio
CD2 piste 02

Culture Tip

Michelle Obama was born on January 17, 1964. She is married to the 44th President of the United States Barack Obama and served as First Lady between 2009 and 2017. She supports many causes including poverty awareness, and healthy eating and living. Her memoir *Becoming* was published in 2018 and immediately became a best seller.

GROUP B

Audio
CD2 piste 03

Culture Tip

Kurtis Blow (born in 1959) is an American rapper, DJ, songwriter, producer and minister. He grew up in New York City and, at the age of 20, was the first rapper to be signed by a major record label. He is considered the first commercially successful rap artist. Throughout his career, Kurtis Blow has released 15 albums.

Prepare your project

Choose a rap song and show its poetic interest. You can talk about the rhythm, the emotions of the author and the ones you feel, and the message.

Grammar Tip Précis → p. 230

Justify your choice by using **verbs of perception** and **verbs expressing emotions**.

Memory Challenge

Play hangman. Use words related to the themes of rap and poetry.

E A lively debate

The short answer is "no", of course. To state the obvious[1], things can share certain attributes and not be the same sort of thing, and asking whether[2] rap is poetry has always struck[3] me as a useless question. Both rap and poetry use literary devices[4] like assonance and alliteration. Both use words. Both are spoken. But rap is a musical-verbal art and poetry is a verbal-musical-typographical one. So why make the comparison?

There is no such thing as high or low culture. There is *interesting* culture and *boring* culture. There are works of art that show great skill and those that don't.
So by all means, defend hip-hop or rap or poetry, but let's avoid defending them by association. Let the songs or poems speak for themselves.

✦ Micah Mattix, *The American Conservative*, July 1, 2014

1. say what is evident 2. if 3. appeared to 4. tools

1 Find the question to the answer "no".

2 Explain how the author of the text classifies culture.

4 Recap briefly the author's opinion on rap and poetry.

F Shakespearean swag

Culture Tip

William Shakespeare was born in 1564 in Stratford-upon-Avon. He was an English actor, playwright and poet. He died in 1616. He wrote about 154 sonnets and 37 plays, the major ones being *Romeo and Juliet*, *Othello*, *Hamlet* and *Macbeth*.

1 Spot the traditional and modern elements in William Shakespeare's portrait.

2 Imagine why the artist modernised this portrait of Shakespeare.

3 Write a speech bubble in which Shakespeare explains his new look.

G Refreshing Shakespeare

Classe inversée

Audio
CD2 piste 04
MP3 n°91

E-workbook
Classe inversée
hatier-clic.fr/lmu063

1 Listen to Devon Glover. Note in two columns the words related to transformation and music. Explain how and why he uses Shakespeare's work.

2 Spot the similarities between rap and Shakespeare's work. Show how rappers relate to Shakespeare.

3 Identify the popular opinion about Shakespeare. Explain what Devon Glover wants to prove.

4 Convince your teacher to invite the Sonnet Man to your school.

Grammar Spot

Linking words Tools → p. 132
"So why make the comparison?"

Word Spot

clothing style
earphones
punchline
creative: innovative
make a reference to: allude to
inspire
create a bridge: make a link with

H Shakespeare in rap

Vidéo DVD

1 Watch the video and identify the topics of Shakespeare's plays.

2 List the literary devices mentioned.

3 Name the plays that have inspired rap songs.

4 Write a blog post to convince a rapper that she or he should refer to Shakespeare in her or his songs.

I The Bard vs. Rappers

The Oxford English Dictionary credits[1] William Shakespeare with coining up to[2] 2,000 words we use today. But linguists from Manchester have found that rappers, such as Eminem and London-based Akala, are actually more adept at creating lyrics and prose than the 16th century poet. By studying rap lyrics, the experts said that traditional and complex rhyming comes so easy to hip-hop artists, the skill[3] is almost 'second nature' to them. […]

While Shakespeare and poet John Keats, as examples, may have had a better style when it came to rhyming couplets and more traditional verse, modern rappers excel at rearranging sentences to make them fit. This includes creating […] half rhymes[4], which are typically much harder to create because traditionalists view them as incorrect. […]

[The researcher] thinks that hip-hop has the most sophisticated use of rhyme of any genre and when written down it reads just like poetry.

✦ Victoria Woollaston, *The Daily Mail*, February 11, 2015 (adapted)

1. attributes to 2. inventing as many as 3. ability 4. see Culture Tip

1 Pick out the names referring to artists and classify them into two categories.

2 Spot the words related to poetry. Present the subject of the study.

3 List the words expressing comparison and talent. Explain the results of the research in your own words.

4 Write a short review about the research on your high school website. Justify your rating.

Culture Tip

Half rhyme, also called **imperfect rhyme**, are words that have only their final consonant sounds in common (such as "stopped" and "wept", or "parable" and "shell").

www.britannica.com

Prepare your project

PAIR WORK Debate whether rappers are the new poets. Defend your point of view. One has a more traditional opinion and the other a modern one.

Grammar Tip

Précis → p. 201

Use **adjectives** to give qualities to both poets and rappers.

Memory Challenge

Create a rotating battle. Build small teams and ask your opponents questions about the relation between Shakespeare and rappers.

Tools in the Spotlight

Entraînez-vous sur la plateforme ***Let's Meet Up!***
reussirenlangues.fr

Practise your grammar

Précis grammatical, p. 192

L'expression du but

• **Formation**

Le but est exprimé par l'infinitif en *to* + base verbale, ou par *in order (not) to* + base verbale ou *so as (not) to* + base verbale.

• **Emploi**

Si le sujet est identique, on utilise *to, in order to* ou *so as to*.

*Nowadays, kids combine rap and education **to** create amazing songs.*

*Devon Glover raps Shakespeare **in order to** make his plays accessible.*

*You need to see someone amazing reading it **so as to** understand the power of poetry.*

*You also have to pay attention to the lyrics **so as not to** miss the main message.*

Toutefois la proposition de but est introduite par *so (that)* lorsque les deux sujets sont différents.

*Devon Glover goes into school **so that** students learn more about Shakespeare.*

⚠ ***For*** n'exprime pas le but, mais peut être utilisé pour indiquer le sujet de la proposition infinitive.

*Here are the lyrics of the song **for** you to learn.*

Les mots de liaison

• Les mots de liaison lient des mots, des propositions ou des phrases afin de relier des idées entre elles.

***Although** rhyming isn't always present in rap or poetry, it certainly is common.*

• Les mots de liaison permettent :
- d'introduire (*first*, *first of all*...)
- d'ajouter (*and*, *also*...)
- de conclure (*finally*, *to conclude*...)
- d'exprimer la cause (*because*, *thanks to*...)
- d'exprimer la conséquence (*so*, *therefore*, *that is why*, *thus*...)
- de marquer l'opposition (*but*, *yet*...)
- de marquer la concession (*though*, *although*, *even if*)
- d'exprimer la simultanéité (*while*)
- de souligner le contraste (*whereas*, *while*).

1 **Complétez avec *to, in order (not) to, so as (not) to*.**

a. He sang the tune softly ... wake her up.
b. She bought the MP3 ... learn the song.
c. They had to hurry ... miss the concert.
d. ... offend people, we asked the poet to avoid vulgar language.
e. Jay-Z visited the school ... listen to students' presentations.

2 **Reformulez les phrases suivantes en exprimant le but avec *to, in order (not) to, so as (not) to*.**

a. She is planning to study the lyrics. She wants to find out the rapper's main message.
b. He has turned down the radio. He doesn't want to disturb his neighbour.
c. He needs to pay attention to every single word. He is planning to check if it rhymes with poetry.
d. They used the beat of a drum. They told stories rhythmically.
e. Music producers took notice of the emerging musical genre. They developed rap back in the 1980s.
f. You need to have both texts. You want to compare poets and rappers.
g. You should include graffiting, deejaying, breakdancing and emceeing. You want to have a complete definition of hip-hop.

3 **Remettez les mots de liaison au bon endroit.**

because • also • first • to conclude • so • and • although

Of course, I am a poet. If you ... look at the definition of a poet, it is someone who uses the art of rhythmical composition. ... that's what all rappers do every time they compose a rap song. Rap is still poetry, ... it is only spoken. Rappers ... like to play on words ... to use language to strike the imagination. Obviously, it has some specificities like any other poetic genres. For instance, a rap song must tell a story. It all depends on the poet's mood ... when he writes, he has an intention. I think the image of the poet has changed over time. ... , I would say that rappers are the poets of today.

Improve your pronunciation

Précis de phonologie, p. 242

Les diphtongues /eɪ/ et /aɪ/

Audio CD2 piste 05 MP3 n°92

La diphtongue /eɪ/ peut correspondre à la graphie :
- a (*age*, *late*, *basis*, *favour*)
- ai (*aim*, *main*, *mail*)
- ay (*say*, *bay*)
- ea (*steak*, *great*, *break*)
- ei (*eight*, *weigh*)
- ey (*they*, *grey*)

• La diphtongue /aɪ/ peut correspondre à la graphie :
- ai (*aisle*)
- ei (*height*)
- ey (*eye*)
- i (*ice*, *ripe*, *wide*, *kind*)
- igh (*high*, *sight*)
- uy (*buy*)
- y (*shy*, *try*, *my*)

4 Pour chaque mot, écrivez le son que vous entendez /eɪ/ ou /aɪ/. Puis vérifiez avec l'enregistrement

Audio CD2 piste 06 MP3 n°93

male • mile • gyre • deejay • vibe • vain • rave • rhyme • line • lane

5 Pour chaque mot, écrivez le son que vous entendez /eɪ/ ou /aɪ/. Puis vérifiez avec l'enregistrement.

Audio CD2 piste 07 MP3 n°94

a. made b. night c. lay d. why e. final f. grade g. side h. tasty i. plain j. lie

Work on your writing skills

L'apostrophe

L'apostrophe a plusieurs sens en anglais.

• L'apostrophe peut correspondre au **génitif**, qui établit souvent un lien de possession entre deux mots.

⚠ L'ordre des mots est inversé par rapport au français.

the rapper's room = la chambre du rappeur = *his room*

my parents' house = la maison de mes parents = *their house*

• On utilise l'apostrophe pour indiquer l'omission d'une ou plusieurs lettres, notamment dans les **formes contractées des auxiliaires.**

⚠ Il ne faut pas confondre ces formes avec un génitif ou un adjectif possessif.

Formes contractées	Formes pleines
's	*is* ou *has*
'd	*had* ou *would*
'm	*am*
'll	*will* ou *shall*
've	*have*
're	*are*
n't	*not*

6 Reformulez les passages en gras de façon à obtenir un génitif.

a. **The father of my girlfriend** lives in the States.
b. **The new manager of my school** is dynamic.
c. **The speech made by the president** was brilliant.
d. **The last concert Tom organised** was great.

7 Classez ces phrases en deux groupes : expression d'une possession • contraction verbale.

a. It's a nice day outside.
b. She isn't supposed to be at the party.
c. Jimmy's father is a doctor.
d. Who's at the door?
e. This is Julia's book.

8 Réécrivez ces phrases sans contractions.

a. Then there's a pair of us – don't tell!
b. They'd banish us, you know.
c. When I'm writing, I'm trapped in between the lines.

Build up your vocabulary

Audio
CD2 piste 08

Rap

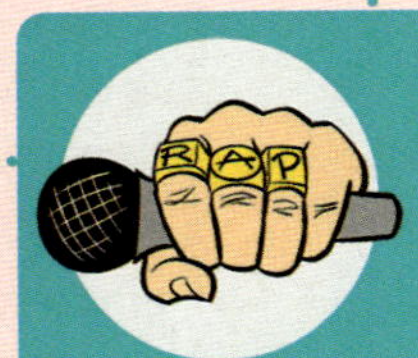

Transform — MP3 n°95

adapt
inspire
invent
modernise
transpose
evolve

Rhythm and sound — MP3 n°99

musical effect
rhythmic speech
quick speech
flow: the rhythm and the rhymes /raɪms/
delivery: tone
cadence /keɪdəns/: the beat
tempo: rhythm
creative: innovative

Message — MP3 n°96

theme
back story
lyrics
punchline
slang
topic
tone: mood
share your feelings
move people: touch people's heart or soul
denounce

Literary device — MP3 n°98

meaning
metaphor
meter: rhythm that repeats a pattern
stanza: a series of lines
rhyme
line: verse
syllable
meter
alliteration
assonance

Debate — MP3 n°97

for instance: for example
nuanced opinion ≠ strict opinion
argument
defy
have a point: have a solid argument
make reference to: make an allusion to
compare oneself
create a bridge: make a link with

Apprenez et révisez le vocabulaire !

Utilisez Quizlet pour vous entraîner en vous amusant.

Quizlet
hatier-clic.fr/lmu064

Utilisez le vocabulaire en contexte.

1 Complétez les phrases suivantes avec des mots de la carte mentale.

a. Real life experiences often ... rappers to write their lyrics.
b. Rappers want to ... people's hearts with their topics.
c. Rappers invent rhyming poems to give ... to the texts.
d. The basis of rap battles are ... and repetitions.
e. The ... is the best line of the song.
f. My friend thinks that ... in rap songs are often repetitive.

2 Complétez ces phrases en utilisant des mots de la carte mentale.

a. I love listening to rap music because...
b. Poetry has a lot of power on people...
c. Rappers innovate when they...
d. Songs can convey a message to people with...

AUTO évaluation

Faites le quiz interactif en ligne et suivez les conseils pour vous préparer à l'évaluation.

Quiz
hatier-clic.fr/lmu065

Project #1

Choose a rap artist and record a speech to convince your teacher to include her or him in a poetry project.

1 Introduce your general opinion.
- ✓ Say which artist you chose.
- ✓ Briefly justify your choice.

2 Find at least three arguments.
- ✓ Focus on the poetic interest of one or several rap songs.
- ✓ You can also use documents from the unit or press articles that make a link between poetry and rap.

3 Find an example for each argument.
- ✓ Choose precise and concrete aspects: rhythm, emotions, messages...

4 Organise your ideas.
- ✓ Write three paragraphs with an argument and an example in each of them. Classify them from the least to the most convincing one.
- ✓ Use linking words: **for example**, **and**, **but**, **in addition**...

5 Conclude your argumentation.
- ✓ Sum up your main ideas. Be convincing!

➤ Fiche de méthodologie N°20 p. 280

Project #2

Create a poster for the rappers' Hall of Fame. Show the link between rap and poetry.

1 Choose your artist.
- ✓ In class, choose which female and male artists you want to talk about.
- ✓ Include artists from various English-speaking countries.

2 Present your artist.
- ✓ Talk about her or him: write a short biography (place and date of birth, career, main achievements...).
- ✓ Talk about her or his most successful songs, rewards, inspiration...
- ✓ You can add pictures.

3 Present a song and link it to poetry.
- ✓ Select an extract from this song.
- ✓ Say which topic it deals with.
- ✓ Explain how it can be considered poetry (literary devices...).

4 Give your opinion.
- ✓ Say if you consider rappers to be poets.
- ✓ Use linking words (**firstly**, **secondly**, **and**, **but**...) to organise your ideas and verbs of opinion (**think**, **believe**...) to express your point of view.

➤ Fiche de méthodologie N°9 p. 261 N°22 p. 284

SÉQUENCE 2

How do musicals reflect the English-speaking world?

A Meaningful entertainment

www.blog.ambient-mixer.com

Have you ever seen a musical? Here are a few reasons why you should get your first ticket!

They teach history

A lot of the current popular musicals you can see on Broadway or in theater are based on historical events. Others may be based on characters or figures from the past. For the most part, the vast majority of them remain[1] closely true to the facts or original story. You and your family can enjoy a musical, while learning about important events in history. […]

Musicals tackle social and political issues

Anyone who wants to watch social and political issues being tackled in a light-hearted way, should watch a musical. Broadway shows take on[2] social and political issues, without being too controversial. The majority of musicals will engage you in the story, without being too biased or insensitive.

Live musicals remind people of how it used to be

[…] People often want to be reminded of times when things were easier to deal with. There were fewer social injustices, strife[3] and chaos going on. The musicals based on past events often take you back to an era when things were great. Or at least easier to deal with.

✦ www.blog.ambient-mixer.com, July 1, 2017

1. stay 2. deal with 3. conflict

1 Read the first paragraph and find two reasons why it is a good idea to go and see a musical.

2 Read the second paragraph. Find four elements that explain why musicals are a great way to learn about social and political issues.

3 Choose the correct statement to summarise the last paragraph.

Musicals deal with social and political problems of the past that seemed easier to deal with.

Musicals deal with social and political problems of the past in a serious and intense way.

Musicals are about comparing social and political problems of the past with the present situation.

Culture Tip

Broadway is a long main street in New York City. It is famous for its musicals and theatre plays. It is so well-known that the term Broadway is used to refer to the whole American theatre industry.
The West End is an area of Central London where many stage productions are shown in numerous theatres. It is the British equivalent of Broadway.

4 Convince your friends! You have decided to go and see a musical with your friends this weekend. Convince them that it is a good idea.

Grammar Spot

Expressing contrast Tools → p. 140

"You can enjoy a musical, **while** learning about important events in history."

Word Spot

- captivating: appealing
- entertaining
- informative: instructive
- educational
- engaging /ɪngeɪdʒɪŋ/: attractive
- tackle: deal with, be about a problem or an issue
- I would like or love to + V
- I feel like + V-ing
- I am not keen on + V-ing

B Hair, the 60s

It is hard to believe that it has been over 50 years since "the American Tribal Love-Rock Musical *HAIR*" came alive [...]. *Hair* was a concept that was a sign of the times. Viet Nam was "happening" despite the protests of those who were facing a war that was not wanted, young men were being drafted[1] [...] and many got married and had a child to avoid[2] the draft, while others enrolled in school to further[3] their education [...].

This was the 1960s. [...] Our set[4] indicates that we are in Greenwich Village, a hippie hangout[5] in New York. [...] *Hair* is a passionate cry for help from those who were facing the future and what this war was about to bring. While it was a defining moment in our history for the teens and young adults of that period, it is still an inspiration today. Think about all the great progress our world has made, and yet, look at the racial situations as well as the treatment of those who are "different". Can one say that our eyes are open wider than they were back then?

✦ www.aroundthetownchicago.com, August 4th, 2017

1. be forced to serve in the army 2. escape 3. continue 4. decor 5. place to meet your friends

The Vietnam War (1955-1975) was fought between North Vietnam (supported by China, the Soviet Union and North Korea) and South Vietnam (supported by the Unites States, Thailand, New Zealand and the Philippines). This conflict was part of the Cold War (between capitalist and communist countries). The Vietnam War was a very controversial conflict and it was the first war to be covered live by television.

Pédagogie différenciée

TRAIL A

1 Match the slogans with their meaning.

a. I saw God and she's black
b. Resist the draft c. Lay, don't slay
d. Peaceful power

1. Make love, not war 2. Don't join the army 3. Non-violence is powerful 4. Be feminist and anti-racist

2 Focus on the first paragraph and find the historical event mentioned. Explain how people reacted to that event.

3 Read the second paragraph. Find three elements that describe where the story takes place.

4 Explain why *Hair* was a "passionate cry for help" (l. 11).

TRAIL B

1 Look at the picture and comment on the characters' appearance. Then focus on the slogans and say what they are protesting against.

2 Read the first paragraph and identify two problems with the war. Explain the solutions young men found to avoid being sent to war.

3 Read the second paragraph and say what *Hair* represented in the 1960s for young people.

4 Focus on line 9 to the end. Explain why *Hair* can be an inspiration today.

Meet up! Answer the question l. 16-17.

Prepare your project

You are a theatre critic for your high school website. Publish a post to encourage students to go and see a musical.

Grammar Tip Précis → p. 227

Use **should** to give advice.

Memory Challenge

Complete the following starters mentally. Remember one item for each starter and then tell your neighbour about it.

I saw... I read... I heard...
I was surprised by...
I didn't understand...

How do musicals reflect the English-speaking world?

C *Rent*, the NYC musical

Classe inversée

Vidéo
DVD
hatier-clic.fr/lmu066

E-workbook
Classe inversée
hatier-clic.fr/lmu067

1 Watch the video and choose three elements to explain why *Rent* is a success.

2 Describe the viewers' reactions.

3 Read the Culture Tip and say why *Rent* is about "hard times and realities".

4 Watch the video again and discuss why it portrays American society at the time.

Culture Tip

Rent was created in 1996 and takes place in the East Village, a neighbourhood in Manhattan, New York City. By the late 1960s, many artists, musicians, students and hippies began to move into the area, attracted by cheap apartment rents. The East Village is known as the birthplace and historical home of many artistic movements, including punk rock. It has also been the site of protests.

D *Billy Elliot*, a sign of the times

Vidéo
hatier-clic.fr/lmu068

Culture Tip

Many coal mines were closed down in the mid-80s, especially in the North East of England and in Wales. Hundreds of workers lost their jobs. They went on strike to get them back. The **1984-85 strike** was the height of the protest movement.

1 Look at the two pictures and say what they have in common. Guess what *Billy Elliot* is about.

2 Focus on the signs and explain what these people are fighting for.

3 Watch the video. Identify and oppose the three main groups.

4 Read the Culture Tip and explain the title of the song *Solidarity*.

Grammar Spot

The superlative — Tools → p. 140

"The **most** polically engaged [...] British musical."
"The **best** musical I have seen in a long time."

Word Spot

signs: notices (here)
asylum seekers
triumph /traɪəmf/: victory
social classes: working class – middle class – upper class
clash: conflict
relevant: appropriate to the time, period, circumstances
united
political
go on strike: stop working to protest
stand up for a cause: defend a cause
show solidarity
support: help sb
move forward
hold a sign
raise your fist
shout: scream
face to face: opposite one another

E Glasgow Girls

Audio
CD2 piste 09

Culture Tip

Written by Cora Bissett, the musical ***Glasgow Girls*** is based on the true story of a tenacious and loyal group of schoolgirls. Together with members of their community, they fought to stop one of their friends being deported back to Kosovo. Their action changed the way that child refugees are treated in Britain.

1 Focus on the girls' hands and faces on the poster and explain what these elements symbolise.

2 Listen to the first part of the recording and choose from the following list the elements that people liked in the musical:

the characters – the songs – the setting – the actors – the special effects – the accent – the humour

3 Listen to the second part of the recording and take notes about the characters, the period and the topics. Write a paragraph with the information you noted.

4 A member of the audience says: "I think it's very relevant." Use this adjective to explain why people should see *Glasgow Girls*.

Prepare your project

Create the flyer of a British or American musical. Choose the name of the musical among the following list: *Girl Power – Money – Yesterday – All Equal*. Write some information about the musical and its topic and add an illustration. Add positive reviews to make it more attractive!

Grammar Tip

Précis → p. 207

You can use **superlatives**.

Memory Challenge

In pairs, make a gesture that you associate with *Glasgow Girls*, *Billy Elliot* or *Rent*. Keep still in that position for three seconds and then explain to your partner why you chose this gesture.

Tools in the Spotlight

Practise your grammar

Précis grammatical, p. 192

Le superlatif

Il sert à comparer plus de deux éléments ou un élément avec **tout le reste**.

• **Le superlatif de supériorité**

Adjectif court (une syllabe ou deux syllabes avec terminaison *-y*)	**Adjectif long** (deux syllabes ou plus)
the + adj. + *-est* ⚠ *y* → *iest*	*the most* + adj.
*This is **the** cheap**est** ticket you can get.*	*Those are **the most** expensive seats.*

Matilda *is **the** smart**est** musical on Broadway.*
Les Misérables *is **the** long**est**-running musical in the West End.*

⚠ La consonne finale est doublée quand elle suit une voyelle unique.

big → *the biggest* mais *great* → *the greatest*

⚠ Les adjectifs irréguliers :

good → *the **best*** *bad* → *the **worst***
far → *the **farthest** or the **furthest***

• **Le superlatif d'infériorité** se forme à l'aide de ***the least***, placé devant l'adjectif, qu'il soit court ou long.

*Choose **the least** cold month if you want to watch an open-air performance!*

*This is **the least** interesting musical I've ever seen.*

L'expression du contraste

unlike (contrairement à)	préposition + nom ou pronom ou groupe nominal ***Unlike** the West End, Broadway has many recent theatres.*
yet / however (pourtant, cependant)	adverbe (souvent placé en début de phrase) *Musicals have a very long history. **And yet**, even today, they still attract so many people.*
whereas / while (tandis que, alors que)	conjonction + subordonnée d'opposition (= sujet + verbe) Matilda *is based on a book **while*** Billy Elliot *was adapted from a film.*

1 Mettez l'adjectif entre parenthèses au superlatif de supériorité.

a. Leonard Bernstein was (talented) ... composer of his generation.
b. *The Phantom of the Opera* is (long-running) ... show in Broadway history.
c. *Billy Elliot* is one of (celebrated) ... musicals of the early 21st century.
d. Musicals can give you (good) ... buzz of all.
e. Florenz Ziegfeld was one of (wealthy) ... New York producers in the early 19th century.
f. The actors of *Billy Elliot* were (adorable) ... on stage.
g. Not being able to go see *Glasgow Girls* because I was sick was (bad) ... experience of my holidays.

2 Mettez l'adjectif entre parenthèses au superlatif d'infériorité.

a. London's West End and New York's Broadway are (risky) places to attend a musical.
b. She managed to get (expensive) tickets.
c. West End tickets are (costly) ones. You usually pay more for Broadway performances.
d. In New York you can find (old) theatres, compared to the West End.
e. Broadway is more condensed, so the venues are (remote).
f. These leaflets provide (detailed) information about the next shows.

3 Complétez les phrases en utilisant chacun de ces mots une seule fois.
yet • unlike • however • whereas • while.

a. ... older musicals, *West Side Story* was filmed in a realistic urban setting.
b. London audiences rarely give a standing ovation ... New Yorkers are usually more demonstrative.
c. The quality of theatre is comparable. And ..., I prefer the West End.
d. Broadway looks to Hollywood for hit movies. ..., adaptations can be risky.
e. *La La Land* is a film ... *Hair* is an onstage musical.

Improve your pronunciation

Précis de phonologie, p. 242

Les énoncés emphatiques

Audio CD2 piste 10 MP3 n° 100

Dans un énoncé, certains mots peuvent être accentués de manière plus forte que les autres : un mot peut être porteur de l'accent de phrase, pour insister sur son importance. On obtient ainsi un **énoncé emphatique**. De manière générale, les **adverbes d'intensité** tels que *so*, *really*, *just*, ainsi que les **superlatifs** tels que *best*, peuvent recevoir cet accent de phrase.

- *This musical is* ***'so*** *fantastic!* : forte accentuation sur l'adverbe ***so***.
- *Broadway is* ***'really*** *awesome!* : forte accentuation sur l'adverbe ***really***.
- *I* ***'just*** *loved the film* Billy Elliot*!* : forte accentuation sur l'adverbe ***just***.
- *It's the* ***'best*** *film I've ever seen!* : forte accentuation sur le superlatif ***best***.

L'insistance peut aussi porter directement sur les adjectifs : *They're* ***'wonderful!***

4 **Écoutez l'enregistrement et repérez les mots accentués dans les phrases suivantes. Notez l'intonation des fins de phrases (↗ ou ↘).**

Audio CD2 piste 11 MP3 n° 101

a. It's so exciting.
b. I really like the characters.
c. It's the best musical I have seen.
d. That's the music from *Grease*, isn't it?

5 **Soulignez les mots qui doivent être accentués dans les énoncés suivants, puis vérifiez avec l'enregistrement.**

Audio CD2 piste 12 MP3 n° 102

a. I really loved the accent.
b. The actors are so energetic.
c. They're incredible.
d. Those girls are just awesome.

6 **Réécoutez les phrases de l'exercice 4 et répétez-les en reproduisant l'accentuation et l'intonation.**

Work on your writing skills

Le point final, d'interrogation et d'exclamation

- La ponctuation est indispensable à la compréhension d'un texte et sert aussi à faciliter sa lecture.

Dans l'exemple suivant, elle peut éviter bien des malentendus !

Let's eat, grandma. ≠ Let's eat grandma.

- Les phrases doivent commencer par une **majuscule** (*capital letter*) et se terminer par un **point** (*full stop*).

- On peut également terminer une phrase par **un point d'interrogation** (*question mark*) s'il s'agit d'une question.

Do you prefer seeing a live musical or a movie?

- On peut également mettre un **point d'exclamation** (*exclamation mark*) pour donner plus d'impact à la phrase.

TIP Attention à ne pas en abuser !

This musical is just great!

7 **Ajoutez la ponctuation (. / ! / ?) et les majuscules qui manquent dans ce texte.**

I went to see *Matilda* last week end it is such a good musical it reminds me of my childhood when I read the book by Road Dahl would you like to come and see it with me I don't mind seeing it again it's so brilliant

8 **Expliquez la différence de sens entre les paires de phrases suivantes.**

a. Charles the First walked and talked. Half an hour after, his head was cut off. • Charles the First walked and talked half an hour after his head was cut off.
b. Most of the time, travellers worry about their luggage. • Most of the time travellers worry about their luggage.
c. I find inspiration in cooking my family and my dog. • I find inspiration in cooking, my family and my dog.
d. A woman, without her man, is nothing. • A woman: without her, man is nothing.

Build up your vocabulary

Audio
CD2 piste 13

Musical

Social message (MP3 n°103)

controversial: debatable
relevant: appropriate to the time, period, circumstances
topical, current: related to the present time
revolutionary
convey a message /mesɪdʒ/
expose: denounce
look forward to sthg

Theatre (MP3 n°104)

theatre (*UK*) / theater (*US*): playhouse
perform a musical: act out a musical
be on (show): be performed at the moment
be named after: have the same name as
play a part / a role

Social conflict (MP3 n°105)

triumph /traɪəmf/: victory
social classes: the working class – the middle class – the upper class
clash: conflict
street protest: demonstration
go on strike: stop working to protest
stand up for a cause: defend a cause
stand up for one's rights: fight for one's rights
show solidarity
go to war
support: help sb
move forward
hold a sign
shout: scream
face to face: opposite one another

Success of musicals (MP3 n°106)

captivating: appealing
entertaining
informative: instructive
educational
engaging /ɪngeɪdʒɪŋ/: attractive
successful film: hit film
musical film (*UK*): musical movie (*US*)
dance number
tackle: deal with, be about a problem or an issue
attract: appeal to: draw
I would like or love to + V
I feel like + V-ing
I am not keen on + V-ing

Apprenez et révisez le vocabulaire !

Utilisez Quizlet pour vous entraîner en vous amusant.

Quizlet
hatier-clic.fr/lmu069

Utilisez le vocabulaire en contexte.

1 Complétez les phrases suivantes avec des mots de la carte mentale.

In the Heights is a musical that was first ... on Broadway in 2008. It is named ... the Hispanic district of Washington Heights. It ... social issues such as integration, poverty, social riots but, at the same time, ... an optimistic message as the community shows ... and friendship as well as a certain pride in what they have achieved. It tells a ... story which sounds genuine with a lively Latin beat and amazing dance ... .

2 Vous êtes le metteur en scène d'une nouvelle comédie musicale anglo-saxonne qui traite d'un sujet d'actualité. Inventez un titre et présentez brièvement cette comédie musicale lors d'une conférence de presse. Écrivez un discours (de quatre ou cinq lignes) en utilisant au moins dix mots ou expressions présents dans la carte mentale ci-dessus.

AUTO évaluation

Faites le quiz interactif en ligne et suivez les conseils pour vous préparer à l'évaluation.

Quiz
hatier-clic.fr/lmu070

Project #1

Become a YouTube influencer. Record a video to push tourists to see a live musical.

1 Start by introducing yourself and the topic of your video briefly.

- ✓ You are a fan of musicals and you have your own YouTube channel.
- ✓ Explain what you are going to talk about.

2 Show that musicals are meaningful.

- ✓ Explain how they reflect the American or British society (history, culture, social conflicts...).
- ✓ Present your arguments using linking words: **what's more**, **in addition**, **yet**...

3 Choose an example of an American or a British musical.

- ✓ Explain how your chosen musical gives an image of a certain period of time.
- ✓ Say what aspect(s) of society it illustrates and / or questions.

4 Don't forget to conclude.

- ✓ Say why it is more fun to see live musicals than watching a musical film.

5 Record your video.

- ✓ Make it personal and effective; to be convincing, you must be convinced!

Fiche de méthodologie N°12 p. 266

Project #2

Write a blog entry to recommend a musical reflecting the American or British society.

1 Choose a musical.

- ✓ You can choose one you studied or one of the following. US: *Grease, Hairspray, Chicago.* UK: *Oliver, Blood Brothers, The Commitments.*

2 Present a list of six reasons to go and see a musical.

- ✓ Say how it reflects the American or British society and what issues it deals with.
- ✓ Write about your experience using **"I"** and address the reader directly using **"you"**.

3 Say why it is better to see it live on Broadway or in the West End.

- ✓ Express comparisons using **more / less + long adj.** or **adj-er + than**.
- ✓ Don't hesitate to use **superlatives**.
- ✓ Express contrast using **unlike**, **yet**, **however**, **whereas** or **while**.

4 Show your enthusiasm!

- ✓ You can add some photos to make your blog entry more attractive.

Fiche de méthodologie N°22 p. 284

Let's RECAP

Lisez les questions-clés et complétez la fiche bilan avec des exemples et des documents que vous avez étudiés ou découverts.

AXE 6 | Creation and relation to arts

SÉQUENCE 1 Does rap rhyme with poetry?

How can rap and poetry be considered as powerful means of expression?
Is rap a modern form of poetry?

E-workbook
Bilan à compléter
hatier-clic.fr/lmu071

#communicateemotions
To what extent do rap and poetry convey emotions through words and rhythm?

#artisticexpression
Are poetry and rap two different artistic means of expressing the same message?

#literarydevices
Which tools do poets and rappers use? To what extent do rap and poetry use the same tools to pass on messages?

#poetry
What is the meaning of poetry in a modern world?

SÉQUENCE 2 How do musicals reflect the English-speaking world?

To what extent are British and American musicals inspired by political and social events?
How do British and American musicals reflect what is happening in society?

E-workbook
Bilan à compléter
hatier-clic.fr/lmu072

#singanddance
How do dancing and singing allow musicals to deal with serious issues and reach a large audience?

#defendacause
To what extent is it relevant to deal with social issues through art?

#thewestend #broadway
How have Broadway and the West End shows evolved through time?

#emotion
How does the combination of dance and words convey emotion?
How can emotions help to convey powerful messages?

#socialissues
Do musicals depict the reality of British and American societies?
Can musicals be socially engaged and denounce societal issues?

GO4IT!

Lisez et écoutez de l'anglais en dehors de la salle de classe ! Voici quelques conseils en lien avec votre séquence.

SÉQUENCE 1

Books

Chuck D Presents this Day in Rap and Hip-Hop History,
CHUCK D, SHEPARD FAIREY, 2017

The Rap Year Book,
SHEA SERRANO, 2015

Hip Hop Family Tree,
ED PISKOR, 2013-2016

TV series, films and documentary

Videos

Rapping, Deconstructed,
VOX
http://bit.ly/1qxOgFT

How to Rap Shakespeare,
CBBC
http://bit.ly/2BnT6jT

Websites

The language of hip-hop,
THE PUDDING
http://bit.ly/2xvlwFG

Quiz: Shakespeare or rap?, ABC
http://ab.co/26ldoAX

SÉQUENCE 2

Books and articles

Musicals, the Definitive Illustrated Story,
DUNCAN TURNER (ED), 2015

The Oxford Handbook of the British Musical,
ROBERT GORDON AND OLAF JUBIN (EDS), 2016

La La Land director Damien Chazelle on why musicals are the most free film genre,
FASTCOMPANY.COM, 2016
http://bit.ly/2neeq4l

Websites

Broadway theatres,
THE CITY OF NEW YORK
http://bit.ly/2nZVBkP

West End theatres,
LONDON THEATRE
http://bit.ly/2k9fQMG

Musical films

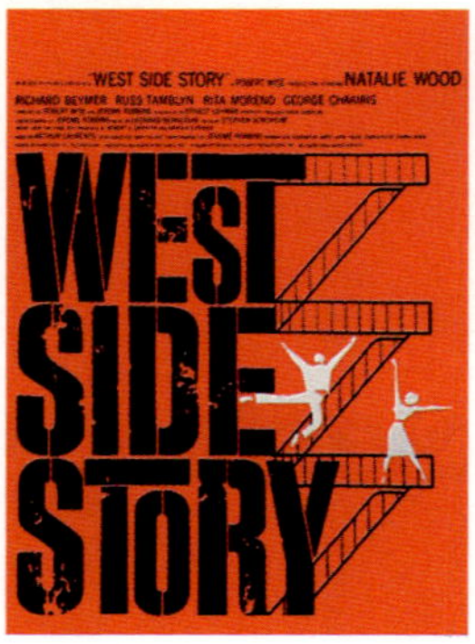

Live musicals

AXE 7

Saving the planet, imagining possible futures

Sauver la planète, penser les futurs possibles

SÉQUENCE 1 How do British citizens deal with sustainability?

Projects

Project #1: On your YouTube channel, announce five new habits you will adopt for a more sustainable lifestyle.

Project #2: You are a member of a youth council in London. Write to the mayor to share your ideas for a more sustainable city.

Tools

Grammaire les adjectifs composés, le futur
Phonologie la prononciation de la voyelle *a*
Écriture les nombres
Vocabulaire le développement durable

SÉQUENCE 2 Can cli-fi save the world?

Projects

Project #1: Let's debate! Can cli-fi change people's behaviour on climate?

Project #2: Create the back cover of a cli-fi story taking place in an English-speaking country.

Tools

Grammaire *can* et *could*, l'hypothèse avec *if* / la projection
Phonologie le suffixe *-ion*
Écriture la rédaction d'une 4e de couverture
Vocabulaire la fiction climatique

#ecology #environmentalpolicies #greencities #sustainablelifestyle #ecofriendly

Climate march in London, November 29, 2015

#climatechange #poweroftliterature #thinkofpossibleworlds #clifi

Polar bear and cub floating on an iceberg in London

SÉQUENCE 1

How do British citizens deal with sustainability?

A Zero-waste tips

Audio
CD2 piste 14

Imogen Lucas, known as "Sustainably Vegan", is a famous British vegan advocate who shares her advice for a low-impact lifestyle on YouTube and Instagram. In this recording, she lists two of her five easy zero-waste tips for teens living at home.

1 Explain what "Sustainably Vegan" advises teens to do.

2 Define "zero-waste".

3 Guess what her three other tips are and write them down.

B Green fashion

Culture Tip

Fashion Revolution is a movement demanding a "fairer, safer, cleaner, more transparent fashion industry".

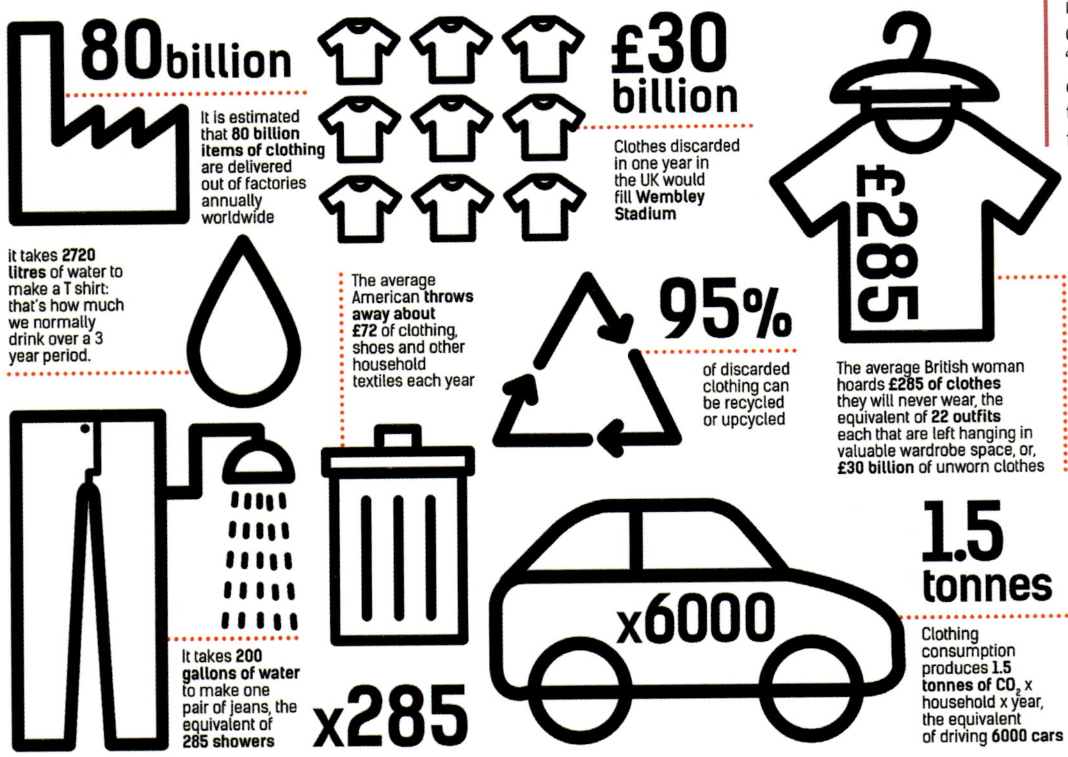

✦ Fashion Revolution

1 Find out how much water is needed to make clothes and the impact on the ozone layer.

2 Comment on the problem of waste in the clothing industry.

3 ***PAIR WORK*** Try to convince your best friend to buy his or her clothes in second-hand shops.

Grammar Spot

Compound adjectives Tools → p. 152

"to buy **pre-loved** clothes affordably"

Word Spot

organic food
selective sorting: recycling
greenhouse gas
rainforest
carbon footprint
thrift shop: charity shop
economical: affordable
disposable: one-use
protect: preserve
avoid
save ≠ waste
discard: throw away
produce
recycle: reuse
upcycle: repurpose
make sbdy aware of sthg

C Upcycling clothes

8th November 2018

Patch Challenge

By Helen Blank, Queen's Park LIS Green Impact

As a follow-up to the British Heart Foundation's Big Stitch event that Queen's Park Library hosted about 18 months ago, we're hoping to hold a Uni-wide[1] pop-up[2] Skills Share event that challenges students and staff to fix and re-purpose their clothes with a little help from volunteers. The idea is that this will benefit the environment by reducing textiles going to waste, and will save money by keeping our clothes wearable in the process – and of course, it's a good opportunity to work together on something useful and fun!

The first event will be held in the Small Hall at Parkgate Road on Friday 7th December 10-2pm alongside the pop-up Share Shop which will be an opportunity for staff, students and the public to buy pre-loved[3] clothes affordably, and all the proceeds[4] go to ShareAid.

This will hopefully be followed by a pop-up Patch Challenge on Queen's Park Campus in the New Year, and we'll take it from there to other campuses if there is interest.

So, we need your help to find some volunteers – staff or students who would be happy to share their 'creative fixing' skills with someone else. Either at one of the pop-up sessions or at a time to suit. It may be that you or someone you know has some great 'cheat' skills using wonderweb or fabric glue and some embellishments, or it may be they are great at upcycling garments[5] into something else completely! All materials will be provided.

If you fancy[6] helping out at one of the events, or if anyone springs to mind over the next few weeks – could you please tell them about the Patch Challenge?

✦ Green Chester, University of Chester

1. everywhere on the university campus 2. ephemeral 3. second-hand, used 4. profits 5. articles of clothing 6. want

1 Spot the proper nouns (places, dates). List the events planned on campus.

2 Show the positive impacts of these events.

3 You have to promote the pop-up Skills Share event. Write out a 50-word text to present it on the Facebook event you have created.

E-workbook
Fiche à imprimer
hatier-clic.fr/lmu073

D One day a week without meat

Classe inversée

✦ The Meat Free Monday Foundation

Audio
hatier-clic.fr/lmu074

E-workbook
Classe inversée
hatier-clic.fr/lmu075

1 Describe the poster and explain what kind of action is promoted.

2 Listen to the recording and use three figures to explain what it is about.

3 Sum up the consequences of animal agriculture on the environment.

4 In groups, draw a parallel between the poster and the audio document. Present your findings to the class.

Culture Tip

Meat Free Monday was launched by Paul, Mary and Stella McCartney in 2009.

Prepare your project

List three things you can do in your daily life to have a more sustainable lifestyle.

Grammar Tip

Précis → p. 227

Use **should** to say what you are ready to change.

Memory Challenge

Form two teams. Each team has to name as many ways as possible to contribute to a zero-waste world.

How do British citizens deal with sustainability?

E Ban on plastic

✦ Advert for Ecostrawz Ltd

UK government announces plans to ban[1] plastic straws, cotton-buds, and stirrers

The U.K. government has laid out plans to prohibit the distribution and sale of plastic straws, stirrers and cotton buds. The ban, which is subject to a consultation launched[2] Monday, would be enforced "at some point between October 2019 and October 2020".

In England alone, the government said that people use an estimated 4.7 billion plastic straws, 316 million plastic stirrers and 1.8 billion plastic-stemmed cotton buds per year.

The environmental impact of using such items is significant, with the government stating that they take hundreds of years to break down. It added that there were more than 150 million tons of plastic in the planet's oceans.

The government said its proposed ban would contain some exemptions and noted that there were scenarios where the use of plastic straws was necessary for medical and accessibility reasons. Citing one example, it said pharmacies would be allowed to sell plastic straws, while bars, pubs and restaurants would be able to stock "some straws for use on request." [...]

The U.K. government has launched several initiatives aimed at tackling the pollution caused by plastic, including a ban on microbeads and a charge on single use plastic bags.

"Our precious oceans and the wildlife within need urgent protection from the devastation throw-away plastic items can cause," Environment Secretary Michael Gove said in a statement Monday. [...]

The proposals were welcomed by environmental organizations. Sam Chetan Welsh, Greenpeace U.K.'s political adviser, said ministers were doing the sensible thing by looking to ban single-use plastic items, but added that [...] the companies producing and selling all this packaging must take responsibility for it and cut down[3] the amount of plastic ending up in our shopping baskets.

✦ Anmar Frangoul, *CNBC*, October 22, 2018

1. prohibit 2. started 3. reduce

1 Describe the advert and say where you could find it.

2 Read the text and focus on the figures. Explain the decision of the British government.

3 Focus on environmental organisations (l. 25-31) and sum up their reactions to the project.

4 Imagine a written message for the customers of a supermarket explaining why they won't find the three plastic items any more.

Grammar Spot

Future Tools → p. 152

If we continue like that, we **will** need three planets!

Word Spot

use (noun) /ju:s/
mindset: ideas and attitudes
green: eco-friendly: ecological
rational: sensible
involved: concerned
contribute to
make sthg easier
take action: act
evolve: develop
be used to + V-ing
adopt new habits: get used to + V-ing
refrain from + V-ing: choose not to
use (verb) /ju:z/
save the planet

F Sustainable communities

✦ *BedZED - The need for sustainable communities*, Bioregional, 2011

Vidéo DVD

E-workbook Fiche à imprimer hatier-clic.fr/lmu076

Culture Tip

BedZED (Beddington Zero Energy Development) is an eco-friendly neighbourhood created in 2002 in the south of London.

Pédagogie différenciée

TRAIL A

1 Explain what is said about the habits of Europeans in their daily lives.

2 Name at least three guiding principles of sustainability BedZED has led to.

3 Pick out the names of cities or countries where BedZED has been developed.

TRAIL B

1 Explain why Europeans need to lead a more sustainable lifestyle.

2 Try to list the 10 guiding principles of sustainability BedZED has led to.

3 Pick out the names of all the cities and countries. Use them to explain the development of the project worldwide.

Meet up! ***PAIR WORK*** Imagine the dialogue between an estate agent and the potential buyer of a sustainable apartment. Speak about the objectives and principles of the creators of BedZED.

G A green policy

Vidéo DVD

✦ *T-charge introduced to tackle London pollution*, ITN, 2017

1 Focus on the figures and places to explain what the T-charge consists in.

2 The mayor of London has a top priority. Use keywords to explain what it is.

3 Write a short paragraph to explain the mayor's plan to London inhabitants on the official website of the city.

Prepare your project

Write a tweet to encourage a British mayor to make his or her city more sustainable. Suggest two decisions he or she could make.

Grammar Tip Précis → p. 209

Use **figures** to back up your arguments.

Memory Challenge

Write five words from p. 150-151 on the board. Go around the class clockwise: the 1st student says a sentence using one word, the 2nd student repeats the sentence and creates a sentence with another word, etc.

Tools in the Spotlight

Entraînez-vous sur la plateforme *Let's Meet Up!*
reussirenlangues.fr

Practise your grammar

Précis grammatical, p.192

Les adjectifs composés

- L'adjectif composé est formé d'**au moins deux mots**.
- De manière générale, le **deuxième mot** peut être un adjectif, un nom, un participe présent ou un participe passé.
  – Adjectif + **adjectif** : *light-**green**, dark-**green***
  – Nom + **adjectif** : *sky-**blue**, nature-**friendly***
  – Adverbe + **adjectif** : *environmentally-**friendly**, eco-**friendly***
  – Adjectif + **nom** + **-ed** : *fair-**haired**, brown-**eyed**, narrow-**minded***
  – Adjectif ou nom + **participe présent** : *good-**looking**, time-**consuming**, energy-**saving***
  – Nom ou adverbe ou préfixe + **participe passé** : *home-**made**, well-**dressed**, pre-**loved***
- D'autres combinaisons sont possibles, notamment avec **trois mots** pour des éléments chiffrés.
  *a **sixteen-year-old** student* *a **two-hundred-euro** budget*
- En anglais britannique, il y a un **trait d'union** entre les deux mots qui forment l'adjectif composé.

⚠ L'adjectif composé, comme tous les adjectifs, reste **invariable**.

1 Indiquez l'adjectif composé qui correspond selon le contexte.

eco-friendly • light-green • time-consuming • nature-friendly • dark-green

a. A ... project respects the environment.
b. These projects are ... . You can spend long hours studying them!
c. Biofuels are ... . They don't harm nature as much as fossil energy!
d. Why did you use ... to paint the leaves? You should have used ... .

2 Formez un adjectif composé à partir des deux mots entre parenthèses.

a. In the countryside we are lucky to live in an (**friendly, environment**) atmosphere.
b. You can contribute to saving the planet if you buy (**hand, second**) clothes.
c. Imogen Lucas is a (**known, well**) vegan advocate in the UK.
d. This lake has turned (**light, green**) because of the water lilies.

Le futur

En anglais, il n'existe pas de temps futur, mais on peut parler de l'avenir en utilisant diverses formulations.

- Le modal ***will*** indique une prédiction, voire une quasi-certitude.
  *If we continue like that, we **will** need three planets!*
- ***be + going to*** indique le futur proche.
  *This environmentally-friendly project **is going to** improve the quality of life in London.*
- Le **présent en *be* + V-*ing*** s'emploie souvent avec un adverbe temporel marquant l'avenir.
  *He **is leaving** for this conference about global warming in New York tomorrow.*
- ***is to*** s'utilise pour parler d'un programme pré-établi.
  *She **is to** make a speech at the meeting on the environment next week.*

3 Complétez par le présent simple ou le présent en *be* + V-*ing*.

a. They always (**sort out**) their rubbish.
b. They (**meet up**) with the leader of this charity tomorrow afternoon.
c. She usually (**wash**) her clothes using eco-friendly products.
d. He (**transfer**) all the signatures of this petition to the mayor next Monday.

4 Complétez par *will*, *be + going to* ou *is to*, selon le contexte.

a. For sure we ... need a lot of green energy like wind farms and biofuels to save the planet!
b. The member of this NGO ... make a speech next month at the Save the Planet conference.
c. I ... collect rubbish by the seashore this afternoon.
d. I ... send you the petition if you want to back up this eco-friendly project.

Improve your pronunciation

Précis de phonologie, p. 242

La prononciation de la voyelle *a*

Audio
CD2 piste 15
MP3 n° 107

En général, la voyelle *a* peut se prononcer au moins de **sept façons différentes** selon le contexte :

– prononciation /ə/ si elle est inaccentuée (*American, sustainable*). On l'appelle **schwa** (*e* muet).
– prononciation /æ/ si elle est accentuée (*attic*) ou suivie de ***ck*** (*black*) ou d'une seule consonne (*ban, van*).
– prononciation /ɑː/ si elle est suivie de la consonne ***r*** (*carbon*) ou de ***lm*** (*calm*).
– prononciation /eɪ/ si elle est suivie d'une consonne elle-même suivie de la voyelle ***e*** (*male, age*) ou si elle est suivie de la voyelle ***i*** (*sustainable*) ou s'il s'agit d'un mot dérivé se terminant par ***ation*** (*organisation*).
– prononciation /ɪ/ dans la terminaison ***age*** (*cottage, message*).
– prononciation /iː/ si elle est précédée de la voyelle ***e*** (*cream, beat*).
– prononciation /ɔː/ si elle est suivie de ***ll*** ou de la voyelle ***u*** (*mall, appalling*).

5 Écrivez les mots suivants. Indiquez si la graphie a soulignée se prononce /ə/, /æ/, /iː/, /ɪ/ ou /eɪ/, puis écoutez l'enregistrement pour confirmer vos réponses.

Audio
CD2 piste 16
MP3 n° 108

leaf • lake • ban • sunbeam • map • lane • cottage • sustainability

6 Écrivez les phrases suivantes. Indiquez le son correspondant à la voyelle a soulignée: /ə/, /æ/, /ɑː/, /eɪ/, /ɪ/, /iː/ ou /ɔː/. Puis écoutez l'enregistrement pour confirmer vos réponses.

Audio
CD2 piste 17
MP3 n° 109

a. We need to be aware of the danger of fossil energy.
b. A thatched cottage is so cosy!
c. You can get some cream at this farm.
d. If the farm is too far away, just go to the local supermarket!

Work on your writing skills

Les nombres

• Pour écrire les nombres de 21 à 99, on ajoute l'unité à la dizaine avec un **trait d'union**.

31: thirty-one *48: forty-eight* *87: eighty-seven*

• Après le mot *hundred* (100), il faut ajouter ***and***.

*3,423: three thousand four hundred **and** twenty-three*

• ***Hundred, thousand, million*** et ***billion*** ne prennent pas de ***s*** quand ils sont précédés de ***several*** ou d'un nombre.

*several **thousand** litres* *two **hundred** years*

En revanche, ils prennent un ***s*** quand ils sont employés comme **noms** et suivis de ***of***.

***Hundreds** of people have recently decided to stop eating meat.*

⚠ Quand on écrit un prix, on place le symbole de la devise **avant** le montant en chiffres ou **après** le montant en lettres.

*£235: two hundred and thirty-five **pounds***

• Les **siècles** s'écrivent en chiffres arabes et non romains.

*the **20th** century* (le xxe siècle)

7 Réécrivez ce texte avec les chiffres en toutes lettres.

In 2017, 24,971 people took part in Veganuary and stopped eating meat for a month. There are 68,841 places in the world where vegans can enjoy a good meal. In London there are 863 different locations in the city centre. The average price of a vegan meal is £15.

8 Réécrivez cet extrait de blog avec les chiffres en toutes lettres.

There are over 7 billion people on planet Earth. How much is 1 billion? It would take you 31 years 259 days, 1 hour, 46 minutes and 40 seconds counting one number a second to reach a billion. If each person buys one shirt and one jacket, how many items would that be on our planet?

Build up your vocabulary

Audio
CD2 piste 18

Sustainability

Green food — MP3 n°116

organic food
vegetarian
vegan /viːgən/
healthy
homemade
natural

Green clothing — MP3 n°110

second-hand clothing
thrift shop: charity shop
ethical /eθɪkəl/
fair: equitable
the 3 Rs: Reduce - Reuse - Recycle
upcycle: repurpose
discard: throw away

Green lifestyle — MP3 n°111

selective sorting: recycling
use (noun) /juːs/
not tested on animals
economical: cheap, inexpensive
zero-waste
disposable: one-use ≠ reusable
adopt new habits: get used to + V-ing
be used to + V-ing
use (verb) /juːz/
save ≠ waste
avoid
refrain from + V-ing: choose not to make sthg easier

Global warming — MP3 n°115

climate change / crisis
greenhouse gas
greenhouse effect
carbon footprint
environmental impact
pollution
rainforest
biodiversity /baɪəʊdaɪvɜːsəti/
wildlife
damage /dæmɪdʒ/

Green cities — MP3 n°112

consumption
clean / renewable energy
biofuel ≠ fossil fuel /fjuːəl/
energy-efficient
energy-saving

Ecology — MP3 n°114

sustainable development
political action
environmental policies
green: eco-friendly: ecological
environmentally-friendly: nature-friendly
protect: preserve
tackle climate change
save the planet

Citizens' involvement — MP3 n°113

petition
demonstration
initiative
commitment: responsibility
mindset: ideas and attitudes
rational: sensible
involved: concerned
conscious
take action: act
advocate: defend
evolve: develop
contribute to
make sbdy aware of sthg

Apprenez et révisez le vocabulaire !

Utilisez Quizlet pour vous entraîner en vous amusant.

Quizlet
hatier-clic.fr/lmu077

Utilisez le vocabulaire en contexte.

1 Complétez les phrases suivantes avec des mots de la carte mentale.

a. An international meeting will be held next year to promote ... development in the world.
b. When they go shopping, my neighbours use ... cotton shopping bags instead of ... plastic bags.
c. Our association aims at making every city greener so please sign this ...!
d. This brand new ... light bulb is great: it creates the same amount of light without creating wasted heat.
e. Last week there was a huge ... that gathered hundreds of people. They marched to demand global action against climate ... .
f. Good food habits and daily physical activity are essential to a ... lifestyle.

2 Pour un magazine en ligne sur l'écologie, écrivez le court portrait d'un·e Londonien·ne engagé·e pour le développement durable et la protection de la planète. Utilisez au moins deux mots de chaque catégorie de la carte mentale.

AUTO évaluation

Faites le quiz interactif en ligne et suivez les conseils pour vous préparer à l'évaluation.

Quiz
hatier-clic.fr/lmu078

Project #1

On your YouTube channel, announce five new habits you will adopt for a more sustainable lifestyle.

1 Choose the five decisions you will make.

- ✓ Use the documents of this unit to find some ideas or this website: http://bit.ly/2UnmwnD.
- ✓ Write down your ideas and number them from the least important to the most interesting.

2 Organise your speech.

- ✓ Use the following words to enumerate: **the first, the second, the third, then, finally**.
- ✓ Use expressions to show how committed you are: **I promise to + V, I commit to + V-ing**...
- ✓ To express the future, use: **will + V** or **be going to + V** and expressions like **From now on**...

3 Rehearse your speech.

- ✓ Check the pronunciation of difficult words using wordreference.com.
- ✓ Practise your speech several times, with a friend or a member of your family if you can.

4 Film yourself!

- ✓ Choose a green setting (a park or a garden) to film yourself.
- ✓ You take a solemn pledge: show how committed you are.
- ✓ Be clear and articulate. Don't speak too fast!

➤ Fiche de méthodologie N°12 p. 266

Project #2

You are a member of a youth council in London. Write to the mayor to share your ideas for a more sustainable city.

1 Think about how to make London more sustainable.

- ✓ You can find some ideas on this website: http://bit.ly/2EPP3fZ or use the documents studied in this unit.

2 Organise the content of your letter.

- ✓ Start a new paragraph for each new argument.
- ✓ Organise your paragraphs with linking words: **first, second, then, to conclude, in addition**...
- ✓ To make suggestions, use the modals **could, should** and expressions such as: **Why not + V-ing ... ? How about + V-ing ... ?**

3 Present your letter properly.

- ✓ Write the date in the top left-hand corner: **Monday, November 5th 2020**.
- ✓ Use the appropriate polite phrases to start your letter: **Dear Mr / Mrs Mayor** and to end it: **Yours sincerely**.
- ✓ Don't forget to sign your letter!

4 Check your text.

- ✓ Read your letter again and focus on the grammar mistakes you usually make.
- ✓ You can use the Cambridge dictionary online to check the spelling of words you don't know.

➤ Fiche de méthodologie N°22 p. 284

SÉQUENCE 2

Can cli-fi save the world?

A Three cli-fi novels

E-workbook
Fiche à imprimer
hatier-clic.fr/lmu079

GROUP WORK

A

B
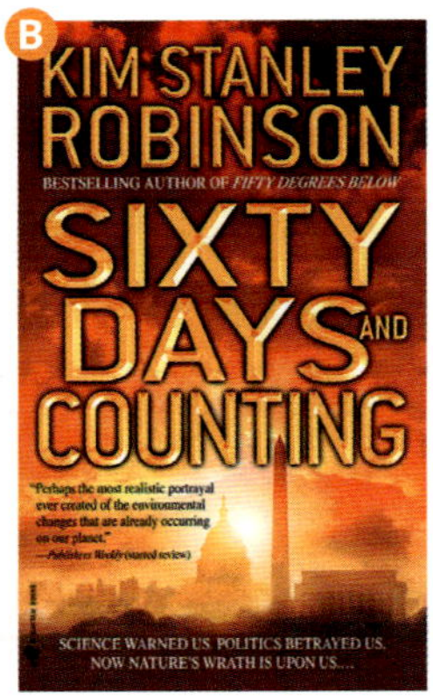

C
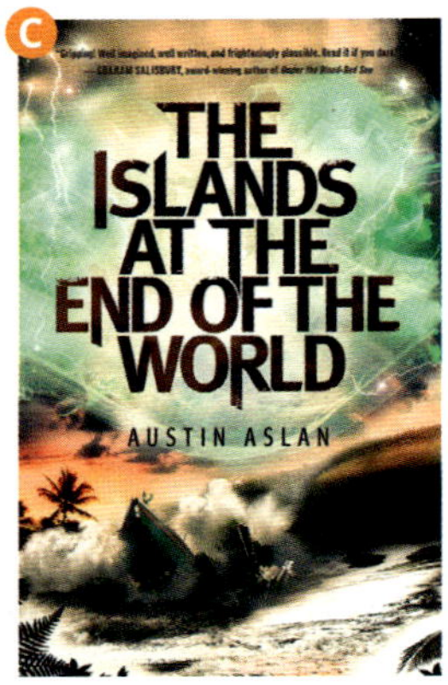

1 Describe the covers: colours, natural elements, buildings...

2 Imagine what the stories are about.

3 Read your group's text and match it with the right cover.

4 In groups, explain the story in your own words and share it with the class.

1 Leilani is a 16-year-old epileptic girl who lives in Hawaii with her family. While she is on an island to take part in a trial for a new medication, the whole planet loses power. Food and water reserves are decreasing and the world is becoming violent. Will Leilani find her way home through chaos, destruction, and lack of electricity?

2 Mitchell Zukor, a brilliant mathematician from New York, has an unusual job. He spends his days calculating worst-case scenarios for Future World, a company that makes big dollars by indemnifying[1] other companies against lawsuits sparked[2] by natural disasters. Just as Mitchell's darkest prediction about Manhattan comes true, he realises he is the only one prepared to face it. But what will it cost him?

1. compensating financially 2. activated

3 By the time Phil Chase is elected president, the world's climate is on its way to irreversible change. In a world full of surveillance and non-existent freedom, the future for the Chase administration looks darker every day. As the latest and most terrible natural disaster is about to happen, it will take a miracle to stop the clock…

B Definition of a genre

Vidéo
hatier-clic.fr/lmu080

1 Introduce the speaker and the topic.

2 Explain the speaker's hope about cli-fi and define the word "cli-fi" precisely.

3 List three literary genres that have been used in cli-fi.

4 Explain the goal of cli-fi and give some examples.

Grammar Spot

Can and could Tools → p. 160

"I never knew that cold **could** kill people like that."

Word Spot

climate change
literary genre
a multi-genre project
YA: young adults
thriller
plot: story line
novel
utopia /juːtəʊpiə/ ≠ dystopia
power cut = blackout
energy consumption
fictional ≠ non-fictional
plausible: realistic, possible
incredible: unbelievable

C Carbon Diaries

Weds, Jan 14th
I woke up this morning and it was freezing, freezing cold. I'm only allowed heat on in my room between 7 and 8. I went and looked at the Smart Meter in the hall. It's this thing that tells you everything that's going on with energy in the house. Even for our one hour of heat Dad's locked the bedroom temp at 15°C. What a joke – it's not even enough to melt the frost on the windows. [...]

Fri, Jan 16th
I've been given an essay to write by next Friday for AS Critical Thinking: *Write an informal personal review of an aspect of your home-life environment in the light of the new carbon rationing system.* [...]

Tues, Jan 20th
We had a powercut[1] in the night. The house is so cold now, it feels like 200 years of evil chill[2] creeping into my bones. Reminds me of the Great Storm. Cuts give me the creeps[3] – you know when you go to switch the light on and it's dead? It was so freezing I went shopping to Waitrose with Mum and Dad just to keep my blood moving. [...]

Thurs, Jan 22nd
Italy has only just got its power back. They've found out the cause of the blackout – a tree fell on a live cable on the Swiss border. A bloody *plant* wiped out a whole country for 60 hours. Loads of old people have died. So strange. I never knew that cold could kill people like that. France is under deep snow now, and it's coming our way.

✦ Saci Lloyd, *The Carbon Diaries 2015*, 2008

1. when the electricity supply stops 2. extreme cold 3. give sbdy the creeps: terrify

1 Pick out the consequences of the carbon restrictions on the narrator's life.

2 Read the highlighted expressions and explain the narrator's feelings in your own words.

3 Explain why the last paragraph is important for the context of the story.

4 Write a short paragraph to describe the impact of climate change on Europeans in the story.

Prepare your project

Write a Wikipedia article giving a definition of cli-fi and explaining why this type of fiction is worth reading.

Grammar Tip Précis → p. 217
Use **can** and **must** to give your opinion.

Memory Challenge

You have one minute to choose three words to define cli-fi. Justify your choice in front of the class.

D Fiction vs. reality

E-workbook
Fiche à imprimer
hatier-clic.fr/lmu081

1 ***PAIR WORK*** Describe your poster to your partner.

2 Discuss which poster you would choose to denounce climate change. Explain why.

E Al Gore's hope to raise awareness

Classe inversée

✦ Al Gore talks about *Truth to Power*, IMDb, 2017

Vidéo
DVD
hatier-clic.fr/lmu082

E-workbook
Classe inversée
hatier-clic.fr/lmu083

1 Watch the video and identify the type of movie that is being discussed (fictional or non-fictional?).

2 Find elements showing the reasons behind Al Gore's film and give its goals.

3 Pick out the arguments which give hope to future generations.

4 Write a review of the movie showing why it is a good way to educate yourself on climate change.

Culture Tip

Al Gore was Vice-President of the USA during Bill Clinton's presidency from 1993 to 2001. He received the Nobel Peace Prize in 2007.

Word Spot

stakes: risks
hourglass: object with sand to measure time
public opinion
fact-based information
worrisome: disturbing
represent: show: feature
rely /rɪlaɪ/ on or upon sthg
raise awareness on sthg
disengage ≠ feel concerned about sthg
appeal to: attract
relate to sbdy or sthg: connect with sbdy or sthg
touch people's heart

Grammar Spot

If clauses TOOLS → p. 160

"If you save the planet, who **will** play you in the superhero movie?"

F From cli-fi to change

Can 'cli-fi' actually make a difference?

Climate scientists [...] tend to bombard their audiences with facts and figures[1] - to convince them how rapidly our planet is warming. [...] A classic example is Al Gore's *An Inconvenient Truth*, and its sequel, which are loaded with graphs and statistics. However, it is becoming ever clearer that these methods don't work as well as we'd like. [...]

One way of potentially tapping into previously unreached audiences[2] is via cli-fi, or climate-fiction. Cli-fi explores how the world may look in the process or aftermath[3] of dealing with climate change, and not just that caused by burning fossil fuels. [...] Climate scientists should not expect everyone to be as concerned as they are when they show a plot of increasing global temperatures. Cli-fi has the potential to work in the exact opposite way, through compelling[4] storylines, dramatic visuals, and characters. By making people care about and individually connect to climate change, it can motivate them to seek out the scientific evidence for themselves. [...] In the long run, cli-fi might encourage audiences to modify their everyday lives (and maybe even who they vote for) to reduce their own carbon footprint.

✦ *London as Venice*, Robert Graves and Didier Madoc-Jones

From personal experience, some audiences tend to disengage from climate change because of how overwhelming[5] the issue may seem. [...]

To this audience, cli-fi also has an important message to deliver – that of hope. That it is not, or will it be ever, too late to combat human-caused climate change.

✦ www.theconversation.com, Sept 5, 2017

1. numbers or statistics 2. tapping into previously unreached audiences: convincing people who were unconvinced 3. consequences 4. fascinating 5. enormous

Pédagogie différenciée

TRAIL A

1 List the vocabulary linked to scientific studies and use it to show it has no impact on people.

2 Explain the solution found to raise people's awareness on climate change.

3 Find some advantages cli-fi has compared to scientific studies.

TRAIL B

1 Explain the method used in *An Inconvenient Truth* and the problem with this method.

2 Pick out three characteristics of cli-fi and explain how they can impact people's minds.

3 Describe the long-term effect cli-fi can have on people.

Meet up! Say what you find more impactful when talking about climate change: scientific facts or cli-fi?

Prepare your project

Choose a climate change documentary or a cli-fi film. Explain your choice and why it is a good way to raise awareness on climate change.

Grammar Tip Précis → p. 219

Use the **present tense** to give your opinion.

Memory Challenge

Look at this lesson for two minutes and close your textbook. Make a list of elements you can remember, count them and challenge someone to have more than you. Then compare your lists!

Entraînez-vous sur la plateforme *Let's Meet Up!*
reussirenlangues.fr

Tools in the Spotlight

Practise your grammar

Précis grammatical, p. 192

Can et could

- ***Can / can't* + V**

Can exprime :

– ce qu'il est **permis** de faire.

*You **can** go outside if you like. It isn't raining.*

– ce que quelqu'un ou quelque chose est **capable** de faire.

*Laura **can** write an essay about carbon cards.*

– la **possibilité** qu'un événement se réalise.

*The weather **can** really **be** erratic nowadays.*

– *Can't* exprime l'**impossibilité**.

*If we **can't** meet today because of the bad weather, we will arrange another appointment.*

- ***Could / couldn't* + V**

Could exprime :

– ce que quelqu'un ou quelque chose **était capable** de faire.

*When she was young, she **could** read stories for hours.*

– une **probabilité**.

*Cli-fi **could** help raise awareness about global warming.*

– *Couldn't* exprime l'**impossibilité** dans le **passé**.

*People **couldn't** read cli-fi 30 years ago, because this literary genre didn't exist.*

1 Donnez la valeur de *can* et *could* dans les phrases suivantes.

a. Politicians can't lie about climate change. We can see it happening.
b. Limiting carbon emissions could slow down the melting of the ice cap.
c. You can demonstrate to fight for a better world.
d. The weather could get a whole lot worse in the years to come.
e. Our grandparents could live their lives without thinking about climate change.
f. "I never knew that cold could kill people like that."*

* Saci Lloyd, *The Carbon Diaries 2015*, 2008

2 Complétez les énoncés à l'aide de *can* ou *could* suivant le contexte donné.

a. (Due to climate change), the UK ... also face threats to its water security and supply.*
b. The government estimates that 27-59 million people ... be living in areas affected by water supply deficits by the 2050s.*
c. Hurricanes (not) ... destroy entire cities.
d. Cli-fi ... help people become aware of global warming.
e. I didn't know that climate change ... affect the planet so rapidly.

* theguardian.com

L'hypothèse avec *if* / la projection

If + présent simple	/	*will / won't* + V
proposition subordonnée		proposition principale

En utilisant ce type de subordonnée, l'énonciateur exprime une situation qu'il ou elle juge **susceptible de se produire**.

***If** people watch films like Geostorm and read cli-fi, they **will** feel more concerned with climate change.*

***If** we don't act quickly, climate change **will** destroy our world.*

3 À l'aide des propositions ci-dessous, rédigez des hypothèses concernant notre avenir liées au changement climatique.

If we do nothing...

the earth's temperatures

the ozone layer

the Antarctic ice sheet

Improve your pronunciation

Précis de phonologie, p. 242

Le suffixe *-ion*

Audio CD2 piste 19 MP3 n° 117

Les mots dérivés se terminant par le suffixe *-ion* sont accentués sur la syllabe qui précède la syllabe *-ion*.

communication /kəmjuːnɪˈkeɪʃən/

admission /ədˈmɪʃən/

fiction /ˈfɪkʃən/

intonation /ɪntəˈneɪʃən/

destruction /dɪˈstrʌkʃən/

consumption /kənˈsʌmpʃən/

⚠ Le mot *television*, qui peut aussi être accentué sur la première syllabe /ˈtelɪvɪʒən/, est une exception à cette règle.

4 **Recopiez et écoutez les mots suivants. Soulignez la syllabe accentuée. Que remarquez-vous ?**

Audio CD2 piste 20 MP3 n° 118

deforestation • condition • emission • station • solution • restriction • pollution • prediction • nation • corporation

5 **Complétez la phrase suivante avec un des choix proposés.**

Les mots terminés par *-ion* sont accentués sur la ... (1re, 2e, etc.) syllabe **avant** cette terminaison.

6 **Lisez les phrases suivantes à voix haute, puis vérifiez votre prononciation.**

Audio CD2 piste 21 MP3 n° 119

a. Living conditions are becoming more and more difficult due to the pollution caused by greenhouse gas emissions.

b. One solution would be to implement restrictions, but the government could be faced with the opposition of the population.

c. The destruction of forests is called deforestation.

Work on your writing skills

La rédaction d'une 4e de couverture

Cette partie de la couverture a pour fonction d'inciter le lecteur à acheter ou à lire le livre. Généralement présentée sous la forme d'un texte court, la 4e de couverture doit, en quelques lignes, présenter l'œuvre : amorcer l'intrigue ou la résumer, préciser le genre littéraire et susciter l'envie de lire le livre. Souvent, elle comporte également un extrait de l'ouvrage.

- Pour rédiger votre texte de 4e de couverture, réfléchissez à une intrigue possible.
- Listez les éléments les plus importants du récit : personnage(s), lieu(x), date(s), événement(s) et impact(s) sur la vie quotidienne des protagonistes.
- Choisissez des personnages qui permettent une identification facile : un ou une adolescent·e par exemple.
- Pensez à situer l'intrigue dans un pays anglophone en utilisant des références identifiables et des lieux précis (*Tower Bridge*, *Manhattan*, etc.).
- Donnez un titre susceptible d'intriguer le lecteur et rédigez une dizaine de lignes.
- Terminez votre texte sur une question directe ou indirecte sur le devenir de votre ou vos personnages.

⚠ *Spoiler alert* : faites attention à ne pas dévoiler la totalité de l'intrigue mais uniquement les éléments qui permettent d'en saisir les grandes lignes.

7 **Pour vous entraîner, imaginez des 4e de couverture à partir des couvertures reproduites p. 156, en vous aidant des synopsis correspondants.**

8 **À partir des éléments suivants, rédigez un texte de 4e de couverture en une dizaine de lignes.**

drought • Florida • spring 2022 • Alison and her family • nature and wild animals • secondary school

Build up your vocabulary

Audio
CD2 piste 22

Cli-fi

Solutions (MP3 n°120)

- solar power
- renewable energy: sustainable energy
- thrilling: exciting
- awesome ≠ terrible
- hopeful ≠ pessimistic
- obligatory: compulsory

Books and literature (MP3 n°123)

- literary genre
- thriller
- cli-fi: climate fiction
- essays
- memoirs
- plot: story line
- novel
- utopia /ju:təʊpɪə/ ≠ dystopia
- fictional ≠ non-fictional
- fact-based information
- represent: show: feature
- rely /rɪlaɪ/ on or upon sthg
- deal with: be about

Climate change (MP3 n°121)

- stakes: risks
- energy consumption
- power cut = blackout
- extreme weather conditions
- heatwave
- human activity
- pollution
- CO_2: carbon dioxide /daɪɒksaɪd/
- carbon emissions
- consequences
- flood
- tornado
- crisis
- destroyed: devastated
- nightmarish
- frightening
- catastrophic
- be freezing cold: be extremely cold
- melt: turn ice into water

Reactions (MP3 n°122)

- public opinion
- plausible: realistic, possible
- incredible: unbelievable
- worrisome: disturbing
- appeal to: attract
- disengage ≠ feel concerned about sthg
- raise awareness of sthg
- relate to sbdy or sthg: connect with sbdy or sthg
- touch people's heart

Apprenez et révisez le vocabulaire !

Utilisez Quizlet pour vous entraîner en vous amusant.

Quizlet
hatier-clic.fr/lmu084

Utilisez le vocabulaire en contexte.

1 Complétez les phrases suivantes avec des mots de la carte mentale.

a. Climate fiction, commonly abbreviated as cli-fi, is a … … .
b. It deals with … … and relies on … … .
c. The … … in cli-fi novels shows the … … of human activities on climate.
d. It aims at raising people's … of climate change issues.
e. Cli-fi novels feature a … and … near future in which characters' stories and actions … … … .

2 Utilisez les documents étudiés en classe pour écrire un courriel à votre correspondant·e américain·e. Vous voulez la ou le convaincre de lire un roman de fiction climatique qui vous a passionné·e. Utilisez dix mots de la carte mentale.

AUTO évaluation

Faites le quiz interactif en ligne et suivez les conseils pour vous préparer à l'évaluation.

Quiz
hatier-clic.fr/lmu085

Project #1

Take part in *The Big Question* on BBC2. Today's debate is: can cli-fi change people's behaviour on climate?

1 **Choose which role you want to play: a British scientist or an American cli-fi author.**

- ✓ Which elements are necessary to play your role (body language, props...)?

2 **Write a few notes with your ideas to remember them.**

- ✓ Think about the pros and cons of your point of view.
- ✓ Research precise examples for each of your arguments.
- ✓ Organise your ideas in a list, a mind map or a diagram.
- ✓ Prepare counter-arguments.

3 **Prepare your speech.**

- ✓ Use linking words: **to begin with**, **in addition**, **on the contrary**, **for example**...
- ✓ Use expressions like **I disagree**, **I see your point but**, **to my mind**, **the way I see it**...

4 **Make sure to speak correctly.**

- ✓ Check your pronunciation on an online dictionary.

5 **Start to debate!**

- ✓ Listen to your classmates' point of view.

➤ Fiche de méthodologie N°20 p. 280

Project #2

Create the back cover of a cli-fi story taking place in an English-speaking country.

1 **Choose the characters and the setting of your story.**

- ✓ Think about a plot which takes place in an English-speaking country.
- ✓ Say when it takes place.
- ✓ Define your characters (number, personality...).

2 **Collect information about the climatic-related issues that will appear in the book.**

- ✓ Think about all the details of your plot: climatic problems, causes and consequences.
- ✓ Use linking words like **consequently**, **for example**, **therefore**, **then**...

3 **Write the back cover.**

- ✓ Find a title for your story.
- ✓ Write a brief description of the plot.
- ✓ Add critics from newspapers or scientists.
- ✓ Say why the story is so appealing using **superlatives**.

4 **Don't spoil the story!**

- ✓ Don't say too much.
- ✓ A back cover intends to attract readers and make people want to buy the book.

➤ Fiche de méthodologie N°22 p. 284

Let's RECAP

Lisez les questions-clés et complétez la fiche bilan avec des exemples et des documents que vous avez étudiés ou découverts.

AXE 7 Saving the planet, imagining possible futures

SÉQUENCE 1 How do British citizens deal with sustainability?

E-workbook
Bilan à compléter
hatier-clic.fr/lmu086

What actions do people take to protect the environment in the UK?
How do they raise awareness for a more sustainable way of life?

#ecology
Is ecology becoming a priority in the UK?

#greencities
How do political measures contribute to a more sustainable way of life?

#environmentalpolicies
Are environmental policies efficient in the UK?

#sustainablelifestyle
How are British citizens changing their habits to be more eco-friendly?

#ecofriendly
What can each Briton do to have a positive impact on the environment?

SÉQUENCE 2 Can cli-fi save the world?

E-workbook
Bilan à compléter
hatier-clic.fr/lmu087

How can cli-fi help raise awareness about climate change?
Is cli-fi more or less efficient than using scientific facts?

#thinkofpossibleworlds
How does cli-fi help us think about alternative futures?

#climatechange
How is climate change addressed both in cli-fi and in scientific publications?

#clifi
What is cli-fi? What are this literary genre's characteristics?

#powerofliterature
How can a literature genre help raise awareness about ecological questions?

GO4IT

Lisez et écoutez de l'anglais en dehors de la salle de classe ! Voici quelques conseils en lien avec votre séquence.

SÉQUENCE 1

Books

Mates, Dates And Saving The Planet, CATHY HOPKINS, 2008

Harmony: A New Way of Looking at Our World, HRH THE PRINCE OF WALES, 2010

Under the Weather: Stories About Climate Change, TONY BRADMAN, 2010

50 Ways to Help the Planet: Easy Ways to Live a Sustainable Life, SIAN BERRY, 2018

There Is No Planet B: A Handbook for the Make or Break Year, MIKE BERNERS-LEE, 2019

Film and documentaries

Songs

When You Gonna Learn, JAMIROQUAI, 1993
https://bit.ly/2qU5H59

The Numbers, RADIOHEAD, 2016
https://bit.ly/2dxgyfJ

Websites

Footprint calculator
footprint.wwf.org.uk/#/questionnaire

Eco-friendly tips
friendsoftheearth.uk/latest/lifestyle

SÉQUENCE 2

Books

Starvation Ridge, RISA STEPHANIE BEAR, 2011

The Carbon Diaries 2017, SACI LLOYD, 2010

Floodland, MARCUS SEDGWICK, 2000

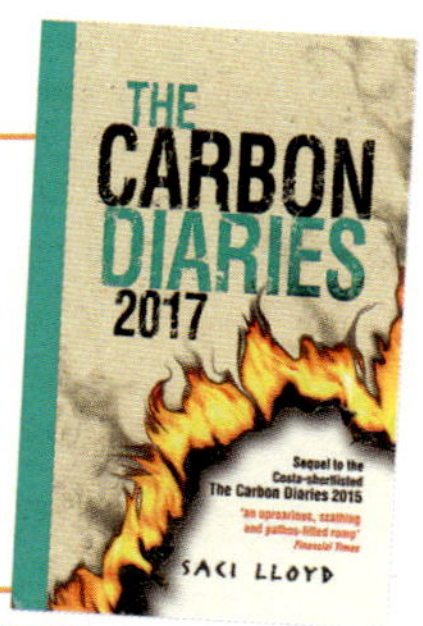

Music

Dear Future Generations: Sorry, PRINCE EA http://bit.ly/1OwxdJQ

Earth Song, MICHAEL JACKSON
http://bit.ly/1igl29b

Love Song To The Earth
http://bit.ly/1M32PdH

Films and documentary

AXE 8

The past in the present

Le passé dans le présent

SÉQUENCE 1

Do American symbols still represent the USA?

Projects

Project #1: Discuss American symbols in a debate.

Project #2: Create a poster for the hall of fame of American symbols.

Tools

Grammaire	le passif, la détermination (Ø et *the*)
Phonologie	l'accent américain
Écriture	l'orthographe américaine
Vocabulaire	les symboles, les valeurs

SÉQUENCE 2

How were Asian immigrants welcomed into the USA?

Projects

Project #1: Make a speech to pay tribute to the Asian immigrants who came to the USA through Angel Island.

Project #2: Write an article to present Angel Island and Asian immigration to the USA.

Tools

Grammaire	le prétérit en *be* + V-*ing*, le *present perfect*
Phonologie	les sons /ɪ/ et /iː/
Écriture	la rédaction d'un article
Vocabulaire	l'immigration, Angel Island

#history #future

#traditions

#memory #identity

Macy's Thanksgiving Parade: the most popular holiday parade in the USA

#immigration #emotions

#identity

#memories #future

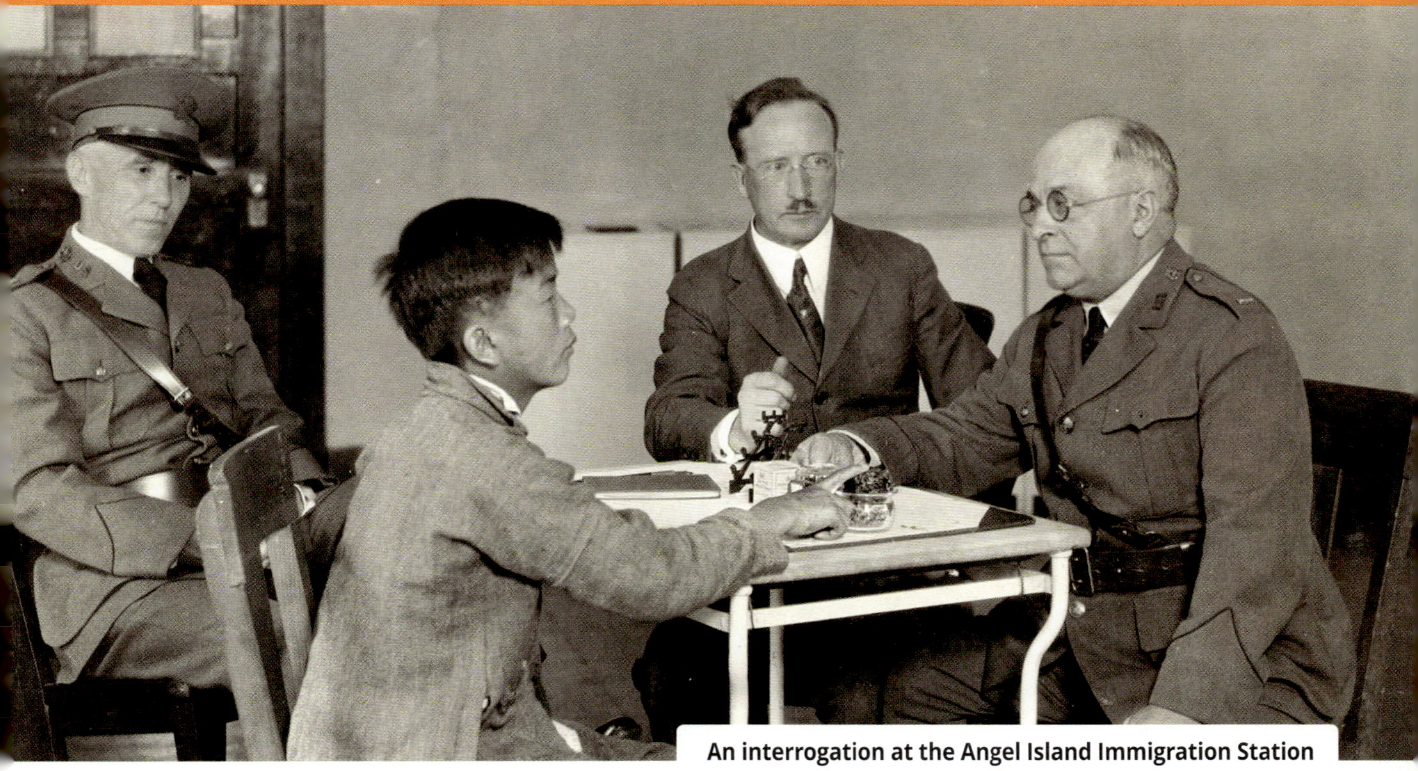

An interrogation at the Angel Island Immigration Station

SÉQUENCE 1 Do American symbols still represent the USA?

A American symbols

GROUP WORK

GROUP A The Great Seal

The most prominent feature is the American bald eagle supporting the shield[1] [...] which is composed of 13 red and white stripes, representing the original States, and a blue top which unites the shield and represents Congress. The motto, *E Pluribus Unum* (Out of many, one), alludes to this union. The olive branch and 13 arrows denote the power of peace and war. [...]

[The Great Seal] appears in some form on coins, postage stamps, stationery[2], publications, flags, military uniforms, public monuments, public buildings, passports. [...] In full color it is displayed[3] above the doors to all US embassies [...] throughout the world.

✦ www.state.gov, July 2003

1. a piece of metal used for protection 2. writing materials especially paper 3. shown

GROUP B American flag: the Stars and Stripes

The flag of the United States of America is a symbol of freedom and liberty to which Americans pledge[1] their allegiance[2] by standing at attention, facing the flag with their right hand over the heart [...]. The flag consists of 13 alternating red and white stripes that represent the 13 original colonies, and 50 white stars on a blue field, with each star representing a state. The colors on the flag represent:

- Red: valor and bravery
- White: purity and innocence
- Blue: vigilance, perseverance, and justice.

✦ www.state.gov, November 8, 2018

1. promise 2. loyalty

Grammar Spot

Articles Ø and the Tools → p. 172

"The flag of the United States of America"

Word Spot

unity	official
value	historical
freedom: liberty	symbolic
symbol: emblem	celebrate
independence	commemorate
pride: to be proud	represent: stand for

GROUP C **Independence Day**

The Fourth of July – also known as Independence Day or July 4th – has been a federal holiday in the United States since 1941, but the tradition of Independence Day celebrations goes back to the 18th century and the American Revolution. On July 2nd, 1776, the Continental Congress voted in favor of independence, and two days later delegates from the 13 colonies adopted the Declaration of Independence, a historic document drafted[1] by Thomas Jefferson. From 1776 to the present day, July 4th has been celebrated as the birth of American independence, with festivities ranging from fireworks, parades and concerts to more casual[2] family gatherings and barbecues.

✦ www.history.com, 2009

1. written 2. informal

GROUP D **The Star-Spangled Banner: the American anthem**

The Star-Spangled Banner[1] is the name given to the national anthem of the USA. The music was adapted from the anthem of a singing club and the words were written by Francis Scott Key. After a century of general use, the four-stanza song was officially adopted as the national anthem by an act of Congress in 1931. […] Key's song became especially popular and a powerful expression of patriotism during the Civil War, with its emotional description of the enduring[2] national flag. […] The national anthem is traditionally sung at the start of major sporting events and it introduced numerous diverse and memorable renditions[3] of *The Star-Spangled Banner*.

✦ www.britannica.com, February 8, 2018 (adapted)

1. flag 2. long existing
3. interpretations

✦ Lady Gaga sings the National Anthem before the Super Bowl, 2016

Pédagogie différenciée

1 Describe your group's picture.

2 Read your text and take notes about the symbol, its meaning and history.

3 Fill in your grid to exchange information about your symbol with other groups.

4 Be ready to answer your classmates' questions.

E-workbook
Fiche à imprimer
hatier-clic.fr/lmu088

Prepare your project

Choose the symbol that you believe best represents the USA. Write a paragraph to explain your choice.

Grammar Tip Précis → p. 207

Use **comparative** and **superlative** forms to justify your choice.

Memory Challenge

Taboo! Choose one symbol and describe it to a classmate without using its name or any of the following words: the USA, freedom, stripes, stars, president, hymn and song.

B A woman for the $20 bill?

Vidéo DVD

E-workbook Fiche à imprimer hatier-clic.fr/lmu089

✦ *Harriet Tubman to replace Andrew Jackson on the $20 bill*, ABC, 2016 (photo by Women On 20s)

Culture Tip

Harriet Tubman (1820-1913) was born as a slave. She escaped to freedom in 1849 and then returned to where she grew up to lead other slaves to freedom. She also became a great advocate for giving women the right to vote.
Andrew Jackson (1767-1845) was the seventh president of the United States. He was a lawyer and a landowner. He founded the Democratic Party and supported slavery's extension into the new western territories. He also played a role in the forced relocation of Native American tribes.

1 Find out the Treasury's plan for the $20 bill.

2 Pick out information about Andrew Jackson and find what opposes him to Harriet Tubman.

3 Focus on the people reacting to the news and describe their reactions.

4 Choose an American celebrity and write the messages he or she posted on social media commenting on Harriet Tubman on the $20 bill.

C Traditions stronger than change

The Trump administration signaled on Thursday that the black abolitionist Harriet Tubman may not replace President Andrew Jackson on the $20 bill after all.
Treasury Secretary Steven Mnuchin declined to endorse[1] the plan for a 2020 redesign of the $20 bill that was announced by the Obama administration last year.
"People have been on the bills for a long period of time," Mr. Mnuchin told CNBC. "This is something we'll consider. Right now we've got a lot more important issues to focus on."
President Trump […] made clear as a candidate that he didn't like the proposal to replace Jackson. "I would love to leave Andrew Jackson […]" he said in April 2016, after the decision was announced.
At the time, Mr. Trump mentioned the $2 bill for Tubman. It circulates in the smallest volume of any bill, about seven times less than the $20. "I think it would be more appropriate," he said.
Mr. Trump […] traveled to Tennessee in March to celebrate Jackson's 250th birthday […] at The Hermitage, the plantation where Jackson kept more than 100 slaves. […] Mr. Trump also put a portrait of Jackson in the Oval Office.

✦ Binyamin Appelbaum, *The New York Times*, August 31, 2017

1. declined to endorse: refused to support

1 Find the connection between the $20 bill, Tubman and Jackson.

2 Describe the opinion of the Trump administration. Explain the disadvantages of choosing the $2 bill for Tubman.

3 Create a mind map showing the differences between the decisions of the Obama and Trump administrations on American symbols. Use it to explain these differences to your history teacher.

Grammar Spot

Passive form TOOLS → p. 172
"The plan that was announced by the Obama administration."

Word Spot

slave owner: sbdy who possesses slaves
the US Department of the Treasury
struggle: fight
abolitionist: person who wanted to end slavery
outstanding: exceptional
deserve: merit, be worthy of

D Taking down Confederate symbols

Classe inversée

Audio
CD2 piste 23
MP3 n° 124

E-workbook
Classe inversée
hatier-clic.fr/lmu090

1 Read the Culture Tip and look at the map. Explain what was wrong with the Confederacy.

2 Listen to the interview and focus on repetitions, proper names and stressed words. Write down as much information as you can.

3 ***PAIR WORK*** Compare the information you have with a classmate and write a short paragraph about the recording.

✦ General Lee's statue taken off, New Orleans, May 19, 2017

Culture Tip

The Confederate States of America was the government of 11 southern states which separated from the Union in 1860–61. They left the Union as they believed that their way of life, based on slavery, was in danger with the election of Abraham Lincoln in 1860. The war between the northern and southern states, also known as the **Civil War**, started in 1861 and ended in 1865 when all the Confederate forces surrendered and the Confederacy ended.

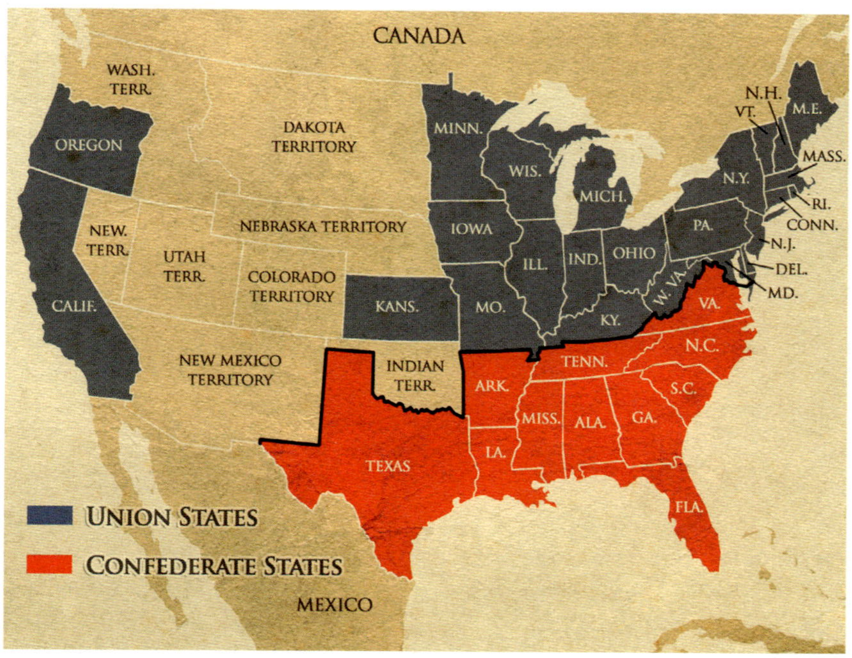

Prepare your project

PAIR WORK Act out an interview between a journalist and an American mayor who decided to remove a Confederate statue.

Student A You are the mayor.

Student B You are the journalist.

Grammar Tip

Précis → p. 214

Pay attention to the word order in your **questions**: (Wh- or How) + aux. + subject + verb + (object)?

Memory Challenge

Words to recap. Write these five words on a piece of paper, close your textbook and tell your classmate what happened in New Orleans.

landmark remove opponents debate Confederate

Tools in the Spotlight

Practise your grammar

Précis grammatical, p. 192

Le passif

- On utilise le passif pour mettre en valeur **ce que quelqu'un ou quelque chose subit**. C'est le sujet de la phrase, mais ce n'est pas lui qui fait l'action.

*The monument **was destroyed**.*

→ Le sujet subit l'action, il n'en est pas à l'origine.

- On utilise aussi le passif comme équivalent du pronom impersonnel « **on** ».

*The athlete **was told** to apologise.*

→ On ignore ou on ne veut pas dévoiler l'identité de l'auteur de l'action.

- Le passif se forme avec l'auxiliaire *be* (à tous les temps) + participe passé (+ *by*).
  - participe passé → verbe + *-d ou -ed* ou verbes irréguliers p. 231
  - *by* introduit celui ou celle à l'origine de l'action (le complément d'agent)

*The statue **was taken** down **by** the city.*

La détermination : Ø et *the*

- Le déterminant zéro (Ø) est très courant et, comme son nom l'indique, consiste en l'absence de déterminant.

On l'utilise :
  - devant des **noms dénombrables indéfinis.**

"A nationwide debate over Ø Confederate symbols."

→ des symboles indéfinis
  - pour renvoyer à une **notion**, une **idée** (abstraite) ou un **nom indénombrable** (*water*, *bread*...).

"Some argue they represent Ø slavery and Ø injustice."

→ les notions d'esclavage et d'injustice

- Le déterminant *the* correspond à « le, la, les » en français. L'article défini s'emploie quand on pense que son interlocuteur·trice sait déjà de quoi on parle ou pour parler d'un **élément précis**. Sa valeur s'apparente à celle du démonstratif français. On le trouve aussi devant certains noms de pays (*the USA*).

*"**The** statues were erected decades after **the** Civil War."*

→ les statues dont on vient de parler : celles-ci

*"Ignoring **the** terror that it actually stood for."*

→ la terreur qu'elle représente : pas n'importe laquelle

1 Mettez les phrases suivantes au passif.

a. New Orleans Council is removing four statues.
b. The mayor of Baltimore ordered the removal of four monuments.
c. Protesters took down a statue of a Confederate soldier in Durham.
d. The City Council in Lexington approved a proposal to remove two statues.

2 Observez cette photo et utilisez les informations et les verbes proposés pour écrire un court article au passif.

remove • set up • express

Landmark: statue of Robert E. Lee
Place: Bronx Community College
Installation: 1923
Reactions: some: relief; others: anger

3 Complétez ce texte avec Ø ou *the*.

... state of Louisiana in ... USA is considering a measure to remove ... war memorials including those from ... Civil War. ... law would let ... local governments take down a statue, for example, if ... voters approved it during a referendum.
In ... South Carolina, a Confederate flag was removed from ... statehouse grounds after ... people protested for ... decades because it is a symbol of ... Confederacy. ... activists were happy with the removal. ... flag had been placed on ... Capitol dome in ... 1960s.

4 Utilisez les mots suivants pour expliquer pourquoi Harriet Tubman figurera peut-être sur le billet de 20 dollars. Choisissez entre Ø et *the*.

slavery • slaves • fight • southern states • freedom • pride

Improve your pronunciation

Précis de phonologie, p. 242

L'accent américain

Audio CD2 piste 24 MP3 n° 125

• Alors qu'avec l'accent britannique, **le « t »** est toujours prononcé de façon distincte, les Américains ont souvent tendance à le vocaliser afin qu'il soit perçu comme un « d », quand il se trouve au milieu d'un mot. Par exemple : dans *totally*, le premier « t » reste en général prononcé /t/, mais le second devient /d/ en anglais américain.

• Là où l'anglais américain implique de prononcer tous **les « r »** présents dans les mots, en Grande-Bretagne, et surtout en Angleterre, seuls les « r » qui précèdent des voyelles sont prononcés. Par exemple : dans *bird* /bɜrd/, le « r » ne s'entend pas s'il est prononcé avec l'accent anglais.

5 Écoutez l'enregistrement. La lettre « t » dans cette phrase est-elle prononcée /t/ ou /d/ ?

Audio CD2 piste 25 MP3 n° 126

"I want to quote a letter to the editors of the *Times-Picayune*, a writer, a citizen named Charles Foy of Madisonville."

6 Écoutez les mots suivants. Ils sont prononcés avec deux accents différents. Précisez lequel est dit avec l'accent américain.

Audio CD2 piste 26 MP3 n° 127

a. better b. quarterback c. supporting d. voted

7 Écoutez ces mots prononcés par cette présentatrice américaine à propos du nouveau billet de 20 dollars. Puis répétez-les à l'identique.

Audio CD2 piste 27 MP3 n° 128

morning • former • pouring • over • leaders • better

Work on your writing skills

L'orthographe américaine

• L'accent n'est pas la seule différence entre l'anglais britannique et l'américain. Il existe aussi des **différences orthographiques** dont voici les principales.

-our	labour, harbour, honour	-or	labor, harbor, honor
-se	analyse, criticise	-ze	analyze, criticize
-re	centre, litre	-er	center, liter
-amme	programme	-am	program
-ogue	dialogue	-og	dialog
-que	cheque	-ck	check
-ll	cancelled, skillful	-l	canceled, skilful
-l	fulfil	-ll	fulfill
-ence	defence, licence	-ense	defense, license
-ge	judgement	-g	judgment

• Cinq **verbes irréguliers** en anglais britannique sont réguliers en anglais américain : *burn, dream, leap, learn, spell*. Leur prétérit et leur participe passé s'écrivent donc avec *-ed* à la fin.

8 Indiquez si les phrases suivantes sont écrites en anglais britannique ou en américain.

a. She visited the city center, then went to the theater on Broadway.
b. Can you do me a favour and analyse this text by Hemingway, please? Then, I need to memorise it.
c. What is your favorite color? Here is a calalog for you to choose from.
d. He wrote a cheque at Macy's in New York, then cancelled it.

9 Réécrivez en anglais britannique.

a. He likes traveling and received his driver's license in New Orleans.
b. A large skillful labor force was used to build this new harbor in California.
c. The defense of the national anthem is both a priority and an honor. That's why it is on the program in quite a few US high schools.

Build up your vocabulary

Audio
CD2 piste 28

American symbols

Values — MP3 n°129

independence
unity
justice
freedom of speech
trust: confidence ≠ distrust
fairness: justice
fair: just ≠ unfair

Money — MP3 n°130

US Department of the Treasury
Secretary of the Treasury
currency: money used in a country
coin
(bank)note (*UK*): bill (*US*): paper money

Reasons — MP3 n°134

pride: to be proud
outstanding: exceptional
historical
celebrate
commemorate
represent: characterise
deserve: merit, be worthy of
praise: acclaim
stand out: be different from
embody: represent
symbolise

Physical symbols — MP3 n°131

the Founding Fathers
figures: important people
symbol: emblem
landmark: symbolic monument or place
statue
pedestal
official

Challenging symbols — MP3 n°133

crowd: group of people
activist: militant
demonstration: march
opponent ≠ supporter
value
significance
conflicting views: diverging opinions
memory: common knowledge of history
dubious: ambiguous
protest
remove: take down / away
be opposed to ≠ be in favour of
gather: assemble
right a wrong: correct sthg bad

Slavery — MP3 n°132

Confederacy: Confederate States: slave states
abolitionist: person who wanted to end slavery
slave owner: sbdy who possesses slaves
freedom: liberty
struggle: fight

Apprenez et révisez le vocabulaire !

Utilisez Quizlet pour vous entraîner en vous amusant.

Quizlet
hatier-clic.fr/lmu091

Utilisez le vocabulaire en contexte.

1 Complétez les phrases suivantes avec des mots de la carte mentale.

a. The Fourth of July celebrates the ... of the United States.
b. The bear is the ... of California.
c. Having Harriet Tubman on the $20 bill ... ...
d. Statues ... historical figures or events.
e. There was a lot of discussion before deciding to ... the statues of the Confederates.

2 Écrivez trois phrases sur l'évolution des symboles aux États-Unis en utilisant ces mots issus de la carte mentale.

embody | opposed to | commemorate | historical emblem

AUTO évaluation

Faites le quiz interactif en ligne et suivez les conseils pour vous préparer à l'évaluation.

Quiz
hatier-clic.fr/lmu092

Project #1

Discuss American symbols in a debate.

1 **Create your character: an expert in traditional American symbols or a member of an organisation that promotes the evolution of American symbols.**

- ✓ Choose your character depending on what you are more comfortable with.
- ✓ Prepare your character (name, job, personality, etc.).

2 **Prepare your arguments.**

- ✓ Read the unit to find arguments.
- ✓ Use examples to support your views.
- ✓ Use **should** and **must** to say which decisions need to be made.
  Ex: You **should** remove...
  You **must** remember...

3 **Discuss!**

- ✓ Don't read your notes: only use a list of 10 to 15 words.
- ✓ Act and be convincing!
- ✓ Use linking words to structure your arguments: **first**, **moreover**, **however**, **finally**...
- ✓ Watch the time!

➤ Fiche de méthodologie N°19 p. 278

Project #2

Create a poster for the hall of fame of American symbols.

1 **Choose your symbol(s).**

- ✓ Pick your symbol(s) in the unit or other American symbol(s) you are familiar with: be original in your choice!
- ✓ Your symbol can be traditional or modern.

2 **Collect the information you need for your poster.**

- ✓ Use your copybook and the work you have done in class.
- ✓ Do some research on the internet.
- ✓ Don't copy and paste, write your own paragraphs.

3 **Write short paragraphs explaining why you chose that or these symbol(s).**

- ✓ Use linking words to justify your choice: **because**, **that's why**, **since**, **as**...
- ✓ Remember to use the **preterite** when you introduce your choice. Ex: I **chose** this symbol... The symbol I **chose** is...

4 **Now, make your poster. The creations can be put together to form a hall of fame!**

- ✓ There are many ways to present your poster: you can draw your symbol or take an image from the internet.
- ✓ You can use websites like *Canva* or *Youblisher* for a cool layout!

➤ Fiche de méthodologie N°5 p. 254 N°9 p. 261

SÉQUENCE 2

How were Asian immigrants welcomed into the USA?

A Traces from the past

1 Describe the monument and its surroundings.

2 Read the translation below and guess the reason why it was built.

3 List the verbs used in the poem. Explain what they reveal about these immigrants' lives.

"Leaving their homes and villages,
they crossed the ocean
Only to endure confinement in these barracks;
Conquering frontiers and barriers
they pioneered
A new life by the Golden Gate."

NGOOT P. CHIN

✦ Monument near the United States Immigration Station, Angel Island, San Francisco

B The Ellis Island of the West

Vidéo
DVD

1 Pick out information about the person talking (country of origin, dates, family).

2 Focus on numbers and dates to explain what Angel Island consisted in.

3 Focus on emotions and explain how the speaker felt there.

4 Explain the statement: "You have to prove yourself."

✦ *US immigration history preserved on Angel Island*, AP Archive, 2009

Culture Tip

The first major wave of **Asian immigration to the USA** started in the 1850s during the California Gold Rush. The population of Asian immigrants increased until the Chinese Exclusion Act of 1882. Asian immigration was then controlled and it is only after the Second World War that Asian immigrants could become naturalised citizens or own property in the USA.

Grammar Spot

Preterite V-ing Tools → p. 180

"Alexander Weiss **was roaming** the site when he discovered..."

Word Spot

- newcomer
- gatekeeper: a person who controls access
- immigrate
- travel by ship
- be processed (through Angel Island)
- be held in detention: be in captivity: be detained
- disembark
- be intimidated
- endure: experience sthg difficult
- be interrogated: be questioned
- prove yourself: show that you are good
- cross the ocean

C Angel Island Immigration Station

PAIR WORK

✦ The Angel Island Immigration Station today

1 Divide the picture in two parts (right and left) and describe your part to a classmate.

2 Pick out the words carved on the steps on your part and guess what or who they refer to.

3 Make suppositions about the presence of the carved words on the stairs.

D Historical testimonies in poems

Classe inversée

In 1970, Alexander Weiss, a state park ranger at the time, was roaming[1] the site when he discovered that nearly every square inch of its walls was covered in carvings in multiple languages. Some were simple messages, affirmations like "I was here" followed by a date. Others were impassioned works of poetry, cries of anger, frustration, sorrow, and despair from the detainees[2] whose dreams of a better life in the land of opportunity were brutally cut short by racist legislation. Mostly written in Chinese by poets who spoke Cantonese or Toisanese dialects, the poems as much speak about the poverty-stricken, turbulent pasts the authors left behind and their current frustrations as they reach out to immigrants to come, encouraging them to work hard to succeed in the United States. Numbering nearly 135, the poems seem to have been the result of collaborative efforts on the part of multiple authors detained at the station for a period of months or years, who, by the poems' various allusions to Confucius or Chinese literary or folkloric heroes, were well educated and highly literate[3]. Meticulous restoration of the carvings, obscured by age and a government covering up its missteps[4], is now underway[5]. We can understand how Weiss knew immediately that the site had to be saved.

✦ www.ked.com, March 16, 2014

1. walking around 2. forced residents, prisoners 3. well educated 4. errors, mistakes 5. in progress

E-workbook
Classe inversée
hatier-clic.fr/lmu093

1 Explain how the poems were discovered and who wrote them.

2 Find out how and why they were written. Summarise the feelings they convey.

3 Find out two reasons why the carvings had to be restored (l. 21-25).

4 Explain in your own words why it is important to restore such sites.

Culture Tip

The **Angel Island Immigration Station** opened in 1910 and closed in 1940. During these thirty years, a total of 500,000 immigrants were processed through the Immigration Station. Most of them were Chinese and were detained for weeks, even months.

Prepare your project

Convince a friend to come visit the Angel Island Immigration Station with you. Explain why it is interesting and important to go there.

Grammar Tip Précis → p. 227
Use **should** to express advice.

Memory Challenge

In pairs, choose five adjectives each to describe detention on Angel Island. Compare your choices.

E David, 8 years old : "paper son"

Alone on Angel Island: David Leong's story

His [family] put eight-year-old David on the boat for America to join his father who was already in the United States. […]

David came to the United States in 1940 as a paper son, the son of a son of a native. He used false papers his father had purchased[1], and he had to familiarize himself with his fake[2] story and family history. He also had a set of "coaching papers," which described where he was living, how many siblings[3] he had, his father's name, and other basic family information. […]

While David's aunt and cousins – American citizens – disembarked at San Francisco, David was sent on to Angel Island. […]

Three to four weeks after arriving at Angel Island, it was finally time for David's interrogation. He entered a small […] room with just a desk and several chairs. There, a Caucasian[4] interrogator, assisted by an interpreter, peppered[5] him with questions about his parents, siblings, and birthplace. […] On paper, David's name was Chan Way Tong. The initial interrogation lasted just thirty to forty-five minutes, although David underwent two or three interrogations before leaving Angel Island. When David learned he passed[6] the interrogation process, he remembers feeling proud. But reuniting with his father was a somewhat strange experience, as his father felt like a stranger to David.

✦ www.aiisf.org (adapted)

1. bought 2. not true 3. brothers and sisters 4. white person 5. (here) asked him many questions 6. succeeded

Culture Tip

The Chinese Exclusion Act was a federal law signed in 1882 following an anti-Chinese movement in the second half of the 19th century. This act prohibited the immigration of Chinese workers to the USA. It was the first law that prohibited a specific group from immigrating. It was abandoned in 1943. Chinese immigration started to increase again from 1952 onwards.

Pédagogie différenciée

TRAIL A

1 Find information about David (age, family).

2 Focus on the type of information on coaching papers and create an empty one. Explain why they were used.

3 In the last paragraph, pick out information about the interrogations and show they were difficult for an 8-year-old.

4 Explain what the role of interrogations was.

TRAIL B

1 Find as much information as possible on David.

2 Focus on the type of information on coaching papers and create one. Try to complete it for David. Explain why they were used.

3 Use some words taken from the text and form a sentence to show why interrogations were difficult.

4 Explain why David was happy when he succeeded the interrogation process.

Meet up! You are David's biographer. Write about his experience as a paper son and his experience on Angel Island.

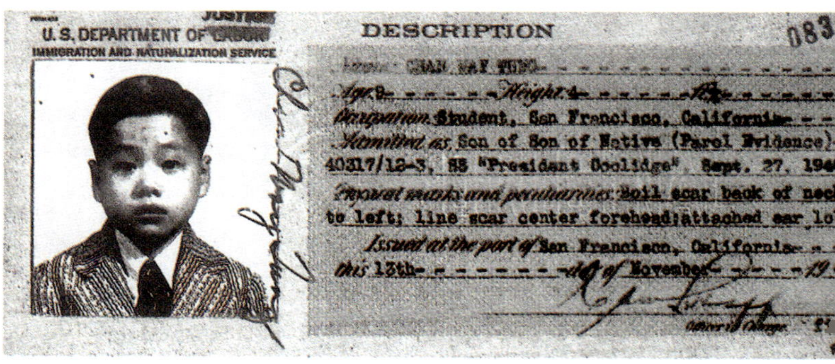

Grammar Spot

Present perfect TOOLS → p. 180

"an organization that **has researched** paper sons"

Word Spot

last name: family name: surname
relative: member of your family
illegally
recall: remember
disembark
assume or take a new identity
be deported: be forced to leave a country

F "Paper sons"

Audio
CD2 piste 29

1 Listen to the recording and state the woman's name and which family member she is speaking about.

2 Explain her discovery and her reactions to that discovery.

3 Explain the consequences this revelation has on her descendants today.

4 Give the reasons why the "paper sons" system was invented.

G Don Lee: my arrival and my interrogation

While I was at the Angel Island Immigration Station, I went for interrogations. […] I know I gave wrong answers and all that. That's why they kept me there 28 days. […]
I was interrogated maybe three or four times. They lasted up to half an hour. I was intimidated because I was only 11 years old. […] There was an official sitting there, with a secretary, typing. There was a translator, and there was a guard. […] The Chinese interpreter was pretty much professional. He wasn't smiling. He didn't try to help me. […] There was a blackboard with the numbers on it. Everybody's got a number. I think my number — I wrote it down — is 80340. They would put your number up there on the blackboard, and you know you have to go to interrogation. They didn't use names. […] The only other thing I remember is that on the day they let you go, your number is on the blackboard and it says "San Francisco".

✦ www.aiisf.org

1 Find information about Don Lee (age, nationality, place of detention).

2 Focus on numbers. Describe the interrogation and find out how many times Don Lee was interrogated.

3 Pick out expressions of feelings and show that the time spent on Angel Island was difficult.

4 In your own words, write a tweet about Don Lee's story. Use hashtags for your key words to make your tweet more visible.

H Memorial of all Asian immigrants

✦ *Preserving Angel Islands' role in US immigration history*, Assembly CA, 2016

Vidéo
DVD

E-workbook
Fiche à imprimer
hatier-clic.fr/lmu094

1 Watch the video. Focus on nationalities and places and try to deduce the goal of this speech.

2 Pick out information and visual details explaining why the speaker compares Angel Island to Ellis Island.

3 Explain why it is important to celebrate Angel Island as a historical spot.

Prepare your project

You are a journalist for the *San Francisco Chronicle*. Write a short article about a person who came to the United States as a "paper son or daughter".

Grammar Tip Précis → p. 220

Use the **preterite** to tell his or her story.

Memory Challenge

Talk about the "paper son or daughter system" without using the words immigration, Chinese, detention, USA and exclusion.

Entraînez-vous sur la plateforme *Let's Meet Up!*
reussirenlangues.fr

Practise your grammar

Précis grammatical, p. 192

Le prétérit en *be* + V-*ing*

- Le prétérit en *be* + V-*ing* signale qu'**une action** était **en cours** à un moment du passé.
- À la différence du prétérit simple qui indique une action vue dans son ensemble, le prétérit en *be* + V-*ing* n'indique pas que la fin de l'action est atteinte.
Il correspond généralement à l'imparfait en français.

*He **was coming** to the Great Hall when the officials stopped him.*

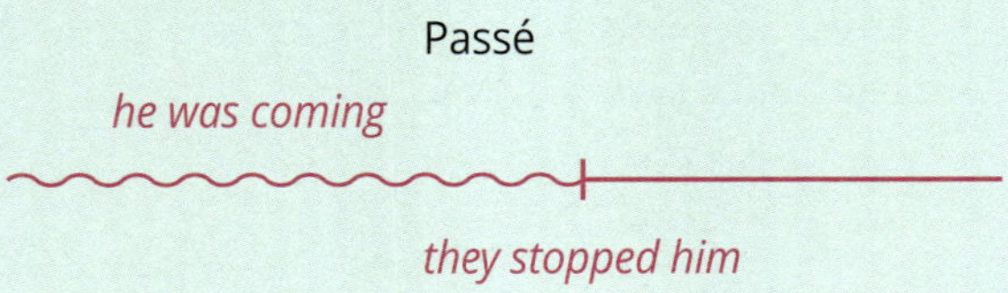

1 Conjuguez le verbe entre parenthèses au prétérit simple ou au prétérit en *be* + V-*ing*.

a. You ... (look) scared when the official ... (ask) you questions.
b. I last ... (see) him in Japan. He ... (tell) me he ... (take) a boat to America and that he ... (try) to fulfil the American Dream.
c. Who ... (talk) to you when I ... (meet) you at the port?
d. She ... (think) about her new life when the boat ... (arrive) in America.
e. The immigrants ... (go) to America when a storm ... (slow) them down.
f. While the officer ... (interview) me, I ... (begin) to panic.
g. When we ... (arrive) on Angel Island, the sun ... (shine).

Le *present perfect*

- Le *present perfect* est un aspect du présent. Il établit **un lien entre un moment passé et un moment présent**. On s'intéresse au **bilan** présent d'un événement passé.
- Il se forme à l'aide de l'auxiliaire *have* et du participe passé du verbe (verbe + *-d* ou *-ed* pour les verbes réguliers, ou verbes irréguliers listés p. 231).

*Angel Island **hasn't acquired** the same reputation as its counterpart, Ellis Island, on the East Coast.*

➝ **notion de bilan** : Angel Island n'a pas réussi à être aussi connue qu'Ellis Island à l'est des États-Unis.

- Le *present perfect* est souvent accompagné d'**adverbes** qui établissent un lien entre le présent et un événement passé : *already*, *ever*, *never*, *yet*, *just*, *since*, *for*, *recently*, *lately*.

__Have__ you ever __been__ to Angel Island?
No, I __have__ never __been__ there.

*He **has** already **visited** Angel Island twice.*

*She **has** recently **discovered** that her grandfather was a paper son.*

2 Conjuguez au *present perfect* le verbe donné à la forme indiquée.

Ex. travel (I) / forme affirmative ➝ I have travelled.
a. visit the Angel Island museum (he) / forme négative.
b. leave (they) / forme interrogative
c. spend days on Angel Island (he) / forme affirmative
d. forget (we) / forme négative
e. think about your family (you) / forme interrogative

3 Dans les phrases suivantes, conjuguez le verbe entre parenthèses au prétérit ou au *present perfect*.

a. I ... (not read) about Angel Island last year.
b. I ... (travel) to the USA and ... (settle) down in California fifteen years ago.
c. I ... recently (travel) the world to see the differences with my homeland.
d. You ever ... (see) so many people on a boat?
e. I ... (buy) already my plane ticket to go back to Japan and see my family during the holiday.
f. The immigration officer ... (know) he was interviewing a paper son.
g. Do you know when the Immigration Station ... (close)?

Improve your pronunciation

Précis de phonologie, p. 242

Les sons /ɪ/ et /iː/

Audio
CD2 piste 30
MP3 n° 135

- Le son /ɪ/, voyelle brève, peut correspondre à la graphie :
  - age (*village*, *sausage*, *hostage*)
  - e (*women*)
  - i (*pick*, *sick*, *pin*)
  - o (*women*)
  - u (*minute*)
  - ui (*building*)
  - y (*myth*)
- Le son /iː/, voyelle longue, peut correspondre à la graphie :
  - e (*be*)
  - ea (*meat*, *beat*)
  - ee (*bee*, *meet*)
  - ei (*seize*)
  - i (*police*)
  - ie (*believe*)

4 Écoutez les mots suivants et classez-les en fonction de leur prononciation.

Audio
CD2 piste 31
MP3 n° 136

Chinese • immigration • speak • speech • sea • uneasy • cheap • Pacific • descent • see • citizen • ship • sheep • sleep

/ɪ/	/iː/
...	...

5 Indiquez dans les phrases suivantes si les voyelles soulignées correspondent au son /ɪ/ ou /iː/, puis vérifiez avec l'enregistrement.

Audio
CD2 piste 32
MP3 n° 137

a. Asian immigrant history leads us to study Angel Island.
b. Some Chinese workers decided to leave America.
c. Immigrants suffered from the heat when California was hit by dog days.
d. Industrious immigrants keep working hard.

Work on your writing skills

La rédaction d'un article

- Le rôle d'un article de presse est d'informer et de permettre au lecteur de se faire une opinion personnelle. Il convient donc de rester neutre et de faire intervenir des avis extérieurs en citant ses sources.
- Le premier paragraphe résume l'idée principale (*who*, *where*, *when*, *what*), les suivants déclinent des aspects précis (un paragraphe = un aspect).
- Mentionnez les faits, les circonstances, les causes et éventuelles conséquences dans un registre courant mais soigné. Évitez donc les contractions.
- Les arguments employés doivent être illustrés par des exemples concrets et des repères temporels pour ancrer la situation.
- Les mots de liaison doivent faire apparaître la logique de votre propos.
- Donnez un titre clair, concis à votre article après l'avoir rédigé. Vous pouvez également ajouter un sous-titre explicatif.

6 Reliez les phrases suivantes avec le mot de liaison adapté.

and yet • consequently • because • although

a. Many immigrants were separated from their families ... they felt isolated.
b. Some Chinese immigrants were lost ... they didn't speak English.
c. Some other immigrants did not speak English ... they could understand some words.
d. ... it was a difficult experience, she never regretted coming to the USA.

7 Rédigez le premier paragraphe d'un article sur les immigrés passés par Angel Island intitulé *Painful memories*.

Build up your vocabulary

Audio
CD2 piste 33

天使島 Angel Island

Detention
MP3 n°142

newcomer
gatekeeper: a person who controls access
travel by ship
be processed (through Angel Island)
be held in detention: be in captivity: be detained
be intimidated
endure: experience sthg difficult
be interrogated: be questioned
prove yourself: show that you are good

Negative emotions
MP3 n°138

alone
lonely
miserable
worried: concerned
afraid: scared
horrified
embarrassed: ashamed
uneasy: uncomfortable

Museums and memories
MP3 n°139

preservation
protection
restoration
historical
relevant
interesting
enriching
moving: provoking emotions
carved: engraved
commemorate: pay tribute to
remember
symbolise
preserve
recall: remember
acknowledge: recognise

Immigration
MP3 n°141

immigration station
waves of immigration
illegally
immigrate
disembark
be deported: be forced to leave a country
banish
come over by ship: cross by ship
cross the ocean

Origins and family
MP3 n°140

last name: family name: surname
relative: member of your family
homeland: native country
descent: origins
assume or take a new identity
descend from sb: be related to sb

Apprenez et révisez le vocabulaire !

Utilisez Quizlet pour vous entraîner en vous amusant.

Quizlet
hatier-clic.fr/lmu095

Utilisez le vocabulaire en contexte.

1 Complétez les phrases suivantes avec des mots de la carte mentale.

a. Angel Island is an … … located on the West Coast of the USA.
b. Many people were … through Angel Island.
c. They were … by officers and after, they could be held in detention for days.
d. It was a humiliating experience for many immigrants who felt … and … .
e. The memory of Angel Island lives on through the poems … on the walls.
f. The first Asian … of … to the USA started in the 1850s during the California Gold Rush.

2 Utilisez ce que vous avez appris sur Angel Island pour expliquer pourquoi il est important que les musées conservent les traces du passé. Utilisez dix mots de la carte mentale.

AUTO évaluation

Faites le quiz interactif en ligne et suivez les conseils pour vous préparer à l'évaluation.

Quiz
hatier-clic.fr/lmu096

Project #1

To celebrate Immigrant Day, make a speech to pay tribute to the Asian immigrants who came to the USA through Angel Island.

1 Collect information and organise your thoughts.

- ✓ Use your notes in your copybook and do some research on the internet.
- ✓ Organise your ideas in a list or a mind map.

2 Write short paragraphs. Be careful with the structure of your speech.

- ✓ Write an introduction. Talk about historical events and the role played by Asians in the USA. Don't forget your conclusion!
- ✓ Use linking words: **and**, **that's why**, **furthermore**...

3 Practise.

- ✓ Practice reading your speech aloud and stressing keywords.
- ✓ Check the pronunciation of difficult words on an online dictionary.

4 Deliver your speech.

- ✓ You can use gap fillers to sound more natural: **so**, **well**, **in fact**...
- ✓ Only use a list of ten words when performing your speech.

➤ Fiche de méthodologie N°5 p. 254 N°22 p. 284

Project #2

Write an article to present Angel Island and Asian immigration to the USA.

1 Think about the ideas you want to put forward.

- ✓ Use some strong ideas from the materials you have studied.
- ✓ Do some research on the internet.
- ✓ Organise your ideas by taking notes.

2 Draft an outline of your ideas.

- ✓ Decide which story is the most interesting to tell and use precise examples.
- ✓ Put forward what moved you.

3 Staying on Angel Island.

- ✓ Talk about the detention and interrogation conditions.
- ✓ Express emotions with verbs like **feel**, **fear**, **hope**, **hate**...

4 It's important to remember!

- ✓ Show why we must remember what happened to Asian immigrants in Angel Island.
- ✓ Give your personal opinion.

5 Check your article like a journalist!

- ✓ Read carefully to check for grammar and vocabulary mistakes.
- ✓ Think about the mistakes you usually make.

➤ Fiche de méthodologie N°5 p. 254 N°7 p. 258

Let's RECAP

Lisez les questions-clés et complétez la fiche bilan avec des exemples et des documents que vous avez étudiés ou découverts.

SÉQUENCE 1 Do American symbols still represent the USA?

E-workbook
Bilan à compléter
hatier-clic.fr/lmu097

How is American society dealing with its history?
Are all American symbols still relevant today?

#history
How are American symbols used to commemorate history and traditions?

#future
Can the USA build its future by remembering its past?

#traditions
To what extent are some American traditions criticised today?

#identity
Can symbols shape a nation by bringing people together?

#memory
How are American symbols a way to remember the country's history?

AXE 8 | The past in the present

SÉQUENCE 2 How were Asian immigrants welcomed in the USA?

E-workbook
Bilan à compléter
hatier-clic.fr/lmu098

How can Asian immigration help define what the USA is today?
How essential is it for Asian Americans to remember their past?

#identity
How did the past help Asian immigrants shape their American identity?

#emotions
Is celebrating the past a means of demonstrating that emotions are still vivid today?

#future
Why do you need to know where you come from to build your life?

#memories
Why is Angel Island an important place of memory?

#immigration
Why is it important to learn more about Asian immigration to the USA?

GO4IT!

Lisez et écoutez de l'anglais en dehors de la salle de classe ! Voici quelques conseils en lien avec votre séquence.

SÉQUENCE 1

Books

Alexander Hamilton: The Graphic History of an American Founding Father, Jonathan Hennessey, Justin Greenwood, 2017

Who was Harriet Tubman?, Yona Zeldis McDonough, 2002

Music

10 Best Super Bowl National Anthem Performances, Rolling Stone magazine
http://bit.ly/2go8u35

Video

Deconstructing History: American Flag, History Channel
http://bit.ly/2u7RzLw

Films and documentary

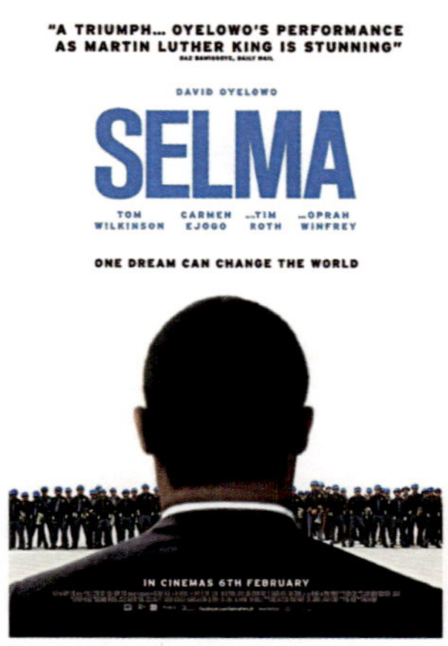

SÉQUENCE 2

Books

Island: Poetry and History of Chinese Immigrants on Angel Island, 1910-1940, Him Mark Lai, Genny Lim & Judy Yung, 1980

Angel Island Immigrant Gateway to America, Erika Lee & Judy Yung, 2010

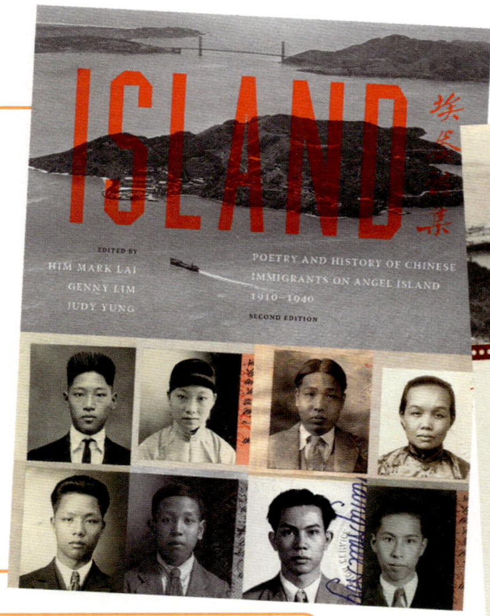

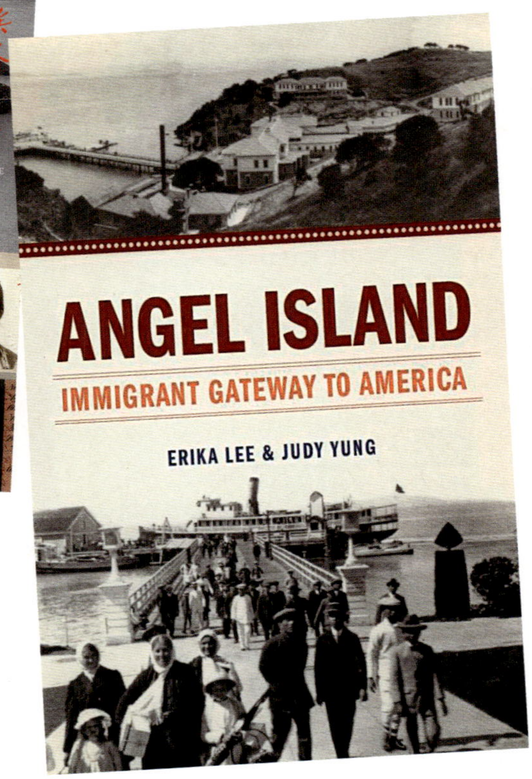

Videos

Channel of the Angel Island Immigration Station Foundation, AIISF
http://bit.ly/2nO53FK

Angel Island Immigration Station Tour, AIISF
http://bit.ly/2FQhQyP

Angel Island: Immigrant Gateway to America, The Gilder Lehrman Institute
http://bit.ly/2FYnQGl

Country ID United Kingdom

Population: 66,040,229

The United Kingdom is made up of England (cap. London), Wales (cap. Cardiff), Scotland (cap. Edinburgh) and Northern Ireland (cap. Belfast). The UK has retained strong links with its former empire through the Commonwealth. The UK has a parliamentary government whose model has spread all over the world: a legacy of its Empire! The parliament is composed of an elected House of Commons and an appointed House of Lords. All bills passed have to be given Royal Assent before becoming a law.

2016
UK votes to leave the European Union in a referendum (BREXIT).

2009
Saci Lloyd, ***The Carbon Diaries***
P.157

1997
Labour Party under **Tony Blair** wins landslide election victory.

1984 - 1985
Miners' strikes.
P.138

1994
Channel Tunnel opened rail link between Britain and rest of Europe.

1981
Prince Charles marries **Lady Diana** Spencer.

1940
Winston Churchill becomes prime minister.

1979
Conservative politician **Margaret Thatcher** becomes prime minister.

1903
Suffragette movement founded

1848
Robert Fortune

1883
Robert Louis Stevenson, ***Treasure Island***

1801
United Kingdom formed by union of the kingdoms of Great Britain and Ireland

1337
Hundred Years' War with France begin.

1746
First recorded performance of a play written by Shakespeare
P.130

1650 - 1730
Golden Age of Piracy

2000 BC
Stonehenge completed

Country ID USA

Population: 327,167,434
The United States is the world's greatest economic power, measured in terms of Gross Domestic product (GDP). It is also the fourth largest country by total area (slightly smaller than Europe, divided into 50 states) and the third most populous country. This is a fairly "young" country (less than 250 years old).
The constitution provides a separation of powers: legislative (Congress, Senate and House of Representatives which make laws), executive (President, Vice-President and Cabinet which carry out laws) and judicial (Supreme Court and other federal courts which interpret laws).

2009
Barack Obama becomes the first African American President of the USA (44th).

2016
Donald Trump elected (45th President of USA)

11th September 2001
Terrorist Attack on the World Trade Center

1996
Tupac murdered
P.129

1996
Rent created
P.138

1920
Women get the right to vote.

4th April 1968
Martin Luther King Jr. assassinated

1954
Beginning of the Civil Rights Movements

2nd July 1964
Segregation abolished in the United States (Civil Rights Act)

1882
Chinese Exclusion Act
P.176

1861 - 1865
Civil War following 11 states seceding from the Union
P.171

1849
Harriet Tubman escapes from slavery on the "Underground Railroad".
P.170

4th July 1776
American independence
P.169

1621
First Thanksgiving

14th May 1607
First permanent English settlement in Jamestown, Virginia
P.98

1492
Christopher Columbus reported to be the 1st European to set foot on the New World.

Country ID Ireland

Population: 6,572,728

Ireland is the second-largest island of the British Isles. It is divided between the Republic of Ireland (officially named Ireland) and Northern Ireland, which is part of the United Kingdom. The Republic of Ireland, whose capital is Dublin, is a parliamentary democracy and is a member of the EU. The government is headed by a prime minister, the Taoiseach. Northern Ireland, whose capital is Belfast, is part of the United Kingdom with a local executive and assembly. The Irish culture has had a significant influence across the world. This is due to the vast number of Irish who emigrated from Ireland in the 19th century (mainly because of the Great Famine from 1845 to 1849). Nowadays, for example,14% of the population of Canada and one third of the Australian population claim Irish descent!

Republic of Ireland

Northern Ireland

2002
Euro replaces punt as national currency.

1992
Ireland signs the Treaty on the European Union at Maastricht.

1998
Good Friday agreement: creation of Northern Ireland Assembly. The Republic of Ireland also agrees to drop its constitutional claim to the six counties which formed Northern Ireland.

30th January 1972
Bloody Sunday: British soldiers shoot 28 unarmed civilians during a peaceful protest march in Derry

1970s - 1990s
Terrorist groups on both sides commit attacks, including bombing bars and discos, killing politicians.

1994
The IRA announces a ceasefire.

1968
Civil rights movement. Catholics complain of unfair treatment at the hands of a largely Protestant political establishment.

1937
Voters approve a new constitution which proclaims Éire as a sovereign, independent, democratic state.

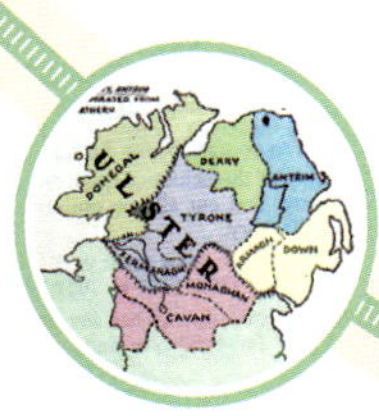

1919 - 1921
War between Ireland and Britain.

1922
Partition. Six counties in the north of the island opt to stay in the United Kingdom while the rest of Ireland becomes independent and later a republic.

1845 - 1849
Great Potato Famine resulted in more than one million deaths; mass immigration to the United States occurred. P.31

445
St. Patrick founded church at Armagh.

1541
Henry VIII of England declared himself King of Ireland.

1695 - 1728
Penal Laws passed against Catholics

1800
Signing of the Act of Union

2017

Trudeau apologises to about 150,000 indigenous children who were separated from their families to have a state-run education during which they were often abused.

Country ID Canada

Population : 36,048,521

Canada is the world's second-largest country by total area. It is divided into ten provinces and three territories. Over 80 percent of its inhabitants are concentrated in large and medium-sized cities. Its capital is Ottawa, and its three largest metropolitan areas are Toronto, Montreal, and Vancouver. Canada is officially bilingual in English and French. The word Canada comes from the Huron-Iroquois word "kanata", it means a village or settlement. About one milion Canadians consider themselves as Inuit, Indian or Métis (of mixed European and Indian ancestry).

2015

Justin Trudeau elected 23rd prime Minister of Canada

1999

The Inuit territory of Nunavut, which covers one-fifth of Canada's landmass, is established.

1903

Canada loses the Alaska boundary dispute with the US.

1989

The Free Trade Agreement between Canada and the US goes into effect

1980

Quebec votes "no" to separatism in a referendum.

1792

George Vancouver begins his explorations of the Pacific Coast.

1841

Act of Union unites Upper and Lower Canada in the Province of Canada.

1763

France is defeated in the Seven Years' War and cedes its North American possessions to Britain in the Treaty of Paris.

1534

The colony of New France is claimed (permanent settlements beginning in 1608).

1818

Canada's border with the United States is defined as the 49th Parallel.

1534

Jacques Cartier visits the Strait of Belle Isle (Newfoundland) and the Gulf of St. Lawrence.

Country ID South Africa

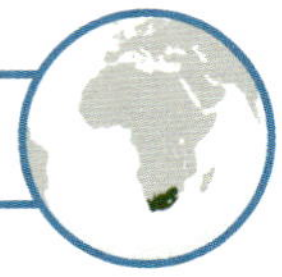

Population: 57,725,600
Home of some of the world's oldest human fossils, South Africa has Portuguese, Dutch and British influences, it is therefore not surprising that at the end of the "apartheid", it was nicknamed the "rainbow nation".
This pluralistic society is reflected also in the fact that its constitution recognizes 11 languages. South Africa is also renowned for its abundant biodiversity. South Africa has three cities that serve as capitals: Pretoria (executive), Cape Town (legislative), and Bloemfontein (judicial). Johannesburg, the largest urban area in the country, is a business centre.

5th December 2013
Nelson Mandela dies, aged 95. Tributes to "the father of the nation" flood in from throughout the world.

2018
MC Ramaphosa elected

2009
ANC wins general election. Parliament elects **Jacob Zuma** as president.

April 1994
April ANC wins first non-racial elections. **Mandela** becomes president.

1990
ANC unbanned, **Mandela** released after 27 years in prison

1964
ANC leader **Nelson Mandela** sentenced to life imprisonment.

1961
South Africa declared a republic, leaves the Commonwealth.

1950
Group Areas Act passed to segregate blacks and whites. Communist Party banned. ANC responds with campaign of civil disobedience, led by **Nelson Mandela**.

1960
Seventy black demonstrators killed at Sharpeville. ANC banned

1948
Policy of apartheid (separateness) adopted by National Party (NP)

1899
Second Anglo-Boer War begins.

1912
Native National Congress founded, later renamed the African National Congress (ANC).

1795
British forces seize Cape Colony from the Netherlands.

1652
Jan van Riebeeck, representing the Dutch East India Company, founds the Cape Colony at Table Bay.

1880 - 1881
Boers rebel against the British, sparking the first Anglo-Boer War.

Country ID India

Population : 1,324,171,354
India is the seventh largest country by area, the second most populous country and the most populous democracy in the world. There is no national language. Hindi, with the largest number of speakers, is the official language of the goverment. English is used in business and administration and has the status of a "subsidiary official language".

2014
Kailash Satyarthi receives the Nobel Peace Prize for his work against child labour.

1984
Indira Gandhi's assassination

1947
India becomes free and independent from the British Empire.

1948
Gandhi's assassination

1947
Jawaharlal Nehru becomes India's Prime minister.

1950
India's constitution

1947
Partition of India

1876
Queen Victoria becomes Empress of India.

1919
Satyagraha civil disobedience (launched by **Mahatma Gandhi**)

1857
Large-scale rebellion in northern and central India against the British East India Company rule.

IV century BC - IV century
Mahabharata (the other major Sanskrit epic of ancient India).

1856
The British control most of India.

1498
Vasco de Gama discovers India.

VII century BC - III century
Ramayana (one of the two major Sanskrit epics of ancient India).

500
First temples built and still visible today: Sanchi (Madhya Pradesh), Dashavatara (Uttar Pradesh), Lad Khan (Karnataka).

Le groupe nominal

1. Les articles

→ L'article zéro : Ø

On parle d'article zéro (**Ø**) pour signaler l'**absence d'article** devant un nom.

Valeur : expression de la généralité

Quand on utilise l'article zéro, on s'intéresse au nom sans lui ajouter le moindre commentaire, c'est pourquoi il exprime souvent une généralité. Dans ce cas, en français, on le traduit par « le / la / les ».

She doesn't like **Ø** tea. Elle n'aime pas le thé.

Cela fonctionne quelle que soit la nature du nom, qu'il soit indénombrable (toujours au singulier) ou dénombrable au pluriel.

You can find **Ø** wonderful works of art in this museum.
Vous pouvez trouver de magnifiques œuvres d'art dans ce musée.

Et devant *man*, *woman*, *nature*, *love*, *society* qui font référence à des généralités.

Ø Nature is stronger than **Ø** man. La nature est plus forte que l'homme.

Quelques cas particuliers

- Les noms de **pays**, de **continents** s'emploient avec **Ø**.
  Ø Germany, **Ø** France, **Ø** China, etc. **Ø** America, **Ø** Africa, **Ø** Asia, etc.
  Sauf les noms de pays au pluriel comme *the USA*, *the Netherlands*... et pour *the United Kingdom*.
- Les **noms de repas** s'emploient avec **Ø** (sauf s'ils sont précédés d'un adjectif).
  I had **Ø** lunch in a wonderful teashop. J'ai déjeuné dans un magnifique salon de thé.
  I had **a wonderful** lunch in that teashop. J'ai eu un magnifique déjeuner dans ce salon de thé.
- Certains noms (***bed***, ***school***, ***jail***) exigent **Ø dans certaines expressions**. Avec un autre article, ils désignent un élément précis
  I go to **Ø** school at 7:30 a.m. Je vais à l'école à 7h30 le matin.
  I go to **Ø** bed at 10:30 p.m. Je me couche à 22h30.
- On utilise **Ø** devant les **noms de titre suivis d'un nom propre**.
  Ø President Trump, **Ø** Queen Elizabeth II, etc.

→ L'article indéfini : *a/an*

Pour désigner un élément parmi d'autres, on emploie ***a*** / ***an*** (« un » ou « une » en français).

She bought **a** new car. Elle a acheté une nouvelle voiture. [une parmi d'autres possibles]

On emploie ***a*** **devant un son consonne**.

A boy, **a** girl, **a** car Un garçon, une fille, une voiture

! **Attention**, certains mots commencent par une voyelle, mais il s'agit d'un son consonne : /j/.
A university /j/, **a Eu**ropean country /j/ Une université, un pays européen

On emploie ***an*** devant un son voyelle.

An elephant, **an** island, **an** egg Un éléphant, une île, un œuf

L'article indéfini est également utilisé (avec un nom dénombrable au singulier) :

- pour parler d'un métier :

John is **an** engineer. He works as **a** consultant for this company.
John est ingénieur. Il travaille comme consultant pour cette entreprise.

- dans des exclamations (au singulier) :

What **a** nice day! Quelle belle journée !
He's such **an** interesting boy! C'est un garçon tellement intéressant !

- pour indiquer des prix par unité de mesure. On peut ici remplacer *a* par ***per*** :

The sausages are £3 **a** kilo. Milk is 50p **a** litre. Les saucisses sont à 3 livres le kilo. Le lait est à 50 pence le litre.

- pour indiquer une fréquence :

He visits us once **a** year. Il nous rend visite une fois par an.
His mother comes here twice **a** month. Sa mère vient ici deux fois par mois.

→ L'article défini : *the*

Pour désigner **un élément précis**, on emploie ***the***. Cet article renvoie à du connu, un élément déjà identifié. L'énonciateur et le co-énonciateur savent à quoi on fait référence.

Where did you put **the** keys? Où as-tu mis les clés ?
[On sait très bien de quelles clés il s'agit.]

On emploie également ***the*** :

- pour **parler d'un élément de culture** partagé par chacun.

The sun, **the** world, **the** media, **the** future Le soleil, le monde, les médias, le futur

- pour faire référence à une **généralité**.

The dog is man's best friend. Le chien est le meilleur ami de l'homme.

Devant un adjectif utilisé comme adjectif substantivé pour indiquer un **ensemble de personnes** (il sera suivi d'un verbe au pluriel) :

The blind, **the** unemployed, **the** old, **the** rich... Les aveugles, les chômeurs, les vieux, les riches…

- devant des **collectivités entières** :

The French, **the** Spanish, **the** Russians, **the** Americans, **the** Germans...
Les Français, les Espagnols, les Russes, les Américains, les Allemands…

- devant les **noms propres déterminés** :

The Prince of Wales, **the** Queen of England, **the** President of the United States.
Le prince de Galles, la reine d'Angleterre, le président des États-Unis…

- devant les **numéraux ordinaux** :

The first page, **the** second platform, **the** eleventh gate... La première page, le second quai, la onzième porte…

- avec ***to play*** suivi d'un instrument de musique :

He plays **the** piano, **the** trumpet, **the** trombone... Il joue du piano, de la trompette, du trombone…

Your turn!

1 Complétez les phrases avec l'article qui convient.

a. I went to ... USA last summer. I arrived in ... California where I decided to visit Angel Island. It was ... wonderful experience.
b. Donald Trump is ... President of the USA.
c. I met ... old man and ... woman at ... tea shop. The man came from ... China and gave me information about tea.
d. ... young people are often addicted to their phones.
e. I love watching ... horror movies.

2. Les noms dénombrables et indénombrables

Il y a deux types de noms :

- les **dénombrables** (les noms **que l'on peut dénombrer, compter**).
- les **indénombrables** (les noms **qu'on ne peut pas dénombrer, compter**).

Afin de bien comprendre le fonctionnement de ces noms, **il faut se détacher du français** et voir les choses différemment : ce qui est indénombrable en français ne l'est pas nécessairement en anglais.

Les indénombrables ne peuvent jamais être précédés de *a, an, one, two*... Ils ne peuvent pas non plus être utilisés au pluriel.

Les indénombrables les plus courants	Ce qui est souvent indénombrable
advice un (des) conseil(s) bread du pain furniture des meubles information / news des renseignements luggage des bagages progress le progrès work le travail	• Les noms qui font référence à **une matière** : water de l'eau, steel de l'acier, cotton du coton, ... • Les noms qui font référence à **une notion abstraite** : courage le courage, love l'amour, hate la haine, patience la patience, ... • Les noms qui font référence à **une activité humaine** : driving, working, watching TV, basketball, badminton, ... • Les noms de **langue** : Japanese, Chinese, French, ... • Les noms de **couleur** : white, red, green, ...

! **Attention**, certains mots sont parfois dénombrables, parfois indénombrables :

Fonctionnement indénombrable	Fonctionnement dénombrable
business les affaires	a business une entreprise
coffee le café (la boisson, en général)	a coffee un café (une tasse de café)
work le travail	a work une œuvre d'art
time du temps	times des fois

3. Le pluriel des noms

Le pluriel des noms réguliers se forme par ajout d'un ***-s*** : *a dog,* → *two dog***s**.

Certains noms ont un pluriel irrégulier :

a child → 2 child**ren**
a man → two m**e**n
a goose → two g**ee**se
a foot → two f**ee**t
a tooth → two t**ee**th
a mouse → two m**ice**

a wife → two wi**ves**
a knife → two kni**ves**
a half → two hal**ves**
a thief → two th**ieves**
a wolf → two wol**ves**

Certains noms sont invariables

a sheep → two sheep
a series → two series
a deer → two deer

! **Attention**, contrairement au français, les noms de famille prennent un ***-s*** au pluriel.
The Smith**s**, the Miller**s**

Your turn!

2 Dans les phrases suivantes, mettez les noms entre parenthèses au pluriel.

a. The (*man*) ... who lived in that house disappeared seven years ago.
b. For her birthday, my niece was given two (*mouse*) ... and a rabbit.
c. The (knife) ... were found in the flat of the (*thief*) ... .
d. He was playing basketball with his three (*child*) ... when he fell and broke two (*tooth*) ... .
e. I was having a walk when I saw two (*deer*) ... running in the (*field*) ... .

4. Les noms composés

Dans un nom composé, c'est le **deuxième élément** qui est le **mot principal**. Le premier élément sert à préciser le sens du deuxième.

A paper **bag**, a tea **bag**, a doggy **bag**, a hand**bag** Un sac en papier, un sachet de thé, un sac à emporter, un sac à main

Certains mots composés s'écrivent en un seul mot car leur utilisation est entrée dans le langage courant.

A toothbrush, a handbag. Une brosse à dent, un sac à main.

! **Attention**, les mots composés ne sont pas toujours séparés ou reliés par un tiret ou une espace.
A dining room, a classmate, a coffee-maker Une salle à manger, un camarade de classe, une cafetière

→ Nom + nom principal

Le nom 1 indique...	Exemples de noms composés :
... **à quoi** sert le nom principal	teaspoon cuillère à thé / petite cuillère fish fork fourchette à poisson breadknife couteau à pain
... **comment fonctionne** le nom principal	gas cooker cuisinière à gaz steamboat bateau à vapeur petrol engine moteur à essence

Le nom 1 indique...	Exemples de noms composés :
... **la matière** du nom principal	silver chain chaîne en argent glass building immeuble en verre wood frame encadrement en bois
... **la fonction** ou ce que contient le nom principal	teapot théière wine glass verre à vin bookshelf étagère pour des livres
... **le genre** du nom principal	boyfriend petit ami female driver conductrice girl soprano une soprano
... **le lieu ou le moment** du nom principal	seabird oiseau de mer streetlamp réverbère night train train de nuit morning paper journal du matin
... **le métier** ou la fonction du nom principal	businesswoman femme d'affaires schoolgirl écolière real estate agent agent immobilier

→ Nom + forme verbale

	La forme verbale désigne...	Exemples de mots composés
Nom + verbe + ***er***	... la personne ou l'instrument qui fait l'action	taxi driver chauffeur·se de taxi opera singer chanteur·teuse d'opéra song writer compositeur·trice de chansons piano player joueur·euse de piano
Nom + verbe en ***-ing***	... une activité	sightseeing faire du tourisme mountain climbing faire de l'escalade en montagne / de l'alpinisme bird-watching aller observer les oiseaux / faire de l'ornithologie
Verbe en ***-ing*** + nom	... l'usage d'un objet	washing machine machine à laver racing car voiture de course fishing rod canne à pêche

Your turn!

3 Complétez les phrases avec le nom composé qui convient.
Indiquez quelle forme vous avez utilisée et ce qu'elle désigne.

Exemple : I would like to listen to music, where are my .... ? *(écouter - oreille)*

→ Where are my earphones? [les écouteurs servent à écouter de la musique dans les oreilles]

a. It was really hot yesterday. We went to the .... . (*piscine*)
b. We are all going to celebrate Matthew's ... next Friday. (*anniversaire*).
c. I love horses and races, so what about going to see a ...? (*course de chevaux*)
d. Come on, we are late! Why does she always speak to the ...? (*conducteur de bus*)
e. All students need to find a good ... to buy cheap books. (*librairie*)

5. Le génitif

Le génitif signale une **relation étroite** entre deux noms.

→ Formation

Nom singulier + **'s**	The girl**'s** books
Nom pluriel + **'**	The girls' books
Nom pluriel irrégulier + **'s**	The children**'s** books, the men**'s** books
Nom propre qui se termine par *s* + **'s**	James**'s** books

→ Valeur

Le génitif unit deux noms. Souvent la relation exprime l'**appartenance** ou une **relation proche de l'appartenance**.

My sister**'s** children Les enfants de ma sœur

The neighbour**'s** dog Le chien du voisin

Le nom à droite du génitif peut être **sous-entendu** quand il désigne **un lieu**.

I need some bread. I'm going to the baker**'s** (*shop*).
J'ai besoin de pain. Je vais chez le·la boulanger·ère.

Les noms qui peuvent être employés au génitif incluent :

- les **personnes**, les **animaux**, les **noms de lieux**, de **pays**, d'**institutions**.

  The cat**'s** ball La balle du chat

  The school**'s** district Le quartier de l'école

- les noms qui font référence à un moment, une durée ou à l'argent.

  A year**'s** break Une année sabbatique

  A day**'s** work Une journée de travail

  Yesterday**'s** newspaper Le journal d'hier

  Two hundred dollar**s'** worth of merchandise Deux cent dollars de marchandise

Sauf pour les cas indiqués ci-dessus, lorsque le possesseur n'est pas un être animé, alors on emploie une structure en *of*.

Mary's foot is broken. Le pied de Mary est cassé.

The foot **of** the table is broken. Le pied de la table est cassé. [table = inanimé]

Your turn!

4 **Reliez les mots ensemble à l'aide d'un génitif lorsque c'est possible. (Sinon, optez pour une structure avec *of*.)**

a. the cakes / the baker → ...
b. the book / the end → ...
c. the pens / the students → ...
d. the world / yesterday → ...
e. a cup / tea → ...
f. my brother / his bike → ...
g. the plays / Shakespeare → ...
h. friends / the children → ...

6. Les démonstratifs : *this/these* et *that/those*

This (+ nom au singulier) et son puriel ***these*** (+ nom pluriel) s'emploient pour désigner **ce qui est proche de l'énonciateur** dans l'espace, le temps ou ressenti comme proche.

This book is wonderful. Ce livre (que j'apprécie) est merveilleux.

That (+ nom au singulier) et son pluriel ***those*** (+ nom pluriel) s'emploient pour désigner **ce qui est éloigné de l'énonciateur** dans l'espace, le temps ou ressenti comme éloigné.

I hate **that** book. It is so boring. Je déteste ce livre. Il est si ennuyeux.

Your turn!

5 Complétez avec le démonstratif qui convient.

a. ... is the best movie I've seen this year.
b. ... biscuits are really good, don't you think?
c. I went to California last summer. ... was a very nice trip.
d. ... happened two weeks ago so I don't remember all the details.
e. Look here, ... is my favourite teashop.

7. Les adjectifs et noms de nationalité

En français, pour faire référence à la nationalité, on utilise un seul et même mot pour l'adjectif (avec une minuscule) et le nom (avec une majuscule).

En anglais, parfois l'adjectif est différent du nom (*Spanish / a Spaniard*) , mais les deux commencent par une majuscule. Par ailleurs, on utilise des mots différents pour faire référence à un individu (*a Frenchman*), quelques individus (*some French people*), et tous les individus (*the French*).

Il existe quatre types d'adjectifs de nationalité :

- Ceux se terminant par ***-sh*** ou ***-ch***

PAYS	Adjectif	Un individu	Quelques individus	Tous
Britain Ireland	British Irish	a British person an Irishman/woman	some British people some Irish people	the British the Irish

- Ceux se terminant par ***-ese***

Pays	Adjectif	Un individu	Quelques individus	Tous
China Japan Portugal	Chinese Japanese Portuguese	a Chinese a Japanese a Portuguese	some Chinese people some Japanese people some Portuguese people	the Chinese the Japanese the Portuguese

- Ceux qui se terminent en ***-an***

Pays / continent	Adjectif	Un individu	Quelques individus	Tous
America Africa Canada Italy	American African Canadian Italian	an American an African a Canadian an Italian	some American people some African people some Canadian people some Italian people	the Americans the Africans the Canadians the Italians

• Ceux qui ont un ***adjectif différent du nom***

Pays	Adjectif	Un individu	Tous les individus
Denmark Poland Scotland Spain	Danish Polish Scottish Spanish	a Dane a Pole a Scot a Spaniard	the Danes the Poles the Scots the Spaniards / the Spanish

8. L'ordre des adjectifs

En anglais les adjectifs sont **invariables**, c'est-à-dire qu'ils ne prennent jamais de marque au pluriel.

→ Les adjectifs épithètes

L'adjectif épithète se place avant le nom.

It was a **difficult** experience. C'était une expérience difficile.

→ Ordre des adjectifs épithètes

Généralement, les adjectifs se placent **du plus subjectif au plus objectif**.

Opinion	Taille	Âge	Couleur	Origine	Matière
	forme, dimension			nationalité, religion, origine géographique ou politique	
beautiful	big	young	red	American	wooden

Il suffit de retenir: **OTACOM** (Opinion, Taille, Age, Couleur, Origine, Matière)
Si on a plus de deux adjectifs, ils sont séparés par une virgule, sauf s'ils sont courts.

It is an impressive, gigantic, rocky mountain. C'est une grande montagne rocheuse impressionante.

A big black cat. Un gros chat noir.

→ Les adjectifs attributs

Certains adjectifs sont toujours attributs. Dans ce cas, ils se placent après un verbe d'état comme ***be*** :

alive, asleep, afraid, awake, cross, ill, glad

Your turn!

6 Insérez les adjectifs dans les phrases suivantes. Attention à l'ordre des mots !

a. We went to the cinema and watched a ... movie. (*recent / American / brilliant*)
b. They live in a ... house. (*huge / wooden*)
c. You should really go to that restaurant. They serve ... food. (*Chinese / wonderful*)
d. She keeps her jewellery in a ... box. (*metal / small*)
e. He is a very ... man. (*attractive / young / Canadian*)
f. She is very interested in ... literature. (*English / old / boring*)
g. I think he's going to buy this ... car. (*beautiful / German / sports*)
h. I hate her. She's a ... woman. (*old / stupid*)

9. Les adjectifs en *-ed* et *-ing*

Les adjectifs en ***-ed*** ont un **sens passif**. Alors que les adjectifs en ***-ing*** ont un **sens actif**.

You are surpris**ed** if something is surprisi**ng**.
Vous êtes surpris·e [« victime » de surprise] si quelque chose est surprenant [provoque la surprise].

You are interest**ed** if something is interest**ing**. Vous êtes intéressé·e si quelque chose est intéressant.

Sens passif	Sens actif
amazed /d/ étonné·e	amazing étonnant·e
astonished /t/ stupéfait·e	astonishing stupéfiant·e
bored /d/ ennuyé·e	boring ennuyant·e
disappointed /ɪd/ déçu·e	disappointing décevant·e
excited /ɪd/ excité·e	exciting excitant·e
frightened /d/ effrayé·e	frightening effrayant·e
interested /ɪd/ interessé·e	interesting intéressant·e

Your turn!

7 Complétez les phrases suivantes avec un adjectif en *-ed* ou en *-ing*.

a. Her job is based on repeating the same actions over and over again, so she finds it very bor… .
b. You should really watch that movie. It's amaz… .
c. When the teacher asked her a question, she was so embarrass… that she blushed.
d. Some people like eating snails, but others find it disgust… .
e. That was a terrible accident. Everybody was shock… .
f. I have already explained this to you. I'm surpris… that you can't remember.
g. My little brother is always writing on my notebook. He's really annoy… .

10. Les quantifieurs : *some*, *any*, *no* ou *not any*

Some et ***any*** servent à indiquer une « certaine » quantité.

On rencontre souvent ***some*** en contexte affirmatif et interrogatif pour proposer quelque chose, ***any*** en contexte négatif et interrogatif.

No et ***not any*** servent à indiquer une quantité nulle.

	Indénombrables	Dénombrables pluriels
Affirmation	There's **some** coffee. Il y a du café.	There are **some** cakes on the table. Il y a des gâteaux sur la table.
Question pour proposer qqch	Would you like **some** tea? Voudrais-tu / Voudriez-vous du thé ?	Would you like **some** scones? Voudrais-tu / Voudriez-vous des scones ?
Interrogation	Is there **any** tea in the pot? Y a-t-il du thé dans la théière ?	Are there **any** scones left? Reste-t-il des scones ?
Négation ***Not any*** + nom	There is**n't any** tea. Il n'y pas de thé.	There are**n't any** scones. Il n'y pas de scones.
Négation ***No*** + nom	There is **no** tea. Il n'y pas de thé.	There are **no** scones. Il n'y pas de scones.

Your turn!

8 Complétez les phrases suivantes avec *some, any, no, not any*.

a. I have bought ... chocolate. Would you like ...?
b. I'm not sure there is ... coffee left.
c. This is difficult so if you have ... problems, don't hesitate to contact me.
d. There are ... questions that I would like to answer.
e. I cannot take ... risks.
f. There are ... photographs that I would like to show you.
g. Do you have ... questions?
h. I have lost all my money. I don't have ... money left!
i. Unfortunately, there are ... buses at that time.

11. Les quantifieurs : *a lot, much, many*

Ces trois outils servent à **exprimer une grande quantité**.

→ *A lot of*

A lot of est plus courant que ***much*** ou ***many***. Il peut être suivi d'un nom au singulier ou au pluriel.

I drank **a lot of** tea this afternoon. J'ai bu beaucoup de thé cet après-midi.

I took **a lot of** pictures when I was on Angel Island. J'ai pris beaucoup de photos quand j'étais à Angel Island.

D'autres expressions sont proches de *a lot of* : ***a large number of*** + nom pluriel, ***a great deal of*** + nom singulier. ***Plenty of*** et ***lots of*** + nom singulier ou pluriel.

→ *Much et many*

Ces deux quantifieurs s'emploient souvent dans des **énoncés interrogatifs et négatifs**.

Much est suivi d'un nom **indénombrable**.

Did the teacher give you **much** homework? Le·La professeur·e vous a-t-il donné beaucoup de devoirs ?
[*homework* = indénombrable]

Many est suivi d'un nom **dénombrable**.

Did the teacher give you **many** exercises? Le·La professeur·e vous a-t-il donné beaucoup d'exercices ?
[*exercices* = dénombrable]

How much... ? et ***How many... ?*** signifient « Combien de... ? », « Quelle quantité de... ? »

How much is this book? Combien coûte ce livre ?
How many pages are there in this book? Combien de pages y a-t-il dans ce livre ?

Your turn!

9 Complétez les phrases suivantes à l'aide de *much, many* ou *a lot of*.

a. How ... pictures did you take while you were in the USA?
b. How ... time do you have for me this afternoon?
c. Have you got ... pets?
d. She spent ... money on clothes.
e. How ... does that car cost?
f. There is ... homework for tomorrow and I haven't started yet.
g. Were there ... people at the cinema?
h. When I'm on holiday, I have ... free time so I read ... books.

12. Les quantifieurs : *a little, a few, little, few*

A little, ***a few***, ***little***, ***few*** font partie des quantifieurs. Ils désignent une petite quantité et ont le même fonctionnement que ***much*** et ***many***.

→ *A little et a few*

A little + nom singulier renvoie à une petite quantité de... (« un peu de... »).
On l'emploie devant un nom indénombrable (*love, hate, courage, homework, water*...).

Could you give me **a little** more time to finish, please?
Pouvez-vous me donner un peu plus de temps pour terminer, s'il vous plait ?

A few + nom au pluriel renvoie à un petit nombre de... (« quelques... »).
Le nom peut être sous-entendu.

I arrived two weeks ago and I have already made **a few** friends.
Je suis arrivé·e il y a deux semaines et je me suis déjà fait quelques amis.

Bad people? I've met a few. Des personnes méchantes ? J'en ai rencontré quelques-unes.
[sous-entendu : *bad people*]

→ *Little et few*

Avec ***little*** et ***few*** (sans *a*), on estime une quantité insuffisante (« peu de... »).

I have **little** time and so many things to do. J'ai peu de temps et tellement de choses à faire.
[*little* + indénombrable]

She is arrogant, so she has **few** friends. Elle est arrogante, donc elle a peu d'amis.
[*few* + dénombrable]

Little et ***few*** peuvent être précédés d'adverbes : ***very, too, extremely***...

I've got **too little** time. J'ai trop peu de temps.

She has **too few** friends. Elle a trop peu d'amis.

Your turn!

10 **Complétez les phrases suivantes avec *little, a little, few, a few*.**

a. There were ... students at school because of the snow.
b. "When did she leave?" "She left ... minutes ago."
c. I cannot answer this question right now. I need ... time to think about it.
d. There was ... traffic so we arrived early.
e. ... students know the answer to that question because it is very specific.
f. "Would you like some tea?" "Yes, please ... ."
g. The weather is really hot in this region. There is ... rain.
h. Can I call you? I have ... questions to ask you.

13. Les pronoms personnels

Les pronoms personnels sujets et compléments permettent de **remplacer un nom** dans une phrase et d'éviter ainsi sa répétition.

Ellen saw Maureen at school today. Ellen a vu Maureen à l'école aujourd'hui.

She saw **her** at school today. Elle l'a vue à l'école aujourd'hui.
[*She* : Ellen] [*her* : Maureen]

→ Formes

	Fonction sujet	Fonction complément
1ᵉ pers. du singulier	I	me
2ᵉ pers.	you	you
3ᵉ pers.	he she it	him her it
1ᵉ pers. du pluriel	we	us
2ᵉ pers.	you	you
3ᵉ pers.	they	them

Le pronom sujet est placé avant le verbe.

I'm studying. J'étudie.

Le pronom complément est placé après le verbe.

Mary talked to **her**. Mary lui a parlé.

We didn't want **you** to come so early. Nous ne voulions pas que vous veniez si tôt.
[Pronom sujet] [Pronom complément]

It reminds **me** of the great storm. Cela me rappelle la grande tempête.
[Pronom sujet] [Pronom complément]

À noter :

He / him (masculin) et *she / her* (féminin) s'emploient **pour les êtres humains et les animaux familiers**.

It s'emploie **pour les autres animaux et les objets**.

They / them remplacent l'ensemble.

He loves **his dog**. He brought **him** to work last week.
Il aime son chien, il l'a amené au travail la semaine dernière.

All of a sudden, we saw **a cow** close to the road! **It** didn't look surprised. Maybe there were **others**, but we didn't see **them**.
Soudain, nous avons vu une vache au bord de la route ! Elle n'avait pas l'air étonnée. Peut-être qu'il y en avait d'autres, mais nous ne les avons pas vues.

Your turn!

11 Complétez l'email avec les pronoms personnels sujets ou compléments.

Dear Laura,

Let me tell ... about my family. I live in Swansea with my mum. ... works as a nurse at the city hospital. My mum's name is Katy, ... loves reading books about climate fiction and always debates about ... with me. ... has long brown hair and ... is not very tall. My dad lives in Cardiff. ... is a civil servant and ... is proud of helping people. I've got a cat, Iris and a goldfish. ... is a lovely cat. I really love ... . But I don't mind about the fish! ... is not a sociable pet!

See you, love

Meghan

14. Les pronoms et déterminants possessifs

Le lien de possession peut s'exprimer de différentes manières :

- avec un déterminant possessif : I have left **my** book at home. J'ai laissé mon livre à la maison.
- avec un pronom possessif : This teapot is **mine.** Cette théière est à moi.

→ Formes

Possesseur	Déterminants	Pronoms
1ᵉ pers. du singulier	my	mine
2ᵉ pers.	your	yours
3ᵉ pers.	his her its	his hers -
1ᵉ pers. du pluriel	our	ours
2ᵉ pers.	your	yours
3ᵉ pers.	their	theirs

Contrairement au français, on utilise un déterminant possessif devant les **parties du corps** ou les **vêtements**.

Paul had **his** hands in **his** pockets. Paul avait les mains dans les poches.

> À la différence du français, les déterminants et les pronoms possessifs s'accordent en genre et en nombre **avec le possesseur** (*his car* si possesseur masculin, *her car* si possesseur féminin, alors qu'en français, c'est « sa voiture » que le possesseur soit masculin ou féminin).
>
> Elizabeth had **her** hair cut yesterday. Elizabeth s'est fait couper les cheveux hier.
>
> Paul and John visited the castle with **their** parents. Paul et John ont visité le château avec leurs parents.

Les pronoms possessifs servent à **remplacer des noms** précédés d'un déterminant possessif. Ils remplissent les fonctions des groupes nominaux qu'ils remplacent.

My carrot cake is too sweet. Mon gâteau à la carotte est trop sucré.

Mine is excellent. Le mien est excellent.
[*Mine* est sujet ici]

Don't touch it, this piece of cake is **mine**. N'y touche pas, cette part de gâteau est à moi.
[*mine* est pronom possessif attribut]

Pour dire « un(e) de mes/tes/ses/nos/vos/leurs » + groupe nominal, on emploie : groupe nominal + *of* + pronom possessif.

She is a cousin **of mine**. C'est une de mes cousines.

I met a friend **of yours** last week. J'ai rencontré un de tes amis l'autre jour.

En anglais lorsqu'il y a plusieurs objets possédés et plusieurs possesseurs, on utilise **le pluriel pour les objets possédés**. C'est ce qu'on appelle le pluriel idiomatique.

Nina and Juliet ride **their** bikes to school. Nina et Juliet vont à l'école à vélo.

Your turn!

12 Remplacez le groupe nominal souligné par un déterminant ou pronom possessif.

a. I've found Linda's wallet but I can't find your wallet and my wallet.
b. I don't like Al Gore's documentary.
c. Are you still reading Saci Lloyd's latest novel. I'd like to read it.
d. This story is not about David Leong's testimony, it's about another Chinese immigrant.
e. I saw this nice jumper yesterday in your room, so I thought that this one might be one of your jumpers.
f. Each school has a board of teachers to vote decisions. Your school has just presented its board too.

15. Les pronoms réfléchis et réciproques

→ Les pronoms réfléchis

Base de formation	Pronom réfléchi
Déterminant possessif : my	**my**self
Déterminant possessif : your	**your**self
Pronom fonction complément : him	**him**self
Pronom fonction complément : her	**her**self
Pronom fonction complément : it	**it**self
Déterminant possessif : our	**our**selves
Déterminant possessif : your	**your**selves
Pronom fonction complément : them	**them**selves

On emploie un pronom réfléchi en anglais quand le **sujet** et l'**objet** sont **la même personne**.

He looked at **himself** in the mirror. **Il se** regarda dans la glace.
Sujet et **complément** sont la même personne.

Le pronom réfléchi peut aussi permettre d'**insister** sur une personne ou un objet.

Why don't you clean it **yourself** ? Pourquoi ne le laves-tu pas **toi-même** ?

Certains verbes français se construisent avec le pronom réfléchi alors qu'en anglais, ce n'est pas le cas.

se sentir = to feel	se raser = to shave
se laver = to wash	s'excuser = to apologise
se rencontrer = to meet	se baigner = to have a bath / swim
se lever = to stand up	s'habiller = to dress

Your turn!

13 Traduisez en anglais à l'aide des verbes indiqués.

a. Excuse-toi quand tu dis une grossièreté! (*to swear*)
b. Je l'ai dessiné toute seule. (*to draw*)
c. Ma mère s'est fait mal en réparant la voiture. (*to hurt/to mend*)
d. Mon frère s'est préparé un plateau télé pour le match de ce soir. (*to prepare*)
e. J'ai toujours trouvé qu'il s'habillait bien. (*to dress*)

→ Les pronoms réciproques

Pour exprimer l'idée d'**échange entre des personnes**, on utilise :

- ***each other*** pour deux personnes,
- ***one another*** pour deux ou plusieurs personnes.

The lovers kissed **each other**. Les amoureux se sont embrassés.

The members of the family supported **one another** when there were difficult times.
Les membres de la famille se soutenaient lors des moments difficiles.

Your turn!

14 Complétez avec le pronom réciproque le plus adapté.

a. Lisa, Mary and Paul have sent gifts to ... since they were children.
b. With my brother, we phone ... every other day.
c. We have known ... for six years now. I would like to organize a party with Jill to celebrate!
d. I know very little about ...'s work in the office.

16. Le comparatif et le superlatif

→ Formation

Le comparatif et le superlatif de supériorité se forment de façon différente selon la longueur de l'adjectif :

	Comparatif de supériorité	Superlatif de supériorité
Adjectif court : - 1 syllabe - 2 syllabes se terminant par *–y, -er, -ow, -le*	adjectif + -er cheap**er** heavi**er**, clever**er**, narrow**er**, simpl**er**	the + adjective + -est the cheap**est** the heavi**est**, the clever**est**, the narrow**est**, the simpl**est**
Adjectif long : - 2 syllabes (autres) - 3 syllabes ou plus	more + adjectif **more** modern **more** expensive	the most + adjectif **the most** modern **the most** expensive

À noter

- Adjectifs en -y :
  funny (amusant) → funn**ier** → the funn**iest**
- Adjectifs d'une syllabe qui comportent une seule voyelle suivie d'une seule consonne :
  big (grand) → bigger → the biggest
- Adjectifs irréguliers :
  good (bon) → **better** → the **best**
  bad (mauvais) → worse → the **worst**
  far (loin) → **farther** (distance) / **further** (sens imagé) → the **farthest** /the **furthest**

→ Le comparatif de supériorité (plus... que)

Il sert à comparer **deux éléments entre eux**. L'élément comparé est introduit par *than*.
On peut renforcer la comparaison avec *much* ou *far*.

Matilda is **more successful than** *Charlie and the Chocolate Factory.*
Matilda a plus de succès que *Charlie and the Chocolate Factory.*

The Book of Mormon is **far more recent than** *The Phantom of the Opera.*
The Book of Mormon est bien plus récent que *The Phantom of the Opera.*

Les Miserables is much **longer than** *High School Musicals.*
Les Misérables est beaucoup plus long que *High School Musicals.*

→ Le superlatif de supériorité (le plus)

Il sert à comparer **un ou plusieurs élément(s) avec tout le reste**.

Wicked is **the most successful** musical in the West End at the moment.
Wicked est la comédie musicale qui a le plus de succès dans le West End en ce moment.

→ Le comparatif d'égalité (aussi ... que)

as + adj. + ***as***

An American in Paris is **as famous as** *Singing in the Rain.*
Un Américain à Paris est aussi célèbre que *Chantons sous la pluie.*

→ Le comparatif d'infériorité (moins... que)

Less + adj. + ***than / not as*** + adj. + ***as*** / ***not so*** + adj. + ***as***

La première structure est plutôt utilisée avec les adjectifs longs.

This theatre is **less popular than** the Haymarket. Ce théâtre est moins populaire que le Haymarket.
This theatre is not **as new as** the Bridge. Ce théâtre n'est pas aussi récent que le Bridge.
This theatre is not **so big as** the Lyceum. Ce théâtre n'est pas aussi grand que le Lyceum.

→ Le superlatif d'infériorité (le moins...)

The least + adj.

Cette structure est plutôt utilisée avec les adjectifs longs.

This is **the least comfortable** theatre I know. C'est le théâtre le moins confortable que je connaisse.

Your turn!

15 Complétez avec l'adjectif au comparatif ou au superlatif de supériorité.

a. We chose ... seats in the theatre. *(expensive)*
b. Which is ... theatre on Broadway? *(large)*
c. *Charlie and the Chocolate Factory* is ... musical film I have ever seen. *(great)*
d. The choreography is ... than the songs. *(spectacular)*
e. Andrew Lloyd Webber is probably one of ... British musical composers. *(well-known)*
f. English theatres are beautiful but American theatres usually have ... facilities. *(good)*
g. I have found last minute tickets at only £ 15. They are much ... than yours. *(cheap)*

16 Complétez les phrases avec un des adjectifs ci-dessous au comparatif d'égalité (*as* + adj. + *as*).

close – expensive – big – busy – fast

a. I'm sorry I'm a bit late, I got here ... I could.
b. My ticket costs £20. It isn't ... yours.
c. Matinees aren't ... night performances.
d. The stage is three times ... it is in most venues.
e. I would like to be ... possible to the stage.

17. Les chiffres et les nombres

→ Les nombres cardinaux

Ils indiquent une **quantité** et sont **invariables**.

More than **ten million** people have diabetes in the USA.
Plus de dix millions de personnes souffrent de diabète aux États-Unis.

Hundred, ***thousand***, ***million***, ***billion*** (milliard) sont invariables lorsqu'ils sont précédés d'un nombre.

Two hundred_ people Deux cent personnes

Mais ils s'emploient également au pluriel et sont suivis de ***of*** pour exprimer une quantité indéfinie.

Hundred**s** of people Des centaines de personnes
Thousand**s** of birds Des milliers d'oiseaux
Million**s** of dollars Des millions de dollars
Billion**s** of insects Des milliards d'insectes

! **Attention** à l'orthographe.

4 = four	14 = fourteen	40 = f**o**rty
5 = five	15 = fi**f**teen	50 = fi**f**ty

- En lettres, on sépare les dizaines et les unités par un **trait d'union**: forty**-**seven years
- En chiffres, on sépare les milliers et les centaines par une **virgule**. En lettres, on sépare les centaines et les dizaines par ***and***.

2**,**298 = two thousand two hundred **and** ninety-eight
24**,**200 = twenty-four thousand **and** two hundred
191**,**568 = one hundred ninety-one thousand five hundred **and** sixty-eight

- Les décimales sont précédées d'un point qui se prononce.

4.38 cm = four **point** thirty-eight centimetres

Oh!

O se dit ***nought*** /nɔːt/ en anglais et ***zero*** /ˈzɪərəʊ/ en anglais américain, mais se lit comme la lettre *o* /əʊ/ dans les numéros de téléphone, bus, de chambre d'hôtel, etc.

Lors d'un résultat sportif, 0 se dit ***love*** /lʌv/ au tennis et ***nil*** /nɪl/ pour les autres sports comme le football.

He beat Federer three sets to **love**. Il a battu Federer trois sets à zéro.
They beat Italy one-**nil** in the final. Ils ont battu l'Italie un-zéro en finale.

→ Les nombres ordinaux

Les nombres ordinaux indiquent un **rang** ou un **ordre**. On les utilise notamment pour exprimer une **date**.

On les forme à partir des nombres cardinaux auxquels on ajoute ***st***, ***nd***, ***rd*** ou ***th***.

1**st** = first	21**st** = twenty-first	31**st** = thirty-first
2**nd** = second	22**nd** = twenty-second	
3**rd** = third	23**rd** = twenty-third	
4**th** = fourth	24**th** = twenty-fourth	

On les utilise pour former des **fractions** et indiquer des **proportions**.

1/5 = one fifth

! **Attention**, certaines fractions sont irrégulières.
1/2 = one half 2/3 = two-thirds 3/4 = three-quarters

Your turn!

17 Écrivez en toutes lettres les données chiffrées suivantes.

a. 1,455
b. 5,333,258
c. 21/02/2018
d. 2/4 of the students have a room on the campus.
e. England won the football game 0-2.

18. *Not anymore, no more, none, never*

Pour signifier l'**absence** d'un ou plusieurs éléments , on peut utiliser ***no*** ou ***none*** suivant sa nature.

There is **no** salt in this meal. Il n'y a pas de sel dans ce plat.
[*no* est le **déterminant** de *salt*]

Is there any salt in this meal? No, there's **none**. Y a-t-il du sel dans ce plat ? Non, il n'y en a pas.
[*none* est **pronom**, il remplace *salt* et indique son absence.]

Pour exprimer le fait qu'**il n'y a plus** de quelque chose (un ou plusieurs éléments), on utilise en anglais ***no more*** ou ***not anymore*** :

There is **no more** salt in the ingredients. / There is**n't anymore** salt in the ingredients.
Il n'y a plus de sel dans les ingrédients.

No more et ***not anymore*** peuvent aussi être employés en adverbe et signifier qu'une situation ou un fait est **définitivement terminé** :

This won't happen **anymore**! Cela n'arrivera plus !

We should fear **no more**! Nous ne devrions plus avoir peur !

Pour exprimer l'équivalent de **jamais**, on utilise en anglais ***never*** et ***not ever*** (toujours avec la forme négative). Les deux expressions sont équivalentes mais ***never*** est celle qui est la plus utilisée.

She has **never** been a friend of ours. Elle n'a jamais été notre amie.

Your turn!

18 Complétez les énoncés avec la forme voulue par le contexte.

a. I've got ... time to waste.
b. I'm looking for flour to make some pancakes. I'm afraid there is ... left.
c. Peter was always looking for inspiration, but it ... came.
d. Everyone is relieved. The power cuts will ... happen ... .
e. Have you ever been to South Africa ? No, I have ... been to South Africa, but I hope I will go there one day.

19. Date, heure et âge

→ La date

Pour situer dans le temps en précisant le moment où l'événement a lieu, on utilise :

- ***in*** + une année / ***in*** + le mois

  Shakespeare was born in 1564, **in** April. Shakespeare est né en 1564, en avril.

- ***on*** + la date ou un jour de la semaine

  I'll be meeting you **on** Monday 21st April **at** 6pm. Je vous rencontrerai lundi 21 avril à 6h.

- ***in*** + un moment de la journée

  I'd rather have a cup of coffee **in** the morning. Je préfère boire une tassé de café le matin.

- ***at*** + une heure

  Your English lesson starts **at** 8:15 am, don't be late! Ton cours d'anglais commence à 8h15, ne sois pas en retard !

Il y a deux manières de donner la date :

– l'une plus américaine :

Tuesday, April 21st 2019

Tuesday, April the twenty-first twenty nineteen

– l'autre plus britannique :

Tuesday 21st April 2019

Tuesday, the twenty-first of April twenty nineteen

Les nombres ordinaux sont employés dans les dates en anglais.

1st, 2nd, 3rd, 4th, … 21st, 22nd, 23rd, 24th, …

Comment dire les années ?

Jusqu'à 2000, on sépare les deux premiers chiffres et les derniers. 1999 = nineteen ninety-nine

Mais de **2001 à 2009** : 2001 = two thousand and one / two… and nine

Puis **à partir de 2010**, on peut utiliser les deux : 2019 : twenty nineteen ou two thousand and nineteen.

Your turn!

19 Écrivez la mini-biographie de Shakespeare à partir de ces informations.

a. **Occupation:** Playwright, actor and poet
b. **Born:** April 26th, 1564 baptized in Stratford-upon-Avon, England - April 23rd
c. **Died:** April 23rd, 1616 in Stratford-upon-Avon, England
d. **Best known for:** Writing plays such as *Romeo and Juliet*, *Hamlet* and *Macbeth*

→ L'heure

Il existe deux manières différentes d'exprimer l'heure.

La manière la plus couramment utilisée

12 : It's … **o'clock.**
1 : It's five **past** …
2 : It's ten **past** …
3 : It's (a) quarter **past** …
4 : It's twenty **past** …
5 : It's twenty-five **past** …
6 : It's half **past** …
7 : It's twenty-five **to** …
8 : It's twenty **to** …
9 : It's (a) quarter **to** …
10 : It's ten **to** …
11 : It's five **to** …

On utilise les nombres de 1 à 12 pour exprimer les heures et on ajoute :

- pour les heures avant midi : **in the morning**
- pour les heures après-midi : **in the afternoon**
- Minuit : **midnight**
- Midi : **midday** ou **noon**

Une autre façon de dire l'heure

On peut dire comme en français, d'abord l'heure puis les minutes.

7:45 pm: seven forty-five pm — **am**: in the morning (**a**vant **m**idi)
6:15 am: six fifteen am — **pm**: in the afternoon (a**p**rès **m**idi)

Your turn!

20 Écrivez les heures en toutes lettres des deux manières possibles.

Every day, I wake up at (*6 am*) … . I get up at (*6:15 am*) … . I make myself a cup of tea, add some milk and have some cereals. I have a shower and get dressed at (*7:20 am*) … . I usually wear jeans, a blouse, a jumper or a cardigan and boots. At (*7:30 am*) … I do my hair and put on my make-up. I pack my bag with all my things. I then put on my coat and leave the house. I catch the bus at (*8:15 am*) … , and then I validate my bus pass and sit down. It takes about 45 minutes to get to my destination three miles away. Classes start at (*9:25 am*) … and end at (*11:25 am*) … . School finishes at (*3:20 pm*) … every day and that's really great.

→ L'âge

Pour parler de l'âge, on emploie **toujours** *to be*.

How old **are** you? Quel âge as-tu ?

I **am** 15 years old. ou I'**m** 15. J'ai 15 ans.

We **are** the same age. Nous avons le même âge.

When I **was** your age, I didn't speak good English. À ton âge, je ne parlais pas bien l'anglais.

! Pour exprimer l'âge :
- en français on utilise le verbe «avoir»,
- en anglais on utilise le verbe «être».

Quand on ne connaît pas précisément l'âge de quelqu'un mais qu'on pense qu'il a une vingtaine, trentaine, quarantaine... d'années, on utilise l'expression : *to be in one's twenties / thirties / forties...*

He is in his **20's**. Il a une vingtaine d'années.
Shakespeare died in his mid **50's**. Shakespeare est mort dans les 55 ans.
She started traveling in her late **twenties**. Elle s'est mise à voyager peu avant 30 ans.

On peut transformer l'énoncé suivant en groupe nominal.

a boy is fifteen years old → a fifteen-year-old boy

Fifteen-year-old devient l'adjectif de *boy*.
Les adjectifs en anglais ne s'accordent ni en genre ni en nombre, donc le *–s* disparaît !

Your turn!

21 Indiquez l'âge du prince Harry.

a. Prince Harry was born on 15th September 1984. He is a ... young man.
b. He lost his mother when he was a ... boy in 1997.
c. In May 2005, at ... he entered the Royal Military Academy of Sandhurst.
d. In 2014, he ... launched the Invictus Games.
e. He first met Meghan Markle on a blind date in July 2016, he ... .

Le groupe verbal

→ Introduction

La communication est basée sur un message adressé au destinataire par l'énonciateur.
Le choix du verbe permet d'informer le destinataire du message :

Énonciateur → **MESSAGE** → Destinataire

Le verbe est l'élément principal du groupe verbal, il traite de l'état ou de l'activité du sujet.

Il porte
- la marque *-s* à la 3e personne du singulier au présent simple,
- la marque de temps base verbale au présent *-ed* au passé,
- la marque d'aspect *V + ing* ou *V + en*.

Il peut être utilisé seul ou avec un auxiliaire (*be*, *have*, *do*) ou avec un modal (*can*, *must*, *will*).

Temps et aspects

Dans la grammaire, « temps » (*tense*) fait référence à la valeur temporelle d'un verbe : quand l'action a lieu. En anglais, il y a deux temps : le présent et le passé. À la différence du français, l'anglais n'a pas de temps futur. On parle de l'avenir soit avec le modal *will* soit avec le présent en *be + ing*.

Pour chaque temps il y a une sous-catégorie de formes qu'on appelle « aspects ». L'aspect d'un verbe fait référence à la durée. Autrement dit, l'aspect nous permet de mieux comprendre comment un événement se déroule à travers le temps. L'anglais a quatre aspects : simple (*simple*), progressif (*progressive*), parfait (*perfect*) et parfait progressif (*perfect progressive*).

1. Les auxiliaires

Les auxiliaires sont au centre du groupe verbal et aident à conjuguer les verbes. Ils servent à former le présent et le passé à la forme *be + ing*, la forme interrogative et la forme négative. *Have* et *be* servent à former les temps composés.

Be, do, have sont aussi des verbes lexicaux (des verbes comme les autres).

Superman **is** a famous superhero who **has** superpowers and **does** extraordinary things.
Superman est un célèbre super héros qui possède des super pouvoirs et réalise des choses extraordinaires.

→ Formes de *be*

	Présent	Passé
Forme affirmative	I **am**… You / we / they **are**… He / she / it **is**…	I / she / he / it **was**… We / you / they **were**…
Forme négative	**Au présent et au passé on ajoute *not* après *be*.**	
	I am **not**…	I was **not**…
Forme interrogative	**On inverse le sujet et l'auxiliaire.**	
	Am I… ?	**Was** I… ?

Les **formes contractées** sont très fréquentes.

Formes affirmatives	Formes négatives
am → *'m*	*am not* → *'m not*
are → *'re*	*are not* → *'re not / aren't*
is → *'s*	*is not* → *'s not / isn't*
Au passé on ne contracte que le not.	
was not → *wasn't*	*were not* → *weren't*

→ Emploi

Be base verbale sert à former le **présent** et le **passé** à la forme *be* + *V-ing* et à la **voix passive**.

Présent	**Are** you **working** on Friday? Est-ce que tu travailles vendredi ?
Passé	They **were watching** a film after dinner, when I called. Ils regardaient un film après le dîner, lorsque j'ai téléphoné.
Présent à la voix passive	His books **are sold** in all the bookshops. Ses livres sont vendus dans toutes les librairies.
Passé à la voix passive	This picture **was taken** in 1925 by a famous photographer. Cette photo a été prise en 1925 par un célèbre photographe.

Attention, *be* ne se traduit pas toujours par "être".

I am Mary.	Je **m'appelle** Mary.	Définir ou nommer
He is 14.	Il **a** 14 ans.	Exprimer l'âge
There is a park in the village.	**Il y a** un parc dans ce village.	Situer un élément dans l'espace
She is hungry.	Elle **a** faim.	Expressions
What's up?	Qu'est ce qui **se passe** ?	
He is afraid of the dark.	Il **a** peur du noir.	

→ Formes de *do*

Do auxiliaire porte la marque du temps (*do/does* au présent et *did* au passé). En tant qu'auxiliaire, ***do*** est employé dans les phrases interrogatives et négatives. Il peut aussi être utilisé dans les phrases affirmatives où il souligne l'emphase, c'est-à-dire l'insistance.

Forme affirmative	I / you / we / they **do** work in a British firm. Je travaille bien dans une entreprise britannique. (énoncé emphatique)
	He / she / it **does** work in a British firm. Il travaille bien dans une entreprise britannique.
Forme négative	I / you / we / they **don't** eat here. Je ne mange pas ici.
	He / she / it **doesn't** eat here. Il ne mange pas ici.
Forme interrogative	Where **do** you / we / they live? Où habites-tu?
	Does he / she / it live here? Vit-il ici ?

Les **formes contractées** sont très fréquentes.
- Présent : *do not = don't* *does not = doesn't*
- Prétérit : *did not = didn't*

! Attention : Il ne faut pas confondre ***do*** auxiliaire et ***do*** verbe lexical. Par exemple :
He **didn't do** the dishes. Il n'a pas fait la vaisselle
didn't est auxiliaire, mais *do* est verbe lexical ici.
Par ailleurs, l'auxiliaire ***do*** est aussi employé en présence de ***have*** verbe lexical.

→ Formes de *have* verbe lexical

Comme verbe lexical (« avoir », « posséder »)

	Présent	Passé
Forme affirmative	I / you / we / they **have**…	I / you / he / she / it / we / they **had**…
	He / she / it **has**…	
Forme négative	**On utilise l'auxiliaire *do*.**	
	I / you / he / she / it / we / they **don't have**…	I / you / he / she / it / we / they **didn't have**…
Forme interrogative	**On utilise l'auxiliaire *do*.**	
	Do I / you / we / they **have**…?	**Did** I / you / he / she / it / we / they **have**…?
	Does he / she / it **have**…?	

"**Do** you have this book?" – "Yes I **do**, it's a classic." « As-tu ce livre ? – Oui je l'ai, c'est un classique. »

! Attention : He **has** a car. Il a une voiture. [= « possède »]
He **has to go to** school at 8. Il doit aller à l'école à 8h. [obligation]

→ Emplois de *have* auxiliaire

Have est l'auxiliaire du ***present perfect*** et du ***past perfect***. Dans ce cas il est suivi du participe passé.

I **have** met this boy at school. J'ai rencontré ce garçon à l'école.

He **had** spent a lot of money to take his driving test.
Il avait dépensé beaucoup d'argent pour passer son permis de conduire.

Have est souvent contracté quand il est auxiliaire.

I**'ve got** a scooter. J'ai un scooter.

He**'s got** a car. Il a une voiture.

He **hasn't** got a car. Il n'a pas de voiture.

Your turn!

22 Complétez les phrases avec un auxiliaire : *isn't - did - do - don't - does not - didn't*.

a. "… you go to the cinema yesterday evening?" "No I didn't, I decided to stay home."
b. "John bought a new video game." "… he?"
c. … be afraid of the dog. It is a good dog that … bite.
d. "The waitress is very busy, … she?" "She hasn't come yet."
e. … you know who lives next door? He is very noisy.

2. La modalité

Le modal sert à interpréter et à commenter des faits ou des paroles. La modalité est une prise de position par rapport à celui ou celle qui parle.

Le modal est un auxiliaire, donc :
- il ne peut pas être utilisé avec *to*,
- on n'emploie pas *do* dans les interrogations ou négations,
- il ne prend pas de -*s* à la 3e personne du singulier présent,
- impossible d'utiliser deux modaux à la suite.

→ Formes et emplois

	Valeur	Exemple	Traduction
Can	Demande	**Can** I have this book?	Puis-je avoir ce livre ?
	Permission	**Can** I go out to play?	Puis-je sortir pour jouer ?
	Capacité [physique ou intellectuelle]	He **can** read.	Il sait lire.
Can't	Incapacité	He **can't** come tonight.	Il ne peut pas venir ce soir.
Could	Hypothèse	I **could** help you if you asked.	Je pourrais t'aider si tu le demandais.
	Can au passé	They **could** not help me.	Ils ne pouvaient pas m'aider.
May	Permission	You **may** go out.	Tu peux sortir.
	Possibilité [choix entre deux options]	It **may** rain.	Il se peut qu'il pleuve.
	Demande polie	**May** I have this pen?	Puis-je avoir ce stylo ?
May not	Interdiction	You **may** not see him because he is contagious.	Il est interdit de le voir car il est contagieux.
Might	Incertitude	He **might** be ill.	Il se pourrait qu'il soit malade.
Must	Obligation forte	The dog **must** go out now.	Le chien doit sortir maintenant.
	Nécessité quasi-certitude	She **must** be very young.	Elle doit être très jeune.
Mustn't (must not)	Interdiction	They **must** not come back.	Ils ne doivent pas revenir.
Shall	Énoncer une loi	You **shall** not kill.	Tu ne tueras point.
	Faire une suggestion	**Shall** we go for a drink?	Et si on allait prendre un verre ?
Should	Donner un conseil	You **should** ask the bus driver for the right stop.	Tu devrais demander au chauffeur pour connaître le bon arrêt.
	Regret	I **should** have stayed with you!	J'aurais dû rester avec vous !

	Valeur	Exemple	Traduction
Will	Coutume	Boys **will** be boys.	Les garçons resteront toujours des garçons.
Would	Habitude	He **would** go home, have lunch and go to the pool in the afternoon.	Il rentrait, déjeunait et passait l'après-midi à la piscine.

3. Modalité : équivalents des modaux

→ Formes et emplois

Modal et son équivalent	Passé	Futur	Valeur
CAN = to be able to	I arrived on time and **was able to** catch the train. Je suis arrivé·e à l'heure et j'ai pu prendre le train.	You **will be able to** join the team of course! Bien sûr, tu pourras rejoindre l'équipe.	Capacité
	She was so small that she **was not able to** carry her bag. Elle était si petite qu'elle ne pouvait pas porter son sac.	They **won't be able to** breathe on Mars. Ils ne pourront pas respirer sur Mars.	Incapacité
MAY = to be allowed to	He **was allowed to** try a second time. Il a été autorisé à faire un deuxième essai.	You **will be allowed to** get in if you have a passport. Vous pourrez rentrer si vous présentez votre passeport.	Permission
	They **were not allowed to** leave the country. Ils n'étaient pas autorisés à quitter le pays.	You **will not be allowed to** get in if you do not have a passport. Vous ne pourrez pas rentrer si vous n'avez pas de passeport.	Interdiction
MUST = to have to	I **had to** leave early to catch the 6 o'clock train. Il fallait que je parte tôt pour prendre le train de 6 heures.	You **will have to** buy some bread for tonight. Il faudra que tu achètes du pain pour ce soir.	Obligation
	You **didn't have to** buy all the books mentioned on the list. Vous n'étiez pas obligés d'acheter tous les livres de la liste.	You **won't have to** wait this time! Tu ne seras pas obligé·e d'attendre cette fois-ci.	Absence d'obligation

Your turn!

23 **Complétez les phrases avec les modaux suivants : *can - could - might - must - should - would*.**

a. I ... remind her to buy some flowers for the party.
b. She is very nice and she ... speak 3 languages.
c. We ... spend a weekend in London if we save enough money.
d. It ... be an adventure, as we have never been abroad.
e. If I have one piece of advice to give you, I think you ... send your job application as soon as possible.

4. Le présent simple

→ Formation

Base verbale sans auxiliaire.

Forme affirmative	I / you / we / they **play**…
	He / she / it **plays**…
Forme négative	On utilise l'auxiliaire *do*.
	I / you / we / they **do not play**…
	He / she / it **does not play**…
Forme interrogative	On utilise l'auxiliaire *do*.
	Do I / you / we / they **play**…?
	Does he / she / it **play**…?

Formes contractées: *do not* → *don't* / *does not* → *doesn't*

→ Emploi

Le présent simple sert à **décrire une action** de manière objective, sans donner d'opinion. L'énonciateur informe sans commenter.

Il n'y a pas de repérage temporel précis, toutefois on le rencontre souvent avec des **adverbes de fréquence** tels que ***always***, ***never***, ***often***, ***sometimes***, ***usually***…

Il peut aussi indiquer **une propriété permanente** du sujet : habitude, action répétée, instructions.

Caractéristique du sujet	Jane **plays** the piano. Ted and Joe **like** hip hop. Joe **plays** tennis. Jane joue du piano. Ted et Joe aiment le hip hop. Joe joue au tennis.
Actions habituelles	Lisa **works** in a shop every Sunday morning. Lisa travaille dans une boutique tous les dimanches matin.
Suite d'actions	Mary **gets up** at 8, **has** breakfast and **goes** to school. Mary se lève à 8h, prend le petit-déjeuner et va à l'école.
Faits sans commentaire	A lot of Japanese people **live** in this area. Beaucoup de Japonai·se·s vivent dans ce quartier.
Exprimer des vérités	The Sun **sets** in the West. Le soleil se couche à l'ouest.

Your turn!

24 **Choisissez l'adverbe qui convient :** ***always, never, sometimes, usually, often.***

a. She likes tea so she … drinks coffee.
b. They… open the shop on Saturday nights.
c. You … play the same tune, try another one!
d. His granddad … needs to have a nap in the afternoon.
e. She … travels to India because she loves Indian culture.

5. Le présent en *be* + V-*ing*

→ Formation

Be au présent + *V-ing*

Forme affirmative	I **am playing**…
	He / she / it **is playing**…
	You / we / they **are playing**…
Forme négative	I **am not playing**…
	He / she / it **is not playing**…
	You / we / they **are not playing**…
Forme interrogative	**Am** I **playing**… ?
	Is he / she / it **playing**…?
	Are you / we / they **playing**…?

→ Emploi

Le présent en ***be* + *V-ing*** sert à décrire et commenter une action en cours au moment de l'élocution. Il est différent du présent simple. L'énonciateur observe, comme s'il filmait l'action avec une caméra.

Look! They **are shooting** a film in the street.
Regarde ! Ils tournent un film dans la rue.

The policeman said: "We **are looking** for two men."
Le policier dit : « Nous cherchons deux hommes. »

Are you **writing** an email to your cousin?
Écris-tu un mail à ton cousin ?

Your turn!

25 Conjuguez le verbe entre parenthèses au présent en *be* + *V-ing*.

a. Listen! Eddie ... (play) the piano!
b. Where are the girls? They ... (play) tennis.
c. No, they ... (be). They ... (watch) TV!
d. What ... you ... (do)? I ... (work).

6. Le prétérit simple

→ Formation

Base verbale + *-ed* (sauf pour les verbes irréguliers)

! Les **verbes irréguliers** doivent être appris **par cœur** (→ page 237).

Forme affirmative	Forme interrogative	Forme négative	Forme contractée
I work**ed**	**Did** I work…?	I **did not** work	
You work**ed**	**Did** you work…?	You **did not** work	*did not* → *didn't*
He / she / it work**ed**	**Did** she / he / it work…?	He / she / it **did not** work	

L'auxiliaire *did* est obligatoire pour les formes négatives et interrogatives.

Did John **buy** a new car? I didn't think his car was that old!
John a-t-il acheté une nouvelle voiture ? Je ne pensais pas que sa voiture était si vieille !

He **cooked** dinner for me. Il m'a fait à manger.

Bill **did not** (**didn't**) come to my birthday party. Bill n'est pas venu à ma fête d'anniversaire.

→ Emploi

Le prétérit sert à exprimer une rupture par rapport au présent. L'énonciateur parle d'un fait daté, révolu, détaché du présent. C'est pourquoi le moment de l'action est souvent déterminé par une date, une heure, un adverbe ou une préposition, par exemple : ***last week***, ***ago***, ***before***, ***yesterday***. C'est le temps du récit. Il sert aussi à exprimer des situations irréelles ou non réalisables.

Fait passé / histoire	Shakespeare **was born** in 1564 in Stratford-upon-Avon. Shakespeare est né en 1564 à Stratford-upon-Avon.
Expression d'une situation	Bob **felt** very lonely after his children **left** home. Bob se sentit très seul quand les enfants quittèrent la maison.
Récit	Lea **was** seasick so Bill **had** to look after her all through the trip. Léa avait le mal de mer, donc Bill a dû s'occuper d'elle pendant tout le voyage.
Récit au passé	My friends **were** jealous because I **spent** two weeks in London last June. Mes amis étaient jaloux parce que j'ai passé deux semaines à Londres en juin dernier.
Récit / conte	Once upon a time, **there was** a prince who **lived** in a castle. Il était une fois un prince qui vivait dans un château.
Récit / roman	His left leg **was cut off** and he **carried** a crutch. Sa jambe gauche était amputée et il avait une béquille.
Hypothèse réalisable	If I **lived** in the USA, I **would live** in San Francisco. Si je vivais aux États-Unis, je vivrais à San Francisco.

Your turn!

26 Mettez les verbes à la forme qui convient.

a. Jill (*miss*) ... the train on Friday so she (*be*) ... late for work.
b. Jack (*send*) ... me an email last week.
c. He (*read*) ... *Oliver Twist* by Dickens when he (*be*) ... 10 years old.
d. Yesterday they (*fly*) ... to London and they (*land*) ... at Heathrow airport.
e. He never (*admit*) ... the crime.

27 Complétez avec les verbes suivants au prétérit : *build* - *say* - *go* - *burn* - *know* - *be* - *live*.

A strange story

An old woman (a)... in a small cottage near the railway station. People (b)... that she (c)... a witch because she was weird. When her house (d)... she disappeared. Finally they (e)... another house in the same place. Nobody ever (f)... where she (g)... .

7. Le prétérit en *be* + V-*ing*

→ Formation

Be au passé + *V-ing*

Il sert à la description d'une action en cours dans le passé, qui contraste avec le prétérit simple.

I **was reading** when she came in. Je lisais quand elle est entrée.
[j'étais en train de lire]

What **were** you **doing** last night at 10? Que faisais-tu hier soir à 10h ?

Plusieurs actions peuvent se croiser ou coïncider.

He **played** tennis yesterday. Il a joué au tennis hier.
[action passée, datée]

I **was playing** tennis when a storm broke out. Je jouais au tennis quand un orage a éclaté.
[action interrompue par un événement ponctuel]

En français on utilise l'imparfait pour décrire l'action en cours. Le passé simple ou le passé composé marque la rupture.

Leo **was surfing** on the Internet when his father **came** in. Léo surfait sur le net quand son père est entré.
[action en cours] [événement qui survient]

Your turn!

28 **Conjuguez les verbes entre parenthèses au prétérit en *be* + *V-ing*.**

a. What ... you ... (*do*) yesterday at 10pm?
b. We ... (*watch*) TV.
c. I ... (*drink*) a cup of tea and my husband (*eat*) ... sweets.
d. We ... (*not work*). It was really nice!

8. Le *present perfect*

→ Formation

Le ***present perfect*** se forme avec l'auxiliaire ***have*** et le participe passé du verbe : *have* + participe passé.

Affirmatif	Interrogatif	Négatif
I **have** finish**ed**	**Have** I finish**ed**...?	I have **not** finish**ed**
He / she / it **has** finish**ed**	**Has** he / she / it finish**ed**...?	He / she / it **has not** finish**ed**
You / we / they **have** finish**ed**	**Have** you / we / they finish**ed**...?	You / we / they **have not** finish**ed**

→ Emploi

Le *present perfect* est un aspect du présent. Il établit un lien entre un moment passé et un moment présent. Il désigne le **résultat d'une action**. Ainsi, on s'intéresse au bilan présent d'un événement passé.

This boy **has not done** his homework. Ce garçon n'a pas fait ses devoirs.

Look! The birds **have eaten** all the plums! Regarde, les oiseaux ont mangé toutes les prunes !

Have you **finished** reading the newspaper? As-tu fini de lire le journal ?

He **has not finished** his work yet. Il n'a pas encore fini son travail.

I **have lost** my keys! I can't open the door. J'ai perdu mes clés ! Je ne peux pas ouvrir la porte.

→ Les marqueurs temporels du *present perfect*

Le *present perfect* est souvent accompagné d'adverbes qui établissent un lien entre le présent et un événement passé.

- ***Just*** : l'action vient de se produire, elle est très proche du présent.

  I have **just** called your boss. Je viens d'appeler votre patron.

- ***Yet***, ***already*** : l'accent est mis sur l'action déjà ou pas encore réalisée.

  I have **already** been to New York. Je suis déjà allé·e à New York.

- ***Since***, ***for*** : on insiste sur la durée.

  I've lived in Dublin **for** two years, **since** 2016. J'habite à Dublin depuis deux ans, depuis 2016.
  [durée] [date de départ] [nous sommes en 2018]

- ***Never***, ***ever*** : on fait le bilan, au moment présent, sur une période de temps.

  I've **never** been to London. Je ne suis jamais allé·e à Londres.

  Have you **ever** been to New York? Es-tu déjà allé·e à New York ?

- Il est aussi accompagné d'adverbes qui ont un lien fort avec le présent : ***recently***, ***lately***, ***so far***.

  She's been very tired **lately**. Elle a été très fatiguée ces derniers temps.

Le *present perfect* sert également à dresser un ***bilan***, en particulier chiffré.

He **has taken** twelve pictures. Il a pris douze photos.

I **have worked** with them for five years now. Cela fait cinq ans que je travaille avec eux.

Le *present perfect* est obligatoire avec ***It's the first time***... , car c'est aussi un bilan.

It's the first time I **have taken** the train. C'est la première fois que je prends le train.

9. Le *present perfect* en *be* + *V-ing*

→ Formation

Le ***present perfect*** en *be* + *V-ing* se forme avec l'auxiliaire *have* suivi de *been* et le verbe en *V-ing*.

We'**ve been waiting** for a long time. Nous attendons depuis longtemps.

Forme affirmative	I / you / we / they **have been playing**…
	He / she / it **has been playing**…
Forme négative	I / you / we / they **have not been playing**…
	He / she / it **has not been playing** …
Forme interrogative	**Have** I / you / we / they **been playing**…?
	Has he / she / it **been playing**…?

Formes contractées

have been → *'ve been*

has been → *'s been*

have not been → *haven't been* ou *'ve not been*

has not been → *hasn't been* ou *'s not been*

→ Emploi

Avec le *present perfect* en *be* + V-*ing* on met l'accent sur l'**action** et **non le résultat**. Ici, peu importe que l'action soit terminée ou non.

She **has been walking** along the sea for six hours. Elle se promène le long de la mer depuis six heures.
[Que fait-elle depuis six heures ? Elle se promène le long de la mer.]

He **has been trying** to contact you all day. Il a tenté de vous joindre toute la journée.
[ici on insiste sur l'action et son échec]

***Present perfect* en *be* + *V-ing* avec *for* et *since*.**

For indique la **durée** d'une action. ***Since*** indique le **point de départ** d'une action.

They have been living here **for** two months. Ils habitent ici depuis deux mois. [durée]

They **have been living** here since September. Ils habitent ici depuis le mois de septembre.
[septembre = point de départ]

It's midnight and she's been sitting at her desk **for** 8 hours now, **since** 4 p.m.
Il est minuit et cela fait 8 heures qu'elle est assise à son bureau, depuis 16h.

Point de départ	Durée	Point d'arrivée
since 4 p.m.	**for 8 hours**	**midnight**

Your turn!

29 Mettez les verbes au *present perfect* ou au *present perfect* en *be* + *V-ing*.

a. Look it's 5pm and he ... (*work*) since 8am!
b. I ... (*write*) invitations for the wedding for 2 hours and I ... (*manage*) to write 20.
c. How long ... you ... (*play*) the piano? And how many concerts ... you ... (*do*)?
d. I ... (*study*) English for 10 years and I can speak fluently!

30 Mettez le verbe à la forme qui convient : prétérit ou *present perfect*.

a. Although we (*live*) ... in this town for several years, we still don't know many people.
b. What you ... (*do*) ... with my camera? It (*disappear*) ... .
c. Sam! What a surprise! I (not *see*) ... you since we (*leave*) ... Boston.
d. I (*meet*) ... this man in 2010.
e. We (*be*) ... friends for 8 years now.
f. This is the man who (*follow*) ... us yesterday.

10. Le *past perfect*

→ Formation

Forme identique à toutes les personnes : **auxiliaire *had*** (*'d*) **+ participe passé**.

She arrived late because she **had missed** her bus. Elle est arrivée en retard parce qu'elle avait raté son bus.

→ Emploi

Ce temps correspond généralement au plus-que-parfait français.

L'énonciateur établit un lien entre deux moments qui appartiennent au passé.

Once the children **had left** I **sat down** and relaxed. Après le départ des enfants, je me suis assis pour me reposer.
[2 actions passées, la plus ancienne au *past perfect*]

I **had** just **finished** eating my dinner when you **called** me. Je venais de finir mon dîner quand tu as appelé.

Le past perfect peut avoir une valeur de flashback, qui souligne une rétrospection entre deux moments temporels diamétralement opposés.

I will always remember my first year in my junior high school – I **had waited** the whole week before meeting all my new teachers!

Je me souviendrai toujours de ma première année dans mon collège… J'avais attendu toute une semaine avant de rencontrer tous mes nouveaux professeurs !

Le *past perfect* s'utilise aussi pour exprimer la durée (« depuis »). Cela correspond à un imparfait français.

They had been playing tennis **for** 2 hours. Ils jouaient au tennis **depuis** 2 heures.

How long had they been playing golf? **Depuis** combien de temps jouaient-ils au golf ?

Your turn!

31 Conjuguez les verbes entre parenthèses au *past perfect*.

a. When he woke up this morning, his alarm clock … already … (*ring*) twice.
b. She looked so different: she … (*have*) her hair cut !
c. She … (*cry*) all morning. Her eyes were red.
d. He arrived late to school because his mother … (*not - wake*) him up.

11. L'expression du futur, référence à l'avenir

L'anglais ne dispose pas d'un temps "futur" à proprement parler. Différentes structures permettent de faire référence à l'avenir :

- les modaux ***will*** (***shall***),
- certaines tournures du présent, ***be*** + V-***ing*** et ***be going to*** + verbe,
- certaines expressions du futur avec *be* et *to*.

Il convient de choisir entre ces formes selon le contexte.

Forme	Exemple	Valeur
Will	My sister **will be** 16 next month. Ma sœur aura 16 ans dans un mois.	Fait daté inévitable
	She **will marry** him. Elle va l'épouser.	Volonté ou certitude
	The weather forecast is bad I think it **will rain** tomorrow. La météo est mauvaise, je crois qu'il va pleuvoir.	Hypothèse quasi certaine (probabilité, valeur de prédiction)
	John **has gone out** to play cricket. He **won't** be back before dark. John est parti jouer au cricket. Il ne sera pas de retour avant la nuit.	Actions prévues, organisées
Shall	It's getting late. **Shall** we **go** home? Il se fait est tard, on va rentrer.	Valeur de futur proche
	Shall we **meet** again next week? Et si on se revoyait la semaine prochaine ?	Proposition

Forme	Exemple	Valeur
Présent en *be* + *V-ing*	We **are spending** Christmas at my parents' this year. Nous passerons Noël chez mes parents cette année.	Fait anticipé, organisé à l'avance
	Who**'s playing** tonight? Qui joue ce soir ?	Valeur de futur proche
Be going to + *V*	She**'s going to teach** in a new school in September. Elle va enseigner dans une nouvelle école en septembre.	Valeur de futur proche
Expressions du futur avec *be* et *to*	Come on! The show **is about to start**! Allez, venez vite ! Le spectacle est sur le point de commencer !	Action imminente, sur le point de se produire
	He **is bound to** come back. Il va sûrement revenir.	Forte probabilité
	This **is likely to** happen again. Cela est susceptible de se reproduire. / Il y a de fortes chances que cela se reproduise.	Probabilité
	The senate **is to debate** a new law next week. Le sénat doit débattre une nouvelle loi demain.	Acte officiel prévu qui aura lieu

→ Subordonnées de temps en *when* et futur

On peut faire des suppositions sur l'avenir en utilisant ***when*** ou ***if***. Dans ce cas, ils ont la même valeur.

Les subordonnées introduites par ***when*** (quand), ***as soon as*** (dès que), ***until*** (jusqu'à ce que), ***before*** (avant que), ***while*** (pendant que) sont suivies du présent.

I will meet you **when I come back** from New York.
Je vous rencontrerai quand je rentrerai de / à mon retour de New York.

I will call him **as soon as I can spare** a moment. Je l'appellerai dès que j'aurai un instant de libre.

Your turn!

32 Choisissez la bonne réponse.

a. What ... tonight?
1 *are you doing* - 2 *do you* - 3 *do you do*

b. You ... thirsty after all this exercising, I guess.
1 *will have felt* - 2 *will be feeling* - 3 *are to feel* - 4 *felt*

c. They ... feel better after they have taken the medicine.
1 *will* - 2 *will take* - 3 *are taking* - 4 *won't take*

d. He says he ... come to the match with us because he is very sick.
1 *will* - 2 *won't* - 3 *isn't going to* - 4 *was not*

e. Tomorrow ... Friday .
1 *is going to be* - 2 *is to be* - 3 *is* - 4 *is about to be*

f. Meghan Markle says she wants to have children as soon as she ... .
1 will be married - 2 won't be married - 3 gets married - 4 gets divorced

12. *Should*

→ Formation

Forme affirmative	I / you / he / she / it / we / they **should play**…
Forme négative	I / you / he / she / it / we / they **should not play**…
Forme interrogative	**Should** I / you / he / she / it / we / they **play**…?

→ Emploi

Should peut exprimer différentes valeurs :

- une **probabilité**

  He **should be** back soon. Il devrait bientôt arriver.

- un **conseil**

  You **should leave** her alone. Tu devrais la laisser tranquille.

  You **should do** your exercise. Tu devrais faire ton exercice.

- un **reproche ou un regret**

  He **should not** spend so much time on the computer. Il ne devrait pas passer autant de temps sur l'ordinateur.

  I **shouldn't have eaten** the plums. Je n'aurais pas dû manger les prunes.

- une **anticipation**

  I **should get** a good mark in the test. Je devrais avoir une bonne note au devoir.
  [sous-entendu j'ai bien travaillé !]

Your turn!

33 **Indiquez la valeur de *should* : *devoir - conseil - reproche/regret - anticipation*.**

a. You should stop smoking.
b. She should come to the gig. It will be good fun.
c. You should get there on time if you take an early train.
d. They should stop arguing.
e. Lisa should have come to the party.
f. Jim should try to eat fewer sweets.

34 **Rédigez une phrase avec chaque valeur de *should* avec les mots suivants en anglais : *neiger, faire tes devoirs, donner son mot de passe, passer de bonnes vacances*.**

13. Le conditionnel : *would*

On utilise *would* pour exprimer le conditionnel, c'est à dire une hypothèse irréelle ou peu probable.

If + **prétérit modal** puis sujet + *would* + V

If I **won** the lottery, I **would buy** a boat. Si je gagnais à la loterie, j'achèterais un bateau.

Attention, le verbe dans la structure *if* + V-*ed* est un prétérit modal. On utilise *were* et non *was*.

If I **were** you, I **would revise** for the test. Si j'étais toi, je réviserais pour le devoir.

Your turn!

35 Compléter ces phrases avec *would*.

a. If I could be an animal, … .
b. If they practised more often as a band, they … .
c. He … if he had better marks at school.
d. She … if her father agreed.
e. My favourite team … if they could afford better players.

14. Les énoncés à l'impératif

L'impératif sert à donner un ordre.

→ Formation

Ordre donné à *you*	Forme affirmative : base verbale	**Look** at me! Regarde-moi !
	Forme négative : *Don't* + V	**Don't** cry! Ne pleure pas !
Ordre donné à *we*	Forme affirmative : *Let's* + V	**Let's** go home! Rentrons à la maison !
	Forme négative : *Let's not* + V	**Let's not** forget the cake! N'oublions pas le gâteau !

Your turn!

36 Traduisez en anglais.

a. Dépêche-toi !
b. Appelle-moi bientôt !
c. Croyez-moi, je ne plaisante pas. (*joke*)
d. Arrête tout de suite !
e. Ouvre la fenêtre !

15. La voix passive

→ Formation

***Be* + participe passé**

L'auxiliaire de la voix passive est ***be***. Le verbe qui suit est au participe passé.
Le complément d'agent est celui qui fait l'action, quand il est mentionné.

Présent	This film **is awarded** an Oscar.	Ce film est récompensé d'un Oscar.
Présent *be + V-ing*	This film **is being awarded** an Oscar.	
Prétérit	This film **was awarded** an Oscar.	Ce film a été récompensé d'un Oscar.
Prétérit en *be + V-ing*	This film **was being awarded** an Oscar.	
Present perfect	This film **has been awarded** an Oscar.	Ce film avait été récompensé d'un Oscar.
Futur	This film **will be awarded** an Oscar.	Ce film sera récompensé d'un Oscar.

Attention, la voix active met l'accent sur le **sujet de l'action**.
La voix passive met l'accent sur l'**objet de l'action**.
Le **complément d'agent** est celui qui fait l'action. Il est mentionné quand il est important.

Voix active	**The public** applauded **the winner**. Le public a applaudi le gagnant. [sujet] [objet]
Voix passive	**The winner** was applauded **by the public**. Le gagnant a été applaudi par le public. [agent]

This novel **was written by** Dickens. Ce roman a été écrit par Dickens.
The mouse **should be caught** by the cat. La souris devrait être attrapée par le chat.
A body **was found** at the bottom of the lake. Un corps a été trouvé au fond du lac.
Joe **has been hired by** a big firm. Joe vient d'être embauché par une grosse entreprise.
English **is spoken** here! Ici on parle anglais !

Your turn!

37 **Transformez les phrases au passif en gardant le même temps.**

a. The postman collects the letters every evening.
b. Someone stole my car.
c. You should make a decision.
d. My uncle gave him a bike. (*2 réponses possibles*)
e. The river is flooding the house.

16. La subordonnée relative

Les pronoms relatifs ***who***, ***which***, ***that*** et ***whose*** permettent d'introduire une proposition subordonnée relative. Le choix du pronom relatif dépend de la nature de l'antécédent (personne ou chose).

→ Pronom relatif avec antécédent animé

Who s'emploie avec un antécédent animé, une personne, en position de sujet de la phrase.

The woman, **who** has just parked her car, is my neighbour. La femme, qui vient de garer sa voiture, est ma voisine.

En position de complément d'objet direct ou indirect, le pronom relatif est en général omis.

The man **Ø** she spoke to is her brother. L'homme à qui elle a parlé est son frère.

→ Pronom relatif avec antécédent inanimé

The book, **which** was on the desk yesterday, is Tom's. Le livre, qui était sur le bureau hier, est celui de Tom.

Il s'agit d'une proposition **relative appositive**, précédée d'une virgule.

→ Pronom relatif *that*

Le pronom relatif ***that*** s'emploie indifféremment avec une personne ou une chose. Il permet d'introduire une **relative déterminative**. Il n'y a pas de virgule avant le pronom relatif.

The train **that** was cancelled last Monday had a technical problem. Le train qui a été annulé lundi dernier avait un problème technique.

→ *Whose* et la possession

Whose est employé pour établir une relation de possession entre deux éléments.

The house **whose** roof is red is the mayor's. La maison dont le toit est rouge est celle du maire.

Your turn!

38 Complétez par le pronom relatif qui convient : *who, which, that, whose*.

a. The train, ... has just left the platform, is the Liverpool one.

b. Her cricket instructor, ... came from Cardiff yesterday, has already gone.

c. The suitcase ... was left unattended was finally destroyed by the customs officer.

d. The mayor ... second home was broken into reported to the police.

17. Les verbes d'état

Les verbes d'état expriment les émotions, les croyances, la perception et l'activité mentale du sujet. Ces verbes n'admettent généralement pas la forme en *be* + *V-ing*.

Il arrive que ces verbes s'emploient au présent en *be* + *V-ing*. Dans ce cas ils font référence à des actions.

He **is thinking** of moving to another country. Il pense sérieusement à s'installer dans un autre pays.

→ Quelques verbes d'état

Les idées abstraites	be être, believe croire, exist exister, forget oublier, imagine imaginer, know savoir, mean signifier, need avoir besoin de, remember se rappeler, think penser, understand comprendre…
Les émotions	care s'occuper de/soigner, dislike détester, envy jalouser, fear craindre, hate haïr, like aimer, love adorer…
La perception	feel éprouver, hear entendre, see voir, seem sembler, smell sentir, taste goûter…
La possession	belong appartenir, have avoir, possess avoir, own posséder…

Your turn!

39 Mettez le verbe au présent simple ou au présent en *be* + *V-ing*.

a. Joe ... (*think*) it is difficult to learn English .

b. She ... (*enjoy*) her life as a student at the moment.

c. My friends ... (*not like*) waiting for the bus.

d. I ... (*feel*) bad for what just happened.

e. Tea ... (*remain*) the most popular drink in Great Britain.

Verbes irréguliers

	Base verbale	Prétérit	Participe passé	Traduction
	Trois formes identiques			
1	cost	cost	cost	*coûter*
2	cut /ʌ/	cut /ʌ/	cut /ʌ/	*couper*
3	hit	hit	hit	*frapper*
4	hurt /ɜː/	hurt /ɜː/	hurt /ɜː/	*blesser*
5	let /e/	let /e/	let /e/	*permettre, louer*
6	put /ʊ/	put /ʊ/	put /ʊ/	*mettre, poser*
7	read /iː/	read /e/	read /e/	*lire*
8	set /e/	set /e/	set /e/	*fixer*
9	shut /ʌ/	shut /ʌ/	shut /ʌ/	*fermer*
	Prétérit et participe passé identiques			
10	bend /e/	bent /e/	bent /e/	*(se) courber*
11	bring /ɪ/	brought /ɔː/	brought /ɔː/	*apporter*
12	build /ɪ/	built /ɪ/	built /ɪ/	*construire*
13	burn /ɜː/	burnt /ɜː/	burnt /ɜː/	*brûler*
14	buy /aɪ/	bought /ɔː/	bought /ɔː/	*acheter*
15	catch /æ/	caught /ɔː/	caught /ɔː/	*attraper*
16	deal /iː/	dealt /e/	dealt /e/	*distribuer*
17	dream /iː/	dreamt /e/	dreamt /e/	*rêver*
18	feel /iː/	felt /e/	felt /e/	*(se) sentir, éprouver*
19	fight /aɪ/	fought /ɔː/	fought /ɔː/	*se battre, combattre*
20	find /aɪ/	found /aʊ/	found /aʊ/	*trouver*
21	get /e/	got /ɒ/	got /ɒ/	*obtenir*
22	have /æ/	had /æ/	had /æ/	*avoir*
23	hear /ɪə/	heard /ɜː/	heard /ɜː/	*entendre*
24	hold /əʊ/	held /e/	held /e/	*tenir*
25	keep /iː/	kept /e/	kept /e/	*garder*
26	lead /iː/	led /e/	led /e/	*mener, guider*
27	learn /ɜː/	learnt /ɜː/	learnt /ɜː/	*apprendre*
28	leave /iː/	left /e/	left /e/	*laisser, quitter, partir*
29	lend /e/	lent /e/	lent /e/	*prêter*
30	light /aɪ/	lit /ɪ/	lit /ɪ/	*allumer, éclairer*

	Base verbale	Prétérit	Participe passé	Traduction
31	lose /uː/	lost /ɒ/	lost /ɒ/	*perdre*
32	make /eɪ/	made /eɪ/	made /eɪ/	*faire, fabriquer*
33	mean /iː/	meant /e/	meant /e/	*signifier, vouloir dire*
34	meet /iː/	met /e/	met /e/	*rencontrer*
35	pay /eɪ/	paid /eɪ/	paid /eɪ/	*payer*
36	say /eɪ/	said /e/	said /e/	*dire (pas à qqun)*
37	sell /e/	sold /əʊ/	sold /əʊ/	*vendre*
38	send /e/	sent /e/	sent /e/	*envoyer*
39	shoot /uː/	shot /ɒ/	shot /ɒ/	*tirer*
40	sit /ɪ/	sat /æ/	sat /æ/	*être assis*
41	sleep /iː/	slept /e/	slept /e/	*dormir*
42	smell /e/	smelt /e/	smelt /e/	*sentir (odeur)*
43	spend /e/	spent /e/	spent /e/	*dépenser, passer (temps)*
44	stand /æ/	stood /ʊ/	stood /ʊ/	*être debout*
45	stick /ɪ/	stuck /ʌ/	stuck /ʌ/	*coller*
46	strike /aɪ/	struck /ʌ/	struck /ʌ/	*frapper*
47	teach /iː/	taught /ɔː/	taught /ɔː/	*enseigner*
48	tell/e/	told /əʊ/	told /əʊ/	*dire (à qqn)*
49	think /ɪ/	thought /ɔː/	thought /ɔː/	*penser*
50	understand /ʌ/ /ə/ /æ/	understood /ʌ/ /ə/ /ʊ/	understood /ʌ/ /ə/ /ʊ/	*comprendre*
51	win /ɪ/	won /ʌ/	won /ʌ/	*gagner*

Deux formes identiques

52	beat /iː/	beat /iː/	beaten /iː/ /ə/	*battre*
53	become /ɪ/ /ʌ/	became /ɪ/ /eɪ/	become /ɪ/ /ʌ/	*devenir*
54	come /ʌ/	came /eɪ/	come /ʌ/	*venir*
55	run /ʌ/	ran /æ/	run /ʌ/	*courir*

Trois formes différentes

56	awake /ə/ /eɪ/	awoke /ə/ /əʊ/	awoken /ə/ /əʊ/ /ə/	*(se) réveiller*
57	be /iː/	was /ɒ/- were /ɜː/	been /iː/	*être*
58	bear /eə/	bore /ɔː/	borne /ɔː/	*supporter*
59	begin /ɪ/ /ɪ/	began /ɪ/ /æ/	begun /ɪ/ /ʌ/	*commencer*
60	bite /aɪ/	bit /ɪ/	bitten /ɪ/ /ə/	*mordre*
61	blow /əʊ/	blew /uː/	blown /əʊ/	*souffler*
62	break /eɪ/	broke /əʊ/	broken /əʊ/ /ə/	*casser*
63	choose /uː/	chose /əʊ/	chosen /əʊ/ /ə/	*choisir*

	Base verbale	Prétérit	Participe passé	Traduction
64	do /uː/	did /ɪ/	done /ʌ/	*faire*
65	draw /ɔː/	drew /uː/	drawn /ɔː/	*dessiner*
66	drink /ɪ/	drank /æ/	drunk /ʌ/	*boire*
67	drive /aɪ/	drove /əʊ/	driven /ɪ/ /ə/	*conduire*
68	eat /iː/	ate /eɪ/	eaten /iː/ /ə/	*manger*
69	fall /ɔː/	fell /e/	fallen /ɔː/ /ə/	*tomber*
70	fly /aɪ/	flew /uː/	flown /əʊ/	*voler (dans les airs)*
71	forbid /ə/ /ɪ/	forbade /ə/ /eɪ/	forbidden /ə/ /ɪ/ /ə/	*interdire*
72	foresee /ɔː/ /iː/	foresaw /ɔː/ /ɔː/	foreseen /ɔː/ /iː/	*prévoir*
73	forget /ə/ /e/	forgot /ə/ /ɒ/	forgotten /ə/ /ɒ/ /ə/	*oublier*
74	forgive /ə/ /ɪ/	forgave /ə/ /eɪ/	forgiven /ə/ /ɪ/ /ə/	*pardonner*
75	freeze /iː/	froze /əʊ/	frozen /əʊ/ /ə/	*geler*
76	give /ɪ/	gave /eɪ/	given /ɪ/ /ə/	*donner*
77	go /əʊ/	went /e/	gone /ɒ/	*aller*
78	grow /əʊ/	grew /uː/	grown /əʊ/	*grandir, croître*
79	hide /aɪ/	hid /ɪ/	hidden /ɪ/ /ə/	*(se) cacher*
80	know /əʊ/	knew /njuː/	known /əʊ/	*savoir, connaître*
81	lie /aɪ/	lay /eɪ/	lain /eɪ/	*être étendu*
82	ride /aɪ/	rode /əʊ/	ridden /ɪ/ /ə/	*aller (à cheval, à vélo)*
83	ring /ɪ/	rang /æ/	rung /ʌ/	*sonner*
84	rise /aɪ/	rose /əʊ/	risen /ɪ/ /ə/	*s'élever, se lever*
85	see /iː/	saw /ɔː/	seen /iː/	*voir*
86	shake /eɪ/	shook /ʊ/	shaken /eɪ/ /ə/	*secouer*
87	show /əʊ/	showed /əʊ/	shown /əʊ/	*montrer*
88	sing /ɪ/	sang /æ/	sung /ʌ/	*chanter*
89	speak /iː/	spoke /əʊ/	spoken /əʊ/ /ə/	*parler*
90	steal /iː/	stole /əʊ/	stolen /əʊ/ /ə/	*voler, dérober*
91	swear /eə/	swore /ɔː/	sworn /ɔː/	*jurer*
92	swim /ɪ/	swam /æ/	swum /ʌ/	*nager*
93	take /eɪ/	took /ʊ/	taken /eɪ/ /ə/	*prendre*
94	tear /eə/	tore /ɔː/	torn /ɔː/	*déchirer*
95	throw /əʊ/	threw /uː/	thrown /əʊ/	*jeter*
96	undergo /ʌ/ /ə/ /əʊ/	underwent /ʌ/ /ə/ /e/	undergone /ʌ/ /ə/ /ɒ/	*subir*
97	undertake /ʌ/ /ə/ /eɪ/	undertook /ʌ/ /ə/ /ʊ/	undertaken /ʌ/ /eɪ/ /ə/	*entreprendre*
98	wear /eə/	wore /ɔː/	worn /ɔː/	*porter (sur soi)*
99	weep /iː/	wept /e/	wept /e/	*pleurer*
100	write /aɪ/	wrote /əʊ/	written /ɪ/ /ə/	*écrire*

Banque d'exercices

Le groupe nominal

1. Les articles

1 Mettez l'article qui convient : *a, an, the* ou *Ø*.

a. ... insect is ... small creature and ... owl is ... bird.
b. I don't believe you, it must be ... joke. Tell me ... truth!
c. He went to ... window, looked at ... sky and saw ... falling star.
d. ... people believe that ... English language is easier than ... French.
e. There are plenty of ... stereotypes about ... Irish and ... Irish immigrants.
f. After breaking ... window, ... robbers came into ... house and stole ... jewels and ... expensive objects.

2 Mettez l'article qui convient : *a, an, the* ou *Ø*.

a. ... children usually get ... toys for ... Christmas.
b. Sam plays ... piano; his sister prefers playing ... football.
c. Some people suffer from ... obesity because of ... fast food.
d. ... honesty is ... best policy.
e. ... Sun is essential to all life-forms on ... Earth.
f. ... Los Angeles flight is now leaving at ... gate 20.

3 Mettez l'article qui convient : *a, an, the* ou *Ø*.

a. I live in ... Great Britain.
b. What ... unusual car! It's Fred's, he's ... university student.
c. My grandfather was ... M.P. (Member of Parliament).
d. ... potatoes are expensive this year.
e. Have you seen ... dress I bought this morning?
f. My friend is ... English teacher.

4 Mettez l'article qui convient : *a, an, the* ou *Ø*.

a. He left on ... foot, but came back by ... car.
b. ... man I saw was ... electrician.
c. ... whales are in risk of ... extinction.
d. What ... exciting adventure we had!
e. Have you ever seen ... U.F.O.?
f. I'm hungry. Could you give me ... few biscuits, please?

2. Les noms dénombrables et indénombrables

5 Relevez les noms et classez-les selon qu'ils sont dénombrables ou indénombrables.

a. I decided to follow your advice, I can't find solutions by myself.
b. My best wishes: happiness, love and health!
c. They took a lot of things for the trip: food, water, books and even music.
d. I need some cash: dollars, euros, coins, bills... any currency is fine.
e. As a child, I used to drink milk but now I prefer coffee.
f. You bought a nice piece of furniture and a TV set at the second-hand shop.
g. Please contact the office for more information.

3. Le pluriel des noms

6 Mettez les noms soulignés au pluriel et faites les accords nécessaires.

a. My foot is sore, I need to take off my shoe.
b. This tooth is starting to fall.
c. The police arrested the thief inside the bank.
d. When I was in the forest, I heard the cry of a wolf.
e. What is your favourite series?
f. This is the best country in the world.

4. Les noms composés

7 À l'aide du dictionnaire, sélectionnez la forme correcte entre parenthèses.

a. Look at my hair, I need a ... . (*haircut / hair-cut*)
b. Jane's ... is very sweet. (*mother in law / mother-in-law*)
c. Once in the police station, they took my ... . (*finger prints / finger-prints*)
d. Read carefully and check all the ... . (*typing errors / typing-errors*)
e. On New Year's Eve, I always go and watch the ... . (*fire works / fireworks*)
f. If you are victim of bullying, talk to a ... . (*grown up / grown-up*)

5. Le génitif

8 Transformez le groupe de mots souligné afin d'utiliser un génitif.

a. It's <u>a cottage of a farm-labourer</u>.
b. Someone has stolen <u>the necklace of Diana</u>.
c. James brought <u>the cycle of the little boy</u> from the garden.
d. <u>The mother of the husband</u> paid a bail to avoid him prison.
e. He must be <u>the successor of Chief Krotoa</u>.
f. <u>The lips of Mrs Turner</u> are painted red.
g. <u>The sons of Charles</u> are William and Harry.

9 Transformez les phrases afin d'utiliser un génitif.

a. The medicine of Doctor Kamal gives me no relief.
b. The tallest building of Cape Town is collapsing.
c. The concert of the artist was great.
d. When the steak of Martin was served, he started eating.
e. I decided to wait for a while at the house of Moira.
f. The ideas of Christopher were getting a bit confused.
g. The wizard of J.K. Rowling is famous.

6. Les démonstratifs : *this/these* et *that/those*

10 Complétez avec *this*, *these*, *that* ou *those*.

a. I know, but we are the guests in ... house.
b. ... is what we do in these situations.
c. At the meeting, we all agreed on ... rules.
d. "Are there people in ... room?" asked the wizard.
e. I remember ... black and white silent films.
f. ... are my other two daughters, Sophina and Brenda.
g. How is your family doing ... days?

7. Les adjectifs et noms de nationalité

11 Retrouvez les noms ou les adjectifs de nationalité correspondant aux pays entre parenthèses.

a. I was a little ... boy who didn't know about my country. (*Poland*)
b. The ... officer was standing in front of his office. (*Germany*)
c. Do you know the song "I'm a ... in New York"? (*Jamaica*)
d. The ... arrived in South Africa in 1820. (*Britain*)
e. My boyfriend is from Spain, he likes to speak ... . (*Spain*)
f. ... are as ... as the ... . (*Scotland / Britain / England*)
g. Haggis is a famous ... dish. (*Scotland*)

8. L'ordre des adjectifs

12 Remettez les adjectifs qualificatifs dans l'ordre.

a. Catherine was an French/ young /energetic woman with bulging / blue / small eyes.
b. A municipal / new / brick building stood at the far end of the street.
c. I was walking on a soft / large / woolen / blue carpet.
d. The man was a dark / short man with wavy / black / glossy hair.
e. We are passing through a old / famous / narrow street.
f. People like eating unhealthy / chocolate / giant cookies.

9. Les adjectifs en *-ed* et *-ing*

13 Choisissez entre la forme adjectivale *-ed* ou *-ing* des verbes entre parenthèses.

a. The archaeologists are looking for an ... vessel. (*undiscover*)
b. Your behaviour is simply ... . (*revolt*)
c. She seems ... and ... at the same time. (*shock – fascinate*)
d. He emigrated to the ... land. (*promise*)
e. It is ... to see Helen with her dolls. (*amuse*)
f. I was ... to meet President Obama. (*honour*)

10. Les quantifieurs : *some, any, no* ou *not any*

14 Complétez les phrases à l'aide de *no, any, some, each, every*.

a. This is too much! The TV is switched on at ... hour of the day and night.
b. She poured ... water into her glass as it was empty.
c. You must fry ... side of the fish for just one minute.
d. ... child under the age of 8 should stay alone at home.
e. Suzan liked ... single country she has visited.

15 Complétez les phrases à l'aide des composés de *no, any, some, every*.

a. Nowadays ... is connected!
b. He has lost his keys ... . He can't find them.
c. You're going to have to leave. ... is allowed on these premises.
d. ... you say will be kept strictly confidential.
e. Unfortunately, we have ... to sleep tonight.
f. I heard ... outside, ... must be happening.

11. Les quantifieurs : *a lot, much, many*

16 Complétez avec *a lot of, much* ou *many*.

a. The earthquake has done ... damage to the city.
b. She has ... respect for Martin Luther King.
c. You are asking too ... questions. Don't talk too ... .
d. I spent so ... money for nothing.
e. We visited ... places and saw ... wonderful things.
f. ... of my friends do not live here.

12. Les quantifieurs : *a little, a few, little, few*

17 Complétez avec *a little, a few, little, few*.

a. ... water was spilled on the book.
b. Mr Anderson will join the meeting in ... minutes.
c. Joyce borrowed ... books from the library.
d. He had ... money left when he got out from the casino.
e. Oscar broke his glasses ... days ago.
f. She wasn't feeling well but she ate ... .

13. Les pronoms personnels

18 Remplacez les mots soulignés par le pronom personnel correspondant.

a. Alison married Jonathan a few years ago.
b. The two brothers stood beside the door.
c. Anyone can ask Mary about the hidden treasure.
d. The young man was secretly staring at the girl.
e. Please leave the window open.
f. The voices of the singers were rising.

14. Les pronoms et déterminants possessifs

19 Complétez les phrases à l'aide d'un déterminant possessif équivalent.

a. When he got home, ... wife was sleeping.
b. Snakes kill ... victims slowly.
c. I have missed ... train again.
d. Julia asked one of ... friends to have a walk in the park.
e. He realised the impact of ... lie on ... relationship.
f. Why don't you put the bag in ... room?

20 Remplacez les groupes de mots soulignés par les pronoms possessifs correspondants.

a. Now take their presents and hide them.
b. I say the cows and chickens are my cows and chickens.
c. His hand covered her hands then he held her tenderly.
d. Please, my home is your home for as long as you like.
e. I put my clothes on his clothes.
f. Let's share: the money is our money not my money.

15. Les pronoms réfléchis et réciproques

21 Utilisez le bon pronom réfléchi.

a. DIY means "Do it ... " .
b. They are quite selfish, they always put ... first.
c. Don't help me mum, I want to do it ... .
d. We never buy any ready-made meals, we cook our food ... .
e. This is a self-portrait, she painted it ... .
f. Aaron smiled to ... , satisfied with his victory.

22 Utilisez le bon pronom réciproque : *each other* ou *one another*.

a. They're the perfect couple! They complete ... perfectly.
b. Stop arguing, you two! I want you to look at ... .
c. This meeting is going nowhere, people are not listening to ... .
d. Respect is about not judging ... .

16. Le comparatif et le superlatif

23 Mettez les adjectifs au comparatif demandé.

a. Jacky was getting ... and ... . (*angry* / +)
b. Lee was ... Edgard. (*fortunate* / -)
c. Press ... to open the door. (*hard* /+)
d. Kim is ... her sister. (*lazy* / =)
e. Let's read a ... story, it's too late. (*short* / +)
f. Eating fast-food is ... traditional food. (*healthy* / -)

24 Mettez les adjectifs au superlatif demandé.

a. I had ... day ever. (*extraordinary* / +)
b. This is ... film of all my life. (*interesting* / -)
c. W. Shakespeare is considered ... dramatist of all time. (*great* / +)
d. The Nile is ... river in the world. (*long* / +)
e. Tell me who ... artist is. (*talented* / -)
f. South African art is one of ... forms of art. (*old* / +)

17. Les chiffres et les nombres

25 Prononcez puis écrivez en toutes lettres les nombres suivants.

a. 240
b. 215,999
c. 12.14
d. 1/5
e. 1/4
f. 2/3

26 Traduisez les phrases suivantes.

a. Des centaines de personnes sont venues, trois cent cinquante-huit pour être exact.
b. Le score du match était 0-3.
c. Anna est première et son frère est deuxième du classement.
d. George W. Bush était le 43e président des États-Unis.

18. *Not anymore, no more, none, never*

27 Complétez avec *never, anymore* et *no more*.

a. Kate is ... late.
b. Lulu doesn't live in London ... , she lives in New York.
c. ... chocolate for Mason and Ed, they've had enough!
d. Liverpool's football anthem is "You'll ... walk alone".

28 Votre père vous demande de lui dicter la liste des courses. Vous ouvrez le réfrigérateur et vous lui indiquez ce qu'il n'y a plus. Construisez un dialogue en utilisant au moins une fois les adverbes *not anymore, no more, none* et *never*.

Ex. : Is there any cheese left ? No, there is none.

19. Date, heure et âge

29 Écrivez les dates et les heures suivantes en toutes lettres.

a. 3 septembre 2018
b. 1er août 1990
c. les années 1970
d. 17h45
e. 01h58
f. 19h00

30 Traduisez les phrases suivantes.

a. Stephen Hawking est mort en mars 2018, il était né en 1942, il avait donc 76 ans.
b. Zaman a une trentaine d'années.
c. J'ai 16 ans, je suis né un lundi, en mars, dans la matinée, à 10h15 pour être précis.
d. Le film commence à 16h20, ensuite on ira au restaurant, j'ai le droit de rentrer à minuit !

Le groupe verbal

1. Les auxiliaires

1 Choisissez l'auxiliaire qui convient.

a. You ... not feeling happy today. (*are, have, do*)
b. ... your friends going to watch the football game tonight? (*are, have, do*)
c. Albert ... not want to lose weight. (*is, has, does*)
d. We ... worked for long hours. (*are, have, do*)
e. There ... a big protest in the city center. (*is, has, does*)
f. ... you think this dress suits me? (*are, have, do*)
g. I ... driving back home. (*am, have, do*)
h. ... Alex got a new timetable this year? (*is, has, does*)

2 Choisissez l'auxiliaire qui convient.

a. What ... you ask them again? (*was, had, did*)
b. I ... not working when the phone rang. (*was, had, did*)
c. They ... fallen off the couch. (*were, had, did*)
d. I ... finished my work before you. (*was, had, did*)
e. Joyce ... not expect that kind of reaction from her friends. (*was, had, did*)
f. ... you thinking of her when you received a call? (*were, had, did*)

3 Choisissez *be, have* ou *do* au présent ou au passé.

a. She ... selling her car as she needs money.
b. After Richard ... finished his homework, he went out.
c. They ... not like the exhibition.
d. We ... decided to go to school early today.
e. I ... watching TV when I heard a knock on the door.
f. ... you often go to theatre nowadays?

4 Choisissez *be, have* ou *do* au présent ou au passé.

a. I ... not happy with your attitude today.
b. Catherine and Gailord ... an amazing trip in Wales.
c. Who ... that man in the blue coat?
d. ... you get his phone number?
e. Hanna ... not understand his reactions any more.
f. Jackie and Fleur ... on their way to Australia.

2. La modalité

5 Indiquez la valeur du modal utilisé : permission, capacité, hypothèse, interdiction, incertitude, nécessité, conseil, volonté, futur.

a. I might be able to come to the game.
b. Can I go to the cinema with my mates, please?
c. You must think about what you'll do when you're older.
d. Should I come or should I go?
e. He'll take the plane to Sydney next week.
f. Would you like some tea?
g. The girls could cook much better than us.

6 Choisissez le modal qui convient.

a. I ... face and conquer this challenge. (*can, might, would*)
b. Nasa ... send humans by the 2030s. (*must, can, could*)
c. You look tired. You ... rest a bit. (*should, might, may*)
d. I ... help you if it is possible. (*will, should, would*)
e. The matter is important, the witness ... lie. (*couldn't, may not, mustn't*)
f. They are not here, they ... have missed their train. (*should, may, can*)
g. We ... use recycled paper to avoid deforestation. (*must, might, can*)
h. From that day, they ... visit their grandmother every Saturday. (*should, would, will*)

7 **Complétez avec le modal qui convient : *could, may, might, can, can't, should, must, mustn't.***

a. Laura ... buy a new car if she gets a better job.
b. You ... go out tonight as you're working early tomorrow.
c. Victor ... have an allergy to pollen, he sneezes a lot.
d. He ... have told me that although it's hard to believe.
e. ... we go to the cinema later?
f. John ... understand Japanese but he is not comfortable to speak it.
g. Children ... lie to their parents.
h. We ... protect wild animals before it's too late.

3. Modalité : équivalents des modaux

8 **Remplacez les modaux par un de leurs équivalents au temps demandé : *have to, be allowed to, be able to.***

a. This actor is ambitious, he can take any role. (*futur*)
b. You mustn't believe all her words. (*passé*)
c. Mike must be on time for once. (*futur*)
d. She can go earlier on holiday thanks to her extra hours. (*passé*)
e. Without a parental authorisation, you can't register at the library. (*futur*)
f. At the age of four, Mathilda could read fast and well. (*passé*)

4. Le présent simple
5. Le présent en *be* + V-*ing*

9 **Mettez les verbes au présent simple.**

a. ... life ... beyond Earth? (exist)
b. Even with their mask, they ... me. (*frighten*)
c. I ... to start a new career in finance. (*want*)
d. She ... about my opinion. (*care – not*)
e. What ... you usually ... on Mondays? (*do*)
f. The animals ... dangerous, don't approach them. (*sound*)

10 **Mettez les verbes au présent en *be* + V-*ing*.**

a. Look, someone ... for help. (*ask*)
b. While I ... on the whiteboard, please be quiet. (*write*)
c. Janice ... for an internship at a bank. (*look*)
d. I'm sure they ... tonight for the meeting. (*come*)
e. ... we ... your birthday today? (*celebrate*)
f. You ... to the rap concert tomorrow night. (*go – not*)

11 **Mettez les verbes au présent en *be* + V-*ing* ou au présent simple.**

a. Oscar always ... his glasses at home. (*forget*)
b. ... Lilly ... on the computer right now? (*work*)
c. Ok, I ... with you in a few minutes. (*come*)
d. Where ... poets ... their inspiration from? (*get*)
e. I ... videos from the internet. (*download – not*)
f. Shh! We ... our English lesson. (*study*)
g. You ... very happy nowadays. (*seem*)
h. The food is terrible, I ... it. (*enjoy – not*)
i. ... the clients ... the new offer? (*reconsider*)

12 **Mettez les verbes au présent en *be* + V-*ing* ou au présent simple.**

a. What ... about? I don't understand. (*they – talk*)
b. He often ... his grandparents. (*visit*)
c. Rajeev ... playing tennis. (*love*)
d. Look at her! She ... very fast! (*run*)
e. He isn't here as you can see, he ... . (*work*)
f. Japanese people ... a lot of photos in Paris. (*take*)
g. Why ... darling? (*you – cry*)
h. Please be quiet, ... (*we – sing*)
i. I'm sorry but I ... tea. (*not – like*)
j. He ... a cake. He ... very happy. (*make – seem*)
k. Lions ... animals to survive. They ... dangerous. (*eat – look*)

6. Le prétérit simple

13 **Mettez les verbes au prétérit simple.**

a. Mike ... to become an artist at the age of 14. (*want*)
b. They ... their holidays in Atlanta last year. (*spend*)
c. The 1995 Rugby World Cup ... place in South Africa. (*take*)
d. We ... breakfast early in the morning. (*have*)
e. MLK ... for equal rights in America. (*fight*)
f. Jack London ... famous for his fictions. (*be*)

14 **Posez la question qui porte sur les mots soulignés.**

a. I went to <u>Miami</u> in April.
b. He became famous <u>because of his engaged songs</u>.
c. Charles gave <u>a lovely present</u> to his mother for her birthday.
d. I saw you with your friends <u>last Monday</u>.
e. I ran <u>42 kilometers</u> within 3 hours.
f. <u>Marcus</u> left home without his keys.

7. Le prétérit en *be* + V-*ing*

15 **Mettez les verbes au prétérit simple ou au prétérit en *be* + V-*ing*.**

a. Everyone ... see that he ... her look. (*can – avoid*)
b. While I ... the car in the city center, the engine .... (*drive – fall out*)
c. She ... at her dog, who ... all over the place. (*shout – run*)

d. I just ... that he ... a good job during his internship. (*say – do*)
e. As we ... at the restaurant, the waiter ... water on the table. (*eat / spill*)
f. He ... in such a rage that he ... as red as a beetroot. (*be – go*)

16 Mettez les verbes au prétérit en *be* +V-*ing*.

a. It was already late. We ... asleep. (*fall*)
b. While they ... under the tree, a bird landed on a branch. (*sit*)
c. As he ... the ball, the goalkeeper hurt himself. (*catch*)
d. I can still tell you what Jess ... that day. (*wear*)
e. We saw a scar on her arm when she ... her coat. (*take off*)
f. It was shown that the company ... evidence. (*hide*)

17 Mettez les verbes au prétérit simple ou au prétérit en *be* + V-*ing*.

a. I ... (have) a bath yesterday when the phone ... (*ring*).
b. According to the police officer, the thief ... (*escape*) through a back door while the jewelry store owner ... (*open*) the safe.
c. The girls ... (*play*) when their dad ... (*come*) home.
d. Her husband ... (*cook*) while she ... (*have*) a bath.
e. His dog ... (*run away*) as he ... (*walk*) it in the park.

8. Le *present perfect*

18 Mettez les verbes au *present perfect* simple.

a. ... you ... Miss Jones? (*see*)
b. At 5pm they ... work for the day. (*finish*)
c. The family ... because they want a greener environment. (*move*)
d. A new store ... on Fifth Avenue. (*open – just*)
e. I ... new shoes since the summer sales. (*buy – not*)
f. He didn't like his real name, that's why he ... it to Kevin. (*change*)

19 Mettez les verbes au prétérit simple ou au *present perfect* simple.

a. The defense team ... their mistakes two days ago. (*admit*)
b. ... you ... a hurling game? (*watch – ever*)
c. We ... the chess club in 2010. (*join*)
d. I ... from my deck since the lesson ... (*move – not / begin*)
e. When I arrived in front of the school, the caretaker ... the door. (*lock – already*)
f. "Try to remember everything you ... these last few days." ... the teacher. (*learn / say*)

9. Le *present perfect* en *be* + V-*ing*

20 Mettez les verbes au *present perfect* en *be* + V-*ing*.

a. We ... you since this morning. (*follow*)
b. I ... much about the accident. (*think – not*)
c. He ... in South Africa since 1994. (*live*)
d. How ... you ... over the past few months? (*feel*)
e. The scholars ... for seven years now. (*study*)
f. When you ... books for as long as I have, you need to write everyday. (*write*)

21 Mettez les verbes au *present perfect* simple ou au *present perfect* en *be* + V-*ing*.

a. The fridge is totally empty, someone ... all the leftovers. (*eat*)
b. Something strange ... over the last few days. (*happen*)
c. I ... him for a long time, you can trust him. (*watch*)
d. How long ... you ... ? (*drive*)
e. Bryan ... for three hours. (*shop*)
f. They ... to the emails. (*reply – not*)

22 Choisissez entre le prétérit simple, le *present perfect* simple ou le *present perfect* en *be* + V-*ing*.

a. Ella ... (*swim*) for 10 years now.
b. Liz ... (*never – be*) to Lebanon but she ... (*already – visit*) Syria twice.
c. She ... (*say – not*) yes to his proposal yet!
d. How long ... (*Tiffany, wait*) for me?
e. James ... (*never – manage*) to be on time. But ... (*he – ever – hurry*)?
f. So, how much money ... (*spend – you*) at Marks and Spencer?
g. Emma ... (*start*) playing the piano in 1979 and she ... (*play*) since.

10. Le *past perfect*

23 Mettez les verbes au *past perfect*.

a. I knew what ... (*happen*)
b. He ... a few paces when he heard a scream. (*walk*)
c. Gloria ... the book before she went to bed. (*finish*)
d. When the policemen arrived on the scene, the robbers ... . (*go – already*)
e. People looked at me as if I ... something wrong. (*say*)
f. Richard told me that he ... his cousin in India. (*meet*)

24 Mettez les verbes au *past perfect* en *be* + V-*ing*.

a. It ... for many hours. (*snow*)
b. ... Chris ... a bad day? (*have*)
c. We ... European coins until the introduction of the Euro. (*collect*)
d. Michelle ... with friends once again. (*argue*)
e. You ... with your passport. (*travel*)
f. I ... of calling my doctor. (*think*)

25 **Choisissez entre le *past perfect* et le *past perfect* en *be* + V-*ing*.**

a. All her family was proud that Tiana ... the competition. (*win*)
b. How long ... you ... to get a taxi? (*wait*)
c. Peter ... his hands until the water stopped running. (*wash*)
d. I wish I ... more with my family. (*stay*)
e. She ... how she could help her. (*wonder*)
f. They ... such a reception for the book launch. (*expect – not*)

26 **Choisissez entre le prétérit simple ou le *past perfect* simple.**

a. I ... you ... interest in everything. (*see – lose*)
b. After the children ... , the coach ... in his office. (*leave – stay*)
c. My father ... when one of his colleagues ... for him. (*go – ask*)
d. Dan ... Janice because she ... him back. (*call – pay*)
e. I ... he ... come to the party. (*hope – can*)
f. He ... she ... a mistake. (*know – make*)

11. L'expression du futur

27 **Indiquez la valeur de la structure qui fait référence à l'avenir : fait daté inévitable, volonté ou certitude, fait anticipé/organisé à l'avance, suggestion, action imminente, probabilité.**

a. It is likely he will be late.
b. Fleur will get married to Eddy in October.
c. The plane is about to take off.
d. I'm sure it will be sunny tomorrow.
e. We will be in 2030 in a few years!
f. He's coming back for his sister's baby shower in May.
g. Shall we take the tube or a black cab?

28 **Choisissez la forme qui convient pour exprimer le futur selon la situation.**

a. Hurry up, the bus ... . (is about to leave – will leave)
b. We ... to the park as soon as we have finished eating. (*will go – are about to go*)
c. Look at the clouds, it ... . (*rains / is going to rain*)
d. I'm happy. The holidays ... in two weeks. (*start / will start*)
e. I ... to finish the race in less than 2 hours. (*am trying / will try*)
f. What ... now? (*is going to happen – is happening*)

29 **Complétez les phrases avec l'expression du futur qui convient le mieux. Justifiez votre choix à l'oral.**

a. I had enough, I ... tonight. (*come back – not*)
b. Wait, the President ... a speech. (*deliver*)
c. NASA ... a robotic mission to the moon in the next few years. (*send*)
d. What ... future generations ... about us? (*say*)
e. Judith ... you how to fix the problem when she finds the error. (*show*)
f. ... the author ... to publish his latest book? We do not know yet. (*manage*)

30 **Mettez les verbes au présent ou au futur avec *will* pour exprimer le futur.**

a. You will understand when you ... older. (*be*)
b. As long as you ... such a behaviour, you won't play video games. (*have*)
c. I don't know when he ... live independently. (*be able to*)
d. They think they ... their exams effortlessly. (*pass*)
e. Elizabeth will stay at school until I ... her. (*fetch*)
f. As soon as the plane ... , the steward will allow us to switch on our devices. (*land*)

12. *Should*
13. Le conditionnel : *would*

31 **Formez des phrases au conditionnel avec les éléments suivants.**

Ex. : go to the hairdresser / have hair → He would go to the hairdresser if he had hair.
a. Come to see you / have time
b. Go more often on holiday / afford it
c. Let you in / have the key
d. Win the lottery / buy a new house
e. go to the seaside / the weather improve
f. invite you / more time
g. pass the exam / work more

32 **Complétez par *would* ou *should*.**

a. ... you please fill in the form?
b. ... we stay longer with you?
c. Valentine ... take extra lessons to improve her marks.
d. If Jonas were wise, he ... play with his friends.
e. Anna ... like to tell the truth about what happened.
f. It is getting late, you ... go now.

14. Les énoncés à l'impératif

33 **Mettez les verbes à l'impératif, à la personne et à la forme demandées.**

a. ... at school! (*swear* – 2e personne – forme négative)
b. ... a new world! (*imagine* – 1re personne du pluriel – forme positive).
c. ... the window and ... me your driver's licence! (*open / give* – 2e personne – forme affirmative)
d. ... late! (*be* – 1re personne du pluriel – forme négative)
e. Please ... a hair of my head. (*harm* – 2e personne – forme négative)
f. Please ... ! (*stand up* – 2e personne – forme affirmative)

15. La voix passive

34 Transformez les phrases à la voix passive.

a. A lot of Irish people play Gaelic football.
b. Madonna will release a new album in October.
c. Columbus didn't discover America.
d. Cuba has bought thousands of American cars.
e. The court had declared the man innocent.
f. Young artists are playing nice music outside.
g. George Clooney won an Oscar.
h. Robert Fortune stole tea from China.

35 Transformez à la voix active en utilisant le sujet entre parenthèses.

a. The treasure was found under a tree in a tropical forest. (*the pirates*)
b. Please wait a few minutes, your computer is still being repaired. (*the technician*)
c. Most of the books are printed in a European country. (*publishing houses*)
d. All the sweets have been eaten. (*someone*)
e. The 2024 Olympics will be played in Paris. (*we*)
f. The thief had been caught before the police arrived. (*the security guards*)

36 Transformez les phrases à la voix opposée. Inventez un sujet si nécessaire.

a. A new museum has recently been opened.
b. He was seen in the swimming pool last week.
c. Every year motorists injure thousands of people on roads.
d. Dany's car had been stolen.
e. Everyone will welcome the next poetry festival.
f. The students are using the laptops.

16. La subordonnée relative

37 Complétez par le pronom relatif qui convient.

a. The tourists ... wanted to visit Loch Ness had to wake up very early.
b. The Highlands, ... are one of the most visited places in Scotland, are so picturesque!
c. The bagpiper, ... played the bagpipes at the fair, comes from Glasgow.
d. The man ... car was found near Loch Lomond is English.
e. Those ... want to apply for this language school have to be trilingual!

38 Indiquez s'il est possible d'omettre le pronom relatif.

a. The Brighton bus whose driver is sick is not running today, unfortunately!
b. The education catchment area which Kate depends on is the largest one in New York.
c. The coach, who is Scottish, is in charge of the organisation of the next tournament.
d. This Brooklyn school, which is quite a good one, welcomes all students.
e. The trip that you talked about was just fantastic.

17. Les verbes d'état

39 Choisissez la forme correcte du verbe.

a. Link what you are hearing / hear to what you know.
b. This story is seeming / seems unbelievable.
c. They are having / have too much fun.
d. You are understanding / understand what he is meaning / means.
e. Now I am remembering / remember!
f. So you say I am imagining / imagine things.

40 Conjuguez les verbes au présent simple ou présent en *be* + V-*ing*.

a. Agathe ... a bath, she can't come. (*have*)
b. Agathe ... a lot of problems. (*have*)
c. All you ... about is yourself. (*care*)
d. The father ... for his children. (*care*)
e. We ... hungry, let's go and eat. (*feel*)
f. I really ... happy! (*feel*)

41 Exprimez chaque phrase sous la forme d'un ordre ou d'une interdiction.

a. We must wear school uniforms at school.
b. You must not forget your umbrella.
c. You must call your parents now.
d. We must not damage the walls.
e. You must finish the book before tomorrow.
f. We must open the window to get fresh air.
g. You must protect the environment for future generations.
h. You must not drive too fast.

Précis de phonologie

Vous connaissez tous cette phrase grâce aux films de 007, vous savez exactement comment elle se prononce. Pourtant, les mots qui la composent vous demandent une réflexion particulière car ils ne se prononceraient pas ainsi en Français – vous êtes donc un as de la phonétique !

D'autres mots peuvent poser problème mais nous allons voir comment contourner ces difficultés ensemble. Par exemple, certains mots des titres des unités de votre manuel, comme *pirate, musical, native* ont une phonie très différente de la manière dont ils s'écrivent : /paɪrət/, /mju:zɪkəl/, /neɪtɪv/.

L'alphabet phonétique est un outil qui vous permettra de mieux prononcer les mots dont vous ne connaissez pas la prononciation. Ce précis phonétique vous donnera un aperçu des principaux points de vigilance à avoir.

Voyelles courtes

Audio
CD2 piste 34
MP3 n° 143

/ɪ/ T**i**n 

/æ/ C**a**t 

/ʌ/ B**u**s 

/ɒ/ D**o**g 

/ʊ/ B**oo**k 

/e/ B**e**d 

/ə/ B**a**nan**a** 

Voyelles longues

Audio
CD2 piste 35
MP3 n° 144

/i:/ Tr**ee** 

/ɑ:/ C**ar** 

/ɜ:/ B**ir**d 

/ɔ:/ D**oo**r 

/u:/ Bl**ue** 

Diphtongues

Audio
CD2 piste 36
MP3 n° 145

/ɪə/ **Ea**r 

/ɔɪ/ B**oy** 

/ʊə/ T**ou**rist 

/eɪ/ C**a**ke 

/eə/ P**ea**r 

/aɪ/ M**i**ce 

/əʊ/ B**oa**t 

Triphtongues

Audio
CD2 piste 37
MP3 n° 146

/aɪə/ F**ire** 

/ɔɪə/ R**oya**l 

/aʊə/ Sh**ower** 

/əʊə/ M**ower** 

Consonnes

Audio
CD2 piste 38
MP3 n° 147

/ʒ/ Gara**ge**, /ʃ/ **Sh**oe, /ŋ/ Si**ng**, /w/ **W**ater, /θ/ **Th**ank, /ð/ Mo**th**er, /tʃ/**Ch**ampion,/dʒ/**J**ump,/j/**Y**ellow, /h/ **H**at, /k/ **K**angaroo

A. Des outils pour vous aider en classe et hors de la classe

1. En classe

Sans le son

- Les **dictionnaires unilingues et bilingues** : ils proposent une retranscription phonétique des mots. Même sans maîtriser l'alphabet phonétique, il vous sera possible de vous rapprocher de leur prononciation.
- Les **affichages dans la salle de classe** : votre professeur a peut-être accroché un poster avec certains sons transcrits en phonétique.

Avec le son

- Certains **dictionnaires électroniques** proposent aussi une fonction qui permet d'entendre la prononciation.
- Votre **professeur·e** : n'hésitez pas à le solliciter et à jouer le jeu des répétitions individuelles et chorales (on a moins peur de se tromper quand on est noyé dans la masse ☺).

2. Hors de la classe

Toujours avec le son ! Sur votre ordinateur, votre tablette ou votre smartphone, de nombreux sites internet et applications peuvent vous permettre de parfaire votre prononciation :

- **YouTube** : si vous avez un doute, tapez le mot et ajouter *pronunciation* et vous trouverez certainement une vidéo où un anglophone répète le mot. Répétez-le lors des pauses et réécoutez la vidéo jusqu'à sentir que vous produisez un son similaire.
- **WordReference** propose deux dictionnaires Français-Anglais, le dictionnaire *WordReference* et le dictionnaire *Collins*. Vous y retrouverez la transcription phonétique des mots, des enregistrements de la prononciation des mots, déclinés avec plusieurs accents : différentes régions de la Grande Bretagne et des États-Unis, l'Irlande, l'Écosse, la Jamaïque, l'Australie...
- **macmillandictionary** propose la transcription phonétique des mots, des enregistrements de la prononciation des mots.
- **linguee** propose des enregistrements de la prononciation des mots avec les accents britannique et américain.
- **howjsay** propose des enregistrements de la prononciation des mots avec l'accent britannique.

B. Le son et la graphie

L'orthographe anglaise ne permet pas toujours de savoir comment un mot se prononce. Lorsque vous apprenez un mot, il est essentiel d'apprendre en même temps la prononciation. Il est donc important de pouvoir lire l'**alphabet phonétique**.

1 Identifiez des sons identiques mais orthographiés différemment :

Audio
CD2 piste 39
MP3 n° 148

/iː/ I went to the sea to see my niece who was dancing on the ceiling!
/eɪ/ I'm late to send a mail to say I can't make it.
/ʊ/ I read the full book and it's good.
/e/ Yesterday I read the story of a man who said he had a red bed.
/ɔɪ/ Oh boy, I think I lost my voice!
/aɪ/ I think it's nice to always get the right reply.
/uː/ The new moon is not blue, you don't have a clue, you only say what suits you!
/ɔː/ He was born on the lawn and they thought it was funny!
/əʊ/ Go get me a rose!

Certaines **consonnes** ne se prononcent pas.

2 Écoutez et repérez dans ces mots les consonnes que vous n'entendez pas :

Audio
CD2 piste 40
MP3 n° 149

climb, debt; Wednesday, sandwich; design, foreign; honest, ghost; knee, knife; muscle, science; could, talk; hymn, column; island, debris; castle, Christmas; wrap, who

Pour les **terminaisons**, une même orthographe correspond parfois à plusieurs sons et d'autres fois, on n'entend pas la fin du mot.

3 **Écoutez ces mots :**
high, thought, find, table, optimism, attraction, torture

Audio CD2 piste 41 MP3 n° 150

La **marque *-ed*** se prononce soit /d/, /t/ ou /ɪd/.

4 **Écoutez les mots suivants et indiquez la bonne prononciation /d/, /t/ ou /ɪd/ :**
asked – followed – proceeded – damaged – connected – fished – used – decided – wanted – stayed – stopped – sailed

Audio CD2 piste 42 MP3 n° 151

Déduisez la règle !
La prononciation change en fonction du son final du radical du verbe. Attention, on parle bien du son final et non de la dernière lettre finale. On doit s'intéresser au son et non à la lettre.

Complétez avec les sons suivants /d/, /t/ ou /ɪd/ :

- ... en règle générale, c'est-à-dire qu'on le prononce comme s'il y avait un 'd' à la fin.
  EXEMPLES : *lived, arrived, enjoyed, played...*
  Audio CD2 piste 43 MP3 n° 152
- ... après certains sons: si le verbe se termine par le son /p/, /k/, /f/, /s/, /θ/, /t/, /ʃ/
  EXEMPLES : *worked* (son /k/), *watched* /tʃ/, *stopped* /p/, *washed* /ʃ/
  Audio CD2 piste 44 MP3 n° 153
- ... après les sons /d/ et /t/.
  EXEMPLES : *decided, started, wanted, needed*
  Audio CD2 piste 45 MP3 n° 154

C. Erreurs fréquentes

Le TH

Le TH en anglais est un son qui n'existe pas dans la langue française. Contrairement à ce qu'on entend parfois, le TH ne se prononce ni /s/ ou /z/, ni /f/ ou /v/. Pour produire ce son correctement, il faut placer le bout de sa langue entre ses dents et expirer. **Il existe deux façons de prononcer le TH** : comme dans *thanks* ou *math*, noté /θ/, et comme dans *the* ou *although*, noté /ð/.

LE CAS DU SCHWA /ə/

C'est le signe le plus employé en phonétique pour l'anglais. Il est pourtant bien discret car **il correspond à une atténuation** et se rapproche du « e » muet français. Il est très important de le repérer pour comprendre comment certains mots « sonnent » très différemment qu'ils ne s'écrivent.

Le H

Contrairement au français où le H ne se prononce pas en début de mot, en anglais il est **marqué et « aspiré »** : pour le prononcer, il faut expirer le début du mot de façon forcée.

Il existe toutefois quelques exceptions : *hour, honour, honesty, heir* (ainsi que leurs dérivés).

D. L'accent de mot

Comme vous l'avez vu dans les *word spots* de votre manuel, certaines syllabes sont en couleur. Il s'agit des syllabes accentuées qui sont très importantes pour respecter la « musique » de la langue. Mais comment trouver la syllabe accentuée ?

Voici quelques pistes :

- **Repérer la terminaison :** elle détermine souvent la position de l'accent qui est sur la première voyelle qui précède la terminaison.

Audio
CD2 piste 46
MP3 n° 155

Accent sur la syllabe avant les terminaisons suivantes	
-ion: interro**ga**tion	-ety: anx**i**ety
-ish: a**bol**ish	-ity: ca**pac**ity
-sive: compre**hen**sive	-ic: spe**cif**ic
-ible: re**spon**sible	

- **Repérer les suffixes « neutres » :** ce sont des suffixes qui ne modifient pas l'accentuation du mot auquel ils sont accolés.

Audio
CD2 piste 47
MP3 n° 156

Pas de modifications d'accent	
-dom: freedom	-less: sleepless
-ful: handful	-ness: brightness
-ly: slowly	-ship: citizenship
-hood: neigbourhood	

E. La phrase

Nous abordons maintenant la question de l'accentuation de la phrase qui est l'accentuation de certains mots dans une phrase. Les mots accentués sont les mots importants pour le message. La voix monte et descend alternativement et l'accentuation de la fin de phrase dépend du type de discours.

Les cas les plus fréquents d'intonation descendante

L'intonation la plus répandue est lorsque la voix descend en fin de phrase : **questions qui débutent par un mot interrogatif, ordres, phrases courtes, exclamations**.

Les cas les plus fréquents d'intonation montante

L'intonation peut remonter en fin de phrase pour **les *yes-no* questions, l'expression de la surprise, des ordres polis (*please*), l'expression du refus**.

5 Entraînez-vous à prononcer à voix haute le texte suivant puis écoutez-le. Répétez l'exercice jusqu'à sentir que votre intonation et vos liaisons « calquent » celles de l'orateur.

Audio
CD2 piste 48
MP3 n° 157

Hi everyone! So, lately, I've been doing a lot of research into London's West End theatre district, taking a look at their different shows and different theatres. And one of the things that I kept finding intriguing as I was going through my research is the number of shows that have had incredibly long runs there. And I was wondering to myself: why doesn't Broadway have shows that have runs this long?

F. Les accents

Les accents de l'anglais sont nombreux et variés. C'est aussi pour cette raison que l'anglais est une langue si vivante. Les légères différences entre l'anglais d'un texan et celui parlé en Afrique du Sud ne sont pas si légères que cela… Alors voici quelques grandes différences à avoir en tête :

Voyelles simples

La plupart des voyelles simples restent inchangées entre l'anglais britannique et l'anglais américain. Toutefois, la **voyelle /ɒ/** disparaît en anglais américains pour devenir /a/ comme dans *stop* ou *job*, ou /ɔ/ comme dans *dog* ou *cost*.

Diphtongues

La seule diphtongue qui se trouve toujours transformée est **/əʊ/ en accent britannique, qui devient en général /oʊ/ chez les Américains**.

Par exemple : le mot *boat*, prononcé /bəʊt/ au Royaume-Uni, devient /boʊt/ aux États-Unis.

Le R

Là où l'anglais des États-Unis implique de prononcer tous les R présents dans les mots, en Grande-Bretagne, et surtout en Angleterre, seuls les R qui précèdent des voyelles sont prononcés.

Par exemple : dans *bird* /bɜːd/, le R ne s'entend pas s'il est prononcé avec l'accent anglais.

Le T

Alors qu'avec l'accent britannique, le T est toujours prononcé de façon distincte, les Américains ont souvent tendance à le vocaliser de façon à ce qu'il soit perçu comme un D, quand il se trouve au milieu d'un mot.

Par exemple : dans *totally*, le premier T reste en général prononcé /t/, mais le second devient /d/ en anglais américain.

Quelques mots dont la prononciation diffère complètement

Dans certains cas, sans que ces mots ne suivent une règle de prononciation particulière, leur prononciation diffère d'un côté ou l'autre de l'Atlantique. Ces mots sont assez rares, mais ils sont de bons indices pour déterminer l'accent de votre interlocuteur, en cas de doute.

Par exemple **Audio** CD2 piste 49 MP3 n° 158

	Anglais britannique	Anglais américain
advertisement	/ədˈvɜːtɪsmənt/	/ædvɜrˈtaɪzmənt/
either	/ˈaɪðə/	/ˈiːðə^{r}/
mobile	/ˈməʊbaɪl/	/ˈmoʊbəl/
schedule	/ˈʃedʒuːl/	/ˈskedʒuːl/
tomato	/təˈmɑːtəʊ/	/təˈmeɪtəʊ/
privacy	/ˈprɪvəsi/	/ˈpraɪvəsi/

Quelques mots dont l'orthographe diffère également

L'une des différences les plus notables est celle de la terminaison des **mots en *-our* au Royaume-Uni, qui devient *-or*** de l'autre côté de l'Atlantique.

De même, la terminaison ***-re*** devient souvent ***-er***.

Par exemple **Audio** CD2 piste 50 MP3 n° 159

Anglais britannique	Anglais américain
colour, neighbour centre, theatre	color, neighbor center, theater

Fiches de méthodologie

Pour mieux travailler

Pour réaliser les projets

Pour vous entraîner dans les différentes activités langagières

Fiche N° 1

S'organiser

La règle d'or

Mieux vaut travailler une fois bien que deux fois mal !

Chez vous

Mettez-vous au travail **rapidement** !

Prenez au minimum **20 minutes le soir** pour apprendre votre cours d'anglais. Fractionnez votre temps de travail pour être plus efficace : prévoyez une pause après avoir étudié 45 mn.

Planifiez votre travail en fonction de votre emploi du temps et de la répartition de vos cours d'anglais dans la semaine. Par exemple, si vous avez deux grosses journées consécutives, arrangez-vous pour ne pas être débordé·e de travail le soir même.

Espacez les périodes de révision. De cette façon, vous « oublierez » les connaissances pour mieux les réactiver. En faisant cela régulièrement, vous consolidez vos acquis.

Fixez-vous des objectifs dans votre progression. Par exemple : connaître entre 5 et 10 mots nouveaux par jour, faire des phrases avec tous les mots de liaison vus en classe, etc.

Pour enrichir votre pratique, **lisez** des articles ou des blogs en anglais sur un sujet qui vous intéresse, écoutez des podcasts ou des chansons, **regardez** des films ou des séries en version originale sous-titrée, etc.

Prévoyez du temps pour vous entraîner seul·e avec des **outils multimédia** (par exemple Quizlet, sites de grammaire, dictionnaires en ligne...).

Vous avez **manqué un cours** ? Pensez à le rattraper le plus vite possible !

En classe

Tenez bien votre cahier ou classeur. Prenez en notes tout le cours qui figure au tableau et **structurez vos notes**. Soulignez les points importants des leçons : titres, points de grammaire, mots nouveaux, structures particulières, éléments orthographiques qui sont causes d'erreur...

Si vous utilisez un classeur, pensez à apporter les dernières pages de cours et les documents que vous êtes en train d'étudier.

Notez précisément **les devoirs à faire** et la date de rendu.

Tenez à jour un agenda avec **les dates importantes** : devoirs à rendre, contrôles, examens...

Fiche N° 2 Apprendre son cours

Les 5 règles d'or

- **Relisez**
- **Répétez**
- **Recopiez**
- **Réutilisez**
- **Racontez**

En classe

Soyez attentif·ve et concentré·e. Impliquez-vous en participant activement.

Copiez le cours de manière lisible en soulignant les mots importants, en utilisant des couleurs pour le rendre attractif. Cela vous avancera pour votre travail à la maison.

Chez vous

Préparez-vous

Essayez de vous souvenir du contenu du cours ou des phrases faites avec le ou la professeur·e.

Pour cela, demandez-vous :

- Aujourd'hui, j'ai vu…
- J'ai entendu…
- J'ai retenu…
- J'ai aimé…
- J'ai été surpris·e par…
- Je n'ai pas compris…

Apprendre du vocabulaire, c'est :
- Savoir ce qu'il signifie,
- Savoir l'orthographier,
- Savoir le prononcer et l'accentuer,
- Savoir comment il se construit (ex. : *to be angry **with** somebody*),
- Savoir l'inclure dans des phrases.

Apprenez

Relisez votre cours en vous assurant de bien comprendre ce que vous lisez. Pour cela, vous pouvez utiliser le *Word Spot* du manuel, un dictionnaire en ligne ou demander de l'aide à un·e camarade ou à un membre de votre famille.

Vérifiez la prononciation des mots nouveaux à l'aide de *Wordreference* ou *Lexilogos*. Répétez ces mots **à voix haute**. Vous pouvez vous enregistrer en les cachant. Vérifiez-les ensuite dans votre cahier.

Recopiez-les sur des fiches ou un cahier que vous compléterez au fur et à mesure de l'année ou bien créez un Quizlet. Entraînez-vous à réécrire ces mots de mémoire puis vérifiez-les.

Restituez ce que vous avez appris

Reconstituez la trace écrite du cours (**à l'oral et à l'écrit**) en essayant d'être le plus proche possible du modèle. Cela vous permet de réutiliser les mots nouveaux et les structures pour vous les approprier.

Faites vos propres phrases avec ces mots et ces structures.

Demandez à un·e ami·e ou à un membre de votre famille de vous interroger, ou expliquez-lui ce que vous avez appris.

> N'oubliez pas de revoir votre cours dans la semaine qui suit pour bien mémoriser ce que vous avez appris !

Trucs et astuces pour vous motiver :

- Fixez-vous d'abord de petits objectifs (ex. : 5 ou 10 mots à apprendre, reproduire une phrase complète du cours) avant de viser des objectifs plus ambitieux (ex. : reconstituer le cours complet).
- Vous pouvez organiser de petits concours sous forme de jeux avec un·e ou plusieurs camarades. Par exemple, chacun donne un verbe irrégulier à l'infinitif et indique ses formes au prétérit et participe passé. Le·la premier·ère qui est à court d'idées a perdu.

Fiche N° 3

Mémoriser

Les 3 règles d'or

- Triez
- Organisez
- Reliez

La mémoire

On distingue la mémoire à court terme (savoir son cours pour l'heure qui suit, voire pour le lendemain) et la mémoire à long terme (pour la tâche finale, pour le bac, pour vos études…).

Pour mémoriser quelque chose, mieux vaut l'avoir compris. Donc n'hésitez pas à poser des questions au·à la professeur·e pendant ou à la fin du cours. Entraînez-vous à l'aide des *Memory Challenges* proposés dans le manuel et avec les activités ludiques de Quizlet.

Les trois principaux modes de mémorisation

Nous apprenons tou·te·s de façon différente en faisant appel à nos sens (souvent l'ouïe et la vue mais parfois aussi par le mouvement).

Essayez tous ces moyens et voyez lequel / lesquels vous convien(nen)t le mieux. La lecture seule ne suffit pas toujours !

Mémoire visuelle ?
Lisez et écrivez, dessinez, associez des images mentales visuelles à ce que vous devez retenir (ex : mémorisez des prépositions de lieu en visualisant un lieu précis que vous aimez).

Mémoire auditive ?
Lisez à haute voix, répétez en chantant, enregistrez-vous sur votre smartphone et réécoutez dès que vous pouvez, expliquez à des camarades afin de vous faire entendre.

Mémoire kinesthésique ?
Lisez puis récitez à voix haute, en marchant, en dansant, en faisant des gestes associés (comme les acteurs qui apprennent un texte).

Utilisez des Post-it® pour noter les points importants et mettez-les dans des endroits où vous les verrez souvent, comme par exemple sur la porte de votre chambre !

Le traitement des informations

Pour mémoriser et être capable de restituer les connaissances plusieurs semaines, plusieurs mois ou même des années plus tard, classez et reliez les informations nouvelles à ce que vous connaissez déjà.

Appliquez la méthode **TOR** !
Trois mots-clés : **T**rier - **O**rganiser - **R**elier

Triez ce qui est utile et ce qui ne l'est pas. Inutile de retenir tout le vocabulaire d'un texte par exemple, le vocabulaire principal suffit.

Organisez les connaissances, c'est-à-dire regroupez-les par thèmes, par catégories, par ressemblance, etc.

Reliez les éléments en établissant des liens logiques entre ce qui est nouveau et ce que vous connaissez déjà.

Les outils

Les *mind maps*

Fabiquez des aides visuelles du type carte mentale, sur support papier ou numérique.

Classez les éléments selon leur importance à l'aide de titres.

Faites ressortir les éléments-clés : utilisez un code de couleurs vives, surlignez, soulignez, encadrez, entourez d'un cercle...

Outils numériques
Xmind8
Popplet
Mindnode
Vocabulary Box pour tablettes

Placez **le thème au centre d'un cercle**. Dessinez les branches principales et indiquez les titres au bout de chaque branche. En dessous de chaque titre, listez le vocabulaire, les idées, les faits à retenir... Utilisez des couleurs pour plus d'efficacité.

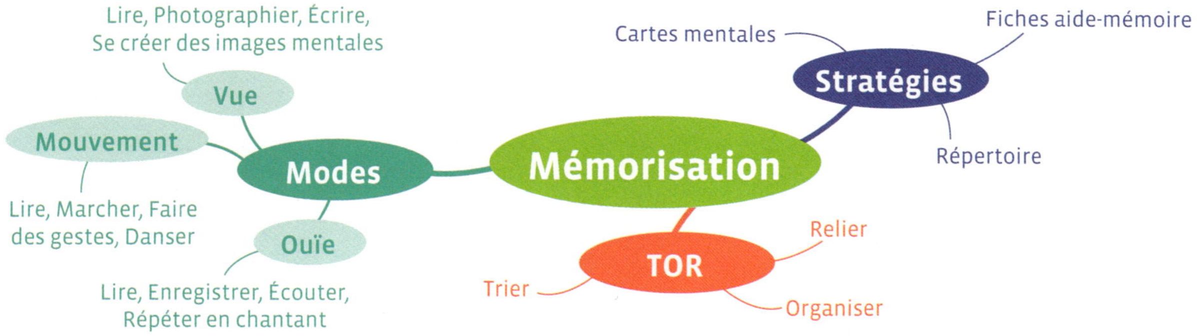

Les fiches thématiques et répertoires

Vous pouvez faire des fiches **par thème** ou **par notion**, comprenant du lexique, des idées, des faits culturels (ou les 3) vus en classe. Ajoutez des titres, des sous-titres, des dessins... qui constitueront des repères pour la mémoire.

Réalisez un lexique classé par ordre alphabétique.

Utilisez un carnet, une liste sur votre smartphone ou un fichier Excel par exemple.

Vous pouvez créer votre propre liste de mots avec leur traduction, leur construction, suivies d'un exemple de phrase incluant le mot. Vous pouvez ajouter la transcription phonétique si le mot pose des problèmes de prononciation.

Fiche N° 4

Comprendre les consignes

Spot

Pick out two elements showing…
Relevez deux éléments qui montrent que…

Find out who lives…
Trouvez qui habite…

Describe

Collect the information…
Relevez les informations…

List / **Mention** the elements…
Listez / Mentionnez les éléments…

Locate the place on the map.
Placez l'endroit / le lieu sur la carte.

Situate the events in time.
Situez les événements dans le temps.

Identify the main characters.
Identifiez les personnages principaux.

Rephrase

Rephrase the sentence.
Reformulez la phrase.

Sum up

Summarise the excerpt / extract.
Résumez l'extrait.

Write **a summary** of the text in your own words.
Résumez le texte avec vos propres mots.

Quote

Justify with **a quote**.
Justifiez à l'aide d'une citation.

Give **a quotation**.
Citez.

Choose

Underline the key words.
Soulignez les mots clés.

Tick the correct answer.
Cochez la réponse correcte.

Pick out phrases / expressions showing that...
Relevez des expressions qui montrent que...

Complete

Fill in the grid below.
Remplissez la grille ci-dessous.

Complete the blanks.
Complétez les blancs.

Match

Match the following words with their definitions.
Associez les mots suivants à leur définition.

Choose the words that are linked to / connected with...
Sélectionnez les mots associés à...

Imagine

Imagine the sequel.
Imaginez la suite.

Guess what happened.
Devinez ce qui s'est passé.

Deduce

Infer / **deduce** the meaning of...
Déduisez le sens de...

Analyse

Comment on the following statement.
Commentez la phrase suivante.

Find out words applying to/ referring to...
Trouvez des mots qui s'appliquent à / font référence à...

Explain

Explain how the characters are related.
Expliquez les liens entre les personnages.

Give the reasons accounting for...
Donnez les raisons expliquant...

Fiche N° 5 Faire une recherche internet

Les 2 règles d'or

- Repérer les *fake news*
- Se recentrer régulièrement sur le sujet

Avant de se connecter

Prévoyez un **« journal de recherche »**, papier ou numérique, où prendre des notes au fur et à mesure de la recherche.

Ouvrez par exemple un document Word, dans lequel vous pourrez copier-coller les informations intéressantes.

Notez le sujet de la recherche en titre. Et faites un rapide *brainstorming* autour du sujet. Les idées que vous notez sont les **mots-clés** que vous allez utiliser pour votre recherche.

Les moteurs de recherche

Commencez d'abord par une recherche large : pas plus de trois mots.
Ajoutez ensuite vos mots-clés pour affiner la recherche.

Vous pouvez encore orienter votre recherche grâce aux outils suivants :

Les opérateurs de recherche :

- Pour chercher uniquement **sur les réseaux sociaux**, tapez @ devant le mot recherché.
- Pour chercher un **hashtag**, tapez **#** devant le mot.
  Exemple : #hatier
- Pour **exclure un mot** de votre recherche, tapez **-** devant le mot à exclure.
  Exemple : mammifères marins -baleine
- Pour rechercher **une expression exacte**, mettez-la entre **guillemets**.
  Exemple : "the life of pi" (titre de livre ou de film)
- Pour associer des recherches, tapez **OR** entre chaque mot.
  Exemple : marathon OR course

Les options des moteurs de recherche :

- **« Image »**
- **« Vidéo »**
  } pour rechercher ce type de fichiers uniquement.
- **« Actualités / news »** pour rechercher sur les sites d'information (journaux, magazines, TV, radio...).
- **« Maps »** pour chercher un lieu, localiser

Les principaux moteurs de recherche

www.google.fr
www.qwant.com
www.bing.com
uk.yahoo.com / us.yahoo.com

Attention, si vous êtes en France, vous avez probablement accès par défaut à la version française du moteur de recherche. Les premiers résultats sont alors en français. Mais vous pouvez modifier **la langue** pour obtenir des résultats en anglais :

- Google vous le propose sur la page d'accueil : « Google disponible en : *English* ».
- Bing vous propose dans les paramètres de limiter la recherche à une langue spécifique.

! Évitez les **traductions** automatiques proposées par les moteurs de recherche, elles sont souvent fausses ou très approximatives.

Les encyclopédies en ligne

Vous y trouverez des informations plus structurées. Elles vous permettent d'avoir une **vision globale d'un sujet** et elles vous donnent des pistes vers des sujets voisins, ce qui vous permet d'enrichir ou corriger votre liste de mots-clés.

QUELQUES ENCYCLOPÉDIES GRATUITES EN ANGLAIS

www.britannica.com
www.scholarpedia.org
www.infoplease.com
www.wikipedia.org

Wikipédia est souvent un bon point de départ. En bas d'une fiche (→ *Liens externes*), vous trouverez notamment des liens vers des sites ou des documents consacrés au sujet.

! Mais attention, Wikipédia est une encyclopédie collaborative : toutes les pages ne sont pas de qualité égale et certaines ne sont pas fiables. Il faut l'utiliser en parallèle avec d'autres sources.

Évaluer la fiabilité d'une information

Les informations que vous trouvez en ligne ne sont pas toutes... des informations. Il y a aussi des *fake news* ! Quelques questions à se poser pour évaluer **la fiabilité** d'une information ou d'un document :

- **La nature de l'information.** S'agit-il d'une donnée objective ou bien d'une opinion personnelle ? D'un fait réel ou bien d'une histoire fictive ? Est-ce que ça pourrait être un mensonge ?
- **La nature du site.** S'agit-il d'un site institutionnel, associatif, commercial ? S'agit-il d'un blog, d'un site personnel ? La compétence de l'auteur·e sur le sujet est-elle reconnue ?
- **L'auteur·e.** Est-il·elle identifié·e ? Peut-on le·la contacter ? Est-ce un·e spécialiste du domaine ? S'exprime-t-il·elle au nom d'une institution ? Quel est son objectif ?
- **Les limites de l'information :**
  - **géographiques.** L'information concerne-t-elle un pays particulier ? L'information est-elle valable partout ?
  - **temporelles.** De quand date la page sur laquelle je me trouve ? Est-ce que je peux vérifier si elle a été mise à jour récemment ?

Quel que soit le sujet de votre recherche, vous êtes comme un·e inspecteur·rice ou un·e journaliste d'investigation : vous menez une enquête. Si vos sources sont fiables, vous aurez des résultats solides. Sinon, vous allez suivre des fausses pistes !

Conserver les informations

À chaque fois que vous trouvez une **information intéressante**, copiez-la dans votre journal de recherche, avec quelques mots de commentaire.

Copiez toujours le lien complet vers une page qui vous intéresse.

Une page web peut vous paraître facile à retrouver quand vous êtes dessus... Mais quand vous aurez vu vingt autres pages, vous aurez oublié le chemin que vous avez parcouru !

Créez un **dossier** sur le disque dur. Vous y sauvegardez votre feuille de recherche si c'est un document Word.

Vous pouvez aussi envoyer le lien par email à un·e camarade pour attirer son attention ou lui demander son opinion.

Quand vous trouvez **une image** intéressante, vous pouvez la copier-coller dans votre journal de recherche. Et vous pouvez sauvegarder les PDF, les audios ou les vidéos dans un dossier de recherche :

Clic droit
/ « Enregistrer l'image sous... »

Quand vous trouvez une information ou un document intéressant sur votre **smartphone**, gardez-en une trace. Vous pouvez par exemple vous envoyer le lien par email, ou bien prendre une note écrite ou enregistrer un mémo vocal.

Fiche N° 6 Utiliser un dictionnaire en ligne

La règle d'or

Un doute, un clic !

Votre devez avoir un dictionnaire de référence toujours **facile d'accès**.

Mettez un dictionnaire **en favori dans votre navigateur**. Testez d'abord tous ceux qui sont présentés ici pendant quelque temps. Puis quand vous vous sentirez plus à l'aise avec l'un d'entre eux, faites-en votre outil de référence, facile à consulter.

Si vous avez un smartphone, installez une application gratuite, *dictionary.com* ou *linguee.fr* par exemple.

Les dictionnaires bilingues

DICTIONNAIRES BILINGUES EN LIGNE

www.lexilogos.com : propose un répertoire de dictionnaires en ligne dans toutes les langues. Cliquez sur « anglais » pour la liste des nombreux outils disponibles.

Testez en priorité :
www.dictionary.com
www.wordreference.com/enfr/
www.reverso.net
www.larousse.fr
www.linguee.fr

Devenez curieux·euse des mots que vous rencontrez. Prenez l'habitude de vous poser toutes sortes de questions :

- Comment se prononce *Edinburgh* ?
- Quel est le pluriel de *foot* ?
- Quel est le contraire de *slow* ?
- Quelle signification ont en commun les mots qui commencent par *inter-* ?
- Quelle est l'origine du mot *sister* ?

Les dictionnaires ne vous donnent pas seulement la traduction d'un mot, mais aussi :

la manière dont il il se prononce	*dictionary.com* permet de lire au choix la transcription en alphabet phonétique ou en transcription facile. l'application *linguee* vous permet d'avoir accès facilement aux prononciations UK et US. *wordreference* donne les prononciations UK et US, mais encore six autres prononciations (irlandais, écossais, jamaïcain...) pour les mots les plus courants.
ses synonymes	*dictionary* et *wordreference* proposent un onglet *Synonyms*.
son étymologie	*dictionary* propose un onglet *Word origin*.

Les expressions idiomatiques

N'oubliez pas qu'une langue a ses propres structures et des expressions qui lui sont propres, et qu'on ne peut pas traduire mot à mot. Par exemple :

- « en faire tout un fromage » a un sens en français, mais la traduction mot à mot n'en a pas en anglais !
- *to make a storm in a cup of tea* a un sens en anglais, mais « faire une tempête dans une tasse de thé » n'en a pas en français !

> Vous allez souvent trouver des expressions idiomatiques dans les exemples donnés par les différents dictionnaires bilingues. Mais voici aussi un outil spécifique pour les reconnaître et les traduire plus facilement : **context.reverso.net**
>
> Au fur et à mesure que vous saissisez des mots, le site vous propose des expressions dans lesquelles elles apparaissent.
>
> Par exemple : *cats...* → *it's raining cats and dogs* (« il pleut des cordes »)

Les dictionnaires unilingues

Si vous ne trouvez pas le mot que vous cherchez dans les dictionnaires bilingues, vous pouvez utiliser un dictionnaire anglais-anglais.

Ils vous donnent des définitions plus complètes et indiquent un plus grande nombre de nuances.

- *Oxford* donne pour chaque mot un très grand nombre d'exemples et de synonymes.
- *Cambridge* présente sous forme de nuage de mots tous les autres mots reliés au mot cherché (option « Thesaurus »).
- *Merriam Webster* intégre aussi les noms propres (personnages, villes, etc.).

Dictionnaires unilingues
oxforddictionaries.com
dictionary.cambridge.org
www.merriam-webster.com

comment l'utiliser dans les phrases	*larousse.fr* indique de manière claire et synthétique (en vert) le contexte et les nuances de chaque traduction. *linguee* donne de longues listes d'exemples authentiques traduits.
des options pratiques	*wordreference* et *linguee* proposent des mots au fur et à mesure que vous saisissez les premières lettres. *wordreference* et *reverso* donnent accès aux articles du dictionnaire papier de référence Collins.

Fiche N° 7

Relire un devoir écrit

La règle d'or

Garder le temps nécessaire pour deux relectures (minimum 5 mn) !

Une relecture en 2 temps

1. Lisez une première fois pour revoir la cohérence globale et l'enchaînement des idées.

Si vous le pouvez, laissez passer quelques minutes avant la deuxième lecture pour avoir un regard neuf.

2. Faites **une deuxième lecture** en vous concentrant uniquement sur la langue (orthographe, grammaire, syntaxe), la mise en forme (alinéas, présentation propre au type de sujet : lettre, dialogue, article de journal, etc.) et la ponctuation.

Pensez à repérer tout au long de l'année les erreurs que vous avez tendance à faire fréquemment. Vérifiez tout particulièrement ces points dans votre relecture.

Les *Grammy Awards* de la grammaire !

Pour vous aider à éviter les erreurs les plus courantes, voici **notre top 10 des classiques de la pop anglo-saxonne**.

Écoutez les chansons sur internet et **mémorisez les refrains** pour retenir les points de langue qu'ils illustrent.

1. *Anyone Can Play Guitar*, by Radiohead

Les auxiliaires modaux sont **toujours** suivis de la base verbale.
(auxilaires modaux : *can, could, must, may, might, shall, should, will, would*)

2. *Why Do I Feel so Sad?* by Alicia Keys

Une question se forme généralement selon le schéma suivant :
(pronom interrogatif) + auxiliaire + sujet + verbe + complément?

3. *Born To Be Wild*, by Steppenwolf

Pour exprimer le but (« pour » + verbe), on utilise *to* + base verbale.

4. *Last Christmas I gave you my heart*, by Wham

Quand vous racontez un fait passé et daté, vous utilisez le prétérit.

5. *She moves far away*, by Alle Farben

À la 3e personne du singulier du présent simple, le verbe prend un *-s*.

6. *I Don't Wanna Live Forever*, by Taylor Swift

wanna = want to (et *gonna = going to*)
« Vouloir » se dit *want* (et pas ~~*will / would*~~)

Pour dire « vouloir + verbe », on utilise *want + to* + base verbale.

7. *Single Ladies*, by Beyoncé

Les adjectifs ne prennent **jamais** de *-s* en anglais.

8. *People Are Strange*, by The Doors

Au pluriel, *person* devient *people*.
Et *people* est un nom pluriel.

9. *Give Peace a Chance*, by John Lennon

Devant un nom employé dans un sens général, on ne met pas l'article *the*.

10. *The Man Who Never*, by Maroon 5

WH☺ renvoie à une personne. *Which* renvoie à une chose ou une idée.

Ma check list

Ma Check List

Est-ce que…

- ☐ j'ai bien traité le sujet, tout le sujet et rien que le sujet ?
- ☐ j'ai répondu aux questions posées ?
- ☐ j'ai tenu compte des consignes (type de production, nombre de mots, …) ?
- ☐ j'ai fait l'effort de structurer le devoir ?
- ☐ les idées s'enchaînent de façon logique avec des mots de liaison et ce que je veux dire est-il clair ?
- ☐ j'ai illustré mon travail avec des exemples concrets ?
- ☐ j'ai fait des paragraphes en allant à la ligne ?
- ☐ le contenu est intéressant (suivant le type de devoir : références culturelles, humour, originalité…) ?
- ☐ j'ai évité les répétitions d'idées ou de mots ?
- ☐ j'ai utilisé une langue riche (c'est-à-dire un vocabulaire varié, de nouvelles structures…) ?
- ☐ j'ai vérifié l'orthographe ?
- ☐ j'ai respecté la ponctuation (points, virgules…) et mis des majuscules en début de phrase et aux noms propres ?
- ☐ j'ai écrit proprement et lisiblement ?

Fiche N° 8 Travailler en groupe

La règle d'or

Écouter, coopérer, intégrer… et parler anglais !

Pourquoi travailler à plusieurs ?

- Pour **effectuer des tâches** qui seraient plus difficiles à faire seul·e.
- Pour **développer la confiance en soi** : exprimer ses idées dans un petit groupe et voir qu'elles sont prises en compte par les autres donne plus d'assurance.
- Pour **s'entraider** : expliquer aux autres permet de mieux s'approprier les connaissances. Demander de l'aide permet de mieux comprendre.
- Pour développer des qualités de travail en **équipe** qui seront utiles dans des situations de la vie courante (club, équipe sportive…), dans sa vie de citoyen·ne et dans un milieu professionnel.

Comment ?

- Mettez-vous tout de suite au travail. Ne commencez pas à discuter d'autre chose avec votre voisin·e et ne restez pas sans rien faire !
- Si cela n'est pas déjà fait, installez rapidement les tables de façon à voir tous les membres du groupe.
- Écoutez attentivement les consignes données par le·la professeur·e et assurez-vous que tout le monde les a comprises.
- Décidez ensemble de ce qui est important (contenu, forme, restitution…).
- Répartissez-vous les tâches si besoin (dans le cas de la préparation d'une affiche, par exemple, ou d'un PowerPoint).
- Prenez des initiatives, apportez votre contribution et ne vous contentez pas de regarder.
- Laissez chacun prendre la parole et écoutez les autres. Quand vous voulez vous exprimer, attendez que celui ou celle qui est en train de parler ait fini.
- Gardez un volume sonore approprié.
- Effectuez le travail dans le temps imparti.

> Restez concentré·e sur le sujet, évitez de passer trop de temps sur des choses qui ne sont pas en lien avec le projet commun.

- Prenez tous des notes sur le travail effectué.
- Contribuez à l'esprit d'équipe par votre bonne humeur et votre envie de travailler.

! Rappelez-vous : pour améliorer votre anglais, il faut parler anglais !

Fiche N° 9 Créer une affiche ou un dépliant

Définir le type de document

Identifiez le **type de production** demandée. De quel type de document s'agit-il ? Un dépliant, une brochure, un *flyer*, une couverture de livre, un poster ?

Identifiez le **contexte de réalisation** :

- Quel est l'**objectif** du document ?
- À qui le document est-il destiné ?
- Combien de temps avons-nous à y consacrer en classe et/ou à la maison ?
- Quels outils ou matériels pourraient nous être utiles (feuille A3, imprimante, colle, feutres ou sites avec des modèles) ?

La règle d'or

L'important c'est que le message passe ou soit immédiatement visible.

Organiser un contenu

- Listez vos idées, cherchez des illustrations en rapport avec votre thématique.
- Trouvez un titre accrocheur (un groupe nominal de préférence).
- Rédigez des énoncés clairs que vous organiserez en paragraphes courts.
- Pour trouver des illustrations, n'hésitez pas à consulter les sites qui proposent des images libres de droits. Ils sont respectueux de la propriété intellectuelle.

IMAGES LIBRES DE DROIT

www.splitshire.com
pablo.buffer.com
gratisography.com
ccsearch.creativecommons.org

Mettre en forme

Vous pouvez choisir de la réaliser à la main en imprimant des documents couleurs scannés ou copiés sur un site et en organisant leur assemblage comme vous le souhaitez sur un format A3 ou A4. Les solutions les plus simples sont parfois les meilleures.

Trucs et astuces.

Vous pouvez utiliser des *templates* ou modèles de documents, qui sont disponibles sur certaines suites avec traitement de texte comme Word.

Pensez aussi aux sites ou applis gratuits, qui vous permettent de réaliser en ligne des documents de qualité. Il suffit de créer un compte gratuit pour avoir accès aux fonctionnalités de base. Et vous trouverez en cliquant sur le lien pour chacune d'elles un tuto pour vous aider dans leur utilisation.

- **madmagz.com** vous permet de créer tout un magazine en ligne. Il vous donne accès à deux *templates* gratuites.

- **about.easil.com** est un outil de création graphique qui vous permet d'élaborer des *flyers*, des cartes, des couvertures de livres, des posters ou dépliants à partir de modèles proposés. Cliquez sur *Start now it's free* et créez un compte gratuit.

- **desygner.com** permet également de créer des visuels de qualité avec différents modèles de *flyers*, de posters, etc.

TEMPLATES EN LIGNE

madmagz.com/fr
about.easil.com
desygner.com/fr

Fiche N° 10

Créer un PowerPoint

La règle d'or : OCASA !

- **Organisé**
- **Clair**
- **Aéré**
- **Simple**
- **Agréable**

Vous devez faire un exposé ? Un PowerPoint vous aidera à illustrer chaque point, à faire une présentation dynamique et, en même temps, vous servira d'aide-mémoire.

Le contenu

Demandez-vous d'abord quelle est l'idée essentielle que vous voulez faire passer.
Puis recherchez les éléments qui figureront dans votre exposé : idées, arguments, exemples, etc.
Faites un plan pour structurer votre présentation et sélectionnez les informations qui doivent apparaître sur chaque diapo.

> Appliquez la règle de clarté : 1 diapo = 1 idée.

Cherchez sur internet des photos libres de droits pour illustrer les points principaux de votre présentation. Mais limitez le nombre d'illustrations par diapo.

Vous pouvez également télécharger des sons, des dialogues en format mp3 ou une vidéo pour les insérer dans votre PowerPoint.

Les diapos

Annoncer le sujet

Sur la **première diapo**, indiquez clairement le **titre** de votre exposé et ajoutez une photo ou un dessin pour l'illustrer.

Vous pouvez aussi mentionner votre **nom**.

> **Mon exposé**
>
> **Mon nom**
>
> *Photo ou dessin*

Sur la **deuxième diapo**, vous pouvez indiquer le **plan de votre présentation**.

Les diapos suivantes mettront en valeur chaque point de votre plan.

> **Mon exposé**
>
> **Plan**
>
> 1. Mon premier point
> 2. Mon deuxième point
> 3. Mon troisième point
> 4. Mon quatrième point
>
> …

Pour insérer des documents

Vous pouvez enrichir vos diapos avec des images ou même des enregistrements. Pour cela, cliquez sur « Insérer » et sélectionnez « Photo » ou « Audio » puis l'endroit où ils se trouvent sur le disque dur. Vous pouvez aussi insérer une vidéo ou un lien web de la même manière.

Présenter ses idées

Mon exposé

1. Mon premier point

→ Un argument / un mot-clé
→ Un exemple
→ …

Photo

Vous pouvez répéter en haut de chaque diapo le titre de votre exposé en petits caractères : pour les retardataires ! Ils·Elles sauront de quoi vous êtes en train de parler.

Mon exposé

1. Mon deuxième point

Schéma

→ Un argument / un mot-clé
→ Un exemple
→ …

Harmonisez le style des diapos (même police, même mise en forme, etc.). Mais variez parfois la disposition des éléments pour rythmer la présentation.

Sur vos diapos, présentez **à chaque fois une idée** de manière claire. Et appuyez-la par un argument, un exemple concret, une photo, un dessin ou un schéma.

- Vos diapos doivent être bien lisibles, même pour celles et ceux du fond de la salle !
- Ne mettez pas dans les diapos tout ce que vous avez à dire. Écrivez des phrases courtes, ou même uniquement des mots-clés, avec une police de caractères bien lisible.
- Prévoyez des légendes brèves pour les illustrations qui ne sont pas assez claires.
- Limitez les effets spéciaux.
- Adaptez le nombre de diapositives à la durée de votre exposé (de 4 à 8 en moyenne).

La présentation orale

- **Regardez votre auditoire** et ne tournez pas le dos pour lire vos diapos. Pour cela, vous pouvez utiliser comme aide-mémoire votre plan ou une liste de mots-clés notés sur un papier annexe.
- **Étoffez à l'oral** les points mentionnés sur les diapos. Prenez votre temps pour les développer.
- Parlez assez fort, pour qu'on vous entende même au fond de la salle.
- Soyez attentif·ve aux mimiques et aux réactions de l'auditoire pour vous assurer que tout le monde vous comprend.
- Soyez souriant·e, énergique et convaincu·e !

Si vous avez accès à l'endroit où vous ferez votre exposé, faites un test en conditions réelles : vérifiez le TBI ou l'ordinateur, le vidéoprojecteur, testez l'ouverture de votre fichier PowerPoint. Sauvegardez toujours une version PDF de votre présentation, au cas où !

Fiche N° 11

Analyser une image

La règle d'or

- Identifier
- Décrire
- Interpréter

Pour comprendre et analyser le message délivré par une image, il faut suivre trois étapes :

1. **Identifier** le type de document, sa source et le moment de sa création.
2. **Décrire** objectivement les éléments qui la composent ainsi que la manière dont ces éléments sont organisés.
3. **Proposer une interprétation** personnelle en prenant appui sur les éléments décrits.

Une image fixe

Repérer les informations données dans la légende (*caption*)

Le **nom** de l'artiste, le **titre** de l'œuvre et sa **date** de création.

La **nature** de l'œuvre :

- *an advertisement, an advert, an ad* = une publicité
- *a cartoon* = un dessin humoristique
- *a comic strip* = une bande dessinée
- *a drawing* = un dessin
- *a painting* = une peinture
- *a photograph* = une photographie
- *a poster* = une affiche
- *a still from a film* = une image de film

Situer les différents éléments de l'image

Nommer les différents éléments de l'image :

- *a character / characters*
- *a person / people*
- *the setting* = le décor
- *a caption* = une légende
- *a balloon* = une bulle

Utiliser des énoncés simples pour décrire les éléments :

- *I can see...*
- *There is / there are...*
- *The characters are standing next to...* (*be* + V-*ing* pour décrire)
- *They look cold and sad...*
- *The focus is on...*

Une image animée

Repérer les informations sur la source :

- *a film, a movie, a flick, a blockbuster, a disaster film, a trailer,*
- *a YouTube video,*
- *a TV show, a report, a news bulletin* (journal télévisé),
- *an advertising campaign, a TV commercial,*
- *a documentary...*

Repérer les éléments principaux :

- *Who? The characters or people involved are...*
- *What? The document is about / deals with...*
- *Where? The scene takes place in a...*
- *The setting is a...*
- *The scene was shot in a...*
- *When? The story takes place in...*

Identifier les différents plans et angles :

A long shot

A low-angle shot

A high-angle shot

A full-shot

Interpréter une image fixe ou animée

Exprimer ses premières réactions

- *What strikes me most in... is...*
- *I think it is about...*
- *I find it interesting / surprising / strange / funny / unsual / disturbing that...*
- *We get a feeling of...*

Formuler des hypothèses

- *It makes me think of...*
- *I have the feeling that...*
- *If we pay attention to... we can deduce that...*
- *For me, it's about... because...*

Interpréter ce que vous avez décrit

- *The director's aim / goal / purpose is to...*
- *The atmosphere is tense / strained....*
- *It makes me think of... / It reminds me of...*
- *It illustrates... / It represents...*
- *It is a symbol of...*
- *It criticises... / It denounces...*

Fiche N° 12 Réaliser une vidéo

La règle d'or

Plus le story-board est précis, plus le tournage et la vidéo seront réussis !

La préparation

Prévoyez d'abord un temps de conception pour bien définir le projet et prévoir tout ce dont vous aurez besoin.

Choisir le bon type de vidéo

Réfléchissez ensemble à ce que sera votre film, son **objectif**, son **format**, son **genre** :

- un clip informatif ? une publicité ? un sketch ? un reportage ? un tutoriel ?
- une mini-fiction ? basée sur un scénario original ? adaptée d'un livre ?
- un documentaire ? sur un lieu, un événement, une personne ? une interview ?
- une animation ? une pixilation (image par image, comme *Wallace and Gromit*) ?

Visionnez ensemble des films et des vidéos pour vous inspirer.

Formaliser l'idée principale de la vidéo

Rédigez un **synopsis** : une courte description de ce que sera le film (½ page).

Résumez aussi votre synopsis en une seule phrase : un ***pitch***. S'il est accrocheur, il vous aidera à présenter votre projet à tou·te·s les intervenant·e·s que vous allez solliciter !

Écrivez le scénario.

1. À partir du synopsis, découpez l'histoire en **séquences** (une séquence = 1 lieu, 1 action).
2. Écrivez pour chaque séquence les divers éléments **descriptifs** et les **dialogues**.
3. Découpez chaque séquence en différents **plans** (ou prises de vue). Décrivez-les très précisément : lieu, décor, accessoires, comédiens, répliques, cadrage, bruitages, musique…

Écrivez votre **story-board** aussi précisément que possible, plan par plan.

Plan n°	Nom du plan + description	Lieu + décor	Personnages + répliques	Costumes et accessoires
1				
2				

Vous pouvez vous répartir les séquences ou les plans pour travailler en plus petits groupes.

Le tournage

Un plan, ou une prise de vue, c'est ce qu'on filme entre le moment où on dit « Action ! » et celui où on dit « Coupez ! »

L'équipe

Répartissez les **rôles dans l'équipe** : acteur·rice·s, cadreur·euse, responsable des décors, des costumes, de la prise de son, etc. Faites pour chacun une liste des tâches et du matériel dont il est responsable.

Prévoyez à l'avance **dans quel ordre vous allez filmer** les différents plans.

Soyez patient·e·s. Certains plans d'une minute demandent parfois une après-midi entière de tournage.

Vérifiez – et vérifiez encore – que vous n'avez oublié aucun plan.
Et dans le doute, refaites-le !

QUELLE CAMÉRA ?
- un caméscope
- un appareil photo hybride
- un smartphone ou une tablette

N'oubliez pas de prévenir en amont les personnes sur le lieu de tournage afin d'éviter les bruits parasites ou interventions inopportunes.

Rapprochez-vous de votre professeur·e pour demander les autorisations pour filmer un lieu public ou utiliser un extrait de film ou de musique.

Le montage

Il faut maintenant **assembler les plans** bout à bout, sans oublier la bande-son, pour former les séquences en reprenant votre story-board.

Organisez des **séances de visionnage** en commun pour prendre ensemble les décisions importantes.

Prévoyez un temps confortable pour le montage car c'est souvent à cette étape qu'on prend conscience d'oublis ou de ratés.
Il faut alors parfois prévoir une nouvelle séance de tournage pour refaire certains plans ou enregistrer certains sons.

LOGICIELS DE MONTAGE
VSDC Free Video Editor
VideoPad
Movie Maker

LOGICIELS POUR FILMER SON ÉCRAN (POUR FAIRE DES TUTOS)
Apowersoft
CamStudio

POUR UNE ANIMATION EN PIXILATION
FrameByFrame
MonkeyJam

Fiche N° 13 Poster sur les réseaux sociaux

La règle d'or

Pensez toujours aux réactions de vos lecteurs·rices

Ce qu'on peut poster...		Quel avantage ? Quel conseil ?
sur **Twitter**	des textes limités à 280 caractères + des images et des vidéos	Réagissez en temps réel à une audience large. ! *Utilisez les bons symboles : # (« hashtag ») pour les mots-clés et @ (« arobase ») pour un·e utilisateur·rice.*
sur **Facebook**	tous types de documents (sauf les PDF)	Partagez en temps réel avec ses ami·e·s. ! *Réglez les paramètres de confidentialité pour bien cibler vos destinataires.*
sur **YouTube** et **Dailymotion**	des vidéos	Créez votre propre chaîne. ! *Pourquoi pas créer vos propres vidéos ?*
sur **Snapchat**	des photos, vidéos et messages éphémères	Personnalisez vos messages en les modifiant avec des filtres, des smileys, des masques... ! *Réfléchissez bien avant de publier.*
sur **Instagram**	des images et vidéos courtes	Partagez ce que vous voyez. ! *Choisissez des mots-clés pertinents précédés de # (hashtag).*

Protéger son image et sa vie privée

Sur internet, vous laissez des traces personnelles, volontaires ou involontaires. Soyez prudent·e quand vous montrez votre vie privée, ne publiez pas toutes sortes d'images de vous.
Adoptez les bons réflexes : utilisez un pseudo, ne révélez pas de données personnelles, vérifiez les paramètres de confidentialité de votre profil, optez le plus souvent pour le mode « privé »...

Avez-vous envie qu'on retrouve cette photo un peu gênante dans dix ans ? Non ? Alors ne la publiez pas ou bien restreignez-en l'accès à vos proches.

Sécurisez vos identifiants et mots de passe.
À chaque réseau, un mot de passe choisi avec soin !
Soyez aussi prudent avec votre smartphone, votre tablette qu'avec votre ordinateur.
N'acceptez pas des inconnu·e·s dans vos réseaux d'amis.

personnel·le innovant·e # observateur·rice vigilant·e bref·ve respectueux·euse surprenant·e imaginatif·ve

Soyez

@ créatif·ve percutant·e visuel·le poète bienveillant·e vous-même reconnaissant·e

Avoir une attitude et un langage respectueux

N'oubliez pas que vous vous adressez à un grand nombre de personnes, dont certaines ne vous connaissent pas. Demandez-vous : est-ce que je dirais telle ou telle chose et de cette manière **si j'étais face à de vraies personnes** ?
Pensez toujours aux réactions de vos lecteurs·rices.
Et évitez les propos qui peuvent blesser ou les images qui peuvent choquer.

> N'écrivez pas en majuscules : c'est comme CRIER dans les oreilles !

Ne pas propager de *fake news*

Avant toute publication, apprenez **à vérifier les sources et les contenus** afin de ne pas propager de fausses informations ou des informations erronées... Sur internet, vous trouvez des milliers d'informations mais beaucoup sont fausses. Alors dépouillez, comparez et vérifiez l'information pour mieux publier.

Rester sous la vigilance parentale

Certains réseaux sociaux demandent une **autorisation** des parents pour les mineurs·es, il faut vous renseigner avant de vous y inscrire. Dans tous les cas, le contrôle des parents reste primordial pour utiliser les réseaux en toute sécurité, discutez-en avec eux. C'est un moyen de se protéger contre le **cyber-harcèlement**. En cas de problème, demandez de l'aide à un adulte.

Respecter le cadre légal

Respectez le droit d'auteur et le droit à l'image. Si vous citez des extraits de texte, indiquez-en la source. Si vous voulez utiliser des documents qui ne vous appartiennent pas, assurez-vous d'en avoir le droit.
Pour cela, préférez les licences *Creative Commons* (CC) gratuites qui précisent les conditions d'utilisation.

> Si vous interviewez des personnes, demandez une autorisation pour diffuser leur image et leur voix.

Fiche N° 14
Écrire une lettre de motivation

La règle d'or

CQFD : montrez votre motivation !

Avant de rédiger la lettre

Lisez attentivement l'annonce ou les consignes pour mieux cerner l'emploi pour lequel vous postulez (nature du travail, compétences et qualités requises, détails importants).

Si vous devez aussi rédiger un CV, mieux vaut commencer par le CV plutôt que la lettre (voir fiche n° 15 p. 272).

Pour rédiger la lettre

> Les bases :

- Pensez à la date, aux noms et adresses et aux formules de politesse.
- Soyez précis·e et concis·e (150 -200 mots suffisent pour le corps de la lettre).
- N'utilisez pas d'abréviations.
- Faites une présentation aux normes (voir modèle ci-contre).

> Le déroulé :

- Présentez-vous rapidement, mentionnez les raisons pour lesquelles vous postulez et en quoi vous pensez correspondre à l'emploi.
- Ne répétez pas ce qui est écrit dans votre CV (sauf un ou deux faits essentiels).
- Précisez votre disponibilité pour un entretien.

Après avoir rédigé votre lettre

Relisez la lettre de motivation au moins deux fois !

> Première relecture :

Vérifiez que l'articulation est cohérente et que vous n'avez rien oublié.

> Deuxième relecture :

Faites la chasse aux erreurs, relisez en vous concentrant sur l'orthographe et la grammaire.
Si vous avez un doute, n'hésitez pas à vérifier les mots à l'aide d'un dictionnaire et / ou à utiliser le précis grammatical.

Exemple de lettre type

Voici un modèle de lettre pour demander à travailler à l'étranger comme bénévole dans une association caritative.

Alexandre Hatier
8, rue d'Assas
75006 Paris
France
01 01 01 01 01
alexandre.hatier@letsmeetup.com

15 April 2019

Ms Liz Chapman
WSH Charity
12 Sumner Park
Manchester QLD 4074
UK

Dear Ms Chapman

I would like to apply for a job as a volunteer in your charity. I have heard of you from a friend, Mathilde Courot, who worked with you last summer.

I am a 15-year-old pupil currently studying in a secondary school in Paris, France. In spite of my age, I have already done volunteer work in the past for the Red Cross (*Croix-Rouge* in France) and I am very keen on helping other people in need. I can do all kinds of tasks such as carrying and distributing food or other supplies, supervising and taking care of children, doing paperwork... I like working as part of a team and can easily integrate. I am adaptable and hard-working. My English skills correspond to B1 and even though I am not quite fluent, I can understand instructions very well and hold a conversation about everyday topics.

In the future, I would like to specialise in humanitarian aid ; that is why I would like to get experience in that field. I am available next summer (July and August) and can join your charity whenever you like.

I am available for a Skype interview any time and I look forward to hearing from you soon.

Thanking you in advance.

Yours sincerely

Alexandre Hatier

Fiche N° 15

Écrire un CV

1 Commencez par indiquer vos informations personnelles.

⚠ Si vous envoyez votre CV aux États-Unis, indiquez votre date de naissance en commençant par le mois : 05/16/2004.

2 Avant d'entrer dans le détail de vos études et de votre expérience, écrivez une phrase qui résume votre profil et vos attentes. C'est le moment de mettre en avant vos atouts !

3 Mentionnez votre parcours scolaire et les diplômes obtenus. Vous pouvez écrire votre niveau d'études en français et préciser l'équivalent en anglais ou écrire directement *Secondary School – Year 11* (*UK*) ou *High School - 10th Grade, Sophomore year* (*US*).

4 Ajoutez votre expérience professionnelle en précisant les dates, les lieux mais également les responsabilités et tâches réalisées.

5 Indiquez les langues étrangères que vous maîtrisez en séparant les aptitudes orales des aptitudes écrites si elles sont différentes. Pour définir votre niveau vous pouvez utiliser les niveaux du CECRL ou utiliser les niveaux suivants : *beginner, elementary, intermediate, advanced, fluent, mother tongue*.

---

1 **Alexandre Hatier**
8, rue d'Assas
75006 Paris

01 01 01 01 01
alexandre.hatier@letsmeetup.com
Nationality : French | 16/05/2004 in Paris (France)

2 **Profile**

Young student, serious and dynamic, looking for an internship.

3 **Education**

2019 > 2020 > **Seconde générale, Lycée Montaigne (Paris, France)**

June 2019 > **Diplôme National du Brevet, Mention très bien,**
Collège Montaigne (Paris, France)
(equivalent to the GCSE with distinction)

4 **Work experience**

Sep. 2019 > Present > **Volunteer Work for the Croix-Rouge Française,**
Sorting clothes and plastic caps, giving out food and clothes.

Jan. 2019 > Feb. 2019 > **Professional work placement, Clinique vétérinaire du Grand Parc, Paris**
Care of animals, service and observation of surgeries in a veterinary clinic

5 **Languages**

> **French:** Mother tongue
> **English:** Speaking: B2 – Writing: B1
> **Spanish:** Speaking: B1 – Writing: A2

6 **Computer skills**

> **Microsoft Office:** Avanced level
> **Adobe Creative:** Working knowledge

7 **Interests and other activities**

> Acting / Drama
> Football school club
> Travelling: Spain, England

---

6 Ajoutez vos compétences informatiques. Vous pouvez les préciser en indiquant votre niveau (*working knowledge, intermediate / advanced level, proficiency*) ou schématiser avec des ronds sur cinq par exemple (Microsoft Office: ●●●●○)

7 Terminez par vos centres d'intérêt et activités extrascolaires. Vous pouvez aussi ajouter vos voyages à l'étranger !

Fiche N° 16 Médiation

Qu'est-ce que la médiation ?

Définition : La médiation consiste à transmettre à quelqu'un les informations contenues dans un document ou un échange écrit ou oral. Il faut avoir compris le contenu du document ou de la conversation afin de pouvoir le reformuler, en anglais ou en français. Il s'agit de jouer le **rôle d'intermédiaire**.

Les descripteurs du Cadre européen et des exemples concrets – B1

- **Transmettre une information, interpréter**
  Écouter une conversation sur un sujet vu en cours et être capable de transmettre l'essentiel du contenu à une autre personne en anglais ou en français suivant la situation.
- **Traiter un texte ou un dossier documentaire**
  Expliciter un fait culturel (*Thanksgiving* par exemple) à une personne qui ne connaît pas ce fait, en anglais ou en français suivant la situation.
- **Faciliter la coopération**
  Participer à un travail de groupe et guider ses camarades à travers des reformulations, des commentaires afin d'accomplir la tâche demandée.
- **Mener un travail collectif**
  Expliquer à un·e camarade une consigne dans ses propres mots en anglais ou en français.
- **Faciliter la communication**
  Animer un débat et faciliter les échanges en clarifiant les malentendus et en faisant émerger les différents points de vue.
- **Établir un espace pluriculturel**
  Rencontrer des personnes de cultures et de langues différentes (en voyage scolaire, en vacances) et être capable de tenir compte de leurs différences, savoir comparer sa culture à celle des autres et lever les ambiguïtés afin de favoriser les échanges.

⚠ La médiation n'est pas de la traduction, le passage par la traduction est une stratégie parmi d'autres.

Stratégies

> **Faire des repérages** pour bien comprendre le contenu des documents ou de la conversation (lexique, dimension culturelle…).

> **Synthétiser et identifier** ce que l'on veut communiquer.

> **Écouter activement** pour vérifier que son interlocuteur·rice comprend ce que l'on dit et reformuler si besoin.

> **Se mettre à la place de l'autre** pour anticiper ses problèmes et trouver des solutions.

> **Être capable de trouver les mots dans une autre langue** que celle des documents ou de la conversation (de l'anglais vers le français par exemple).

Fiche N° 17 Compréhension orale

Les descripteurs du Cadre européen - B1

- Comprendre les points essentiels d'une intervention énoncée dans un langage clair et standard.
- Comprendre ce qui est dit pour réaliser une tâche en situation réelle ou simulée.
- Comprendre une information factuelle sur des sujets de la vie quotidienne ou étudiés.
- Suivre une conversation en situation réelle ou simulée.
- Comprendre les points principaux d'une intervention sur des sujets familiers ou étudiés y compris des récits courts.
- Suivre le plan général d'un exposé court sur un sujet connu.
- Comprendre les points principaux de bulletins d'information et de documents enregistrés simples portant sur des sujets connus.

Faites une expérience

1. **Prenez** la vidéo *Inside These Lines* page 111.
2. **Anticipez** à partir du titre : quel sera le sujet ?
3. **Notez** tous les mots que vous comprenez, accentués ou qui vous semblent importants.
4. **Faites des hypothèses** sur le contenu à partir des mots relevés.
5. **Réécoutez** pour confirmer ou infirmer vos hypothèses.
6. **Récapitulez** ce que vous avez compris.

Que vous apprend cette expérience ?

Vous voyez que comprendre un audio, ce n'est pas forcément le comprendre intégralement. Il est normal d'être confronté·e à des zones d'ombres. Cela arrive même dans notre langue maternelle, mais ça ne nous empêche pas de comprendre l'essentiel de la situation et du contexte.

Comprendre un audio consiste **à élucider les passages flous à partir de ce que l'on connaît** : le contexte, les mots-clés, les noms propres, etc. Comme lorsque la conversation téléphonique est brouillée car vous passez dans un tunnel ! Vous avez souvent suffisamment d'informations pour deviner / inférer le passage manquant !

Avant l'écoute

Anticiper à partir du titre, du·de la locuteur·rice et des images

Essayez de **comprendre les termes utilisés** dans le titre, de les relier à ce que vous savez de la notion et de **les associer à des images mentales**. Ces images vous permettront d'**émettre des hypothèses** sur le contenu. **Utilisez** aussi des éléments visuels qui peuvent entourer le document sonore.

Le titre de la vidéo *Inside These Lines* ainsi que sa légende *National Football League, 2017* nous indiquent qu'il va être question de football américain. L'image accompagnant le document, qui montre deux joueurs lors d'un match, le confirme.

Titre : informations sur la thématique, le sujet, la notion.

On en déduit :

- qu'il s'agit d'un support authentique : une vidéo de promotion de la National Football League (NFL) à propos de ce sport, symbole des États-Unis, dans le cadre de l'axe des programmes intitulé « Sports et société ».
- qu'il est probable que l'on entende une ou plusieurs voix, peut-être des témoignages. Il y a de grandes chances pour que le débit soit plutôt lent afin que le message passe facilement.

Avant même d'écouter, vous êtes capable de faire des **hypothèses sur son contenu**.

La première écoute

Saisir les informations principales

Soyez actif·ve·s ! Il faut noter toutes les informations que vous pouvez voir ou entendre et qui faciliteront votre compréhension globale. Votre prise de notes doit être active dès le début et tout au long des écoutes. Écrivez en laissant de la place pour compléter vos notes ou au fur et à mesure des écoutes suivantes. Quel que soit le document, il faut essayer de repérer les informations suivantes :

- le **type de document** : un reportage ? un extrait de journal télévisé ? une interview ? un monologue ? une bande-annonce ? une publicité ? un discours ?
- les **personnes** présentes dans le document : métier, nom, attitude, etc. Aidez-vous de leur apparence, de leur gestuelle, du bandeau indiquant leur nom s'il y en a un.
- les **chiffres**, les **dates**, les **noms propres** : notez-les si / quand ils apparaissent à l'écran.
- le **sujet principal** / le **problème traité**. En général, le titre a introduit le thème. Écoutez bien et associez le titre et les images pour comprendre de quoi il s'agit.

Qu'avez-vous noté ?

Voici un exemple de prise de note possible :

Inside these lines
- place destination.
- differences us.
- game easy fight
- victories
- best united.

Faites un premier bilan : quelles **hypothèses** émettre sur le contenu du document ?

Établissez des **liens entre les informations** : il s'agit de raconter une histoire, donc tentez de lier les éléments trouvés pour créer du sens grâce à vos notes.

Les écoutes suivantes

Réécouter plusieurs fois

Complétez vos notes et **ajoutez des détails**.

Ne cherchez pas à écrire des phrases entières.

Soyez **attentif·ve·s** :
- au **ton des personnes qui parlent** : neutre ? en colère ? révolté ? joyeux ? choqué ?
- au **sujet présenté** : Pourquoi fait-il débat ? Parle-t-on des enjeux, des causes, des conséquences ?

Qu'avez-vous noté ?

Voici un exemple de prise de notes possible :

Inside these lines
- ... don't have to come from the same place to help each other reach the same destination.
- we may have our differences ... more that unites us.
- it's a game of ... no such thing as an easy ... when you're fighting to move forward.
- ... not only defined by our victories but by the way we ... our defeats?
- ... bring out the best in each other and live united.

Après ces écoutes, vous êtes maintenant capable de comprendre les **enjeux** du document, les **références**, le **contexte**.

Après les écoutes

Relisez vos notes et synthétisez-les.

Vérifiez que tous les éléments repérés pendant les écoutes figurent dans vos notes.

Vous êtes maintenant capable de **résumer les idées principales** du document à l'oral ou à l'écrit.

Synthétisez ces idées et écrivez ces idées sous forme de liste ou de *mind map* par exemple. Ainsi vous les aurez en tête au moment de la mise en commun avec vos camarades ou votre professeur·e.

Fiche N° 18 Compréhension écrite

Les descripteurs du Cadre européen - B1

- Comprendre des textes essentiellement rédigés dans une langue courante.
- Comprendre des instructions et consignes détaillées.
- Comprendre suffisamment pour entretenir une correspondance suivie.
- Localiser des informations recherchées ou pertinentes pour s'informer et réaliser une tâche.
- Comprendre un enchaînement de faits.
- Reconnaître les grandes lignes d'un schéma argumentatif.

Faites une expérience

1. **Prenez un texte** de votre choix (ou bien prenez le texte *Tubman on the $20 bill*, page 170).
2. **Effacez** tous les mots inconnus.
3. **Essayez de résumer** le texte à partir des éléments restants.
4. **Relisez** ensuite le texte intégral. Aidez-vous cette fois d'un dictionnaire.
5. **Constatez** votre progrès dans la compréhension du texte.

Que vous apprend cette expérience ?

Vous voyez que comprendre un texte, ce n'est pas forcément le traduire de bout en bout. Il est normal d'être confronté·e à des mots inconnus. Cela arrive même dans notre langue maternelle (on ne finit jamais d'apprendre !).

Comprendre un texte consiste **à élucider les passages flous à partir de ce que l'on connaît** : le contexte, les mots-clés, les mots transparents, les noms propres, etc.

Avant de lire

Anticiper à partir du titre et du paratexte

Essayez de **comprendre les termes utilisés** dans le titre et de **les associer à des images mentales**. Ces images vous permettront d'émettre des hypothèses sur le contenu.

Lisez le **paratexte**. Il vous renseigne sur le **type** d'écrit dont il s'agit, la **date** à laquelle il a été écrit, son **auteur·e**.

> Vous pouvez être confrontés·es à deux types de supports authentiques : **le texte littéraire** et **l'article de presse**. On parle de l'**auteur·e** pour un texte littéraire et du **journaliste** pour l'article de presse.

> **Paratexte :** informations autour du texte, souvent situées en bas de page.

Lisez de plus près le **sous-titre** (pour un article) ou le **paragraphe introductif**, généralement en italiques, s'il s'agit d'un texte littéraire. Ils vous donnent des informations importantes sur le contexte, dans le cas où le paratexte ne serait pas assez éclairant.

Vous êtes maintenant capable de résumer l'**idée générale du texte** et de faire des **hypothèses sur son contenu**.

Lecture

Plusieurs lectures du texte sont nécessaires.

Lecture 1

Pour comprendre le **sens global** du texte et le confronter aux **hypothèses** émises avant la lecture.

Lecture 2

Qui est qui ?
Vous devez **identifier les personnages** et les liens qu'ils entretiennent entre eux.

Dans le cas d'un texte littéraire, un travail sur les pronoms sujets ou compléments (voir Précis grammatical p. 192) peut vous aider à repérer les liens.

Dans le cas d'un article de presse, il s'agit de comprendre la fonction des personnes citées et de faire attention à leurs propos : sont-ils rapportés au discours direct ou indirect ?

→ À la fin de cette deuxième lecture, vous devez être capable de dire quels sont les personnages qui ont un rôle central, quels sont ceux qui sont simplement mentionnés dans le texte.

Lecture 3

Vous allez vous concentrer sur les **lieux**, les **nombres**, ainsi que les **objectifs** principaux (dénoncer, déplorer, accuser, montrer) dans le cas d'un article de presse.

Vous allez aussi approfondir le rôle des personnages grâce aux éléments descriptifs, et identifier le type de **narrateur** ainsi que son rôle.

> Utilisez des couleurs différentes pour souligner les différents éléments.

> Après ces trois lectures, vous êtes maintenant capable de préciser les **intentions** de l'auteur·e ou du journaliste, le rôle des **personnages**, les **références**, le **contexte**.

Relecture

Lire entre les lignes !

Une dernière lecture va vous aider à comprendre **la logique du texte** et à vous saisir de sa progression entre le début et la fin.

Certains **repères** s'avèrent très utiles pour lire entre les lignes :

- dans un texte littéraire : les mots de liaison, le retour à la ligne, la répartition des échanges dans un dialogue. Par exemple, si un des personnages monopolise la parole cela interroge sur ses intentions.

> L'**auteur·e**, c'est celui ou celle qui écrit le texte. Le·la narrateur·rice, c'est celui ou celle qui s'exprime dans le texte. Dans un texte littéraire, il ne s'agit pas forcément de la même personne !

- dans un article de presse : la répartition des paragraphes (en général un paragraphe exprime une idée, une étape de l'argumentation du journaliste), les mots de liaison.

> Un article de presse n'est pas forcément objectif.

Deviner

Deviner le sens des mots inconnus à partir des mots connus fait aussi partie des stratégies à acquérir. Celle-ci s'appelle **l'inférence**. **Inférer** c'est chercher, enquêter à partir de trois éléments dont on se souvient avec le nom de code **RAS**.

R	pour **racine** : enlever le suffixe ou le préfixe pour comprendre comment le mot est créé.
A	pour **atmosphère** : se servir du contexte pour faire sens.
S	pour **syntaxe** : comprendre le rôle du mot dans la phrase (sa fonction).

Synthétiser

Sur une feuille à part, donner un titre synthétique à chaque paragraphe d'un article peut s'avérer être d'une grande aide ; de même que lister les thèmes principaux évoqués ou répétés dans un texte littéraire le sera tout autant.

> Après cette dernière lecture, vous êtes maintenant capable de **résumer les idées** principales du texte.
>
> **Écrivez ces idées** sous forme de liste ou de schéma (*mind map* par exemple). Ainsi vous les aurez sous la main au moment des questions.

Fiche N° 19

Expression orale en interaction

Les descripteurs du Cadre européen - B1

- Faire face à des situations variées avec une relative aisance à condition que la langue soit standard et clairement articulée.
- Engager la conversation et maintenir le contact pour :
  - échanger des informations ;
  - réagir à des sentiments ;
  - exprimer clairement un point de vue.
- Prendre part à une discussion pour expliquer, commenter, comparer et opposer.
- Interviewer et être interviewé·e, conduire un entretien préparé et prendre quelques initiatives.
- Faire aboutir une requête.

Faites un essai !

1. **Réfléchissez à votre sujet :** est-ce un débat ? À deux, à plusieurs ? À la radio, à la télévision ? Enregistré en cours, à la maison ou « en direct » en classe ?
2. **Prenez des notes** en fonction de la forme de votre prise de parole. L'exercice de la prise de parole en interaction impose que vous n'ayez pas des phrases déjà écrites mais des éléments de réponses sous formes de notes. Pour que le débat soit plus naturel, vous devez être spontané·e, dans votre répartie.
3. **Répétez vos arguments** avec des camarades qui ont votre rôle ou imaginez les réponses de vos camarades et affinez votre argumentation !
4. **Utilisez un code couleur** pour vos idées, vos arguments, vos exemples, etc.
5. Notez la **transcription phonétique** des mots difficiles et **surlignez** les mots à accentuer car importants.
6. **Mettez-vous dans votre rôle** (nom, fonction, origine…). Si vous avez un rôle à jouer, celui de présentateur·trice par exemple, vous devez avoir formalisé le début et la fin de votre intervention. Toutefois vos questions doivent se baser sur ce que disent les participants·es et si elles doivent être préparées en amont, elles ne doivent pas être rédigées.
7. **Débattez** avec des camarades !

Que vous apprend cette expérience ?

Vous voyez que prendre la parole en interaction est un exercice difficile et qui vous demande beaucoup d'attention.

Vous devez réussir à donner vos arguments tout en respectant la parole de l'autre. Il vous faut être cordial·e, mais restez suffisamment convaincant·e pour que le débat tourne en votre faveur !

Pour faire passer votre message vous devez être capable de vous adapter aux arguments des autres interlocuteurs·trices et aux questions du·de la camarade qui mène le débat. Il faut donc que votre élocution soit claire, que votre prononciation soit la plus authentique possible, que les mots porteurs de sens soient bien accentués et que l'intonation soit adaptée. Cet exercice nécessite donc de l'entraînement.

> Vous pouvez vous filmer pour revoir et analyser votre performance. Personne n'aime entendre sa propre voix, mais c'est un très bon exercice pour s'améliorer à l'oral !

Avant de parler !

Organiser votre prise de parole

Prendre part à un débat ne signifie pas seulement être pour ou contre mais être capable de nuancer son opinion, argumenter, encourager mais aussi contredire les autres participants.

Parlez à partir de **notes succinctes** mais ne les lisez pas. Vos notes peuvent être sous forme de :

- tirets pour lister vos idées principales,
- d'acronymes ou d'abréviations,
- de carte heuristique (*mind map*) pour schématiser votre pensée.

DEBATE

S'opposer

I don't agree... I disagree... I don't think that... Frankly (*franchement*), I doubt if...

The truth is... I see your point but the problem with your point of view is that...

Donner son opinion

I think... In my opinion... To my mind... The way I see it... (*La façon dont je vois les choses, ...*)

I suppose... I'm sure / certain / convinced that...

I honestly feel that... I strongly believe that...

Without a doubt... (*Sans aucun doute...*)

Argumenter

To start with... The reason why... That's why... For this reason... That's the reason why... Most people think.... It is common knowledge that... For example... For instance...

S'exprimer en interaction

Prenez la parole en vous efforçant de ne **pas lire vos notes** de façon mécanique.

Regardez votre ou vos **interlocuteur·rice·s** !

Attention à votre temps de parole : **n'allez pas trop vite** ou à l'inverse, ne soyez **pas trop long·ue**.

Mettez le ton, il faut jouer **comme un·e acteur·rice**, vous devez défendre votre point de vue !

Entraînez-vous aussi souvent que possible : faites des présentations à la maison ou en cours (seul ou en groupe) et filmez ou enregistrez-vous. Pensez à **l'intelligibilité** de votre discours (accent, prononciation).

Si vous vous trompez – ce n'est pas grave : **reformulez** et pensez à l'autocorrection.

Entraînez-vous à plusieurs !

Vous êtes :

- le présentateur ou la présentatrice → préparez vos questions et vos relances,
- l'un·e des deux débateur·euse·s → réfléchissez au personnage, imaginez son point de vue et préparez vos arguments.

Welcome to *The California Report*, NPR's radio news programme, providing daily news of California. On today's programme, we wonder if... there should be **a bank holiday called *Angel Island day* in California**. We have a descendant of a Chinese immigrant and the descendant of a Russian immigrant who went through Ellis Island...

Fiche N° 20

Expression orale en continu

Les descripteurs du Cadre européen - B1

- S'exprimer de manière simple sur des sujets variés.
- Prendre la parole devant un auditoire, mettre en voix un texte.
- Restituer une information avec ses propres mots éventuellement à partir de notes.
- Relater des expériences vécues, en rendre compte (événements, dialogues, texte écrit ou oral).
- Expliquer un projet, exposer une démarche, préciser un mode d'emploi.
- Exprimer des sentiments, une opinion personnelle.
- Argumenter pour convaincre.

Faites une expérience.

1. **Réfléchissez à votre sujet** : est-ce un discours ? un audioguide ? un vlog ?
2. **Prenez des notes** en fonction de la forme de votre prise de parole. Pour un monologue de théâtre ou un discours, rédigez entièrement. Pour donner votre opinion sur un sujet, prenez seulement des notes afin de garder une part de spontanéité.
3. **Utilisez un code couleur** pour repérer vos idées, vos arguments, vos exemples.
4. Notez la **transcription phonétique** des mots difficiles et **surlignez** les mots à accentuer car importants.
5. **Entraînez-vous** devant un auditoire (ami·e·s, parents, frères et sœurs, ou même un miroir…).

Que vous apprend cette expérience ?

Quelles réactions avez-vous observées chez vos auditeurs·rices ? Vous devez réussir à capter l'attention de votre public en vous adaptant à lui. Il vous faut être agréable et convaincant·e.

Il est surtout nécessaire que le message passe, tant dans la forme que sur le fond.

Il faudra donc que votre prononciation soit la plus authentique possible, que les mots porteurs de sens soient bien accentués, que l'intonation soit adaptée.

Enfin, il faudra être audible pour capter l'attention de votre public. Cet exercice n'est donc pas aisé et nécessite de l'entraînement.

Préparer son intervention

Exemple de prise de notes pour préparer le message vidéo d'un joueur de football américain page 115 :

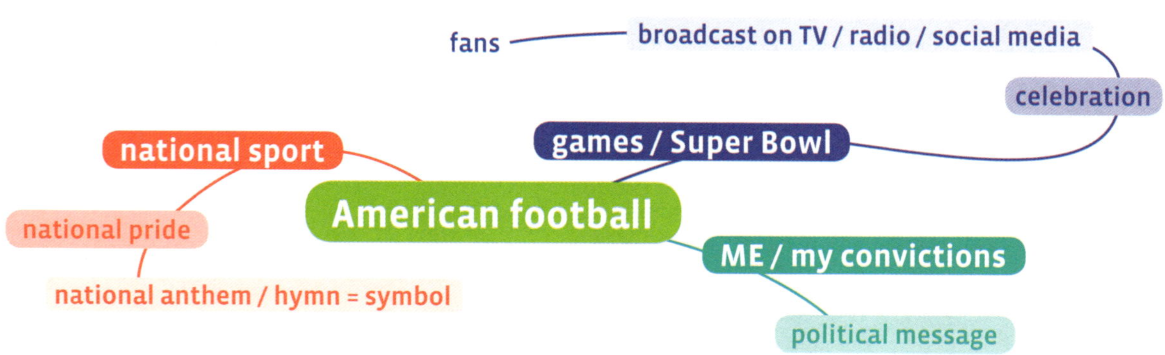

Planifier la prise de parole

> Illustrez vos arguments par des **exemples concrets** : noms propres, dates, chiffres, anecdote historique, actualité récente, etc. Ils vous rendront plus convaincant·e.

1. L'introduction : soyez dynamique !
- Présentez le sujet.
- Introduisez le thème et la question soulevée.

2. Le développement : soyez clair·e !
- **Organisez** votre propos à l'aide des mots de liaison.
- **Expliquez** les questions / problèmes soulevés par le sujet.
- **Illustrez** votre propos en vous appuyant sur des exemples concrets.

3. La conclusion : soyez concis·e !
- **Récapitulez** votre propos rapidement.
- Apportez une **réponse personnelle** au problème et faites une ouverture.

S'exprimer devant un auditoire

Prenez la parole en vous efforçant de ne **pas lire vos notes** de façon mécanique.

Regardez votre auditoire. Si vous vous enregistrez, efforcez-vous de ne pas regarder vos notes !

Mettez le ton. Adaptez-vous au rôle du personnage que vous incarnez ou au format de votre prise de parole : discours, guide de musée, etc.

Pendant votre intervention, faites des pauses, **des silences**. Vous avez besoin de respirer… et ceux qui vous écoutent aussi. Pensez aux discours des hommes politiques : ils accentuent les mots-clés et multiplient les silences. Les silences peuvent servir à souligner une idée importante, ou à capter l'attention de vos auditeurs·rices s'ils ne sont pas assez attentifs·ves – c'est souvent plus efficace que de crier !

Votre **posture** est très importante. Imaginez que vous passez à la télévision ou que vous parlez sur une estrade devant tout le lycée.

Attention à votre temps de parole : veillez à ne **pas aller trop vite** ou à l'inverse, ne soyez **pas trop long·ue**, vous risqueriez de lasser l'auditoire. Respectez les consignes !

Entraînez-vous aussi souvent que possible : faites des présentations à la maison ou en cours (seul·e ou en groupe).

Quelques mots de liaison pour articuler votre discours

Pour commencer un paragraphe	*To begin with… To start with… First of all… The first thing to take into consideration / to take into account is…*
Pour ajouter une idée	*In addition… Moreover… Furthermore… Also… Additionally…*
Pour exprimer un contraste	En début de phrase : *On the contrary… On the other hand…* Entre deux idées : *whereas… while…* En début de phrase ou entre deux idées : *Nevertheless… however… yet… that said…*
Pour donner un exemple	*For example… for instance*
Pour exprimer la conséquence	*As a consequence… consequently… as a result…*
Pour donner son opinion	*To me… as for me… in my opinion… as I see it… I think… I do believe…*
Pour confirmer ou compléter une idée	*As a matter of fact… in fact… actually…*
Pour conclure	*As a conclusion… to conclude…*

Faites un essai !

- **Préparez** vos idées et le plan de votre intervention.
- **Parlez** devant un groupe de camarades si possible.
- Pensez à **l'intelligibilité** de votre discours (accent, prononciation).
- **Si vous vous trompez**, ce n'est pas grave : reformulez et pensez à l'autocorrection.

> **Filmez-vous** afin de pouvoir adopter un regard extérieur sur votre performance. C'est un excellent moyen de repérer vos défauts récurrents pour y remédier. Mais vous verrez aussi des choses que vous faites bien sans en être conscient·e, et vous pourrez les reproduire dans vos interventions suivantes.

Fiche N°
21 Expression écrite en interaction

Qu'est-ce que l'expression écrite en interaction ?

Définition : Il s'agit d'échanges généralement courts entre interlocuteurs·rices à l'écrit.
Ex : échanges personnels (lettre, chat, messagerie instantanée, messages téléphoniques, ...) ou impersonnels (formulaires, ...).
Forme : Le langage est souvent informel, il peut être emprunté au langage oral. Structurer le texte n'est pas la priorité. Il est même possible de demander à clarifier un propos.

Les descripteurs du Cadre européen - B1

- Écrire de **brèves notes simples** en rapport avec des **besoins** immédiats.
- Apporter des **informations** et des idées sur des sujets abstraits et concrets, **vérifier** l'information, **poser** des **questions** sur un **problème** ou **l'exposer** assez précisément.
- Écrire des **lettres personnelles** décrivant en **détail expériences**, **sentiments** et **événements**.
- S'engager dans des échanges en ligne en **temps réel** avec **plus** d'**un·e participant·e**, prendre en compte les intentions communicatives de chaque intervenant·e, mais **peut ne pas comprendre les détails** et les **implications**.

Faites une expérience.

1. **Réfléchissez à votre support** : est-ce un texto ? un email ? plusieurs messages sur un forum de discussion ?
2. **Qui écrit ?** Allez-vous utiliser votre **nom** et **prénom ou** bien un **pseudonyme ?**
3. **Prise de notes** : quelle longueur ? quel registre de langue ? quel sujet ? à qui cela s'adresse-t-il ?
4. **Utilisez un dictionnaire** (papier ou en ligne) pour traduire des mots mais surtout pas des phrases entières.
5. **Entraînez-vous** d'abord sur un brouillon en utilisant des **couleurs différentes** pour chaque participant·e.

Que vous apprend cette expérience ?

Il ne s'agit pas seulement de rédiger mais de réagir à l'écrit à ce que votre interlocuteur·trice vous a écrit ou bien à ce que vous lui avez écrit.

N'oubliez pas que vous pouvez demander des précisions à votre interlocuteur·trice si vous n'avez pas compris ses propos.

Essayez d'adopter un langage correct, mais ne vous concentrez pas trop sur la forme. Vous pouvez vous corriger en temps réel, comme à l'oral.

Communiquer efficacement

Assurez-vous toujours de :

- vous faire bien comprendre en reformulant au besoin (*What I meant is..., I'm sorry, I didn't mean...*),
- prendre en compte la ou les réponses précédentes et les réactions de votre ou vos interlocuteurs·rices,
- mettre en place des stratégies pour communiquer : la coopération, l'illustration, la négociation, etc.

Organiser sa prise de parole à l'écrit

1 **Bien définir le contexte de cette interaction à l'écrit :** pourquoi écrivez-vous ? À qui ? Quelles questions vous posez-vous ? Sur quel support (en ligne, par voie postale, par courrier électronique ...) ? Répondez-vous à quelqu'un, ou bien êtes-vous à l'origine de ce questionnement ?

2 **Préparer son sujet :** prenez des notes et rassemblez les outils dont vous avez besoin. N'écrivez pas de phrases complètes mais réfléchissez au lexique dont vous aurez besoin.

3 **Répéter ses interventions :** imaginez les questions ou les réponses que vous pourriez formuler. Quels éléments pouvez-vous apporter à cette conversation ?

4 **Anticiper une clarification :** rassemblez les outils et expressions que vous pourrez utiliser pour reprendre et clarifier un propos si celui-ci n'a pas été compris par votre interlocuteur·rice.

5 **Mettre le ton :** réfléchissez aux moyens de mettre le ton dans vos écrits (ponctuation, mais aussi symboles, GIFs, images et smileys s'il s'agit d'une conversation personnelle). ☺

Entraînez-vous à plusieurs !

Vous êtes :

- un·e Français·e voulant préparer sa visite du MoMA à New York City pendant ses vacances, et qui veut quelques précisions sur l'entrée, les collections, et quelques artistes,
- un·e New Yorkais·e travaillant pour le service de communication du musée et en charge de répondre aux questions des visiteurs sur internet.

Discutez sur le service de chat du musée pour organiser la visite en toute sérénité.

Vous pouvez vous aider d'un dictionnaire en ligne ! (**Wordreference** ou **Cambridge**)

Simulateurs d'applications de messagerie en ligne

igenerator.eu
ios.foxsash.com
ifaketextmessage.com

Fiche N° 22 Expression écrite

Les descripteurs du Cadre européen - B1

- Peut écrire des **descriptions détaillées non complexes** sur une gamme étendue de sujets familiers dans le cadre de son domaine d'intérêt.
- Peut rédiger une **critique simple** sur un film, un livre ou un programme télévisé, en utilisant une gamme limitée de langage.
- Peut écrire de brefs **essais simples** sur des sujets d'intérêt général.
- Peut écrire un texte sur un sujet actuel en rapport avec son centre d'intérêt, en utilisant un **langage simple** pour lister les avantages et les inconvénients, donner et justifier son opinion.
- Peut intégrer des illustrations, des photos ainsi que des textes courts à un rapport ou une affiche de présentation.

Faites une expérience.

1. D'instinct, comment traduiriez-vous en anglais les deux expressions suivantes ?
   - « Il me fait chanter. »
   - « Il me fait marcher. »

   Des énoncés de type **He makes me sing* ou **He makes me walk* ne sont pas recevables dans ce contexte.
2. Cherchez maintenant ces expressions dans le dictionnaire.
3. Que remarquez-vous sur la démarche même d'écriture ? Pouvez-vous toujours traduire mot à mot ?

Que vous apprend cette expérience ?

Afin d'éviter les confusions, il faut garder en tête qu'écrire ce n'est pas traduire. En effet, penser comme cela évite de passer par le mot à mot et permet d'utiliser une langue de plus en plus authentique. Il convient donc de **penser directement en anglais** et d'acquérir une logique de la langue, en participant activement en classe par exemple, pour se faire corriger.

L'anglais est très global alors que le français est très spécifique. C'est pourquoi le même terme en anglais peut traduire plusieurs idées. Pour chaque mot appris, essayer de retenir trois sens différents est très utile.

Le fond et la forme

Réussir une expression écrite, c'est assurer un équilibre entre **le fond** (les idées) et **la forme** (la façon de les articuler), le tout en répondant à un sujet donné.

Pour cela, appliquez la méthode COOL :

C	pour **comprendre** : bien comprendre le sujet est essentiel (→ Fiche N° 18 Compréhension écrite p. 276).
O	pour **obéir** : il faut suivre la direction donnée par les mots-clés du sujet.
O	pour **organiser** : plus vos idées seront organisées, plus votre devoir sera clair.
L	pour **lire** : lire et relire sa production en entier à la fin sont des étapes capitales.

Écrire un email ou une lettre

Dans ce type d'échanges écrits, tout dépend du **destinataire**. En effet, une lettre à quelqu'un de sa famille sera à distinguer d'une correspondance avec une institution ou encore à un potentiel employeur.

> **Attention**, le langage SMS ne sera pas recevable dans ce type d'écrit.

Présenter un courrier formel

Nom et adresse
de l'expéditeur·rice

Date

Nom et adresse
du·de la destinataire

Dear Madam, Sir

Lettre

...

...

Formule de politesse

Signature

	Un email	Une lettre
Fond	**Pour amener l'objet du courriel** • *I'm writing to you today...* • *The reason why I'm writing is...* • *I really wanted to tell you about...* • *The purpose of my email is to know...* • *I'm writing to find out if...*	**Pour amener l'objet du courrier** • *If I may, I would like to + BV* • *I am writing to inform you about...* • *The subject of my letter is...* • *With all due respect, I would like to inform you that...* • *I wanted to tell you how I was doing.*
Forme	**En ouverture :** • *Dear X* • *Dear Mr/Mrs X* • *Hi (to a friend)* **Pour conclure :** • *Yours sincerely* • *See you soon (to a friend)* • *Xo Xo (to a very good friend)* **Pour parler d'une pièce jointe :** • *You will find the document attached/enclosed* • *As promised please find the document attached/enclosed*	**En ouverture :** • *Dear Madam, Sir* • *To whom it may concern* **Pour conclure :** • *Yours faithfully* • *Kind regards* • *Love from LA* **Point de vigilance :** • Aérer son courrier au maximum. • Changer de ligne ou de paragraphe chaque fois que vous apportez un élément nouveau (dans une lettre formelle). • Utiliser les mots de liaison. • Pas de présentation particulière pour une lettre à un·e proche.

Écrire un dialogue

Attention, un dialogue n'est pas un script. Il ne suffit donc pas d'écrire des répliques échangées entre deux personnages (comme au cinéma ou au théâtre). Il est important de **contextualiser**.

Commencez par **une courte phrase d'introduction** puis donnez des précisions sur **les expressions faciales ou l'atmosphère**, cela permet de rendre le dialogue visuel pour le·la lecteur·rice et donc authentique.

Dans le fond comme dans la forme, un dialogue en anglais s'avère assez différent d'un dialogue en français. Dans le premier cas, le dialogue s'imbrique davantage dans le récit et n'est visible que grâce aux guillemets.

Présentation d'un dialogue	
en français	**en anglais**
« – Un jour je partirai et tu ne me reverras plus jamais ! cria-t-il. – Calme toi d'abord, répondit-elle choquée. »	"Someday, I'll run away, and you will never see me again!" he shouted. "First, calm down," she answered, shocked.
• Les guillemets sont ouverts au début du dialogue et ne sont fermés qu'après la dernière réponse. • Des tirets sont utilisés à chaque ligne pour marquer le changement de personnage.	• Les guillemets sont utilisés au début et à la fin de chaque intervention. • Pas d'inversion sujet/verbe pour les verbes de discours. • Pas de tirets.

Said is dead!
Évitez la répétition du verbe said à chaque ligne, remplacez-le par un autre verbe.
Parler : *tell, say, ask, answer, reply, explain, admit, deny...*
Crier : *scream, shout...*
À voix basse : *mumble, whisper...*
Avec émotion : *cry, laugh, argue...*

Écrire un article

Attention, il faut distinguer l'article du paragraphe argumentatif. Le premier se base sur des faits et non sur l'opinion. Même si un article est rarement objectif, l'opinion n'est pas donnée directement : l'enjeu est de faire comprendre ce que l'on pense dans la manière et pas dans les mots.

À partir du **thème** qui vous est donné, vous devez trouver **un sujet** (un aspect caractéristique ou problématique du thème) autour duquel votre article sera construit.

Le paragraphe introductif doit permettre aux lecteurs de répondre aux questions en *Wh-* (*Who? What? Where? When?* ...) et d'imaginer clairement la situation que vous allez développer dans la suite.

Vous devez maîtriser **les mots de liaison**, rechercher le **vocabulaire spécifique** au sujet que vous traitez, et **répartir vos idées** tout au long de l'article.

Chaque nouveau paragraphe doit apporter des éléments supplémentaires.

N'hésitez pas à utiliser des **citations** de gens connus ou qui interviennent dans les faits relatés.

Pour plus de cohérence et d'inspiration donnez **un titre** à votre article <u>après</u> l'avoir écrit.

Utilisez des formules passives (équivalent du pronom neutre « on ») pour donner à votre article un ton plus objectif.

Écrire un paragraphe argumentatif

Le paragraphe argumentatif n'est pas un plaidoyer. Vous ne devez pas présenter une seule et unique vision de problèmes amenés par le sujet. Il s'agit de **peser le pour et le contre**.

Construisez votre texte en suivant le **principe de l'entonnoir** : de l'argument le plus évident à l'argument le plus réfléchi.

Tout l'enjeu de l'exercice est d'**argumenter**, **relativiser**, **réfuter**, **critiquer**...

Pour cela vous devez maîtriser **les mots de liaison** afin que votre développement soit structuré et suivi de bout en bout par votre lecteur, sans aucune gêne.

Faites bien attention à **trouver les mots justes** pour vous exprimer de façon claire et concise.

Ne confondez pas vos arguments (les idées qui répondent au problème posé en introduction) **et les exemples** (qui rendent les arguments plus concrets en les illustrant).

Vos phrases introductive et conclusive ne doivent pas excéder une à deux lignes.

Notez les guillemets différents :
« ... » : guillemets français,
"..." : guillemets anglais

CREDITS TEXTES

p. 19 © Key Club at West Ranch High School ; **p. 19** *The 39 Best Clubs to Start in High School*, by Dora Seigel, November 15, 2017 © PrepScholar 2018 ; **p. 29** *The Story Of The Claddagh*, by Shannan McQuade, Oct 11, 2016 © Odyssey Media Group, D.R. ; **p. 37** FEATURED WORK. Chris Saunders: The Smarteez. Used with kind permission of The Vitra Design Museum ; **p. 38** *South Africa's 'born-free' generation*, 25 April 2014 © Courtesy of BBC ; **p. 39** © 2012 Alexia Webster ; **p. 48** *Secret Diary of a Camp Counselor*, by Lucy Harper © Bursea Books ; **p. 49** *America's (small) new trend: taking a gap year*, by Hank Pellissier, June 21, 2018 ©2019 GreatSchools.org , D.R. ; **p. 50** https://www.gap-year.com/your-gap-worldwide ; **p. 51** *You decide: is a gap year right for you?* 19/08/2006, The Guardian © Guardian News & Media Ltd 2019 ; **p. 57** *The American Dream has moved to Canada*, by Scott Gilmore, Feb 28, 2017 © Rogers Media 2019, D.R. ; **p. 58** *Canada is a Land of Opportunity*, Rany Ibrahim © Century Initiative ; **p. 68** *Diagnosing Gentrification*, by Erin Schumaker. From Huff Post, 2018-02-12 © 2019 Oath Inc. All rights reserved. Used by permission and protected by the Copyright Laws of the United States. The printing, copying, redistribution, or retransmission of this Content without express written permission is prohibited. ; **p. 71** *From THEM: A Novel*, by Nathan McCall. Copyright © 2007 by Nathan McCall. Reprinted with the permission of Atria Books, a division of Simon & Schuster, Inc. All rights reserved. ; **p. 77** *Maximum City: Bombay Lost and Found*, Suketu Mehta © Penguin UK ; **p. 78** *Ants Among Elephants*, by Sujatha Gidla © MACMILLAN US ; **p. 89** *WE SHOULD ALL BE* FEMINISTS, by Chimamanda Ngozi Adichie. Copyright © 2012, 2014, Chimamanda Ngozi Adichie, used by permission of The Wylie Agency (UK) Limited ; **p. 90** *Young women on Instagram and self-esteem: 'I absolutely feel insecure'*, Mahita Gajanan, 4/11/2015, The Guardian © Guardian News & Media Ltd 2019 ; **p. 97** From *CUSTER DIED FOR YOUR SINS: AN INDIAN MANIFESTO*, by Vine Deloria Jr. Copyright © 1969 by Vine Deloria Jr. Copyright renewed © 1997 by Vine Deloria Jr. Reprinted with the permission of Scribner, a division of Simon & Schuster, Inc. All rights reserved ; **p. 98** *The True Story of Pocahontas*, by Jackie Mansky, MARCH 23, 2017 © 2017 Smithsonian Institution. Reprinted with permission from Smithsonian Enterprises. All rights reserved. Reproduction in any medium is strictly prohibited without permission from Smithsonian Institution. **p. 108** *2018 Super Bowl: Trump brings up national anthem debate in pregame statement*, by Ryan Wilson, 4 February, 2018 © CBS ; **p. 108** *The Power of Super Bowl Advertising*, by Marianne Bickle, Feb 6, 2012 ©2019 Forbes Media ; **p. 108** *Super Bowl Makes 'Heroic' Play To Unify America*, by Anne Zeiser, Columnist, February 5, 2018 © MediaPost ; **p. 108** *What's So Super About Super Bowl Sunday?*, AR and Lydia from OH, wonderopolis.org © National Center for Families Learning **p. 110** *The History Of The National Anthem In Sports*, by Caroline Bologna. From Huff Post, 2018-05-19 © 2019 Oath Inc. All rights reserved. Used by permission and protected by the Copyright Laws of the United States. The printing, copying, redistribution, or retransmission of this Content without express written permission is prohibited ; **p. 117** Dr Andy Clark, Historian, Newcastle University, April 13, 2015 © Working-Class Perspectives ; **p. 118** *Women's football can be the first female team sport to break through into the mainstream*, by Luke Edwards, 7 September 2018 © Telegraph Media Group Limited 2018 ; **p. 119** *Club Charter, Season 2017/18* ©2019 Manchester United Ltd ; **p. 128** *"I'm Nobody! Who are you?"*, in *Poems*, Series 2, by Emily Dickinson, 1891 ; **p. 128** *I know you got soul*, Compositeur / Auteur : BARRIER ERIC, RAKIM ; **p. 128** *Tell Him*, Lauryn Hill © 1998 Sony/ATV Tunes LLC / Obverse Creation Music Inc. Avec l'aimable autorisation de Sony/ATV Music Publishing France. Droits Protégés. ; **p. 128** *Words like Freedom*, Langston Hughes ; **p. 130** *Is Rap Poetry?*, by MICAH MATTIX, July 1, 2014, © The American Conservative 2018 ; **p. 131** *Are rappers better linguists than SHAKESPEARE? Complex rhymes are 'second nature' to hip-hop artists*, by Victoria Woollaston, 11/02/2015 © MailOnline ; **p. 136** *6 Reasons Why Broadway Musicals Are Great* © 2018 The Ambient Mixer Blog, https://blog.ambient-mixer.com ; **p. 137** *Hair: The American Tribal Love-Rock Musical" 50th anniversary celebration!*, by Alan Bresloff, August 4th, 2017 © 2018 Around the Town Chicago, D.R. ; **p. 149** © 2019 University of Chester, D.R. ; **p. 150** *UK government announces plans to ban plastic straws, cotton-buds, and stirrers*, by Anmar Frangoul, 22 Oct 2018 © 2019 CNBC.com ; **p. 157** *The Carbon Diaries 2015*, Saci Lloyd, 2009. D.R ; **p. 159** *Can 'cli-fi' actually make a difference? A climate scientist's perspective*, by Sarah Perkins-Kirkpatrick, 5 septembre 2017, The Conversation France. D.R. ; **p. 168** *The American Flag*, March 26, 2018 © USA.gov ; **p. 168** U.S. Department of State. Bureau of Public Affairs. Washington, D.C. July 2003 ; **p. 169** *The Star-Spangled Banner*, by Naomi Blumberg, 2-8-2018 © 2018 Encyclopædia Britannica, Inc. ; **p. 169** *HISTORY OF THE FOURTH OF JULY*, February 19, 2018, History.com © A&E Networks ; **p. 170** *Mnuchin Doesn't Endorse Placing Harriet Tubman on the New $20 Bill*, by BINYAMIN APPELBAUMAUG. From The New-York Times, 2017.09.01 © 2018 The New York Times. All rights reserved. Used by permission and protected by the Copyright Laws of the United States. The printing, copying, redistribution, or retransmission of the Content without express written permission is prohibited ; **p. 177** *ASIAN MIGRATION AND GLOBAL CITIES*, by Samantha Ching © kqed.org, D.R. ; **p. 179** *My Journey from China to America, Kaiping, Guangdong to San Francisco, CA, Don Yee Fung Lee*, by William Wong (edited by Jordan Yee and Eddie Wong) © Angel Island Immigration Station Foundation.

TABLE DES ILLUSTRATIONS

p. 6-1 ph © The British School of Paris ; **p. 6-2** ph © Courtesy of Lorraine Maher ; **p. 6-3** ph © Chris Saunders- La Belle Façon Talents ; **p. 6-4** ph © potowizard- stock.adobe.com ; **p. 6-4-m** ph © creative soul- stock.adobe.com ; **p. 6-5** ph © Pgiam / iStock / Getty-Images ; **p. 8-1** ph © James and Karla Murray ; **p. 8-2** ph © hadynyah / iStock / Getty-Images ; **p. 8-3** ph © Richard Levine / Alamy Stock Photo ; **p. 8-4** ph © Sidney E. King / Colonial National Historical Park, Yorktown, Virginia, USA. ; **p. 10-1** ph © Patrick Smith / Getty-Images / AFP Photo ; **p. 10-2** ph © Maxim Zmeyev / AFP Photo ; **p. 10-3** ph © AFP Photo / Chris J Ratcliffe / © Adagp, Paris 2019 ; **p. 10-4** ph © Juan Antonio Alonso- www.agefotostock.com ; **p. 12-1** ph © Leon Neal / AFP Photo ; **p. 12-2** ph © Oli Scarff / Getty-Images / AFP Photo ; **p. 12-3** ph © Carlo Allegri / Reuters ; **p. 12-4** ph © Granger / Bridgeman Images ; **p. 15** ph © The British School of Paris ; **p. 16** ph © Gregg Vignal / Alamy Stock Photo ; **p. 18-a** ph © Nerthuz / iStock ; **p. 18-b** ph © portishead1 / iStock ; **p. 18-c** ph © Hero Images / Getty-Images ; **p. 18-d** ph © Richard B. Levine / Alamy Stock Photo ; **p. 18-e** ph © gorodenkoff / iStock ; **p. 20** ph © RosalreneBetancourt 13 / Alamy Stock Photo ; **p. 21-h** ph © VHS Unicef Club / D.R. ; **p. 21-b** ph © Allvisionn / iStock ; **p. 22** ph © ibooo7 / iStock ; **p. 24** ph © Selenophile / Shutterstock ; **p. 25** ph © Duel / Getty-Images ; **p. 27-h** ph © Courtesy of Lorraine Maher ; **p. 27-b** ph © Chris Saunders- La Belle Façon Talents ; **p. 28-1** ph © nordmann- stock.adobe.com ; **p. 28-2** ph © John W Banagan / Getty-Images ; **p. 28-3** ph © Brendan Moran / Sportsfile via Getty-Images ; **p. 28-4** ph © cezzar1981 / iStock ; **p. 28-5** ph © scenicireland.com / Christopher Hill Photographic / Alamy Stock Photo ; **p. 28-6** ph © Derek Brumby / iStock ; **p. 29-h** ph © Silver Spiral Arts / Shutterstock ; **p. 29-g,d** © Courtesy of Midas Productions ; **p. 30-h** ph © What it means to be irish © Charlotte Ryan ; **p. 30-m, b** ph © Courtesy of Lorraine Maher ; **p. 35** © ‹Wide shot of ‹Today› set (2013) © Courtesy of RTÉ Archives ; **p. 36-h** ph © Marco Longari / AFP Photo ; **p. 36-b** © Journeyman Pictures ; **p. 37-h** ph © Per-Anders Pettersson / Getty-Images ; **p. 37-b** © 2018 Between 10 and 5 ; **p. 39-hg, hd** © 2012 Alexia Webster ; **p. 43-h** ph © Sipho Mpongo ; **p. 43-b** ph © Via Vyndal / Alaister Russell / Sunday Times / Gallo Images / Getty-Images ; **p. 45-h-1** © Walk the Blue Fields by Claire Keagan, published by Grove Press, Black Cat, 2008 ; **p. 45-h-2** © From « The Commitments « by Roddy Doyle, Published by William Heinemann. Reproduced by permission of The Random House Group Ltd. © 1897 ; **p. 45-h-3** Brooklyn (Dir: John Crowley), 2016 ph © SunsetBox / AllPix / Aurimages ; **p. 45-h-4** Shadow Dancer (Dir: James Marsh), 2012 ph © BBC Films / Element Pictures / Irish Film Board / The Kobal Collection / Aurimages ; **p. 45-h-5** Angela's Ashes (Dir: Alan Parker), 1999. Coll. Christophel © David Brown productions / Dirty hands productions / Scott Rudin productions ; **p. 45-h-6** The Wind that Shakes the Barley (Dir: Ken Loach), 2006 ph © Mary Evans / Aurimages ; **p. 45-b-1** © The Hidden Star by K. Sello Duiker, published by Umuzi, 2006. Cover design by The Inkman ; **p. 45-b-2** © Book cover from Out of Bounds, by Beverley Naidoo, 2008. Reprinted by permission of HarperCollins Publishers ; **p. 45-b-3** © Book cover from Mama Africa! by Kathryne Erskine & Charly Palmer. Publisher: Farrar, Straus and Giroux (BYR) (Pan Macmillan) ; **p. 45-b-4** Hear me move (Dir: Scottnes L. Smith), 2017 ph © Coal Stove Pictures / BBQ_DFY / Aurimages ; **p. 45-b-5** The African Cypher (Dir: Bryan Little), 2012 ph © Fly on the Wall / Red Bull Media House / BBQ_DFY / Aurimages ; **p. 47-h** ph © potowizard- stock.adobe.com ; **p. 47-hm** ph © creative soul- stock.adobe.com ; **p. 47-b** ph © Pgiam / iStock / Getty-Images ; **p. 48-g** © The University of Adelaide, D.R. ; **p. 48-d** © Lucy Harper, Bursea Books, 2011 ; **p. 49** ph © Toltek / iStock ; **p. 50-h** ph © Anthony Asael / DanitaDelimont.com- www.agefotostock.com ; **p. 50-b** ph © Elizabeth Fitt / Sopa Images / LightRocket via Getty-Images ; **p. 51** ph © Drobot Dean- stock.adobe.com ; **p. 55-h** ph © sturti / iStock / Getty-Images ; **p. 55-b** ph © Robert Daly / Caiaimage / Getty-Images ; **p. 56** ph © Courtesy of Global News ; **p. 58-h** ph © Courtesy of Rany Ibrahim ; **p. 58** ph © www.centuryinitiative.ca ; **p. 59** © Moving2Canada 2019, D.R. ; **p. 63-h** ph © alexskopje / Shutterstock ; **p. 63-b** ph © Ronnie Chua / Shutterstock ; **p. 65-h1** Secret Life of Backpackers: A bunk's-eye view of the tourist trail from Bondi to Cairns by Barry Divola. © A.B.C, 2008 ; **p. 65-h2** Tales from Nowhere by Tim Cahill, Jason Elliot, Don George, Pam Houston, Pico Iyer, Rolf Potts, Anthony Sattin, Danny Wallace, Simon Winchester. © Lonely Planet, 2016 ; **p. 65-h3** Gap Year Adventures: An Essential Pocket Guide to Making It Count by Tamsin King. © Summersdale Publishers, 2016 ; **p. 65-h4** Work Your Way Around the World (17th edition) by Susan Griffith. © Crimson Publishing, 2017 ; **p. 65-h5** Gap Year, serie created by created by Tom Basden, 2017 ph © Eleven / BBQ_DFY / Aurimages ; **p. 65-b1** Souvenir of Canada by Douglas Coupland © Greystone Books, Canada, 1998 ; **p. 65-b2** The Collected Essex County by Jeff Lemire © Top Shelf Productions, 2009 ; **p. 65-b3** One Week (Dir: Michael McGowan), 2008. Coll. Christophel © Mongrel Media ; **p. 65-b4** Scott Pilgrim (Dir: Edgar Wright), 2010. Coll. Christophel © Marc Platt Productions / Big Talk Productions ; **p. 65-b5** Being Canadian (Dir: Robert Cohen), 2015. Coll. Christophel © Grainey Pictures ; **p. 65-b6** The Great Canadian Bucket List: One-of-a-Kind Travel Experiences Paperback by Robin Esrock. © Dundurn, 2017 ; **p. 67-hg,hd** ph © James and Karla Murray ; **p. 67-b** ph © hadynyah / iStock / Getty-Images ; **p. 68** ph © Philip Scalia / Alamy Stock Photo ; **p. 69** ph © Maurizio dalla Palma / © Alberto Serrano (aka Tito Na Rúa) and Alfredo Bennett (aka Royal KingBee) ; **p. 70** ph © Travis Estell ; **p. 71** © CNN ; **p. 75-h** ph © Zuma Press, Inc. / Alamy Stock Photo ; **p. 75-b** ph © Pacific Press / Alamy Stock Photo ; **p. 76-h** © United Nations ; **p. 76-b** © Urban-Think Tank (U-TT), D.R. ; **p. 77** © Headline Review Publishers, 2004 ; **p. 78** ph © Sujatha Gidla / D.R. ; **p. 79-h** ph © Noppasin / iStock / Getty-Images ; **p. 79-m** © CNBC International ; **p. 79-b** © ORF ; **p. 83-h** ph © K M Sharma / The Times of India / AFP Photo ; **p. 83-b** ph © Jon Arnold Images / hemis.fr ; **p. 85-h1** This Side of Home by Renée Watson © Bloomsbury USA Childrens, 2017 ; **p. 85-h2** How to Kill a City: Gentrification, Inequality, and the Fight for the Neighborhood by Peter Moskowitz © Bold Type Books, 2017 ; **p. 85-h3** Do the Right Thing (Dir: Spike Lee), 1989 ph © Universal / The Kobal Collection / Aurimages ; **p. 85-h4** Priced out (Dir: Cornelius Swart), 2016 © Collective Eye Films ; **p. 85-h5** The North pole (Dir: Yvan Iturriaga) ph © Black Square Productions / Movement Generation / BBQ_DFY / Aurimages ; **p. 85-b1** Q & A: A Novel by Vikas Swarup © Scribner, 2005 ; **p. 85-b2** The White Tiger by Aravind Adiga. © HarperCollins, 2009 ; **p. 85-b3** The Lunchbox (Dir: Ritesh Batra), 2013. Coll. Christophel © Sikhya Entertainment / DAR Motion Pictures ; **p. 85-b4** Slumdog Millionaire (Dir: Danny Boyle), 2008. ph © Zuma Press / Aurimages ; **p. 85-b5** India in a day (Dir: Richie Mehta), 2016. ph © Scott Free Productions / BBQ_DFY / Aurimages ; **p. 85-b6** The Ministry of Utmost Happiness by Arundhati Roy. © Hamish Hamilton Ltd, 2017 ; **p. 87-h** ph © Richard Levine / Alamy Stock Photo ; **p. 87-b**

ph © Sidney E. King / Colonial National Historical Park, Yorktown, Virginia, USA. ; **p. 88-g, d** ph © 2019 Hearst Communications, Inc. / D.R. ; **p. 89** ph © Janette Pellegrini / Getty-Images for Girls Write Now / AFP Photo ; **p. 90** ph © Instagram / Essena O'Neill ; **p. 91-hg** ph © Instagram / Beyoncé (https://www.instagram.com/p/qwWCsgPw7N/) ; **p. 91-hd** ph © Time Life Pictures / National Archives / The Life Picture Collection / Getty-Images ; **p. 91-b** © 2018 Magnolia Pictures- Participant media- CNN Films- L'atelier d'images. ; **p. 95-h** ph © Michael Caulfield / Wirelmage for Turner / Getty-Images ; **p. 95-b** ph © Photographer is my life / Getty-Images ; **p. 96-1,2,3,4** ph © Edward S. Curtis Collection (Library of Congress) ; **p. 96-5** ph © D.R. ; **p. 96-6** ph © Photo Heyn / Photo-Re-Pubblic / Leemage ; **p. 96-7** ph © Look and Learn / Elgar Collection / Bridgeman Images ; **p. 96-8** Bury My Heart at Wounded Knee (Dir: Yves Simoneau), 2007. Coll. Christophel © HBO Films / Wolf Films / Travelers Rest Films ; **p. 97-h** ph © Cyrus McCrimmon / The Denver Post via Getty-Images ; **p. 97-b** ph © Smoke Signals, Courtesy of Miramax ; **p. 98** ph © Bianchetti / Leemage ; **p. 99-h** © D.R. ; **p. 99-b** © 6 Misconceptions About Native American People / Teen Vogue ; **p. 103-h** ph © Collection Dagli Orti / Buffalo Bill Center of the West, Cody, Wyoming / Buffalo Bill Center of the West / Aurimages ; **p. 103-b** ph © Cali / Iconotec / Photononstop ; **p. 105-h1** A New Model, What Confidence, Beauty, and Power Really Look Like by Ashley Graham & Rebecca Paley © Dey Street Books (HarperCollins), 2018 ; **p. 105-h2** Dear Ijeawele, or A Feminist Manifesto in Fifteen Suggestions by Chimamanda Ngozi Adichie © Alfred A. Knopf (Random House Children's Books), 2017 ; **p. 105-h3** RBG (Dir: Julie Cohen and Betsy West), 2018 ph © CNN Films / Kobal / Rex / Shutterstock / Aurimages ; **p. 105-h4** I Feel Pretty (Dir: Abby Kohn, Marc Silverstein), 2018 ph © STX Films / Kobal / REX / Shutterstock / Aurimages ; **p. 105-h5** On the Basis of Sex (Dir: Mimi Leder), 2018 ph © Amblin Partners / Participant Media / BBQ_DFY / Aurimages ; **p. 105-b-1** © The Absolutely True Diary of a Part-Time Indian by Sherman Alexie. Publisher: Little, Brown Books for Young Readers, 2009 ; **p. 105-b-2** Dances with wolves (Dir: Kevin Costner), 1990. ph © Mary Evans / Aurimages ; **p. 105-b-3** Rumble: The Indians Who Rocked The World, (Dir: Catherine Bainbridge, Alfonso Maiorana), 2017. ph © Rezolution Pictures / BBQ_DFY / Aurimages ; **p. 105 b-4** Phoenix Arizona, Smoke Signals (Dir: Chris Eyre, Gary Farmer, Irene Bedard, Adam Beach), 1998. ph © ShadowCatcher Entertainment / BBQ_DFY / Aurimages ; **p. 107-h** ph © Patrick Smith / Getty-Images / AFP Photo ; **p. 107-b** ph © Maxim Zmeyev / AFP Photo ; **p. 109-h** © BBC News ; **p. 109-b** ph © Jamie Squire / Getty-Images / AFP Photo ; **p. 110** ph © Michael Zagaris / Getty-Images ; **p. 111-h** ph © Michael Zagaris / Getty-Images / © From Time, The Perilous Flight, 2016-10-03, Time Inc. Used under license. ; **p. 111-b** © NFL, D.R. ; **p. 115-h** ph © Eric S. Lesser / EPA / Maxppp ; **p. 115-b** ph © Kirt Dozier-USA Today Sports / Reuters ; **p. 116** ph © AP / Sipa Press ; **p. 117** © Productions and funded by the Heritage Lottery Fund. D.R. ; **p. 118-h** ph © Nathan Stirk / Getty-Images / AFP Photo ; **p. 118-b** © Sunderland Association Football Club Limited, D.R. ; **p. 119** © Manchester United ; **p. 123-h** ph © Eddie Keogh for FA / REX / Shutterstock / Sipa Press ; **p. 123-b** ph © Darren Walsh / Chelsea FC via Getty-Images ; **p. 125-h1** Friday night lights, TV Serie, 2006. Coll. Christophel © NBC Studios Inc TV ; **p. 125-h2** QB1: Beyond the Lights, TV serie, 2017. Coll. Christophel © Film 45 ; **p. 125-h3** Any Given Sunday (Dir: Oliver Stone), 1999. ph © Prod DB / AllPix / Aurimages © Warner Bros / D.R. ; **p. 125-h4** Remember the Titans (Dir: Boaz Yakin), 2000. Coll. Christophel © Jerry Bruckheimer Films / Run It Up Productions Inc ; **p. 125-h5** The blind side (dir: John Lee Hancock), 2009. ph © Warner Bros. Pictures / The Kobal Collection / Aurimages ; **p. 125-h6** Undefeated (Dir: Daniel Lindsay & T.J. Martin), 2011. Coll. Christophel © Zipper Bros Films ; **p. 125-b1** Fever pitch by Nick Hornby © Penguin, 2014 ; **p. 125-b2** Liverpool!: The Comic Strip History by Bob Bond © Vision Sports Publishing, 2013 ; **p. 125-b3** The Illustrated History of Football by David Squires © Century, 2016 ; **p. 125-b4** Red Men: Liverpool Football Club-The Biography by John Williams © Mainstream Publishing, 2010 ; **p. 125-b5** Bend It Like Beckham (Dir: Gurinder Chadha), 2002. Coll. Christophel © Bend It Films / Roc Media ; **p. 125-b6** Looking for Eric (Dir: Ken Loach), 2009. Coll. Christophel © Sixteen Films / Film Four ; **p. 125-b7** The Pass (Dir: Ben A. Williams), 2016. ph © Toledo Productions / BBQ_DFY / Aurimages ; **p. 127-h ph** © AFP Photo / Chris J Ratcliffe / © Adagp, Paris 2019 ; **p. 127-b ph** © Juan Antonio Alonso- www.agefotostock.com ; **p. 128 ph** © Stuart Forster / Alamy Stock Photo ; **p. 129-h ph** © The Life Picture Collection / Getty-Images ; **p. 129-bg ph** © Chris Delmas / AFP Photo ; **p. 129-bd ph** © Frank Mullen / Wirelmage / Getty-Images ; **p. 130** © Javier Jaén ; **p. 131 ph** © Christopher Polk / Getty-Images for MTV / AFP ; **p. 135-h ph** © Pete Davis / Alamy Stock Photo ; **p. 135-b-1 ph** © Photo by Frank Micelotta / Getty-Images ; **p. 135-b-2 ph** © AP Photo / Gary He / via Sipa Press ; **p. 135-b-3 ph** © Clarence Davis / NY Daily News Archive via Getty-Images ; **p. 135-b-4 ph** © Fredric Reshew / Contour by Getty-Images ; **p. 135-b-5 ph** © Jeff Kravitz / FilmMagic / Getty-Images ; **p. 135-b-6 ph** © Dominique Charriau / Wirelmage / Getty-Images ; **p. 137 ph** © Joan Marcus ; **p. 138-h ph** © Alastaire Muir ; **p. 138-b ph** © Martin Jenkinson Image Library. All rights reserved. DACS / Artimage 2018 / © Adagp, Paris, 2019 ; **p. 139 ©** Robert Day / © National Theatre of Scotland ; **p. 143-h ph** © Marc J. Franklin / Playbill ; **p. 143-b ph** © Black / Alamy Stock Photo ; **p. 145-h-1** © The Rap Year Book by Shea Serrano and illustrated by Arturo Torres. Text © 2015 Shea Serrano. Illustrations © 2015 Arturo Torres. Used with the permission of Express Permissions on behalf of Abrams Images, an imprint of Harry N. Abrams, Inc., New York. All rights reserved. www.abramsbooks.com. ; **p. 145-h-2** The Get Down Serie TV 2017- 2018 USA Saison 1 ph © Netflix / BBQ_DFY / Aurimages ; **p. 145-h-3** Beats Rhymes & Life: Travels of Tribe Called Quest (Dir : Michael Rapaport), DVD, 2011 © Sony Pictures ; **p. 145-h-4** Straight Outta Compton (Dir: F. Gary Gray), 2015. ph © Universal Pictures / BBQ_DFY/ Aurimages ; **p. 145-h-5** Something from Nothing: The Art of Rap (Dir: Ice-T, Andy Baybutt), 2012. DVD © JollyGood Films / Westmount Films / Vivendi Entertainment ; **p. 145-b-1** ph © Mary Evans / Aurimages ; **p. 145-b-2** ph © The Advertising Archive / Aurimages ; **p. 145-b-3** Rent: Filmed Live on Broadway (Dir: Michael John Warren), 2008. ph © RadicalMedia / Hot Ticket / Sony Pictures Home Entertainment ; **p. 145-b-4** Grease (Dir: Randal Kleiser), 1978. ph © Paramount / The Kobal Collection / Aurimages ; **p. 145-b-5** ph © Black Label Media / Summit Entertainment / BBQ_DFY / Aurimages ; **p. 145-b-6** Billy Elliot, The Musical live (Dir : Brett Sullivan, Stephen Daldry), 2014. ph © Universal Pictures / Universal Stage Productions /Working Title Films / Old Vic Productions ; **p. 147-h** ph © Leon Neal / AFP Photo ; **p. 147-b** ph © Oli Scarff / Getty-Images / AFP Photo ; **p. 148** © Fashion Revolution Week ; **p. 149-h** © University of Chester ; **p. 149-b** © The Meat Free Monday Foundation ; **p. 150** © Ecostrawz Ltd ; **p. 151-h** © Bioregional ; **p. 151-b** © T-charge introduced to tackle London pollution» de 5 News ; **p. 155-h** ph © Artem Varnitsin- stock.adobe.com ; **p. 155-b** ph © Simon Turner / Alamy Stock Photo ; **p. 156-1** Odds against tomorrow by Nathaniel Rich. © St Martin's Press, 2014 (Pan McMillan) ; **p. 156-2** Sixty days and counting by Kim Stanley Robinson © Bantam Doubleday Dell Publishing Group / Spectra / Random Penguin House, 2007 ; **p. 156-3** The Islands at the End of the World by Austin Aslan. © Ember/ Random Penguin House, 2015 ; **p. 157** © 2015 Saci Lloyd. All Rights Reserved ; **p. 158-hg** Geostorm (Dir: Dean Devlin), 2017. Coll. Christophel © Warner Bros / Electric entertainment / Jerry Bruckheimer films / Skydance media ; **p. 158-hd** An inconvenient truth (Dir: Davis Guggenheim), 2006. ph © Lawrence Bender Prods. / The Kobal Collection / Aurimages ; **p. 158-b** © IMDb, D.R. ; **p. 159** ph © Robert Graves and Didier Madoc-Jones, aerial photograph by Jason Hawkes / www.postcardsfromthefuture.com ; **p. 163-h** ph © Bernhard Staehli / Shutterstock ; **p. 163-b** ph © mppriv / iStock ; **p. 165-h1** Mates, Dates and Saving the Planet A girl's guide to being green and gorgeous! by Cathy Hopkins © Piccadilly Press Ltd, 2008 ; **p. 165-h2** There Is No Planet B: A Handbook for the Make or Break Years by Mike Berners-Lee © Cambridge University Press, 2019 ; **p. 165-h3** 50 Ways to Help the Planet: Easy ways to live a sustainable life by Sian Berry © Kyle Books, 2019 ; **p. 165-m1** The True Cost movie (Dir: Andrew Morgan), 2015 © With Life Is My Movie Entertainment Company ; **p. 165-m2** Planet Earth II, narrated by David Attenborough, DVD cover, 2016 © 2 Entertain ; **p. 165-m3** Earth, The journey of a lifetime (Dir: Alastair Fothergill and Mark Linfield), 2007. Coll. Christophel © Disneynature / BBC Worldwide ; **p. 165-b-1** © The Carbon Diaries 2017, Kindle Edition, Publisher: Hachette Children›s, 2011 ; **p. 165-b-2** The day after tomorrow (Dir: Roland Emmerich), 2004. ph © 20th Century Fox / The Kobal Collection / Aurimages ; **p. 165-b-3** Waterworld (Dir: Kevin Reynolds), 1995. ph © Universal / The Kobal Collection / Aurimages ; **p. 165-b-4** An Inconvenient Sequel Truth to Power (Dir: Bonni Cohen & Jon Shenk), 2017. Coll. Christophel © Actual films / Participant media ; **p. 165-b-5** Beast of the southern Wild (Dir: Benh Zeitlin), 2012. ph © Cinereach / The Kobal Collection / Aurimages ; **p. 167-h** ph © Carlo Allegri / Reuters ; **p. 167-b** ph © Granger / Bridgeman Images ; **p. 168-h** ph © Brooks Kraft / Corbis / Getty-Images ; **p. 168-b** ph © Bill Chizek / iStock ; **p. 169-h** ph © Ariel Skelley / Getty-Images ; **p. 169-b** ph © Robert Deutsch- USA Today Sports / Reuters ; **p. 170** © Women On 20s ; **p. 171** ph © Jonathan Bachman / Reuters ; **p. 172** ph © Drew Angerer / Getty-Images / AFP Photo ; **p. 175-h** ph © Wavebreakmedia Ltd / Getty-Images ; **p. 175-b** ph © Figura13 / iStock ; **p. 176-h** ph © Wayne Hsieh ; **p. 176-b** © AP archive ; **p. 177** ph © Jenn Yoo / Untapped Cities ; **p. 178** ph © Collection of David Leong / AIISF ; **p. 179** © State of California, D.R. ; **p. 183-h** ph © DGLimages / Alamy Stock Photo / hemis.fr ; **p. 183-b** ph © jacoblund / iStock ; **p. 185-h** © Alexander Hamilton: The Graphic History of an American Founding Father, by Jonathan Hennessey, ill. Justin Greenwood, published by Ten Speed Press, 2017 (Random House UK) ; **p. 185-m-1** Captain America First avenger (Dir: Joe Johnston), 2011. Coll. Christophel © Paramount pictures ; **p. 185-m-2** Forrest gump (Actor: Tom Hanks. Real : Robert Zemeckis), 1994. Coll. Christophel © Paramount Pictures ; **p. 185-m-3** Hamilton's America (Dir: Alex Horwitz), 2016. Coll. Christophel © John D. & Catherine MacArthur Foundation ; **p. 185-m-4** Selma (Dir: Ava Duvernay), 2014. ph © Paramount / Pathe / Harpo Films / The Kobal Collection / Aurimages ; **p. 185-bg** © Lai, Him Mark, Genny Lim and Judy Yung, eds. Island: Poetry and History of Chinese Immigrants on Angel Island, 1910-1940. © 1991. Reprinted with permission of the University of Washington Press. ; **p. 185-bd** © Oxford University Press (www.oup.com) ; **p. 186-1** ph © George Clerk / iStock ; **p. 186-2** ph © Homer Sykes Archive / Alamy Stock Photo ; **p. 186-3** ph © Jeff Morgan 01 / Alamy Stock Photo ; **p. 186-4** ph © Anwar Hussein / Wirelmage / Getty-Images ; **p. 186-5** ph © Paul Fearn / Alamy Stock Photo ; **p. 186-6** © Louis Rhead & Frank E. Schoonover ; **p. 186-7** ph © GL Archive / Alamy Stock Photo ; **p. 186-8** ph © Danita Delimont / Gallo images / Getty-Images ; **p. 187-1** ph © Rhona Wise / AFP Photo ; **p. 187-2** ph © Chuck Kennedy / MCT via Getty-Images ; **p. 187-3** ph © Sean Adair / Reuters ; **p. 187-4** ph © Mitchell Gerber / Corbis / VCG via Getty-Images ; **p. 187-5** ph © Robert W. Kelley / The Life Picture Collection / Getty-Images ; **p. 187-6** ph © Consolidated News Pictures / Getty-Images ; **p. 187-7** ph © Underwood Archives / Getty-Images ; **p. 187-8** Battle of Kenesaw Mountain, 1864 / ph © Universal History Archive / UIG / Bridgeman Images ; **p. 187-9** ph © Akg-Images / Science Source ; **p. 187-10** ph © Mike White / Private Collection / Look and Learn / Bridgeman Images ; **p. 187-11** ph © Granger / Bridgeman Images ; **p. 188-1** ph © Dan Chung / Pool / Files / AFP Photo ; **p. 188-2** ph © William L. Rukeyser / Getty-Images ; **p. 188-3** Civil rights march, Newry, 1969. ph © Courtesy of RTÉ Archives ; **p. 188-4** ph © Universal History Archive/UIG / Bridgeman Images ; **p. 188-5** ph © Ken Welsh / Bridgeman Images ; **p. 188-6** ph © Pat Nicolle, gouache / Private Collection / © Look and Learn / Bridgeman Images ; **p. 188-7** ph © The Irish House of Commons, 1780 by Francis Wheatley / Leeds Museums and Galleries (Lotherton Hall) U.K. / Bridgeman Images ; **p. 188-8** ph © Granger / Bridgeman Images ; **p. 189-1** ph © Andrew Vaughan / AP / Sipa Press ; **p. 189-2** ph © Nicholas Kamm / AFP Photo ; **p. 189-3** ph © Tom Hanson / AFP Photo ; **p. 189-4** ph © North Wind Picture Archives / Akg-Images ; **p. 189-5** ph © Granger / Bridgeman Images ; **p. 190-1** ph © Emilie Chaix / Photononstop / AFP Photo ; **p. 190-2** ph © AFP Photo / Alexander Joe ; **p. 190-3** ph © AFP Photo ; **p. 190-4** ph © Ian Berry / Camerapress / Gamma- Rapho ; **p. 190-5** ph © Michele and Tom Grimm / Alamy Stock Photo ; **p. 190-6** ph © ANC ; **p. 190-7** ph © Look and Learn / Illustrated Papers Collection / Bridgeman Images ; **p. 191-1** ph © Heiko Junge / NTB Scanpix / Pool / Reuters ; **p. 191-2** ph © The Life Picture Collection / Getty-Images ; **p. 191-3** ph © Universal History Archive / UIG via Getty-Images ; **p. 191-4** ph © 1882 / Pictures from History / Alexander Bassano / Bridgeman Images ; **p. 191-5** ph © National Portrait Gallery, London / Aisa / Leemage ; **p. 191-6** ph © Dinodia Photos / Alamy Stock Photo ; **p. 191-7** ph © Britich Library / Science Photo Library / Akg-Images ; **p. 264** ph © Jarek Kilian / iStock ; **p. 265-1** ph © Ianunzio Alessandro / stock.adobe.com ; **p. 265-2** ph © Paul Cowan / Shutterstock ; **p. 265-3** ph © David Schaffer / Caiaimages / Photononstop ; **p. 265-4** ph © John Gomez / Shutterstock

D.R. : Malgré nos efforts, il nous a été impossible de joindre certains photographes ou leurs ayants droits, ainsi que les éditeurs ou leurs ayants droits pour certains documents, afin de solliciter l'autorisation, mais nous avons naturellement réservé en notre comptabilité des droits usuels.

Achevé d'imprimer en Italie par Stige
Dépôt légal n° 05319-9/04 - Juillet 2020